W9-ADK-149

The Later Years
Social Applications of Gerontology

The Later Years
Social Applications of Gerontology

Edited by
Richard A. Kalish
Berkeley, California

Brooks/Cole Publishing Company
Monterey, California
A Division of Wadsworth Publishing Company, Inc.

Printed in the United States of America

10 9 8 7 6 5 4 3 2 1

Library of Congress Cataloging in Publication Data

Main entry under title:

The Later years.

   Includes index.
   1. Aged—United States—Addresses, essays, lectures.
2 Old age—Addresses, essays, lectures. I. Kalish, Richard A.
HQ1064.U5L37   301.43′5′0973   76-58336
ISBN 0-8185-0223-1

Production Editor: *Susan Hannan*
Interior and Cover Design: *Jamie S. Brooks*
Cover photo: *Karen Preuss*
Photos, pages 2, 157, 190, 191, 250, 251, by *Liane Enkelis;* photos, pages 3, 8, 9, 46, 47, 98, 99, 126, 127, 156, 217, 288, 289, 310, 338, 339, by *Karen Preuss;* photo, page 216, by *John Warford.*

Preface

Gerontology is neither a field nor a profession. Rather, it is a specialty within innumerable fields and professions. A gerontologist can be a social scientist, a physician, a psychotherapist, a lawyer, a recreation specialist, an economist, a biologist, a senior-center director, an architect . . . . . The list is endless. It is impossible for anyone to become expert in all these areas of specialization, but it did seem possible that one person could bring together in a single volume the best thoughts of some of the most knowledgeable specialists to provide an integrated picture of what gerontology is about.

The present book focuses on what is often called *social gerontology* or, sometimes more specifically, *applied social gerontology*. It is for those people who are going to work with the elderly by providing direct services, by initiating and developing programs, by planning, and by developing policy. It is also for people teaching others who work with older people in one or more of these ways. I would further hope that those who are more oriented to research or more concerned with theory development will also find this book useful in describing the ends toward which their research endeavors and their theories are directed.

Older people themselves will find this book helpful, not only to learn what people are saying about them, but also to discover options available to them in their later years. For anyone who wants to become politically involved with the concerns of the elderly, for anyone who has been asked to serve on a local committee on aging, or for anyone who wishes to serve as an advocate for the elderly, I believe this book offers many possibilities.

Although the topic is as old as time, the present emphasis on gerontology is very recent. Even a decade ago, there were virtually no regular-credit courses on aging in colleges and universities, and the subject received only the briefest mention in courses on developmental psychology, sociology of the family, cultural anthropology, psychiatric nursing, and human biology. Today the field is burgeoning, and colleges and universities are redesigning curricula to keep up with the rapidly expanding interest in the applications of gerontology.

I have attempted to capture the present excitement of gerontology in this book by using materials from a wide variety of sources: from academic journals and newspapers, from the *Congressional Record* and other government publications, and from books and conference proceedings. I have also included previously unpublished materials.

Of course, more important than the sources are the topics covered and the authors. In each section, the author is expert. The traditional characteristics of aging are discussed comprehensively. Two demographers write about aging populations; a physician discusses the health of the elderly; an internationally renowned economist writes on the financial implications of growing old, and an expert in transportation writes about the need for mobility with advancing age.

Not only have I approached the familiar concerns—social work, housing, health-care services, retirement, leisure, and geriatric institutions—but I have also included matters that are just coming to general attention. This text offers a section on law and the elderly written by a lawyer, and one on sexual functioning written by a psychiatrist. The concept of the hospice for people who are terminally ill is described by the medical director of the first American hospice; criminal victimization of the elderly is discussed by the attorney general of California; and the role of television in the lives of older people is written about by a man with extensive media experience. I have also included materials on aging and ethnicity, each authored or coauthored by members of the ethnic community discussed.

You might wonder, with so many contributors from such diverse backgrounds, how the various sections come together as a book. I can provide two answers. First, each of the ten chapters and each of the selections within them is introduced by some coordinating discussion; this enables us to shift from topic to topic with ease and continuity. Second, each section has been edited to reduce the length. To make certain that the editing left the author's original meaning intact, each section has been reviewed by the person or persons who wrote it, and their suggestions, restorations, and revisions were incorporated in the versions published here.

I must mention the initial selection, *The Musicians of Bremen.* Several years ago, long before I conceptualized this book, I wanted to use that famous Grimm tale in a book on human aging. It tells so poignantly and so effectively of the tragedy of human waste, yet it also shows that, given even a minimal opportunity, the elderly can pool their resources, rout the wicked, and live happily ever after. So much that has been written about being old emphasizes the negative, the depressed, and the exploited that it seemed appropriate to begin a book on aging with a selection that points out what the elderly can do when given the chance.

There are many people I wish to thank for their help with this book. Some are old friends who reviewed earlier versions and did not hesitate to criticize where criticism was needed—Tom Hickey, now at the University of Michigan, M. Powell Lawton at the Philadelphia Geriatric Center, and Frances Scott at the University of Oregon. Others are people I don't know, who were gentler in their criticism but no less helpful—Lynne Bynum of Monterey Peninsula College, Monterey, California, and Margaret Franks of Cypress College, Cypress, California. Of course, I also wish to acknowledge the work of all the authors, not only in writing such excellent pieces initially but also in their additional efforts in reading my edited versions, in commenting on the changes, and in granting me permission to use their contributions. Also I want to thank Sheila Fabricant, who, while she rested from one graduate degree before launching on another, served as secretary, manuscript typist, and organizer during most of the two years this book was in process. And thanks also to the people at Brooks/Cole who were willing to experiment with a new form of textbook.

Finally, as my own life appears to be in transition at this moment, I want to dedicate this book not only to Alice, Rachel, Danny, and Leah, who have been most important to me in the past, but especially to Sidnee, Greta, Chris, and Sandy, who are important to me in the present and will be even more so in the future.

Richard A. Kalish

Contents

The Later Years
Social Applications of Gerontology

Prolog

The Musicians of Bremen: An Adaptation

Richard A. Kalish

Sometimes we forget that the world has a history and that most of what we see today has occurred, in one form or another, in times past. Our history is written not only in textbooks and academic documents, but also in art, music, ritual, and legend. And one highly significant form of legend is the fairy tale, which is used both to preach and to entertain.

The most obvious message in the tale that follows is that frustration with the apparent uselessness of old people is not a phenomenon first observed in the middle of the 20th century. The parable clearly describes what happens to those whose productivity has waned and who lack loving family members or friends. But there is another message—that older people, when they work together and fight for their rights, can be successful, and their reward is to live happily ever after. In most fairy tales, the old are characterized as either wise or wicked, but in The Musicians of Bremen *they are neither. Rather, they are capable, resilient, and able to take advantage of what is offered them. And perhaps that is more like real life.*

A donkey who had labored long and hard in the fields for his master and mistress had grown old. His movements were slower, and more and more frequently he was unable to work. His master, although not a poor man, was not wealthy, and times were hard. One day his master spoke to his mistress, suggesting that the faithful old donkey should be put out of his misery. "For then, perhaps," he said, "we will receive a few marks for his hide and a few more for the rest of him. He will no longer be in pain, and we will have a little money to show for it."

The next day, when the donkey's master came to feed him, the man's eyes were moist, and he put his arm around the donkey in a show of warmth that he had never before expressed. When the man left, the donkey sensed exactly what was going to happen and decided to run away. He had not gone very far when he spied a dog lying under a tree, his head dejectedly placed on his two front paws.

"Why so dejected, friend Growler?" asked the donkey.

"You would be dejected too," said Growler, "if your master and mistress had taken you many leagues from your home and left you in a strange town. Their little boy and their little girl cried and cried, but my master said that I was no longer able to run after the sheep and my mistress said that it was all they could do to get food for the younger dog. So here I am."

"Ah," said the donkey. "That is very much the situation for me also. I have been walking for only one hour, but I have decided what I wish to do.

4

My friends have often told me that I have a fine singing voice and a good sense for music, so I am going to Bremen to earn my way as a musician. Would you like to accompany me?"

"I, too, have been told that I have a fine voice," responded Growler, "and I would very much like to accompany you. Perhaps I could play the violin, and you would obviously have great success with the drums." And the two set off on the road to Bremen.

Soon thereafter they came upon a cat who sat on the stump of a tree and watched the birds nearby but did not move toward them. "Hey, friend Whiskers," called Growler, "have you eaten so well that that excellent dinner does not entice you?"

"Nothing entices me anymore," the cat replied. "I cannot catch birds that fly. I have become so old and slow that I cannot even catch mice, and so my master and mistress have decided that they need me no more. They came upon me last night, pretending to offer me love, then put me in a sack and carried me down to the river. The only reason you see me here is that I created such a commotion in the sack with my cries that a passing farmer thought there was a baby inside. He accosted my master, and in the confusion I escaped. But now what can I do?"

"You can come with us to Bremen," the dog and the donkey said in unison, "and we can all be musicians together. You could play the flute, and I can tell by listening to you that you have a fine singing voice. We will all become town musicians."

The cat looked a little happier. "That sounds like an excellent idea," she said. And the three animals walked off together. But now that each had company, their steps were more sprightly and their manner was more lively.

When the shadows grew long, they heard the loud crow of a cock. "Strange," said the donkey, "for cocks do not crow at the end of the day." And the three hurried to see what it might be.

There, in the shadow of a barn, was a large fowl, crowing with all its might at the fading sun. "Why do you crow at this strange hour?" asked Growler.

"Because I am now old and the dawn does not always find me awake, nor does my call resound across the fields to the farmhouse as it once did. This afternoon, when I was in pain from a stomachache, I heard my mistress tell one of her servants that I would be their dinner for Sunday next. The pain in my stomach has gone, but the pain in my heart is deep. I woke this woman and her servants for many years, but that matters not when now I am old." And the cock crowed a particularly long sad cry.

"Then come with us," said the donkey, "and we will live out our days in the warmth and joy that Bremen offers its musicians. You can pluck the strings of the lute, while Growler plays the violin and Whiskers makes music with the flute and I beat hope and love upon the drums."

"May I sing as well?" the cock asked.

"We shall all sing," replied Whiskers. And the four friends set off together.

But the way to Bremen was longer than they realized, and dark was soon upon them. Their steps became slower and their eagerness turned to weariness. "Let us spend the night by this tree," spoke the donkey.

"I would, but I fear the night in these parts," said the dog. "I know this road from being here with my master. In the daylight it is safe enough, since many tread upon it, but at night the trees seem to close in upon you, and the wind whistles eerily through the branches. It is then that thieves and cut-throats abound. If what my master says be true, we are this moment close to the home of the worst band of robbers in the area."

The four friends all shuddered at once, as though a cold breeze had penetrated to their bones, but their fatigue overcame their fears, and they agreed to remain there to sleep. Worried by the news provided by Growler, however, they agreed to take turns standing watch.

Growler took the first turn, and he moved from rock to bush to hilltop to see that nothing came upon the sleeping group without warning. Then his turn ended, and the donkey roused himself to watch for enemies. Some time later the donkey awakened Whiskers for her watch, which also went peace-fully. The cock, for his turn, flew to the branch of a tree from which he could see the countryside. By now, dawn was only two hours away.

"Ho!!" he shouted. "I see a light. I think a light. Through the trees and over two hills."

"Back to sleep!! Back to sleep!!" his comrades groaned.

"No," answered the cock. "We have not eaten all day. Perhaps the kind people who live in that cabin would permit us a morsel."

"It is too early in the morning to go visiting," the donkey murmured. "Let us sleep now and visit them later." And he turned away and went back to sleep.

A few minutes later the cock was rousing all the animals from their new sleep. "I have flown to the cabin," he explained, still out of breath, "and it is the home of the robbers that Growler has spoken of. Their table is spread with delicious food and drink, and they are all lying about asleep. Their snores alone almost frightened me away."

"I see," the donkey said thoughtfully. "Perhaps, my musician friends, this is the time to practice our singing." And he explained his idea.

Thirty minutes later, still before the dawn, the four friends were out-side the robbers' cabin. The donkey stood outside the only window to the building; the dog stood on his back; the cat stood on his back; the cock stood on her back. All waited and watched. Then the donkey smashed through the window, singing with his loudest brays; the dog leaped into the cabin, howl-ing his loudest howls; the cat raced into the cabin, shrilling her shrillest cries; the cock flew against the lantern and with his wings extinguished the light, as he crowed loudly and triumphantly.

The cabin was in chaos. The robbers thought that the devil and a swarm of helpers had attacked them, and they all raced out the door and ran as quickly as they could to the distant road where the animals had spent the night. Once there, they took to quarreling about whether they should go back to the cabin or move on to begin again. One robber even said that their life of evil was being punished, and he went away that moment and was never heard from after. Finally the robber chieftain agreed to return that very night, to see if they might recapture their cabin from the demons that had beset them.

In the meantime, the donkey, the dog, the cat, and the cock had eaten all the food on the table and some that was still in the pantry. The food and the excitement made them sleepy, and they each found a place that was especially comfortable and fell asleep. Their fatigue was so great that they slept the entire day and were still asleep when night came again.

That night, while the animals still slept, the robber chieftain returned. As he found all was quiet, he thought the demons had left, and he went to the table to light a candle. The cat, asleep on the table, felt his presence and woke suddenly. Seeing the robber bending over her, she spat in his face, shrieked out the most mournful of sounds, then scratched and bit him on the hands and arms and face.

The noise awoke the other animals. The cock immediately flew at the robber's head, flapped his wings in the man's face, and pecked him on the forehead and all about the eyes. As the robber chieftain tried to flee, the dog bit him hard on each ankle, so that he had to sit down until the pain in his legs would leave him and he could walk again. As he stood up to go, he bent over to rub his sore ankles, and the donkey, who had been watching all with glee, dispatched him with one hard swift kick to his backside.

The robber picked himself up and limped away to his friends. "I tell you, my men," he said, "that cabin is inhabited by evil spirits. When I tried to light the lantern, an old witch shouted at me and scratched me with her long fingernails. Then a flying devil stabbed me all over the head, as he flew round and round me. Then a furry devil grabbed my ankles in his teeth and would not let go. When I bent over to rub my ankles, the biggest devil of all, Lucifer I am certain, slammed me in the backside with a blow so hard that it carried me out the door.

Thereafter the robbers never returned to the forest, and the four friends lived out their days in peace and harmony, making music as they desired, not caring that the donkey moved more slowly or that the dog could not run so fast or that the cat could catch only a few mice or that the rooster might sleep beyond dawn. They served each other well, and when their time came they each went to a just reward.

Chapter 1

Who Are the Elderly?

Older people come in all the sizes, shapes, colors, dispositions, and capabilities that we can use to describe people of any age, and we do a disservice both to them and to ourselves by lumping them casually together and reacting to them in terms of our stereotypes. Even worse is the kind of stereotype that is applied—and as often by the elderly themselves as by younger people.

The stereotype, interestingly enough, is often based on one or two experiences, or even on the concepts of others and not on experience at all. "Those old people" is an expression applied to the elderly in general but based on the small portion of the elderly population who are ill, confused, impoverished, irritable, or unpleasant. But these stereotypes carry on. In a study I did with Tom and Louise Hickey some years ago, third-grade children often described the elderly as having beards, although most of them had probably not seen more than one or two old people with beards; in fact, most of these children were much more likely to have seen young people with beards. But the stereotype (did they learn it from fairy tales?) hung on.

When an older person applies the stereotype, he usually isn't referring to himself or to his friends but to "those old people." My 93-year-old uncle sometimes would talk about "those old people" and would mean people like those I described earlier. Thank heaven he was not like "those old people"! Perhaps you have had a similar experience.

In teaching courses on human aging, I frequently assign students the task of interviewing one or two older persons. After the interviews, I ask the students about the people they spoke with, and the single most frequent comment is "The person I interviewed is very atypical." This suggests that most old people are atypical, which, of course, is true. People, young or old, are unique.

Some of the stereotypes applied to the elderly may derive from those of us, whether we are young, middle-aged, or older, who try to function as advocates for the elderly. Advocacy often emphasizes limitations rather than accomplishments and potential. Furthermore, many people who work with the elderly see only those who need help, so the vast majority of older persons are just not known to professionals in the social and health fields.

A related matter is: how should "old" be defined? The most obvious and the simplest way is to use chronological age, and that is what this chapter and most of the other chapters in this book use. We refer to 65, or sometimes 60 or 62 or 70, as the cutoff point. That makes some sense, because Social Security payments, various retirement regulations, and income-tax deductions use one or another of those ages. But "old" can be defined in such other ways as by physical appearance, cognitive competence, health, social role (a grandparent is old), certain physiological changes (bone calcification), or attitude (he acts much younger—or older—than his age).

Individuals, of course, don't all age at the same rate. Thus, one friend of mine, at the age of 78, still jogs; another is so arthritic he can barely walk. One 86-year-old woman still reads voraciously, whereas another of about the same age cannot finish the newspaper without dozing. Nor does any one person age in all ways at the same rate. When considered in terms of her social role, a great-grandmother would rank as quite old, but in terms of health she could be very young. Even more obvious is the man with a cardiovascular system that resembles that of someone 20 years younger but skin so wrinkled that he looks 15 years older than he really is.

Therefore, when the 93-year-old man or woman you are talking with refers to "those old people," don't laugh to yourself about how "cute" it is, but reflect that age classification is based on much more than the number of years ago a person was born.

A Plea
from the Older Individual*

Herbert A. Shore

This brief excerpt provides an amazing overview of the rest of the book. In it, author Shore touches briefly on most of the issues that the subsequent pages present in greater depth. At the same time, Dr. Shore's sensitive insights represent most effectively what 22 million people would say if they could speak with one voice.

It has been said, *"The three saddest words in the English language are, I am old; the five saddest, I am old and poor; the seven saddest, I am old and poor and sick; and the nine saddest, I am old and poor and sick and lonely,"* and I submit to you that in this great and affluent country of ours, these sad indictments should not be allowed to be true, or to persist.

In this presentation I am attempting to distill the comments, pleas and cries of older people I have heard.

I have tried to live my life so that I have been a contributing member to my community and to society. I have always wanted to assume my responsibilities and my obligations as duties. I feel that as an individual there is a reciprocal relationship of society's obligations and responsibilities to me. I do not feel that I should be a second class citizen because I am needy or old.

*Edited from "Herbert Shore's Testimony before the Presidential Task Force on the Elderly," October 25, 1969.

It seems clear to me that the elderly of America ought not be thought of as a homogeneous group, having a singular set of needs requiring a singular set of services but rather a diverse group whose needs and requirements vary in accordance with a variety of characteristics of which chronological age is only one.

What do I want, need, hope for, expect and desire as an older person? May I suggest some of the following:

I want my needs to be met adequately. I want them to be met respecting me as an individual and not as a nameless, faceless recipient of a handout, with payments based on substandard, minimal existence of yesteryear.

There must be a recognition that the standard of assistance considers all my needs at a time of increasing disability. Food, shelter, and utilities are important, but so is my need for a telephone, for continued participation in my church, and for recreation. At my age I may need an increased laundry allowance (I cannot carry my clothes to the laundromat) and a telephone gives me security and communication. Social Security is much more than financial security. I need Social Security to keep me in touch with the world around me and to help my emotional health. Idleness is my greatest scourge, and loneliness my greatest burden.

It appears to me that my medical needs should be met as a right and not as a privilege. As I grow older my bouts with illness increase. I want the services to be available to me so that I can continue to function at the maximum of my capacities. These should include all services which can be brought into my home (and for which funds are available), home care, visiting nurse, homemaker, rehab team. If I get ill, vendor payments should meet true costs so that I can receive the best care available. Continuity of care is vital for me and other elderly.

I should not have to move out of my home because of rent limitations. I have become painfully aware of the fact that for the past century, *indigency* has set the standard for care of the poor aged. If I were very rich I might be able to afford some of the newer, finer and specially planned retirement housing. But since I am poor and have limited resources I must depend on public housing or institutional care.

I believe that adequate housing is a right and every older American is deserving of it. I believe that physical comfort is a basic human need and reasonable requirement for the young and the old, for the affluent and the indigent. I believe that year round weather conditioning, especially air conditioning is not a frill or a luxury but a necessity. I really don't understand how my government can have such great concern for air pollution on the one hand and not permit air conditioning in public housing on the other.

I believe that a full range of facilities and services should be available to me that I can utilize as I wish and as my needs change.

I am not sure that it is in my best interest to continue to suffer from the segregation that comes from my age, my financial condition and all too often my race.

In terms of my housing needs I want to remain as independent as long as I can. I should have those services which will allow me to remain in my own home, be they housekeeping or homemaker or visiting nurse or home care or even meals on wheels. If I need services brought to me for more than 8 hours a day I may need some other arrangement (and help in making the decision). . . .

I never have been able to understand why at a time when my health fails and I need familiar faces and surroundings more than ever—when I have the least resources to make major adjustments—why I have to be moved.

And I don't really understand the devices invented to keep me from benefiting from the programs designed for me. I don't really understand the "spell of illnesses" and the intermediate care and other such developments.[1]

What is most important to me is that I have a choice—that no computer or point system or bureaucratic official makes the decisions for me.

I need more than a roof. Even a beautifully designed building, great improvement that it is in my life, is nothing more than a warehouse cold storage for warm bodies, if the laws that create the facility prevent my having a central food service (I may not always want to, or be able to prepare my meals) or that do not allow the sponsor to include in the rental structure some provision for program services and space.

I want the management to be prepared for me and special needs. I don't want to be thought of as a "tenant." I want the management to be specially trained, to understand me as an individual and the problems I encounter as I age. They have to be more than rent collectors. They have to be service oriented.

In my living arrangement I want a senior center that is a multipurpose service center (that includes a health screening clinic, social security representative, legal services as well as all recreational and educational services) open at all times, professionally staffed with people who have special training.

I should be able to get maximum help from my caseworker—she should have a small enough caseload so that all of the services can be available to me. I should not have to reduce my standard of living to a marked degree. I should have an adequate diet with balanced nutritional meals. I should have opportunities to be useful to myself, to serve others and to serve my community. I should be able to declare what resources I have and then if necessary this can be studied further. My dignity as an individual must always be preserved—what else do I have?

The full resources of the community should be available to me—if I want employment there should be a place toward which I can turn for help in finding it or if I become confused, there should be screening clinics available for early diagnosis and treatment. I don't want to be jailed or committed and then shuttled to a nursing home, especially if that nursing home is not equipped to care for the problems of the senile aged.

I am not looking for a handout. It is not my fault that I am too old to

---

[1]This refers to government regulations affecting payments for services.

work and too young to die. But the dole is a living death. I don't want to lose my vote because I am on a welfare roll. I don't want to feel that because I am poor it is corrupt for me to have a TV. I want to feel that my nation cares enough about me so that it reflects this in uniform national payments for my care.

I want to live life as well as I can, as long as I can, as happily as I can. I want to live it as an individual, not as a ward, not as a statistic, not as a recipient, but as an individual.

That I am old need not be tragedy; it can be the attainment and reward of a full life. That I am poor may not be my fault, but rather the result of an economy in which inflation has shrunken my purchasing power. That I am ill or in poor health is not unusual or unexpected. It means I need more services than I did when I was younger. That I am lonely is not unusual for the older companions of a lifetime are gone. This can be corrected by community awareness, senior centers and programs. That all of these conditions can be relieved or improved is assured if we only wish it so and with the awareness and understanding of our situation by the people of our country, it can be so.

*Older Americans: Who Are They?**

George C. Myers
Beth J. Soldo

Statistics can easily be used to depersonalize very personal issues. Thus, knowing that there are some 22 million people 65 years old and over in the United States can be seen as "interesting" but nothing more. But each one of these 22 million elderly is a human being. Each one has a face, a body, and a brain; each one has thoughts and feelings and hopes and fears; and the face and the fears of each one are different from those of every other one. It is difficult, perhaps impossible, to conceptualize at a personal level what it means for there to be 22 million older people, but think of three or four older people you know, whom you like or dislike, whom you seek out or avoid, and try to realize that each of the 22 million is as uniquely individual as the three or four you know.

For purposes of understanding, of planning, of conceptualizing, we need to know about numbers. We need to know that there are more women than men, that the proportion of elderly who are over age 75 is increasing more rapidly than the proportion between 65 and 74, that the rising proportion of persons in the United States who are elderly is greatly influenced not only by life expectancy but by changes in birth rates and immigration patterns.

The article that follows provides a statistical overview of who older Americans are. Subsequent sections and chapters will add face and form to the bones.

The dynamics of population change express themselves invariably as social concerns. Although the problems of total population size commonly receive extensive treatment in both the popular and the scholarly literature, the more meaningful and enduring issues often are embedded in questions that relate to a population's composition and its territorial distribution and to the changes that occur in these elements over time. When attention is focused on a particular segment of the population, such as the aged, the importance of considering such factors becomes readily apparent. An increase in either the absolute or the relative numbers of the aged, shifts in their composition and spatial distribution, and structural changes in the society and economy resulting from and produced by these alterations dictate the need for a greater awareness of the problems of aging populations. The intent of this section is to highlight some of these changes for the aged population of the United States.

DEMOGRAPHIC ASPECTS OF AGING

Traditionally, demographers have approached the study of aging by examining how fertility (births), mortality (deaths), and migration (moving) interact to produce a given age structure. Although changes in mortality have contributed to the aging of populations, particularly for the Western industrialized nations, the downward trends in fertility have been of even greater significance in producing the higher proportions of the aged. It should be noted, however, that the potential effects of changes in mortality on the number and proportions of the aged are of considerable importance.

A second level of demographic analysis is emerging, however, with wider implications for gerontology and the related social sciences. Aging, in this sense, is a dynamic, multifaceted process. By defining aging as a continuous variable, interest is shifted to social, psychological, economic, and medical variations at different ages. Therefore, attention is directed to those factors that affect the survival conditions of the aged—rates of morbidity, disability, and institutionalization; family composition; and the demographic and socioeconomic determinants and consequences of these factors. For example, we might pose the question "Does a continued decline in births imply more job opportunities for older people as the younger labor-force reserve is reduced?" From this perspective, the aged are treated as a demographically heterogeneous group with respect to a wide range of relevant variables. It should be pointed out that this approach is especially useful for the gerontologist in attempts to understand and anticipate the needs of various elderly groups.

TRENDS IN THE AGED POPULATION

Total Population

The number of persons aged 65 years and over has increased sharply since 1900, whereas the relative percentage change among this segment of the population has shown considerable fluctuation. In 1975, the aged, defined as those 65 years of age and over, numbered approximately 22.4 million of a total population of nearly 214 million (U.S. Bureau of the Census, 1976). Table 1 presents a summary of these data for intercensal periods from 1900 to 1970 and for the year 1975. As the table shows, the median age of the U.S. population rose steadily up to the year 1950, showed a sharp decline during the following 20 years, and has increased gradually in recent years. The median, of course, is sensitive to shifts in the overall age distribution of the population, and the downward trend observed between 1950 and 1970 indicates increases in the young segment of the population (aged 0–24 years). The current rise in the median age suggests, however, that the

Table 1. Selected Measures of the Aged Population, United States, 1900–1970

	Population 65 Years and Over			Percent of Population			Index of	Aged Dependency
			Median	*Under*			*of*	*Dependency*
Year	*Number*	*Change*	*Age*	*15*	*15–64*	*65+*	*Aging**	*Ratio†*
1900	3,080,000	—	22.9	34.4	61.5	4.1	11.8	6.6
1910	3,950,000	+28.2	24.1	32.1	63.6	4.3	13.4	6.8
1920	4,933,000	+24.9	25.3	31.8	63.5	4.7	14.6	7.3
1930	6,634,000	+34.5	26.4	29.4	65.2	5.4	18.4	8.3
1940	9,019,000	+36.0	29.0	25.1	68.1	6.8	27.3	10.0
1950	12,270,000	+36.0	30.2	26.9	65.0	8.1	30.2	12.5
1960‡	16,560,000	+35.0	29.5	31.1	59.7	9.2	29.7	15.5
1970	20,050,000	+21.1	27.9	28.4	61.8	9.8	34.6	15.9
1975	22,400,000[a]	+11.7	28.8[b]	25.1[c]	64.4[c]	10.5	41.8[c]	16.3[c]

*Ratio of population 65 years of age and over to those under 15 years of age.
†Ratio of population 65 years of age and over to those 15–64.
‡Includes Alaska and Hawaii as of 1960.
[a]Demographic Aspects of Aging and the Older Population of the United States, P-23, No. 59 (Washington, D.C., 1976), p. 3, Table 2-1.
[b]Population Estimates and Projections, P-25, No. 614 (Washington, D.C., 1975), p. 5, Table C.
[c]Population Estimates and Projections, P-25, No. 614 (Washington, D.C., 1975), p. 11, Table 1.
Source: Data through 1960 are from U.S. Bureau of Census, 1961, Table 47. Data from 1970 are from U.S. Bureau of the Census, 1971, Table 2.

cohorts that have passed through the age category in which the median falls have been greater than the annual number of births.

An examination of the percentages of population in broad age categories reveals a significant increase in the group categorized as "aged"—from 4.1% in 1900 to 10.5% in 1975. Viewed in a somewhat different manner, it means that roughly every tenth American is 65 years of age or older. The changes revealed in the under-15-years-of-age category reflect primarily the prevailing trends in fertility, with a decline up to 1940, an increase from the postwar baby boom, and a progressive decline in the recent past. While the middle or *active* age category, 15–64 years of age, has fluctuated since 1900, it is interesting to note that in 1975 the proportion of the population in this age classification approximated what it was in 1950. Furthermore, the proportion in 1970 was nearly identical to what it was in 1960.

The two indexes presented in Table 1 relate directly to changes in broad age categories. Both the Index of Aging and the Aged Dependency Ratio (see Table 1 for explanation) show an essentially similar trend toward higher ratios over the period 1900–1975. It is worthwhile to note that the ratio of people aged 65 years and over to the population under 15 years of age has experienced a dramatic increase, particularly in the last five years. The general decline in the birth rate has contributed most significantly to this increase.

From this brief overview, it is evident that the aged population has become an increasing segment of the total population, although the change has been gradual. With a continuation of the present trend of low fertility, we can expect that the median age of the population, as well as the other indexes of aging, will show steady movement reflecting an ever-increasing aged population.

Age Characteristics

An examination of five-year age categories within the broad classification 65 years of age and over provides a revealing picture of the important changes that are taking place. In 1975, the population 65–74 years of age accounted for 61.9% of the aged population; those 75–84 years of age, 29.7%; and those 85 years and over, 8.4%. In the same year, one-half the older population was approximately 73 years of age or older.

Since 1960, the older population has grown faster than the general population, with the aged segment increasing by 35.3%, whereas the population as a whole grew by 19%. Yet, the rate of change for the aged segment during the 1960s was substantially less than that during the 1950s. Table 2 illustrates the differential growth rates of the age groups. During the period 1960–1975, the age groups over 80 years of age increased by much greater amounts than those below 80. Surprisingly, the 65–69 age group experienced a larger percentage increase for the five-year period 1970–1975 than for the preceding decade. The greatest relative growth occurred in the age category 85 years of age and over.

Table 2. Number and Proportion of United States Population by Age Categories 65 Years of Age and Over

Age	1960	Population 1970	1975[a]	Percent Change 1960–70	Percent Change 1970–75	Percent Change 1960–75	Proportion of Aged Population 1960	1970	1975
65–69	6,257,910	6,991,625	8,099,000	11.7	15.8	29.4	37.8	34.8	36.2
70–74	4,738,932	5,443,831	5,775,000	14.9	6.1	21.9	28.6	27.1	25.8
75–79	3,053,559	3,834,834	4,001,000	25.6	4.3	31.0	18.4	19.1	17.9
80–84	1,579,927	2,284,311	2,649,000	44.6	16.0	67.7	9.5	11.4	11.8
85+	929,252	1,510,901	1,877,000	62.6	24.2	102.0	5.6	7.5	8.4

[a]Population Estimates and Projections, P-25, No. 614 (Washington, D.C., 1975), p. 11, Table 1.

Source: "1970 Census of Population, General Population Characteristics," PC(1)-B1, U.S. Summary (Washington, D.C., 1972), p. 269.

Sex

The number of women in the older population greatly exceeds the number of men. The female population 65 years of age and over increased by 46.1% between 1960 and 1975, whereas the male population 65 and over increased by only 22.2%. In 1975, the sex ratio, or the number of males per 100 females, was 69.3 for all those over age 65. As indicated in Table 3, this discrepancy between the number of males and the number of females increases with age, and the gap widened between 1960 and 1975.

Table 3. Sex Ratio by Age Categories 65 Years of Age and Over, United States, 1975

Age	Males per 100 Females 1975[a]	1970	1960
65–69	79.4	80.7	88.1
70–74	73.3	74.0	85.6
75–79	64.7	68.6	80.2
80–84	56.9	62.2	72.7
85+	48.5	56.0	63.9

[a]Population Estimates and Projections, P-25, No. 614 (Washington, D.C., 1975), p. 11, Table 1.

Source: "1970 Census of Population, General Population Characteristics," PC(1)-B1, U.S. Summary (Washington, D.C., 1972), p. 271, Table 52.

Progress in prolonging life is reflected by reductions in age-specific mortality rates, but changes in these rates are not equally distributed among specific population groups. Throughout the life cycle, females experience lower mortality than males, although the extent to which females have lower mortality varies considerably with age. At ages 65 and over, the mortality rate among males is about 40% higher than among females, a smaller differential than that for any other age group except the youngest (Statistical Bulletin, 1964), yet one large enough to contribute to the difference in the number of aged males and the number of aged females.

There have been many biological and social inquiries into the differential survivorship between males and females (Myers, 1975). Duncan (1968), for example, cites stress among working males as a possible explanation. A question frequently asked is "If stress is a contributing factor, can this trend be expected to continue as more women enter the labor force full time and participate equally with men in a range of more stressful activities?" Continued research on this issue is clearly needed. Grannis (1970) makes an interesting case for cigarette smoking as a possible cause of the differential sex composition at older ages. He concludes that "the ratio of widows to widowers has changed during the past 75 years to the extent expected on the basis of national cigarette consumption by males and the known relation of the degree of cigarette smoking to premature mortality by males" (p. 62).

In the past, decreases in mortality from infectious diseases were primarily responsible for increased life expectancy at all ages. But as the chronic, degenerative diseases have gained new importance, their differential impact on males and females has been felt. Will future reductions in these "modern diseases" continue to favor females? Increased life expectancy for both males and females also may hinge on improvements in the delivery of health services. It is known that females generally use medical services more often than males. Will expanded and more accessible health services further contribute to these differentials?

There are numerous direct and indirect effects of differential mortality by sex. Will more elderly women reenter the labor force as successive cohorts of the aged with more education and prior labor-force experience enter the later age groups? Are the present trends of elderly women living alone as widows to be continued? What will be the effect of changing mortality by sex on Social Security and welfare payments?

Demographers, epidemiologists, and gerontologists need to investigate the important factors leading to the female advantage, the future expectations for these differentials, and their implications for labor-force participation, for welfare and Social Security payments, and for family composition and distribution patterns among the elderly.

Cross-cultural studies of this problem area are clearly needed, as are inquiries into the effects of sex roles, life-style, psychological attitudes, and physiological differences on varying patterns of male and female survivorship.

Racial Characteristics

While longevity among non-Whites in the United States has continued to increase, the life expectancy for non-White males and females is distinctly below that for comparable categories of Whites. In 1974, the life expectancy at birth for non-White males was 62.9 years; that for females,

71.2 years (National Center for Health Statistics, 1974). The 8.3-year discrepancy between non-White male and female life expectancy approximates that of the White population (68.9 years and 76.6 years, respectively, with a 7.7-year discrepancy).

In 1975, 7.2% of the non-White population was over 65 years of age, a considerably smaller proportion of aged than in the total population. All non-White age categories over age 65, however, have a much higher growth rate than comparable groups in the total population. Better census coverage and accuracy in age reporting may account for part of this substantial growth. Research is clearly required to determine the effects of improvements in differential mortality and better health-care services as alternative explanations.

Observations on White and non-White mortality rates suggest an advantageous position for the non-White population at the very old ages. This characteristic, as noted from current data, is independent of time interval, measure used, sex differential, or specific cause of death. Although both populations show similar age curves of mortality, the "crossover effect" is generated by more rapidly rising death rates for Whites than for non-Whites after age 55 (Thornton & Nam, 1968). The effects of measurement error or age misstatement among elderly Blacks, however, has not been ascertained. The crossover effect also may indicate poor quality of data. Assuming that a differential exists, however, both biological and social selection would seem to be operating. Additional research into the interaction of these factors at all ages should receive especially high priority. (See the following article, "The Black Aging: A Demographic Overview," for a more complete discussion.)

DISTRIBUTION PATTERNS OF THE AGED

The distribution of the older population is frequently measured by determining the percentage of aged persons among the total population residing in a given area and then comparing these data with the national proportion. From such comparisons it is possible to determine which locales constitute aging areas. Thus, in 1970, 23 states had larger proportions of aged populations than the national average of 9.8%, but only one state— Florida, with 14.5%—exceeded the national average by more than 2.5 percentage points. The other states had less than 9.9% of the population aged, with Hawaii (5.7%) and Alaska (2.3%) at the extreme end of the scale. Similarly, in 1975, the percentage of aged ranged from 2.4% (in Alaska) to 16.1% (in Florida), as compared with a national average of 10.5%.

Although eight states showed decreasing proportions of aged, the national trend has been toward increasing proportions. Forty-two states showed increased percentages of the aged population both in 1950–1960 and in 1960–1970.

Varying proportions of the aged are the result of the interactions among fertility, mortality, and migration. Although a decrease in fertility is the major factor in increasing proportions of the aged, migration is highly significant in altering the geographical distribution of the aged population. An important research concern is to establish whether individual areas are being affected because many of the younger population are leaving or because people are moving in.

The U.S. population as a whole grew by 7.6% between 1960 and 1970 and by an additional 4.3% between 1970 and 1975. Between 1960 and 1970, the aged living in urban areas increased by 6.5%, and the rural aged increased by 7.9%. Clearly, the rural aged contributed more to the growing proportions of the elderly in the United States. Cowgill (1970, pp. 27–70) suggests that the pattern has been quickly shifting, and cities, once havens for the young, have been losing younger population through suburban migration and therefore are left with high proportions of older people.

As the United States becomes increasingly urbanized, the use of a simple urban/rural distinction loses a great deal of meaning. Rural places of 1000 to 2500 inhabitants show the greatest concentration of aged. Whereas 13.6% of the total rural nonfarm population was 65 and over in 1970, the farm population contained only 9.6% aged, which is somewhat below the national average. This suggests that old people have been increasingly moving off the farm at retirement and moving into small towns. Not only are older people migrating to small towns, but young persons are leaving such areas, especially those experiencing depressed economic conditions. Small cities with between 2500 and 10,000 inhabitants show the second highest proportion of aged in 1970—12.2%. Smaller towns and cities appear to predominate as local aging areas. This pattern holds for all age categories over 65.

The sex ratio ranges from 71.0 (males per 100 females) in rural areas of 1000 to 2500 to 92.8 in rural farm areas. This difference reflects the increased proportion of husband/wife families among the aged in rural areas. Of the total population, 30.5% were living with spouse, including 28.8% of the urban aged and 35.1% of the rural aged.

This difference in urban/rural sex ratios also may reflect lower male mortality rates in the rural areas. Sauer and Donnell (1970) found a moderate association between geographic distribution and the rates of cardiovascular/renal diseases and malignant neoplasms for White males aged 35–74. They conclude, however, that "The association is not due to any appreciable extent to the tendency for metropolitan areas to have higher rates for both categories than do non-metropolitan areas" (p. 85). They also found a number of moderate correlations between ecological factors and the risk of death. Additional research along these lines is needed before any definite conclusions may be drawn. The relationships must be well established before the effect of increasing urban residence on mortality rates can be adequately assessed or future trends in distribution patterns of the aged can be projected.

The Black population, although only 7.8% of the total aged population, is distributed in a similar manner to that of Whites. Of the total Black population in urban areas, 6.5% is 65 and over, whereas 8.7% of the rural population is aged. The aged Black population also shows the highest proportions in rural towns between 1000 and 2500 population and in small urban areas of 2500 to 10,000 inhabitants.

The distribution patterns of aged within metropolitan areas point up the increasing central-city concentration of this group. Cowgill (1957) has suggested that "to a measurable extent the central areas of most cities have become specialized as dwelling areas for the aged . . . . [although] the degree of such specialization in relation to the rest of the city is not increasing, and, in fact, shows some tendency to decline" (p. 80).

Recent analysis of 1970 census data confirms the hypothesis that within the central city the aged population has grown faster than the total population (Howard, 1971). In 1970, 10.7% of the population of central cities was aged 65 and over, whereas only 7.8% of the urban fringe or suburban population fell into this category. The aged population increased by an average of 16% from 1960 to 1970 within central cities of the United States. Of the 50 largest standard metropolitan statistical areas in the country, 42 had a larger aged population in their central cities at the end of the decade. Moreover, the growth rate of the aged non-Whites in the central city was substantially higher than for either the White aged population or the total non-White population. The changing racial structure within the aged population in central cities merits considerable research effort.

MOBILITY PATTERNS AMONG THE AGED

Although young adults predominate among movers, the aged population is not completely sedentary. The aged have lower mobility rates than any other age group and generally move for different reasons. Using 1960 census data, Lenzer (1965) found that 64% of the aged remained in the same house, whereas 50% of the total population did so during the five years preceding the 1960 census. Ideally, the type of move (intracounty, intrastate, or interstate), the age of the mover, and the reason for moving should be identified in a study of mobility patterns.

Mobility patterns of the aged remain constant between ages 65 and 74 but increase after age 75. Increased mobility presumably reflects changes associated with widowhood and institutionalization. As those who are single or widowed are more likely to move than married individuals, it is hypothesized that women predominate among elderly movers, in terms of both absolute numbers and proportions.

The elderly tend to move for somewhat different reasons than the young. In contrast to younger people, for whom economic considerations are most commonly cited as reasons for moving (Rossi, 1955), the elderly seek better climates, special housing or care facilities, and opportunities to be near or live with relatives, and possibly lower costs of living. The large net migration to Florida is testimony to a desire for better climate and special housing. In a sample survey of the Los Angeles standard metropolitan statistical area, dissatisfaction with current housing and neighborhood accounted for a large share of the mobility behavior among older persons. Economic and employment reasons explained less than one-fifth of the moves (Goldscheider, 1966). Age, however, is inversely related to long-distance moves, in which economic reasons usually are of major importance.

Cross-tabulation of mobility behavior by age and race is generally lacking. There is some evidence that on both the individual and the aggregate levels elderly non-Whites are as desirous of moving as their White counterparts, but they do not realize these desires as often. Previous residential mobility, stage in the family life-cycle, and home ownership seem to indicate that social stability is conducive to residential stability among the elderly.

In short, there are various interesting questions relating to the spatial distribution and movement of this age group that have received little attention from either gerontologists or demographers. Moreover, the results of such studies would seem to have much importance for policies and plans affecting the allocation of public expenditures and the location of special facilities to serve the aged.

Assessment of both present and future size, composition, and distribution of the aged population is essential to policy formulation. The basically descriptive approach taken in this chapter is only a beginning toward more extensive and probing research into the *determinants* and *consequences* of demographic factors. The requirements for the future must place greater emphasis on developing our knowledge of past trends and taking concerted steps toward predicting future developments. In this effort, more dynamic and longitudinal studies are clearly needed, and a firm commitment must be made toward examining the process of aging. Cross-sectional studies are usually beneficial, but they must be supplemented by more dynamic analyses of aging as well as of the aged.

Aging and Ethnicity

The population of the United States can be looked at as a totality, as we have done in the previous article. It can also be looked at in terms of the various groups that make up this totality: sex; religion; regional, ethnic, or social class; age; and locale, among other classifications. The following readings describe aging within four ethnic groups in the United States: Black, Asian American, Mexican American and Native American. I selected these groups above others because considerable attention has been given to them recently and because the needs of ethnic communities are often not fully understood by persons outside those communities.

The argument might be made that women also deserve a special discussion, and you may disagree with my reasons for not including such a section. Essentially, I feel that so many workers in the field are women and that so much of what has been written on aging includes women, or even focuses on women, that a special section is not necessary.

Each of the authors treats the community discussed in a somewhat different fashion. In the first article, elderly Blacks are viewed from a demographic point of view, and the author takes a strong position on the significance of the data she has brought together; the article on Chinese and Japanese Americans is written from a sociohistorical approach; Native Americans are discussed from a broad perspective; and the Mexican-American article provides a sociocultural approach.

In the preceding article, authors Myers and Soldo make comparisons between Whites and non-Whites. Dr. Jackson, on the other hand, restricts herself primarily to discussing differences within the Black (or, because information is not always available, non-White) segment of the population. Although there is some overlap in these two articles, each uses the information for quite different purposes.

Asian Americans and Native Americans are also included as non-Whites, but they constitute an extremely small percentage of the entire population, and statistics on these groups are not easily available. Persons of Spanish heritage (including, but not limited to, Mexican Americans, Puerto Ricans, Cubans, and those of Central American origin) generally are numbered with Whites, but separate statistics are sometimes available.

It is important to keep in mind, as Dr. Jackson so forcefully states, that differences within these ethnic/racial communities are great and that thinking about or planning for Native Americans or Japanese Americans as though all their elderly are alike would be just as inappropriate as it would be to consider all college students, regardless of race, age, or sex, as a single entity.

One more issue deserves particular emphasis. By selecting four ethnic/ racial communities for attention, I am not saying that these are the only ones that matter. Innumerable other groups could have been included: North Americans whose background is Irish, Italian, Greek, Samoan, Jewish, Czech, Basque, French, and so on. Although many persons belonging to each ethnic community have assimilated into the North American society and have few or no vestiges of their origins (and others are of such mixed origin that they can hardly trace themselves back to non-American ancestry), immense numbers of people in the United States and Canada identify with one or more ethnic communities as well as with their present country. It is a mistake to assume that only those persons who are sometimes termed Third World *ethnic groups retain identification. Many other elderly persons are influenced by their origins.*

The Black Aging:
A Demographic Overview*

Jacquelyne J. Jackson

Poor, illiterate, helpless, dependent, in extended family, in ill health, *et cetera.* Typical imageries of aged blacks. Deprived, disadvantaged, unqualified, inarticulate, *et cetera.* Plus scarce. Recent but now typical imageries of black graduate and professional students. Many aging educationists and other professionals believe (or at least act as if they believe) those or similar descriptions are apt for both aged blacks and black students. But, excepting poverty, such traits are generally uncharacteristic of both groups. These inappropriate conceptions arise out of negative and homogeneous "white middle-class-mind-sets" toward blacks. Most whites label blacks atypical of those traits as "exceptionals," avoiding thereby careful or even superficial examination of their own prejudices.

Ideally blacks should ignore persons with such "mind-sets." But, unfortunately, realism demands confrontation since most aging research, training, and services affecting blacks are controlled by white individuals with those "mind-sets." Thus, blacks and others genuinely concerned about aged blacks must seek to influence favorably those powerholders and eventually gain control over their own lives and destinies.

This presentation is concerned with some 1970 census descriptions suggestive of social stratification among aged blacks (i.e., 65 or more years of age), which underscore a need for planning and training diversification of or for aging blacks.

SOCIAL STRATIFICATION AMONG AGED BLACKS

Aged blacks in the United States in 1970 were not "all just alike." They varied demographically by such variables as age, geographical location, sex, marital status, household composition, and educational and economic levels. While census data do not and cannot permit a precise capturing of social stratification among aged blacks, they are useful in indicating their variations and in suggesting what some of us already know to be so: namely, while by any national classification, a majority of aged blacks are of lower socioeconomic status, some are of middle and others, although fewer, of upper socioeconomic statuses.

*Edited from "Social Stratification of Aged Blacks and Implications for Training Professionals," by J. J. Jackson. In J. J. Jackson (Ed.), *Black Aged in the Future,* mimeographed monograph based on the proceedings of a conference in San Juan, Puerto Rico, December 15–16, 1972, pp. 114–132. All rights reserved. Permission to reprint must be obtained from the author and the publisher.

Age

In 1970, the 1,558,754 aged blacks enumerated by the U.S. Bureau of Census constituted slightly less than 7 percent of the total black population, about half of whom were under 22 years of age. But these aged blacks themselves were not age homogeneous, ranging from 65 to more than 100 years. In fact, about 40 percent or two-fifths were between the ages of 65 and 69, and about two-thirds were under 75. About 16 percent were between 75 and 79, about 9 percent between 80 and 84, and almost 8 percent were 85 or more years of age. As is perhaps well known by now, life expectancies of blacks who attain 69 years of birthdays are longer than those for whites. As I have been emphasizing for at least a decade, very old blacks in the United States are probably most elite and certainly in better health than almost any other group of American aged.

Sex

As expected, a majority of the aged black population was—what else—female. In fact, in 1970, about 52 percent of the black population of all ages was female, and about 57 percent of the aged black population was also female. The aged black sex ratio of 76.5 (i.e., 76.5 males/100 females) was considerably lower than that of 90.8 in the total black population. More interesting, perhaps, was the geographical variation in the aged sex ratio: it was highest in the North Central region (81.3), followed by 76.3 in both the South and the West, and lowest in the Northeast (71.8).

Marital Status

The usual variations in marital status between the sexes in existence prior to 1970 were also present in 1970, as can be seen from Table 1. In addition to showing the percentages of various aged groups by marital status, it also contains the same data for all persons 14 or more years of age by sex. Worth noting are such observations as the following. A majority of black males, 65–79 years of age, were married and living with spouse in 1970. Almost half of the males between 80 and 84 years of age were also married and living with their wives. *In fact, in 1970, a majority of all black males within the United States were married and living with their wives.* Such data should remind us to examine the extent to which federally funded activities for black aged, such as Senior Citizens Centers, are geared toward planning some activities for married couples.

Education

Very often the presumably low educational level of aged blacks is proffered as sufficient rationalization for their underutilization or inappropriate utilization of existing services, and, worse, as adequate explanation for their generally lower income levels when compared with aged whites.

Table 1. Marital Status of Blacks, 14+ Years of Age by Sex and Selected Ages, United States, 1970

| | | % in Each Marital Status | | |
| | | *Married,* | | *Separated or* |
Sex and Age	*Single*	*with Spouse*	*Widowed*	*Divorced*
Male				
14+ years of age	35.5	48.3	4.3	11.9
65–69 years	7.6	60.9	17.9	13.6
70–74 years	7.8	58.2	21.4	12.6
75–79 years	7.6	51.4	29.4	11.5
80–84 years	7.5	46.6	35.4	10.5
85+ years	13.9	36.5	38.1	11.5
Females				
14+ years of age	28.7	41.2	13.3	16.9
65–69 years	5.8	35.2	46.9	12.1
70–74 years	5.6	27.2	57.4	9.8
75–79 years	6.2	19.1	67.0	7.7
80–84 years	6.4	12.1	75.2	6.3
85+ years	8.5	8.7	76.6	6.1

Source: U.S. Bureau of Census. Census of Population: *1970 Detailed Characteristics,* Final Report PC(1)-D1, United States Summary. Washington, D.C.: U.S. Government Printing Office, 1973.

However, it may be more appropriate to examine the conscious or unconscious motives of those engaging in such false rationalizations. In other words, for many aged blacks, the generally low level of formal educational attainment is not only often an insufficient index of their actual educational levels, but has nothing to do with the fact that, as exploited workers, they have been made to work for slave wages. Those who are in poverty are not generally in poverty merely because of education, as absolute income gaps between blacks and whites with equal educational levels have existed for years and years and years.

Further, and also in contradiction with many popular images, some aged blacks are highly educated. Educational levels (i.e., years of completed formal schooling) of blacks 25+ years of age and of aged blacks are shown by sex in Table 2.

The data show that while the median educational level for both sexes of the aged blacks was between five and seven years, and while a higher proportion of each sex within each age group was more likely to have received no formal education than education beyond high school, educational diversity was, nevertheless, present. Some aged blacks have had no formal education, but others are highly educated, including holders of earned terminal graduate or professional degrees, such as a Ph.D., M.D. or D.D.S. In 1970, 33,272 blacks 65 or more years of age had completed a college education or obtained education beyond college. About 37 percent of these highly educated and aged blacks were males. Many were professional educators,

Table 2. Educational Distribution of Aging and Aged Blacks, by Sex, 1970

Sex and Age	None	Highest Completed Year of Schooling						Median (years)
		1–8	*9–11*	*12*	*13–15*	*16*	*17+*	
Males								
% 25+ years	3.9	43.1	22.9	20.0	6.0	2.2	2.0	9.4
% 65–69 years	8.9	71.6	10.2	5.3	2.2	0.9	0.9	6.0
% 70–74 years	11.1	71.5	8.5	4.9	2.2	0.9	0.8	5.6
% 75+ years	15.4	68.8	7.5	4.5	2.1	1.0	0.7	5.1
Females								
% 25+ years	2.7	38.4	26.4	22.2	5.6	2.9	1.7	10.1
% 65–69 years	5.7	68.3	13.7	6.9	2.8	1.7	0.9	7.0
% 70–74 years	7.2	69.8	11.6	6.3	2.8	1.6	0.7	6.7
% 75+ years	11.4	68.2	9.7	5.9	2.6	1.6	0.5	6.1

health practitioners, social scientists, natural scientists, or social workers during their major years of employment. Thus, given the relatively small number of existing training programs in aging, the "scarcity" of educated blacks potentially available for service as short- or long-term professors may well be a figment of the imagination or a result of inadequate or insincere recruitment efforts.

Employment and Occupation

Perhaps it should be stressed that the majority of aged blacks were not, of course, within the labor force at all in 1970. In fact, 76.5 percent of the males and 86.8 percent of the females were outside the labor force. Most interesting is the observation of higher labor force participation among those 85+ years of age than among those 80–84 and 75–84 years of age among males and females respectively. This phenomenon could, no doubt, be attributed to a greater number of very old individuals engaged in farm or farm-related activities.

Table 3 contains percentage data showing occupational distributions of aged blacks by sex. Almost 58 percent of the total number of 265,226 employed black males and females 65 or more years of age were male. About 14 percent of the males and 15 percent of the females were in white collar employment, which indicates some occupational diversification. As can be seen, slightly over one-half of all employed aged females in 1970 were household domestics. This is probably the last generation of aged blacks which will contain such a high proportion of female workers in this category. Almost all of these employed domestics failed to earn sufficient income—despite their long working hours—to place them above the poverty level. Thus, it appears quite probable that reexamination of the extent to which work itself is a viable solution for income problems of many aged blacks is in order. Studies showing that old blacks, at least, desire employ-

Table 3. Occupational Distribution of Aged Black Labor Force Participants by Sex, 1970

Occupational Category	Males	Females
Total Number Employed Persons	153,547	111,679
% Professional, technical, and kindred workers	4.6	6.8
% Managers and administrators, except farm	3.5	1.9
% Sales workers	1.9	1.7
% Clerical and kindred workers	4.0	5.0
% Craftsmen and kindred workers	10.4	1.3
% Operatives, including transport	16.3	8.6
% Laborers, except farm	17.9	1.5
% Farmers and farm managers	4.4	0.3
% Farm laborers and foremen	7.4	1.2
% Service workers, except private household	27.8	20.2
% Private household workers	1.8	51.4

ment must distinguish carefully between those who seek employment after retirement merely because they wish to continue working (but do not need the money), because they need the money (but do not wish to work if their retirement incomes were sufficient), or because they both wish to work and need the money.

Income

Although most aged blacks are plagued by deplorably low incomes, not all aged blacks live in poverty. Table 4 shows the percentage of blacks, 60+ years of age, by various individual income levels in 1969 for those with income in that year. It also contains the median income levels for each age and sex group.

Table 4. Individual Income of Blacks, 60+ Years of Age, in 1969, by Sex

Sex and Age	Income					Median	Mean
	Under $1,000	$1,000– 2,999	$3,000– 5,999	$6,000– 9,999	$10,000+		
Males							
% 60–64 years old	13.6	28.8	32.1	21.5	4.7	$3616	$4164
% 65–69 years old	20.0	48.3	21.4	8.4	2.0	1956	2744
% 70–74 years old	23.2	56.3	16.0	3.6	0.9	1711	2198
% 75+ years old	30.1	55.6	10.9	2.7	0.7	1503	1882
Females							
% 60–64 years old	37.3	39.7	16.2	5.3	1.5	$1466	$2120
% 65–69 years old	44.0	45.8	7.7	1.9	0.5	1170	1530
% 70–74 years old	46.3	47.2	5.2	1.0	0.4	1098	1364
% 75+ years old	51.3	43.4	4.1	0.8	0.3	974	1237

The usual correlations between education and income were present among aged blacks. For example, in 1969, the mean income of aged males with income was $2,319, but it ranged from a mean of $1,807 for those with less than five years of schooling to a mean of $7,934 for those with education beyond college. The mean income for all comparable females was $1,384, with a range of $1,102 for those with less than five years of schooling to $4,959 for those with education beyond college. In each instance, however, even when education and age were held constant, aged whites earned more income than aged blacks.

The same types of income patterns between blacks and whites in the United States over the past few decades are also present between black females and males. That is, the absolute income earnings of whites are becoming continuously larger than those of blacks; the absolute income earnings of black males are also becoming continuously larger than those of black females.

Family

In 1970, among all blacks, aged persons headed 11.8 percent of all families. Almost none of these families had any minor offspring (i.e., own children under 18 years of age) within their homes, but a few did. But—and quite important—*the majority of all black families with heads 65 or more years of age in 1970 contained only two persons.* About 67 percent of these husband-wife families contained only the husband and the wife; and about 54 percent each of the female-headed and the other male-headed families contained only one person in addition to the head. Thus, most aged blacks do not live in large or extended families.

Despite such data as the above, however, myths continue to persist among even aging professionals specializing in the family. Too many continue to believe and teach that most aged blacks reside in large extended families, where, to embellish the myth further, enough family members are available to wait upon them and attend to their various needs. Thus, it may be useful for us to not only stress the generally small family size for most aged blacks, but to provide some additional information about their living arrangements in 1970. Those concerned about "Black aged in the future" also need some information about "Black aged now."

Table 5 depicts living arrangements for both sexes, 65–74 years of age and 75+ years of age. As is evident, almost all aged blacks reside within households. They are rarely institutionalized. As Hobart C. Jackson, Chairman, National Caucus on the Black Aged, has repeatedly emphasized, overinstitutionalization of the aged has never been a problem for aged blacks. The major problems have been underinstitutionalization or inappropriate institutionalization.

About one-fifth of aged black males and one-third of aged black females lived alone (i.e., as primary individuals), and about 27 percent of all aged blacks resided alone in 1970. Thus, once again, most aged blacks either resided with one other person (usually spouse or adult child) or lived alone. Finally, as an aside, while 1.8 percent of all black males, 14+ years of age

Table 5. Living Arrangements of Aged Blacks by Sex and Age, 1970

	Males		Females	
Living Arrangement	*65–74 years*	*75 + years*	*65–74 years*	*75 + years*
Total Number of Persons	468,588	222,364	587,217	303,833
% in Households	96.9	94.7	97.6	94.0
% within Families	71.3	66.2	63.9	59.0
% in Group Quarters	3.1	5.3	2.4	6.0
% Secondary Individual	0.6	0.7	0.4	0.5
% in Institution	2.4	4.6	2.0	5.5
% Mental Hospital or Home for Mentally Handicapped	0.7	1.1	0.7	1.0
% Home for the Aged	1.3	3.0	1.1	4.0
% Correctional Institution	0.2	0.1	—	—
% Other	0.4	0.5	0.2	0.5

were in correctional institutions in 1970 (i.e., over 98 percent of all such black males were not in prison), the rate was substantially lower among aged black males, where, as shown in Table 5 only 0.2 percent were in correctional institutions.

Such data as those presented in Table 5 can be useful in reducing homogeneous "mind-sets" about aged blacks. In general, they reveal considerable heterogeneity among almost 1,600,000 individuals whose only universally shared trait (beyond those shared by all human beings) was that of race.

Aging among Chinese and Japanese Americans*

Richard A. Kalish
Sharon Moriwaki

The first generation Asian American, having been socialized in his early years to a Japanese or Chinese value system, is now growing old and facing death in a milieu much at variance with his beginnings. Hsu (1971) states:

In America the most desired position of the individual is a combination of (a) economic and social independence, (b) successful and rapid achieve-

*Edited from "The World of the Elderly Asian American," by R. A. Kalish and S. Moriwaki, *Journal of Social Issues,* 1973, 29(2), 187–209. Reprinted by permission of the Society for the Psychological Study of Social Issues.

ment of this goal, and (c) the use of creative means in achieving an identity of one's own [p. 86].

Hsu then shows how these values conflict with the values of traditional Chinese society, which discourages financial independence from parents and extended family, while encouraging interdependence, opposes "cutthroat competition for individual ends" [Hsu, p. 87], and rejects "the emphasis upon creativity [which] has given men license for indiscriminate and irresponsible use of any means to pursue an end" [Hsu, p. 87]. Hsu subsequently suggests that the basic root differentiating American and Chinese value systems is the individual-centered orientation and self-reliance of the former vis-à-vis the situation-centered orientation and mutual dependence on the family of the latter.

Financial Independence

For the elderly Chinese American, reared to believe that children should not become financially independent of their parents, contemporary American values must be highly distressing. Except for the handful of very well-to-do, most elderly Chinese have modest or low incomes—some have virtually no income at all. Yet their children, now middle aged, have undoubtedly received better formal education than their parents, and their present earning power and net worth are probably many times that of their parents. Simmons (1945) has shown that respect for the elderly is highest in societies where the elderly maintain meaningful control of property, income, and jobs. The elderly Chinese Americans have little such control. Their only claim to their children's respect is community pressure (and this can be very powerful), plus the shame, guilt, love, and personal respect that have developed over the years. In a stable society, such as China prior to the postwar period, the wholesale upward mobility of an entire generation would be virtually impossible; in the United States and in Canada, it occurred.

A parallel occurs among the Japanese Americans. Because the first generation could not own real property, real estate was purchased in the name of an American citizen, often the natural child of the alien Japanese, but not infrequently the American born child of a very close friend. Although the right of the American citizen child to receive such a gift from his noncitizen parent (or family friend) was contested, the action was upheld as appropriate.

In effect this meant that the first generation could neither own property nor become citizens until so late in their lives that vocational achievement and financial success were very difficult, although Kitano (1969) can say, "Most of them are in comfortable circumstances" [p. 139]. They met many kinds of discrimination in jobs and education and through legal statute that severely limited their progress. The aged Japanese American, with inevitable exceptions, was even less likely to accumulate property because of initial expectations of returning to his homeland.

The relocation camps made matters still worse. The Issei heads of families were unable to forestall the loss of property and were similarly unable to protect their children against incarceration. Not only did their sometimes-limited skills in English and their naiveté regarding American laws and bureaucracy impede their receiving a fair response, but no noncitizen was permitted to hold an administrative office in the Evacuation Centers or the War Relocation Camps. Thus the first generation was ignobly stripped of all status and authority and relegated to second-class roles, even within the context of the internment camps. The Nisei, then largely in their teens and twenties, assumed the offices of managers, block captains, council members, and so forth.

Up until the relocation, there was general acceptance of the idea that the parents (primarily Issei) held the reins of the family by tradition, even when they did not have economic power. The camps would appear to have been responsible for forcing the Issei from power and turning it over to the Nisei.

Upon the postwar return to private life, it was the Nisei who was able to take advantage of educational opportunities and to obtain better jobs, while the Issei, the fruits of his most productive years often destroyed by the lengthy incarceration and his dominant role having been effectively undermined, was forced to return to what he had been doing—often required to work with his sons or sons-in-law not as a respected patriarch, but as an equal or even a subordinate.[1]

Americans, who tend to value financial and social independence, rugged individualism, and freedom from parents, often express deep concern when middle-aged children appear to turn from their elderly parents by not showing proper deference and caring. How much more intense this feeling must be in a culture where independence and self-reliance are negatively valued in the first place.

Competition for Individual Ends

Hsu's (1971) second point was opposition among Chinese to "cutthroat competition for individual ends." The important distinction is that aggressive competition between extended family units or between tongs is not deprecated, but the purpose of the competition is to enhance the family or the group rather than the self. Elderly Chinese who are part of an established extended family will probably have some feeling of belonging and of meaning, through group identification and through carrying along a tradition; not infrequently, their effort in working with the family is required. In a distressing number of instances, however, the aged Chinese American is either lacking such close relationships or is unable to capitalize upon them as his tradition has promised him. And some Chinese have never been part

---

[1]Much of this account is incorporated directly from the notes of Kazue Togasaki, now a San Francisco physician, whose knowledge of the situation was gathered from her own personal experience.

of such an association; they were required to enter the general American work arena, where individual competition is socially reinforced.

Creativity

When Hsu speaks of creativity, we surmise his unhappiness is in response to rapid change in social systems. This kind of creativity, which upsets what seems to be the natural order of things, disrupts traditional relationships. Americans at mid-century and thereafter seem to reward innovation for the sake of innovation, changing styles, changing houses, changing spouses, changing jobs. The elderly of all cultures are conservative in that they wish to conserve—conserve values, conserve strength, conserve money, conserve energy, conserve relationships. The fast-moving world is distressing; new customs and people and rules are no sooner assimilated than they are passé. As memory and vitality diminish, as time boundaries begin to blur, the aged tend to hold more strongly to the values which are familiar to them.

As with independence and competition, if the elderly in our society which is highly supportive of innovation are disturbed by the rapid change of customs and manners, values, and technology, consider how much more disturbed would be persons reared in societies that looked askance at social innovation.

In discussing the traditional Japanese, Kitano (1969) comments that "Japanese reverence for hard work, achievement, self-control, dependability, manners, thrift, and diligence were entirely congruent with American middleclass perceptions" [p. 76]. This is at a different level of abstraction from Hsu's comparison of the Chinese and Americans. Kitano's list of admired qualities points to the norms held by the Japanese immigrants, not their motivations for behavior. These norms derive from values which are similar to those posited by Hsu: the importance of the family and the dependence of the individual on the family group, and obedience and duty to elders.

To an appreciable extent, both Hsu and Kitano have presented values and norms applicable to each other's national group. These cultural maps have been transplanted to a country where the basic axioms of family-centered stable life and rules of proper conduct have little relevance, where rules and roles are in constant flux as the individual moves in different circles of others. We are again reminded of how maladaptive even American value systems are to being old in America; the value systems of Japan and China, as transmitted to Japanese and Chinese Americans, are even more maladaptive for these elderly in this country.

A LOOK BACKWARDS

In traditional East Asia, the kin group was the functioning unit, and the individual was part of a network of primary relations stemming from the family. Among the Japanese, primogeniture was through the eldest son, and as technology decreased the value of small landholdings, the younger son could do little but go for further schooling or move to the cities. Emigration to America to make their fortunes was an attractive alternative for the ambitious. They form the predominant group of Japanese American aged, the Issei.

The Chinese, on the other hand, distributed wealth (land primarily) equally to all sons, and land was felt to belong to the entire family. Thus emigration was due to external causes—the overpopulation problems, political conflicts, and so forth. Both groups of Asians came to the United States and Canada expecting to grow rich in these countries of promise and then to return to leisure and superior status in their own lands. The final result of their migration was to grow old in a foreign land, with a different language, a strange value system, and odd rules of behavior. Changes these immigrants would have encountered in their homeland might have been difficult to accept, but the changes would have occurred in a familiar environment and through a familiar language; they would have been better comprehended, even if not necessarily approved.

If Chinese American, the elderly person is probably a man (the ratio of males to females, all ages combined, in California was 107:100 in 1970; the same ratio among the aged would be higher); although Chinese immigration patterns date back to the middle of the last century, most early arrivals were men and progeny were seldom left to carry on.

If Japanese American, the elderly is more likely a woman (the California ratio of males to females of all ages was 88:100 in the 1970 census, and women tend to live longer than men); the Japanese immigration occurred primarily between the last dozen or fifteen years of the nineteenth century and the first two decades of the twentieth. A modest flow of picture brides, however, continued through the end of 1924; many of these women were the mothers of the Nisei in the relocation camps.

Almost all of today's elderly Japanese Americans arrived in the United States and Canada during the early part of this century, while a moderate number of elderly Chinese Americans arrived more recently, either coming initially as students or businessmen, perhaps seeking political sanctuary, or as part of the very recent immigrant group following the Immigration Acts of the past two decades.

The Asians suffered from discrimination that was codified in law and that explicitly listed them as the victims of the overtly discriminatory laws. The Alien Land Acts, the Alien Exclusion Act, miscegenation laws, the World War II treatment of the Japanese Americans are the most conspicuous of these laws and regulations (although relatively few of Hawaii's Japanese were interned).

Not until 1952 could first-generation Asians become citizens. They were thus unable to vote or exert any but the most marginal political influence. Moreover, they were left in legal jeopardy since they could readily be deported. Even today, first-generation Asian Americans, all but the most recent arrivals having become citizens, are reluctant to become involved with the legal and bureaucratic mechanisms of this nation. Therefore they may refrain from seeking medical care, legal advice, or financial help until their difficulties have reached an extreme stage. If the problems are medical, institutionalization is often required, bringing about an even more stressful situation—alone in an unfamiliar and incomprehensible environment.

Studies of stereotypes during the 1930s and 1940s (for example, Katz & Braly, 1933; Gilbert, 1951) serve as reminders that the elderly Asian American of today faced a very antagonistic white community during his early adult years. The often patronizing, but still favorable, stereotypes their grandchildren complain so vociferously about today would have been a welcome relief from being viewed as inscrutable, superstitious, sly, shrewd, and imitative. Although prejudice and discrimination are not lacking today, it is difficult to recall the intensity of feelings directed against today's first generation when they were young and middle-aged parents and the second generation was growing up.

And They Are Now Old

The Chinese Americans often lived in Chinese enclaves to which new immigrants came upon entering the country; San Francisco's Chinatown is now drawing elderly Chinese from the entire West Coast (from Vancouver to San Diego) and east to Chicago, perhaps in lieu of their ability to return to China. Elderly Japanese Americans, although torn out of their own communities during World War II and although less likely to reside in sections as ethnically dense as Chinatown, have also tended to live an insular existence.

Increasingly over the years return to the homeland became impossible, but effective dealing with the customs, manners, laws, and regulations (most certainly including the bureaucracy) also loomed as impossible. With age come certain kinds of decrements and losses—not inevitably and not for every elderly person (nor only for the elderly), but the relationship between old age on the one hand and illness, reduction of function, and death on the other hand is obvious. The now-elderly Asian Americans must face the varied problems of old age not as they had expected—care and respect in one's family and community—but as strangers in a foreign situation.

SERVICES FOR THE ASIAN AMERICAN ELDERLY

What is being done for this group of elderly? Some preparation for the care of the elderly within their ethnic communities has begun. But the demand exceeds the supply, and many elderly Asian Americans must leave their communities to receive necessary services. An elderly Japanese or Chinese American, at the time of life that—according to his upbringing—would bring him respect, leisure, and attention, now lives in isolation and fear. If he needs long-term care and does not have ethnic facilities available, he will probably be placed in an institution without personnel who speak his language; he will be treated by a physician who understands neither his culture nor his speech; he will eat unfamiliar food (the lack of rice and tea alone would be bad enough); and he may find no one else with whom he can converse or share his thoughts.

For the Asian elderly, this separation is especially critical for it removes them from their families and the rules and explicit norms for behaviors which they have come to follow. In the institution, because of language difficulties and the ethnic differences between himself and the staff, the elderly Asian cannot learn the rules and cannot adequately verbalize his needs.

We do not wish to exaggerate the situation. Relatively few elderly of any ethnicity are in institutions; many elderly Asian Americans in areas of high Asian American density can find physicians and other health care professionals who do speak their language and do understand their customs. Most elderly Issei have living children who are concerned about their aged parents and who do have a modest or better income. The situation for first-generation Chinese Americans is less optimistic, many falling into the category of "geriatric orphan," i.e., an elderly person with no responsible next-of-kin available; but the Chinese American communities are actively moving. While the situation may not be drastic in terms of numbers when compared to other ethnic minorities or to poor whites, it is certainly drastic for those who are affected.

The Mexican American Grows Old*

David Maldonado, Jr.

Social scientists, both within the Mexican-American community and without, have created sociological and psychological theories that supposedly explain and describe the elderly Chicanos (*los viejitos*). Some of the theories have been based on factual data and on observation at some point in history and formerly were justified. This was especially true of the concepts of the extended family and of the patriarchal or matriarchal structure, which refers in this instance to the high status and the roles of the family's older members. However, it is becoming questionable whether these theories now describe this particular segment of the Chicano community. (In this article, the terms "Chicano" and "Mexican American" are used interchangeably.)

*Edited from "The Chicano Aged," by D. Maldonado, Jr., *Social Work*, 1975, *20*(2), 213–216. Reprinted by permission of the National Association of Social Workers.

The Chicano population has experienced rapid and dramatic social change since World War II. Today's elderly Chicanos have seen in their lifetime a phenomenal degree of social change that has greatly affected individuals, their family, their society, and the manner in which each relates to the other. Yet, in general, society's attitudes toward them are more applicable to previous generations of older Chicanos than to those of the present generation, especially if they have lived most of their lives in the United States. The result is a population living today who are treated as if they belonged to a past generation.

Nevertheless, it is important to recognize that there is a constant flow of immigrants from Mexico. Thus, there are some elderly Chicanos who have not gone through this drastic social change and who therefore more closely maintain the traditions expected of them. The variety that is evident among the present older generation makes the stereotyping all the more unjust and invalid.

Back of popular sociological theory is the assumption that aged Mexican Americans are properly cared for because of the extended family pattern. It is also assumed that the aged have the emotional and social support they need to maintain a positive self-esteem and a positive relationship with their environment because of their role and status as the older family members.

These popular viewpoints, although they may be based on historical fact, may today be incomplete and misleading notions. They may well work to the disadvantage of aged Mexican Americans rather than have positive implications for their well-being. For example, public and private social agencies may find it convenient to use these generalizations to cover their inadequate services to older Mexican Americans and their lack of understanding of these people. Governmental social agencies, in "respecting the culture," may be avoiding their responsibility to provide services since they place responsibility on the Chicano family. At the same time, the agencies are not providing the family with the resources for making needed services available to the aged. Social scientists, in their delight at discovering a social theory that contains some truth, seem content to perpetuate the theory without vigorously following it through the extreme social changes that occurred in the last decades.

THE EXTENDED FAMILY

The Mexican-American family has traditionally been characterized by its pattern of extended relationships. The relationships go beyond the nuclear family to include adult relatives (cousins, uncles, or aunts), other dependent children (orphans or children of divorced parents), and the grandparents or even the great-grandparents (Madsen, 1964, pp. 46–47). The extended family may live within one household or in a cluster of homes around its older members, either on a farm or in a *barrio*. The important elements are the interpersonal and intergenerational relationships and the interdependence, rather than the strictly physical or geographical proximity, of family members. As Sotomayor (1971) notes:

> It is a supportive and flexible structure assuming functions in dealing with the environment and with the emotional and psychological aspects of the family unit and individuals [p. 32].

The extended family bends to the needs of the group or its individual members. The group may care for the children of working or unemployed parents and may provide emotional and social support when its adult members need it, either in times of development or in times of stress.

Such a family pattern especially affects the aged. The larger group shares the physical or emotional needs of any member. Thus aging Mexican Americans within the extended family structure face no threat to their physical survival. Biological change, especially loss of physical strength, does not present a threat to the aged; the family will care for them. The group increasingly supports the male when he gradually loses his instrumental role (employment for wages) and the female when she just as gradually becomes limited in her ability to continue her household chores. The conclusion implied is that the aged, regardless of physical or mental capability, will continue to be part of the extended family. Such a pattern does not permit the isolation of older men and women but retains them within both the physical and social life of the family (Clark & Mendelson, 1969). It is common to see a very old man, bedridden at home, but surrounded daily by his children or grandchildren. And it is equally common to see a very old woman in such a situation. In a way, that bedridden person even becomes the center of the family's life.

The aged person in the extended family holds high status and commands the respect and obedience of the younger family members. To quote Sotomayor, "The aged are greatly respected among Mexican Americans; positions of authority are assigned to them regardless of their sex" (p. 321). Within the extended family structure, the aging person grows in prestige and respect. He holds high rank and has influence in the life of the group.

A myth that has developed and has been perpetuated is that the Mexican-American family is a patriarchal structure (Rubel, 1966, pp. 60–70). The oldest male, either son or father, is pictured as playing the dominant role. Closer observation reveals that the woman plays an even more active role as she grows older, to the point that the grandmother plays quite a dominant role in the extended family. This does not mean that the elderly male is playing a lesser role; it probably indicates the high early death rate among the men. But more important, it indicates that the surviving older parent, whether man or woman, continues as head of the hierarchy; the oldest son does not become head merely because he is male.

Many Anglo Americans assume that aging Chicanos, since they supposedly are growing in respect and status, do not face emotional or psychological stress on reaching old age. These people take it for granted that the patriarchal pattern of the extended family provides the support and the roles that help the individual avoid such stress. Thus, the popular view is that the aging Chicano has few special problems either physically or emotionally. The extended family is expected to provide for the elderly. Meanwhile, those planning the research studies about the aging and those responsible for considering the distribution of resources to the needy aged in both the public and private welfare sectors tend to exclude the Chicano.

CHANGING PATTERNS

Just as myths about the Chicano aged maintain images that no longer reflect true conditions, so some stereotypes about them are themselves based on other stereotypes. The popular view is based on conditions that have changed or are rapidly changing; the false image is based on a myth of the Mexican-American family, which is making social adjustments as it reflects the changing situation of the Chicano community in the larger society.

The Chicano community today appears to be transforming the basic social structure of its extended family. There seems to be a gradual movement toward developing and strengthening the nuclear family. The basic need of survival, rather than purposeful planning or modified Chicano values, is probably bringing this about. It would appear that the more deeply Chicanos participate in the urbanized, industrial society of the United States, the greater is the social and economic pressure to adapt their social structures to the society or to accept structures that the system produces. The nuclear family seems to be a product of the modern society.

Agrarian societies produce social structures that are functionally appropriate to them. The extended family is an example of a social structure that is functional in an agrarian society. Such a family provides the society with a balanced distribution of manpower and the persons who can perform the roles necessary for surviving in the system. The family unit in its extended form provides workers (mature men, youths, some younger women), persons having knowledge based on experience (the aged), those who engage in child care (older women), and those who perform other supportive roles (housewives). Together all make it possible for families and individuals to survive.

Such a system provides for individuals of all ages and conditions and develops roles for them. To a considerable degree, the extended family in an agrarian society is self-supporting and independent. Because of its independence from the rest of society and because of the way that work needed for survival is distributed within the group, the family tends to develop a strong sense of group identity and of interdependence. The young workers depend on others for supportive services (for example, meals); the old, when they cannot work, depend on the young. Thus, in an agrarian society, one can readily see how an extended family pattern develops, in which the aging members continue to perform functional roles and even attain higher status than they had when they were younger.

ATTACHMENT TO THE LAND

The Mexican-American community, since World War II, has been experiencing a transformation from a rural to an urban society. A brief historical survey of Mexican Americans reveals an initial agrarian experience. The Chicano culture was established on certain fundamental principles of land distribution, land usage, and love for the land. The Indian reverence for the land and the Spanish methods of land distribution (land grants, communal rights, and so on) blended to give birth to a people deeply attached to the land. The cries of revolution have been *tierra o muerte* (land or death) from the early struggles for independence to the present.

Mexican Americans living in the United States have maintained a history and culture close to the land. For as long a time as they could and as much as possible, they built their lives close to the land. In short, Chicano history is a history of the land.

At the start, most Mexican Americans were in the rural areas of the Southwest. Their survival depended on farming. During the transitional period (from independence, to the Mexican War, to the time Mexican Americans became a minority group in the country) they continued to work the land and maintain the extended family, which proved to be a fairly stable social system encouraging their survival. The extended family, in turn, kept alive the roles and relationships involved in such a pattern. For example, in this system respect for the aged was maintained, useful roles for the elderly were assured, and the immediate family provided for their needs. This pattern is still found in rural areas, among migrant farm workers, and even in some urban *barrios* where families tend to cluster around the older parents.

But Chicanos have not remained on the farm; they have moved into the city. Their migration into the urban areas began with World War I, although its largest thrust was during World War II. Chicanos moved to the city to man the machines; they also left the farm for military service, and they never returned. They left the Rio Grande Valley in Texas to move into San Antonio, Houston, Dallas, Fort Worth; they left rural communities to form *barrios* in Albuquerque, Phoenix, Tucson; they moved into Los Angeles and Denver, even Detroit and Chicago. Chicanos have become urban.

But Chicanos, like all people bred in a particular culture, cannot discard their culture by merely moving away from its source to new surroundings. Cultural forms and values continue. When the parents become too old or too isolated, they may move into the city to be closer to their children. Efforts are made to maintain what has been functional and what has traditional value. But the modern setting exerts strong pressure to change those within it, if they are to survive. The extended family is no longer functional. Despite the great value that its members place on it, the extended family may actually impede their well-being.

Just as Chicanos left the farm for the city, they left farmwork for more skilled jobs, higher wages, and education. Social mobility also exerts pressure. Children are earning more than their parents ever dreamed of earning; their social status has risen with their education or skills. The children have risen higher on the social ladder than their parents, uncles, or even older brothers and sisters.

These phenomena have created pressure to break up the extended family and strengthen the nuclear unit. Young Chicanos have become independent of their parents and their brothers and sisters. Interdependence is decreasing. The young Chicano family is increasingly becoming more distant physically from relatives. It is mobile.

IMPLICATIONS FOR THE AGED

The physical and social mobility of their children has had an equally dramatic effect on aged Mexican Americans. Rapid and dramatic changes for the young have often placed the elderly in an awkward and difficult position. Their social environment has completely changed within their lifetime. Although they were reared within one culture (in a purer form), they now find themselves in a situation for which their early socialization did not prepare them. Tension and disjointedness seem to describe the relationship between this new social environment and the one in which they developed their values, attitudes, and expectations.

Most aged Mexican Americans grew up in a rural community or on a farm. They had a function to perform then, and knew that when they reached old age they would still have a role, because they had seen their grandparents carry important roles in the extended family on the farm. Today the aged Chicanos find themselves in a city, surrounded by a system that does not need their knowledge and skills. Or they find themselves in a small town far from their children. They had prepared themselves for and looked forward to roles in old age that have never materialized.

Thus aged Chicanos are increasingly without a role. They find also that, since their children have moved upward socially and educationally, their own status and respect have relatively decreased. Their children do not need their knowledge to survive today. The values of the aged relate to an agrarian society; their children are living today in an urban industrial setting. The expectations of the aging Chicano do not always coincide with those of the younger generation.

The total effect is a population that may be misunderstood by both the general society and by its own culture. The general society, by having a dated understanding of Chicano culture, believes that the Chicano family can and will provide for its older members. The younger Chicano generation is having an increasingly difficult time in doing so. This does not mean that young Chicanos do not appreciate their parents. It is rather that they must adjust and pay a price for surviving and participating in such a mobile, urban, and industrial society as that in the United States today.

Both the older and younger Chicanos are recognizing the tension and transition. The young will not abandon the elderly for the sake of mere progress. Neither will the elderly cling to the young and demand care. Recent studies have shown that both generations are making adjustments, both are maintaining a strong sense of family, and the young are keeping their respect for the elderly (Carp, 1968). The aged Chicano is independent (Steglich et al., 1968). He does not want to be a burden. He cherishes ownership of his home. The younger generation does much to keep the elderly close by and to provide personal attention. In San Antonio, for example, aging Chicanos did not want to go into a home for the aged, not only because of their strong sense of autonomy, but also because their children did not favor their going into an institution (Carp, 1968).

As the Chicano family adjusts to the mobility and urbanization of the younger generation, the changes and adjustments in family patterns have serious implications for the welfare of the older generation. Yet the old myths of the extended family have blinded both the social scientists who formulate theories and the practitioners who provide social services so that they fail to understand the present crisis of the Chicano aged. Thus all too often elderly Chicanos are limited in the roles they are able to perform, and those who are in need may not receive the services provided to the aged who belong to other cultures.

The Older Native American*

Statistics about Indians, or Native Americans, are frequently inadequate, inaccurate, or not available at all. A survey of the Library of Congress catalogue files revealed, for example, that there are approximately 417 cards on Indian legends and pottery, but none at all for "income" or "population." In fact, there is still confusion in arriving at an acceptable definition for determining who would be classified as an Indian. These conclusions were reached in a brief, but blunt, statement by the Indian Advisory Council to the Senate Committee on Aging.

By whatever standard one would choose to employ, American Indians—and particularly the aged within that group —constitute one of the most deprived segments in our population. Per capita income for Indians, for instance, is estimated to be $1,051, only about one-third the national average for the total population.

Underlying the Advisory Council's statement is a fundamental theme that existing programs for elderly Indians continue to be uncoordinated and fragmented. A major by-product of this dilemma is a low level of visibility for the unique problems of aged Indians. As a consequence, many Indians—the

*From "Developments in Aging: 1974 & January–April, 1975," *Report of the Special Committee on Aging,* United States Senate, 1975, pp. 59–61. Washington, D.C.: U.S. Government Printing Office.

young as well as the old—never receive the full benefits of these programs. To rectify this problem, the panel called for a high-level advocate for elderly Indians. Additionally, this office would coordinate and publicize all programs which are aimed at helping older Indians.

POPULATION

According to the 1970 Census data, there are nearly 792,000 Indians living on and off reservations. It is estimated by Bureau of Indian Affairs officials that there are between 45,000 and 50,000 Indians aged 65 and older, about 6 percent of the total population. A major reason for this comparatively low percentage of aged is that life expectancy for Indians is considerably lower than for the total U.S. population, averaging about 46 years.

Earlier Social Security benefits, in the judgment of the task force, is not the solution to the problem of a shorter longevity expectation. Instead, they maintain that the numerous factors which lead to a shorter life expectancy—such as inadequate nutrition, dilapidated housing, insufficient medical services, poor transportation systems, and others—must be dealt with immediately, forcefully, and effectively to raise the longevity expectation of Indians.

HOUSING

Symptomatic of their deprivation is the appalling lack of acceptable housing for Indians. According to Bureau of Indian Affairs statistics, about 48,500 Indian homes are substandard and are currently in need of replacement or renovation. Approximately 55 percent of the homes have less than 600 square feet of living space. Inadequate heating exists in 63 percent of the units and 21 percent have no electric power available.

Another problem, in the view of the task force, is that little or no consideration is given to the cultural desires of Indian tribes—such as style, location, or building materials in home construction.

EMPLOYMENT

Unemployment for older Indians and the Indian population in general is alarmingly high. At some reservations, the jobless rate runs as high as 80%, nearly 14 times as great as the unacceptable national rate of 6 percent in September, 1971.

To combat this widespread problem, the Advisory Council recommends that:

—Funds should be earmarked by the Bureau of Indian Affairs for public service and community betterment projects for elderly Indians who could participate in a wide variety of capacities, such as community development officers, guides in wilderness areas, counselors, and others.

—Employment programs for older persons, such as Mainstream, should be effectively enforced to insure that aged persons participate in these projects to the extent that Congress intended.

NUTRITION AND HEALTH

Hunger or malnourishment is a way of life for most older Indians. Inadequate diets and limited information about proper eating habits are two major factors for this critical problem. And the impact of malnourishment is seen in many tragic ways for aged and aging Indians—a substantially shorter life expectancy, poorer health, and an inability to work in many instances.

Moreover, present federal programs fall far short of providing the nutritional requirements of the needy. Items in the Commodities Distribution program usually meet less than 80 percent of their caloric requirements and from 30 to 50 percent of their nutritional needs.

Poor health for Indians is further intensified by bad roads, poor communication, and inaccessible health care facilities. One outgrowth of these conditions is that many Indians, especially those in need of immediate medical attention, go to the nearest hospital rather than an Indian Health Service (IHS) facility which may be many more miles away. Another problem for IHS facilities is that there is a high turnover of medical personnel. Many young doctors fulfill their military obligations by serving in these facilities, usually for a two-year period.

However, the Advisory Council noted "The success of Indian Health Service in providing medical care for Indian peoples is worthy of commendation." But it is also warned "Much is left to be done, and no one can relax when the average age at death for the American Indian is 46 years."

Chapter 2

The Older Person: A Psychosocial View

Who are older people? In the first chapter, I tried to respond to that question through demography and through discussion of some of the ethno-racial groups in the United States and Canada. In this chapter I look at the same question from an entirely different point of view—what it means to be old to individuals and to those in their milieu.

The first and most important statement to make about older people is that they are as diverse as any age group. They differ in appearance, vital-ity, roles, competence, friendliness, loneliness, fear, and health just as much as people in any other generation.

The second important statement is that older people have the same needs and wants that all people have. They need food and sleep and air; they need friends and money and housing; they think about their relationship to the infinite and about their relationships with those they love; they want to enjoy themselves and to feel they are loved and to perceive themselves as competent. But their circumstances may alter the ways in which these needs and wants make themselves felt. Thus older people are more likely to have special diets than the nonelderly; they are less likely to have an adequate income; they are more likely to have lost many of their friends through death; they are less likely to be performing work-related tasks that most people do to make themselves feel competent.

A third important statement: older people share certain things among themselves that they are not likely to share with other age groups. Older people will remember the depression of the 1930s and World War II very vividly, and from their own personal experiences; some can recall World War I with equal clarity. They can talk about Joe DiMaggio and Joe Louis as youngsters, about Clark Gable and Jean Harlow when their films first appeared, about automobiles that needed cranking to start and that had no windshield wipers, about iceboxes that were cooled by 25-pound blocks of ice brought by the iceman, about going far out of the town where they lived into the country—which is now lined with housing developments and shopping centers. You can understand their pleasure at reminiscing, but the richness of the common bond produced by shared memories is difficult to grasp fully unless you are at least in your mid-thirties.

Older people share both pleasant and unpleasant circumstances. For example, they are more likely than younger people to have some significant health problem, although they have probably learned to take this in their stride; they are closer to their own deaths, and they take this into account, often in very subtle ways; they are less likely to have access to income through jobs; they are less likely to take risks, since a fall or an accident, a loss of money or property, would be more difficult to overcome.

At the same time, they are probably no longer constrained by having to wake up at a certain time in the morning and hurriedly get ready for work;

they are under less pressure to compete with their neighbors; relationships with children have probably become stable, and relationships with grandchildren often permit lots of love and companionship without the responsibilities of parenthood.

I have been writing in generalities. You all know of good examples of and exceptions to everything I have stated. This chapter will touch on only a handful of concerns, and I hope you will read some of the books and journals available in the field. I also hope you will talk with older people whenever you get the chance and that you will make an effort to let them do most of the talking. Something strange usually happens. You probably will decide that each older person you talk to, each older person you get to know, is "just not a typical older person." Eventually you will realize that the stereotyped "old person," the sickly, cranky, lonely, complaining old person, is about as common as the stereotyped student radical or hard-hearted businessman. That is, they do exist, but they are not familiar. And the only way you will truly believe this is if you learn it through your own experiences.

*Human Behavior and Aging: An Overview**

Let me offer a strongly felt personal opinion: too many people who work in the field of aging attempt to substitute academic knowledge for personal experience. Now let me offer another equally intense personal opinion: too many people who work directly with the elderly attempt to substitute experience for academic knowledge. The greatest strength of the professional comes with the combination of the theoretical with the practical.

This book is in large part my effort to integrate the academic knowledge with that derived from practical experience. The academic is not highly theoretical, and the practical is not a series of cookbook approaches, but there is a body of knowledge about aging. Although many of the specifics and some of the generalities will change over the years, the field is no longer new.

I feel that people who work with the elderly, either through direct services, policy development and implementation, or through organization, need to know about the psychology and sociology of the later years. This chapter in

---

*Edited from "Psychological Aspects of Aging," in *Working with Older People, Vol. II: Biological, Psychological, and Sociological Aspects of Aging*, pp. 24–37. Washington, D.C.: U.S. Government Printing Office, 1970.

general, and the first selection in particular, will help to give this knowledge some focus.

PSYCHOLOGICAL ASPECTS OF AGING

Adult life is a process of continual change, as the individual is faced with new tasks that require him to adapt to new circumstances. While these tasks are unique to the individual, they do form a pattern that can be described as the developmental tasks of the life cycle. Each task is associated with a certain amount of "role uncertainty," whether it occurs in the twenties or in the eighties. Courtship, marriage, childbirth, career changes, changes of residence, retirement, and death of peers and spouse are among the elements that form important parts of the content of the adult life. Changes in appearance, body function, and health also present problems or tasks to which the individual must adapt.

Throughout the adult life span, the individual's capacities to solve problems and to adapt will be challenged by situations that may be novel to him but are characteristic of his age level. Should the individual undergo a reduction in his capacity for adaptation, even though a task is characteristic of a specific age level, the reaction to it may constitute a crisis or an emotional problem. However, adequate adaptation to earlier problems increases the likelihood that he will be able to cope with the tasks unique to later life.

Social Change

Not only do we as individuals change with age, but there are also trends in society that often render our models of age-appropriate behavior out of date. Present trends for early marriage and child rearing result in an "empty nest" period for middle-aged persons when the last child has grown and left the home. Around 1900, the average marriage dissolved through the death of one of the partners before the last child was married. Now, about 15 years of married life together may be expected after the last child marries. This means that there is a long period of family life together after the children leave the home.

The lack of social roles and models in our society for such "pre-retirement" living results in uncertainties about family life. Further uncertainties result from the fact that one way of adapting to the empty nest is for the woman to take a job in middle-age. New psychological issues emerge when the woman moves out of the house into a job at a time when her husband's career has probably stabilized and perhaps become boring. Such events can be midlife turning points for marriages when some improve and others decline in satisfaction for the partners.

Our attitudes toward the appropriate content of family life are complicated because we are in a period of rapid social change. For example, earlier periods of history did not have a large proportion of widows in society. Increasingly, women are living longer than men, and they are gaining more than men in life expectancy. More than 50 percent of the women over 65 are widows, whereas only 22 percent of the men over that age are widowers.

These are but a few indications that not only do individuals change biologically during their lifetime but they also change psychologically, since they are constantly required to adapt to a changing physical and social environment. Nonetheless, despite great social change, adult life maintains a characteristic rhythm. Certain concerns and moods are associated with certain episodes in the adult life span. Middle-aged persons show more sensitivity to problems of health in themselves and friends. An aged adult tends to attach great importance to his immediate physical environment, and his attitude toward a household move contrasts with the easy residential mobility of the younger adult. Such events as moving of place of residence can be turning points in the psychological and social life of the older individual and can precipitate health problems or exacerbate previously existing health conditions.

DETERMINANTS OF AGING

We have grown used to the idea that the individual's heredity plays a role in how long he is likely to live. Less commonly considered is the fact that the individual's psychological and social environments also influence the length as well as the quality of his life. Indeed, at the present time in our society an individual's probable length of life is related more closely to his social/environmental background—sanitation, preventive health care, and accident prevention—than it is to the longevity of his parents and grandparents.

The particular environment in which the individual grows up and grows old determines to a considerable extent how he will express his genetic potentials. As society becomes more supportive of individuals physically, socially, and psychologically, however, then differences in genetic background probably will become more important and eventually dominate longevity and aging.

The Nervous System

Several features of the nervous system warrant emphasis in any discussion of aging. The nervous system is a pathway by which environmental factors have health consequences. The nervous system is unique in having an organization stemming from the genetic background of the species but shaped by the unique experiences of the individual.

Cells that do not divide—fundamental in the nervous system and elsewhere—may be most important in aging. In particular, the cells of the nervous system are critical in influencing functions of the body. As old as the individual, neurons, through their role in integrating functions of the body, are able to spread the effects of age changes to other organ systems and remote tissues. Individuals who escape cardiovascular disease and neoplasms may show senescent changes that are heavily influenced by the aging nervous system. Biological changes of the nervous system underlie deterioration of behavioral capacities and health. Evidence also suggests that important restrictions and other changes in the activity patterns of the individual will produce a chain of crises. Serious, if not terminal, illnesses may be precipitated. For instance, the aging individual whose loss of coordination leads to recurrent falls may surrender his roles in community activities, stay home, become depressed, lose appetite, and become vulnerable to infection.

PERCEPTION

In most sensory systems, acuity declines with advancing age. Reduction can be a consequence of age-related diseases and occupational injuries, as well as changes in the receptors that may be due to primary aging.

From age 20 to age 60, the rate of hearing impairments rises from about 10 to about 75 per 1000 population. However, between ages 60 and 80, the rate accelerates to 250. Thus, 1 out of 4 very aged persons has a significant hearing impairment. In the same age group, about 80 individuals per 1000 population are blind.

Not only does the proportion of persons with sensory defects increase with age, but there is a significant acceleration of this increase past the age of 60. Commonly, therefore, the individual over 60 must adapt to some type of sensory change that reduces the amount of information he receives from his environment. The viscera and the proprioceptors as well as organs of touch, smell, taste, hearing, and seeing provide reduced information on which to base his behavior.

With age, most sensory receptors require more energy to reach a threshold level of stimulation. Turning up the lights or the radio may annoy younger companions, but this is an adaptation by the older adult to increase his sensory input.

One consequence of the reduced sensory input is the need to become more conscious of behavior, to monitor and recheck sensory input before making some movement. Crossing the street may be slow and uncertain for an older person, not only because of the necessity to judge the automobiles and the traffic lights, but also because of the necessity to monitor foot movements. Some evidence suggests that older persons have to monitor their body movements visually in order to secure adequate placement. Because previously automatic actions of walking or eating need to be watched, the aged reduce their attention to the environment.

MOTOR PERFORMANCE

It was suggested earlier that one cause of the cautious voluntary movements of the aged stems from changes in sensory acuity. Many skills that improve with practice, such as walking, riding, or playing a musical instrument, may cease to have the automatic quality they had in earlier years. Movements never involve just one muscle. However simple a skill may appear to be, it is, nevertheless, a complex chain of events integrated by the nervous system. These patterns of finely coordinated voluntary movements involve continuous excitation and inhibition of neural activity. The resulting muscle movements comprise a graded distribution of sequential activity. Hence, if there are delays or reductions in sensory information about a limb position or the contracted state of a muscle, smoothness or speed of the voluntary activity is disrupted.

It is very likely that changes in motor skills in persons over 65 contribute to high accident rates. In individuals over the age of 65, accidents are the sixth largest cause of death. Deaths resulting from falls are more common than deaths from all other sources of accidents combined. Most of the fatal accidents in persons over 65 occur at home, thus ruling out the inexperience or unfamiliarity that might contribute to industrial accidents.

Subtle physical changes are believed to predispose the individual to accidents. Individuals who repeatedly fall appear even at the outset to be less physically fit than those who don't fall. Physical education instructors believe that the aged who maintain a high level of physical activity have better control over their body movements. However, individuals who are affected by certain of the degenerative diseases may constitute distinct subgroups of the aging. For them, sustained gymnastics designed to result in greater agility and the avoidance of accidents can be expected to have a less favorable effect.

Besides, the individual's judgment, in addition to perception and motor skill, can expose him to conditions beyond his physical or physiological limitations. Errors of judgment rank high in automobile accidents of older drivers. In young drivers, speed is a primary contributor to accidents, but drivers over 65 are less likely to drive fast than they are to misjudge speed or improperly manipulate their cars on the road.

Occupational Accidents

Automobile accident rates do not parallel those for industrial accidents. Generally speaking, automobile accident rates decline from a peak around age 20 to a low about age 30. This rate persists to about age 55 and then rises. Industrial injuries, on the other hand, are lowest for workers over 65. One important reason for the difference may be the fact that industry tends to exclude individuals of advanced years and with health defects or other problems. Only the best and most experienced workers remain on the job after the age of 60 or 65. After age 35 men tend to be stable in their jobs. Being more skilled and interested in holding their jobs, they tend to avoid the impulsive acts characteristic of younger workers. Their experience leads to better management in the avoidance of accidents.

MEMORY AND LEARNING

Memory and learning are primary functions of the central nervous system. Our ability to adapt to a changing environment is, to a significant extent, dependent upon our ability to register, retain, and recall experience. Learning may be defined as the relatively permanent modification of behavior as the result of experience. Under most circumstances, age-related changes in the primary ability to learn appear to be small, even when sensory acuity begins to decline. When differences in the ability to learn do appear between individuals in their thirties and in their fifties, these differences seem to be attributable to problems of getting information into the nervous system, and to perception, control of attention, and motivation. Also relevant is general health, especially absence of diseases that might lead to impaired function of the central nervous system. Such factors are to be distinguished from a primary age-related change in the ability to learn.

When there is impairment in learning, one should not infer that some typical process of aging is at work. Rather, one should suspect either some prior incapacity or debilitating change in the individual. Evidence showing an age difference in learning is based mostly on comparing individuals over the age of 65 with individuals in their twenties.

INTELLECTUAL ABILITIES

In addition to his sensory acuity and motor skills, man's ability to adapt to a changing environment depends to a significant degree upon his ability to solve problems. Important to successful problem solving is a clear grasp of the essential nature of the problem facing the individual. If an individual characteristically faces problems with highly familiar elements, he spends less time in analyzing the problems than in solving them by selection from a repertory of mastered solutions.

The greater the interval since formal schooling, the greater the likelihood that an individual will rapidly find a solution from the relevant items in his stored experience. And he will be less likely to take time to analyze the nature of the task confronting him. For example, it has been shown that vocabulary size increases over the adult lifespan. Words recognized serve as an index to the amount of information stored; however, increased stored information does not necessarily imply that the individual will show flexibility in the selection of relevant information. In other words, he may be a stodgy rather than a creative thinker.

The word "rigid" has been used to describe individuals who persist in a particular approach to a problem, even in the face of information that suggests change. Some related evidence suggests that older adults may seek absolute categories of truth or falsity in answering questions.

Again, years since formal schooling can result in a change in the way an individual evaluates his own performance. The person in school is quite sensitive to the quality of his performance in response to external demands.

After many years of successful adaptations to the normal demands of life, the older person may not have the same sensitivity to unusual challenges. All things being equal, therefore, a change in problem-solving attitudes toward unfamiliar tasks occurs as the interval since schooling grows.

PERSONALITY

Personality is difficult to define precisely. It refers to the distinctive styles in which individuals behave or react. How we react to developmental situations like marriage, the growing independence of adolescent children, and retirement is a function of our personality.

The evolving personality or habit system of the individual imposes a bias or type of control over behavior. Thus, the way an individual reacts to body changes and disease is a function of his personality. With advancing age, the adult shows a reduction in drive level that includes reduced spontaneous physical activity as well as reduced sexual behavior. Depending upon his personality characteristics, the individual may regard these changes as an insult to his ego and throw himself into his activities with increased motivation, or he may react by passive retreat. Others may find physical changes not at all insulting and in fact somewhat congenial. One factor of personality underlying the choices of behavior is the individual system of personal values. For example, if the individual places a high value on visible participation in the general social scene, the general drift with age toward lowered activity may be resented.

In the years over 60, there also appears to emerge a quality of effective (emotional) detachment from the environment. Older persons tend to have less emotion or ego involvement in their roles and activities than they had earlier in life. It is not yet clear that this is an adaptation to the fact that the environment is "moving away" from the individual in the sense that peers and relatives die, jobs and careers stop, and children grow up and go away. Possibly, such disengagement reflects reduced "ego energy" on part of the drive system of the individual. If so, older individuals presumably would have a lower capacity for effective involvement with other people, processes, and things.

SEXUAL ACTIVITY

Generally, the frequency of sexual intercourse declines linearly from a peak in the early twenties. To this extent, sexual intercourse follows other declines of activity. Married partners in their nineties may continue to engage in intercourse to orgasm, although less often than in early life. Health changes in the spouse may preclude sexual intercourse. Some aging partners welcome the lower sex drive, since sex for them has always been the source of uncomfortable relationship. There are also those who deeply miss sexual activity and may actively seek a new mate late in life, after the death of the spouse. Novelty in mating does appear to increase temporarily the frequency of intercourse.

MENTAL ILLNESS

Brain disease of late life occurs more frequently but gets less clinical attention than do the characteristic mental illnesses of early life. Because senile individuals have fewer years of life remaining, mental hospitals and mental health clinics may be more concerned with the treatment of young schizophrenics than with senile patients. Between 1 and 2 percent of the population, under current standards of hospitalization, may be expected to be institutionalized for the first time for mental disease late in life. According to a statistical projection based on genetic considerations, senile dementia can be expected in about 4 percent of the population. Senile dementia seems to occur independently of, or in combination with, preexisting disease such as psychoneurosis, schizophrenia, or manic depressive reactions.

Communities vary in the institutionalization of individuals for the same manifest behavior. Deviant behavior tends to be more tolerated in older rather than younger persons. Perhaps deviant behavior in the aged is assumed to be an innocuous, "natural" consequence of aging. An older person is, in fact, more likely to hurt himself than he is to hurt others. Mental disturbance in the young is more likely to lead to harm to others. The extent of "queer behavior" that is tolerated varies with the nature of the community, whether it is rural or urban, or upper or lower socioeconomic class.

Mental illness in older persons can occur commonly as a side effect of somatic illnesses. Infectious diseases and undernutrition may help produce mental symptoms, and these may not disappear until some time after the original conditions are controlled.

Primary anatomical changes in the brain occur in a small proportion of older persons independent of the presence or absence of affective disorders and circulatory disorders. Thus, being schizophrenic neither raises nor lowers the probability of developing a senile brain disorder. The fact that primary senile brain deterioration occurs with the same frequency among those with functional psychosis as it does in the population at large indicates that these diseases have distinct etiologies.

In patients with organic brain disease, cognitive functioning degenerates. However, there is the possibility of a social/psychological cushioning of the consequences of senile brain disorder. An individual with an affective interpersonal relationship with another person, a "confidant," is less likely to be precipitated into a mental crisis requiring hospitalization than is the isolate.

That only a small percentage of persons in the total population is institutionalized for mental illness in late life has two implications. First, it is obvious that a senile pattern of brain deterioration does not commonly accompany advancing age; when it does occur it is likely to be a pathological rather than a normal concomitant of growing old. Second, geriatric psychiatry is giving more emphasis to mixed causes of mental illness in older persons. Rather than search for a single diagnosis, one should seek a mixture of functional and organic factors. Diagnosis therefore tends to be multiple in older persons. Interactions take place among the physical illness, the mental illness, and the social environment.

One of the areas in which stress seriously taxes the individual's physiological limits is in bereavement. There is a marked rise in the death rate of spouses during the first year or two after the death of mates. Bereavement can be especially stressful to an individual who has preexisting health problems. Adaptation to bereavement eventually reduces the stress, but during the first year the surviving individual should receive increased attention from his physician and other health personnel. Health workers should attempt to see the individual several times during the early months and at least twice in the second six months following death of the spouse. Bereavement control measures, cushioning the physiological and psychological consequences in older persons, should be a new focal point of health activities. For the relatively isolated individual, such measures should be emphasized.

Attitudes and Aging: Myths and Realities*

In 1975, the National Council on the Aging (NCOA), in conjunction with the Harris polling organization, published an excellent monograph, titled The Myth and Reality of Aging in America. *The report was based on the results of an extremely extensive poll conducted by the Harris organization, touching on many aspects of what it means to be old. Participants in the study were men and women of all ages, and particular emphasis was given to the Black elderly. The following article reviews some of the highlights of the book itself.*

This study is by far the most extensive ever conducted to determine the public's attitude toward aging and their perceptions of what it's like to be old in this country—and to document older Americans' views and attitudes about themselves and their personal experiences of old age.

The National Council on the Aging (NCOA) commissioned the study to provide definitive data to researchers, writers, students, legislators, and the general public. For too long the people of this country have accepted without question all of the stereotypes and clichés about growing old. We hope the material that follows will separate the myth from the reality.

*From "Developments in Aging: 1974 & January–April, 1975," in *Report of the Special Committee on Aging*, United States Senate, 1975, pp. 59-61. Washington, D.C.: U.S. Government Printing Office.

The study will also provide base data about the attitudes and perceptions of age for NCOA's newest project, the National Media Resource Center on the Aging, and it will be used with other data to evaluate the results of future programs.

Several points should be made about these data:

First, the findings in the area of public policy are extremely significant. An overwhelming 97 percent of the American people believe that Social Security payments to the elderly should automatically increase with the rises in the cost of living. There is no indication that the public supports an arbitrary limitation on this increase.

The study also reveals that 81 percent of the public agree that the Federal Government has the responsibility to use general tax revenues to help support older people. And 86 percent of the people are opposed to mandatory retirement at a fixed age if the worker wants to continue working and is able to do a good job.

The study explored the attitudes of Americans on a wide range of issues related to aging and compared the feelings of older people with the perceptions of those younger.

Second, the conclusion is obvious that most of the older people of this country have the desire and the potential to be productive, contributing members of our society. They do not want to be "put on the shelf" and excluded from social and economic activities.

Third, it is clear that most older people feel that their condition in life is better, economically and socially, than the general public believes it to be. But "most" can be a deceptive term; it is vitally important to remember that many millions of older people are living at, or below, the poverty line. Thus, when 15 percent of people over 65 say that "not having enough money to live on" is a personal problem for them, that percentage translates to some 3 million needy people. The same thing is true of many of the other categories discussed in the pages that follow.

PUBLIC POLICY

A full 87 percent of those responsible for hiring and firing say "Most employers discriminate against older people and make it difficult for them to find jobs," and only 37 percent of these decision makers feel a fixed retirement age for everyone makes sense.

Among the older public now retired, 37 percent, or 4.4 million people, said they did not retire out of choice, and approximately the same number—31 percent—said they would like to be working now.

Not only should the Government provide income for older, retired people, the public feels it should provide them with enough income to live comfortably. By 76 to 19 percent the public agreed that "No matter how much a person earned during his working years, he should be able to have enough money to live on comfortably when older and retired."

There is tremendous potential support for a movement to improve the conditions and social status of people over 65. Those under 65 (81 percent, compared to 70 percent of those 65 and over) are most conscious of this need for focus and organization.

STEREOTYPES AND
PROBLEMS OF OLDER PEOPLE

It is not the young alone who have negative expectations of old age. Recognizing that life is not so terrible for themselves, older people have bought the stereotypes and myths of old age and consider themselves the exception to the rule. In fact, for every older person who feels that his or her own life is worse now than what he/she thought it would be, there are three who say that life is better now than they expected. As many people under 65 feel that their current lives fall short of earlier expectations as people 65 and over. "While I personally am bright and alert," most people 65 and over seem to be saying, "most of my peers simply are not."

A comparison between the problems attributed to "most people over 65" by the public at large and the problems actually experienced personally by older people indicated the extent to which the public has a distorted view of what it is like to grow old. In most cases, the discrepancy is enormous.

Fifty percent of the public felt that "fear of crime" was a very serious problem for the aging, versus 23 percent of older people who thought it a problem for them personally.

Fifty-one percent of the public thought "poor health" a problem for the aging, versus 21 percent of older people who thought it a personal problem.

Sixty-two percent of the public thought "not having enough money to live on" a problem for the aging, versus 15 percent of the elderly who found this a personal problem.

It is striking that in the above examples, people over 65 substantially agreed with those younger that these were problems for "most people over 65." But by the percentages indicated, individual older persons considered themselves exceptions.

Except for health and fear of crime, the "very serious" problems of people 18–64 are very comparable to those who are 65 and older, including not having enough money, job opportunities, medical care, and education.

OLDER PEOPLE,
THEIR LIFE-STYLE AND PERCEPTIONS

It is generally recognized by the public at large that people over 65 represent a larger segment of the population today than 10 or 20 years ago. And, as a group, people over 65 are seen as healthier, better educated, and in better financial shape than in the 1950s or 1960s.

But when queried as to the type of life older people lead, the perception, again, is quite different from the reality.

In the eyes of the public, people over 65 spend a great deal of their time in sedentary, private, and isolated activities. Actually the older public is far more active than imagined.

Sixty-seven percent of the total public expect that most people over 65 spend a lot of time watching television. Only 36 percent of the older group report they do.

Sixty-two percent of the public at large expect that older people spend a lot of time "sitting and thinking." Only 31 percent report they do.

In fact, pastime activities of both young and old are very similar. Comparable numbers of old and young, for example, spend a lot of time sleeping, reading, sitting and thinking, participating in fraternal or community organizations, or going for walks. The only areas in which the two groups part are: older people spend more time watching television than the young, whereas the younger group spends more time in child care, at a job, or engaged in sports.

Additionally, the physical and sexual activity of the over-65 group is misperceived by the general public.

The total public expected that less than half (41 percent) of the older group was "very physically active," whereas 48 percent of those over 65 report that they are. Also, only 5 percent of the total public expected older people to be "very sexually active," compared to the 16 percent of the older men and 7 percent of older women who say they are.

The young picture older people as engaged in passive, sedentary activities and not an active part of society, but older people are unwilling to be relegated to the sidelines. They do not wish to be excluded from things happening around them, or limited to communities for older people. Like the young, three out of four people 65 and over said they prefer to spend their time with people of all different ages.

BECOMING OLD AND SELF-IMAGE
OF OLDER PEOPLE

When does one turn the corner and become old? Public opinion varies. Only half the public (53 percent) picked some specific age as the criterion for "old age"; the other half has a less chronological, numerical concept, citing "retirement," "health," and "it depends" as the criteria.

Of those who do state a fixed age, the largest block (23 percent) feels the average man or woman becomes old in the 60s. And while some may argue that women age faster than men, or vice versa, most people do not feel this way.

Seventeen percent of the public think that women become old before they're 60, compared with 16 percent who feel that way about men.

Age does not appear to influence significantly the way individuals tend to view themselves. The public 65 and over sees itself as being as bright, alert, openminded, adaptable, and as good at getting things done as those 18–64.

Those 65 and over have a higher self-image in terms of being "very useful members of their community" (40 percent) than the younger group (20 percent). Yet the younger public's view of their elders is even lower than their own self-evaluation. Only 21 percent of the younger group consider most people over 65 to be "very useful."

Older whites tend to have a more positive image of themselves than do older blacks. In only a few areas do the two groups come close together in their self-image—in seeing themselves as friendly and warm, wise from experience, and sexually active. Some of the same differences exist between younger blacks and whites, but to a lesser extent.

ADDITIONAL FINDINGS

Like percentages of the young and old feel that parents and grandparents over 65 assist their offspring in various ways. The young credit parents and grandparents with less assistance than the older generation claims in helping out when someone is ill, taking care of grandchildren, and helping out with money. Also, the young say the old give far more advice than the older generation admits.

It is not necessarily surprising that a substantial proportion of those 65 and over (45 percent) feel they get less respect from the young than they deserve. What might be surprising is that a full 71 percent of the public 18 to 64 feel that people over 65 get "too little respect" from young people these days.

Blacks 65 and over feel more than older whites (60 percent versus 43 percent) that they do not receive enough respect from the young.

Managers, officials, and proprietors make up 18 percent of the people past 65 who are still working; salespersons, 10 percent; and service workers, 17 percent. A full 22 percent of retired people were skilled craftsmen or foremen, whereas only 11 percent of those still employed hold those jobs.

The current volunteer force among older people is 4.5 million strong. Another 10 percent of the 65 and over public said they would like to volunteer their services. Thus the potential total number of the volunteer force among older Americans is 6.6 million.

But people 65 and older are not interested in doing volunteer work exclusively. Old and young alike, while willing to accept their share of uncompensated community service, also feel that if a person's work is valuable, he or she should be paid for it.

Few people in this country single out the later years as the most desirable period of one's life. Substantial numbers (69 percent) consider the teens, 20s, and 30s as the "best years of a person's life." Those who did identify the later years as the prime of life associated that period with the advantages of youth—a time of few responsibilities, problems, and pressure, a time to withdraw from productive roles, to take it easy and enjoy life.

Not only do four in five older people look back on their past with satisfaction, three in four feel that their present is as interesting as it ever was, and over half are making plans for their future. Although life could be happier for 45 percent of older people, an even higher 49 percent of those under 65 feel the same. Income, education, and employment status appear to have greater effects on overall life satisfaction than age or race.

The study reported in *The Myth and Reality of Aging in America* might be characterized by this observation from the section "The Experience of Being Older":

> There appears to be no such thing as the typical experience of old age, nor the typical older person. At no point in one's life does a person stop being himself and suddenly turn into an "old person," with all the myths and stereotypes that that term involves. Instead, the social, economic and psychological factors that affected individuals when they were younger often stay with them throughout their lives. Older people share with each other chronological age, but factors more powerful than age alone determine the conditions of their later years.

Social Age and Being "On Time"*

Vern L. Bengtson

On what basis do you judge a person to be old? Appearance: gray hair or balding, lined face, changed body shape? Movement: stiffness, some difficulty in running? Health: more chronic conditions, lowered resistance to illness? Roles: retiree, grandparent? Attitudes, values and behavior—whatever you believe old attitudes, values, and behavior are. Or the number of years the person has lived? Whichever approach you take, you will have developed a partially true thesis. Dr. Bengtson writes about another way of looking at the aging process.

Defining age usually seems such a simple task: one merely counts birthdays or groups individuals into cohorts (e.g., the "Geritol set"). However, chronological age is an arbitrary yardstick that is often meaningless in characterizing functions. When one attempts to analyze everyday behavior as it changes with age, it soon becomes apparent that there are social, as well as biological, psychological, and historical time-clocks which serve as measuring devices and which influence behavior. In this sense age can best be defined as the cumulation of developmental events at a particular point of time in the life of an individual.

We see this social definition of age in everyday circumstances. In the first place, people react to others more on the basis of the statuses or posi-

*Edited from *The Social Psychology of Aging*, by V. L. Bengtson, © 1973 by the Bobbs-Merrill Company, Inc., reprinted by permission of the Bobbs-Merrill Company, Inc.

tions they have (e.g., chairman, chief of staff, executive) than with regard to their actual years. The deference accorded an Admiral is related to his seniority, which may or may not be related to his age. Of course, we react to symbolic cues that are associated with biological aging (such as wrinkled skin, a bald head), but even these are only moderately related to chronological age. In the second place, as Linton (1940) and Wood (1971) have pointed out, such age-status patterns are more pervasive and significant than we usually acknowledge in determining interpersonal behavior. Such positions are related to time in that people are called upon to occupy a fairly orderly succession of statuses in various areas of life as they age. However, although such age-related positions usually are roughly correlated with chronological age, often they are not.

For example, in the medical profession a man may be socially "mature" at chronological age 30, having rapidly gone through medical training and residencies; or he may be an "immature" intern at 35 if he entered medical school late. How he is treated by colleagues and patients depends more on his social age than on his chronological age. Or, consider the difference between the kind of behavior one expects of a 60-year-old who has retired, and a man of the same age who has not. In terms of many kinds of social expectations, the former is "old," the latter is not. For studying the course of aging, the yardstick of social expectations may be more relevant than age measured by birthdays.

There are several implications of this usage of the term age which must be kept in mind. First, in discussing the behavioral characteristics of age groups, or in charting changes in behavior over time, one must always pay attention to the relevant comparison group, social position, or institution used in defining "age." All too often we discuss "the aged" in terms of all persons over age 65, without reference to the substantial individual differences that may make such gross generalizations inappropriate. The aged are not a homogeneous group; chronological age is only an imperfect approximation of social or personal age. What we need is a more precise method of determining the social punctuation points of the life-cycle as they affect individual behavior. Moreover, we should recognize that social definitions of age and its importance in patterning individual behavior vary greatly from one culture or social setting to another.

Second, in charting the course of individuals through the social punctuation points of the life span, there often occurs what Leonard Cain (1964, p. 287) calls "asynchronization": differences in the timing of events in various areas of one individual's life. Consider, for example, a 55-year-old steelworker whom I once interviewed. He had just retired and thus had reached the status of "old age" in the occupational or economic institution. Within the context of the family, however, he was relatively "young," for he had a 13-year-old daughter. In terms of formal voluntary organizations he was "middle aged," having just succeeded to the third highest position in a fraternal order. By what standards should this man's social age be calculated? In which age category does he belong? Such a question would be trivial, were it not for his own anxiety and confusion about his age status:

I'm glad to be through with work because I couldn't take it any more. But now my friends don't know what to call me. They kid me about being an old man, and I don't feel it . . . . My wife doesn't know what to do with me, says I get underfoot being around the house all the time . . . . I guess I've got to find something to do. A man my age shouldn't just sit around.

Third, and most important, social age is relevant because it suggests some guidelines for how we should behave. In the example just cited, the steelworker isn't so much confused over his age, as over what a person his age who doesn't work should do. The importance of age (as socially defined at least) in patterning everyday interaction resides in the expectations it creates regarding appropriate behavior.

One final point is crucial regarding the definition of "old age." The above discussion would appear academic except for the way in which our society adheres to a chronological definition of age to the exclusion of all others. Many tensions arise from the fact that "old age" is defined to begin at age 65 in most occupations, and thus, despite considerations of biological and psychological capacity, to say nothing of social competence, a chronological definition of aging is paramount. One thus sees in the real world many tensions that arise from conflicting criteria of age. With the increased push toward earlier retirement, greater longevity, private pension plans, and better health characterizing the American population, age 65 is increasingly proving to be an arbitrary and less than useful way to mark the "old age" stage of life.

*Social Values and the Elderly**

Richard A. Kalish

According to all logic, the self-esteem of older people should be lower than when they were younger. According to most research studies (see Riley et al., 1968; National Council on the Aging, 1975), self-esteem does not diminish with age. What is the basis for the apparent contradiction? Probably that, even when you are old, you know that you are still you. If you esteemed this "you" when you were younger, you apparently continue to esteem it when you become older. You may become frustrated with new limitations, some imposed by the environment and some imposed by your changing body; you

*Edited from "Social Values and the Elderly," by R. A. Kalish, *Mental Hygiene*, 1971, *55*, 51–54. Reprinted by permission of the Mental Health Association.

may feel that you lack the ability to be as meaningful to others as you once were. But the basic self-esteem appears to remain reasonably constant. Old people may feel that old people are not esteemed by society, but their self-esteem as individuals is still intact.

But when people become old, we know that their intellectual abilities diminish, right? The answer is a resounding "maybe." Some elderly suffer strokes or other physical ailments and definitely lose their previous cognitive powers, but this is much less common than often assumed. True, many elderly people have more trouble recalling names of people they've just met or recalling telephone numbers or other things they have recently experienced, but the more significant aspects of intelligence, such as the ability to reason or to integrate information, appear to diminish very little in the later years. It is only in very old age or when health conditions affect the brain that cognitive losses become serious.

What does all this have to do with social values? Our society places a very high value on those efforts that lead to productivity and achievement. Therefore, older people, who are believed to have reduced intellectual competence, are valued less than younger people. The following article ends on a harsh note, which focuses attention on what society says to the older person. Yet the article does not give full sympathy to the elderly by any means.

Today's elderly have made a Procrustean bed for themselves. Little wonder that they are unhappy lying in it, waiting to be pulled or chopped until they fit the bed that they themselves designed. To use another idiom, Mr. and Mrs. John Q. Citizen, Sr., are their own finks, for it was they who—as young marrieds and middle-aged community leaders—reared, nurtured and taught the generation that today sees little need for them.

It was Mr. Citizen, Sr., who emphasized the importance of being independent and avoiding dependency, of being productive and avoiding unproductive time, of being meaningful to others and avoiding self-centered actions, of being future-directed and avoiding past directedness. Now that old John Q. is retired, he and his wife have more difficulty being independent, productive and meaningful, but the world they live in is dominated by the values they transmitted, and they are paying the penalty. The chances are that they themselves agree with this evaluation of their worth—or lack of worth—and their own voices often join the chorus that deprecates the elderly for the very things that time, health and society conspire to impose upon them.

Youngsters today claim that the values of Americans favor the old, while the oldsters complain that this is a youth-oriented society. They are both wrong. The traditions that have evolved through our history have led to values that reward neither the young nor the old, except to the extent that each can play the game of the middle class and the middle-aged. If our society valued the old, we would not have complaints about the existence of Medicare, about letting grandma move into our house, about grandpa's idiosyncrasies, or about the horrors of age segregation in retirement communities (mostly expressed by people who live in communities segregated by age so as to avoid the elderly).

On the other hand, if we were a youth-centered society, we would welcome equally the youngster who wished to attend college and the one who wished to lounge on the beach; we would applaud the art major as we do the engineering major; we would admire the bearded and the protesting as much as the shaven and the accepting.

But we don't. And that is because we are not youth-oriented. We are oriented only to those youths who show promise of accepting the middle class, middle-age rewards. Young people who indicate that they will follow along tried and true paths of success are given high rewards—after all, they essentially will support the middle-aged in what the latter wish, a variation of the old apprenticeship system. And the bribes to do this, such as college scholarships and good jobs, are substantial.

However, the youngsters who, perhaps themselves believing this to be a youth-oriented society, decide to go their own way soon find that the rewards are few. If they challenge the middle-aged autocracy through words, they are spurned and patronized; if they dare to do so through actions, they are met with substantial opposition both through physical force and through other forms of power.

I wish to focus particularly upon productivity and achievement, independence, meaningfulness and futurity. These values are all very close to the hearts of most Americans, so close, in fact, that few ever stop to think that alternatives even exist. And they are all values that the older retired person can satisfy only in part.

Although we claim not to be a materialistic society, one major complaint about older persons is that they are useless. Usefulness, of course, is about as materialistic a criterion for a person's worth as one could imagine. On the one hand, we require that older people stop working; on the other hand, we adhere to a value system that degrades the non-worker. How much better it would be if we could believe that 40 or 50 years of work entitled a person either to stop work, to reduce his work effort, or to alter his type of work, and that in so doing, he might enhance rather than detract from the image that the community maintains of him. And by work and productivity, I refer to housework and child-rearing as much as to tasks for which pay is given.

Being independent is the second middle class, middle-age source of confusion. No one is independent, although many people work very hard at being "dependent on no one." But we depend upon the building inspector, the teacher, the pilot, and the policeman in our daily actions; we also are dependent upon those whom we love or even those to whom we are mildly attached.

The myth of independence, partly a carryover from our frontier heritage by people who ignore the immense dependence that our pioneer ancestors had upon each other, is difficult to dispel. More to the immediate point, it is accepted by most people as a given. To be independent is good; to be dependent is bad. As people become older, they are likely to need more kinds of support and help from others. Ill health requires help from physicians, nurses and family members; inability to drive requires help from neighbors, friends and relatives; the loss of a spouse brings about the need not only for help in doing certain things, but also for emotional support; increasing difficulty in keeping up with the fast-paced, modern world may call for help in decision-making.

These are the realities of aging for some persons, but they are most painful to accept, because our cultural demand for independence makes it embarrassing and degrading to ask for such help. In addition, those called upon to give help frequently are angry, patronizing or otherwise punishing in their approach.

These responses are understandable, since a dependent person is a demanding person, that is, the very fact that he depends upon us makes a demand upon us. Thus, the physician, the adult child, the recreation leader all turn away from dependent older persons, because they wish to avoid being enmeshed in a relationship that may make unwished-for demands upon them. A dependent infant or young child is acceptable, but not a dependent parent. No wonder that when older people who are part of the same culture find their own need to be dependent increasing, they become anxious and depressed. No wonder that the most common concern I hear is "I don't want to be a burden to my children."

Third, the older person wishes to be meaningful, but he often defines meaningfulness in terms of service to others or productivity. Many people cannot think of being meaningful to themselves, or developing their own capacities and making themselves the best possible persons they can be. Any age is the correct age for self-development; old age is the last possible age to do it.

Yet many people, old as well as younger, try to persuade older persons that they can be meaningful only insofar as they serve others or produce, without recognizing either the moral implications of their demands or the difficulties that some older persons encounter in trying to live up to this standard.

The older person finds it increasingly difficult to be meaningful to others because he is not permitted to work; because his children no longer need him in the same way that they did previously; because his stamina, mobility and sensory-motor capacities are possibly diminished; and because his ways of understanding and dealing with the world may not accord with what the prevailing approaches are. The wisdom and experience that his years have provided may be seen as irrelevant or outmoded, and his lack of power and influence reduces his ability to command consideration.

And fourth, the older person lacks futurity; that is, the likelihood that he will live a substantial number of additional years in good health is limited.

Thus, the older person is not devalued because we have a youth-centered society, but because our society is centered around productivity and achievement, independence, meaningfulness and futurity. (And also such qualities as vigor, sexuality, formal education, technological and scientific skills, and other capabilities that older persons tend to have in lessening amounts.)

Perhaps the underlying, coordinating theme of all this is "the payoff." Using the vocabulary of the stock market, we Americans like to invest our efforts, money, time and emotional involvements in people who will pay off. Society is contrived so that older persons are very unlikely to pay off, since they will probably not be productive in the ways we wish, they will not be able to be as independent as when they were younger, they will be less meaningful, and they have limited futures.

Young people who show promise of fulfilling these demands are worth investments because they will pay off, either through future achievements or by offering us the psychic reward of knowing we have contributed to a potentially long and happy life. The physician or social worker who puts great time and energy and emotional feelings into helping an elderly person receives, as he perceives it, less payoff than when a similar expenditure is made for a younger person. Not only are the odds less that the older person will recover, but if he does recover, it is likely to be for a much briefer time. The payoff, in terms of our values, is much less. The upside potential is slight; the downside risk is great.

Shifting briefly back to the contemporary values of younger America: it can easily be seen that those youngsters who are the most despised by the middle-aged are the very ones who reject the same values that the elderly have permitted to be imposed upon them. That is, some of the students are asking why they should be productive, for whom are they achieving, what is so good about not being a burden, and why bother planning for such an unstable future. In essence, they are retired even before they have begun to work.

The following paragraph attempts to establish a new set of ground rules.

In America, we should no longer focus upon those with high potential future payoff, since there are already enough people who will knock themselves out to produce and achieve. Our main responsibility should be to our older citizens, since they will only be here a relatively short time, while younger people have many decades. The older person, who has already expended his life's energies for his community, needs his reward now, not in the tomorrow that his juniors can look forward to. In addition, the best way to maintain healthy continuity of ideas and values is to reward the old, so that the young will observe the reward system and attempt to emulate the traditional values of the country in order to gain these rewards for themselves in the later years. As an example, we should establish geriatric clinics and do away with our maternal and child care clinics, since: (a) we have too many babies anyway; and (b) a new baby can be brought forth in a matter of months, while it takes 70 or more years to nurture an old person.

Unfair? Insensitive? Obtuse? Ugly? Regressive? Stultifying progress? I have only applied against the very young the reverse of what I often hear directed against the elderly. If we truly respect the dignity and worth of an individual, rather than his potential for material gain and social productivity, then we need to begin to judge people by such criteria as integrity, compassion and humanity, rather than by the criterion of payoff.

*Changing Roles in the Later Years**

Gordon F. Streib

Old age is most certainly a time of role change, but for the most part— except for the work role—the change is gradual. And even the work role does not change all at once, since the individual anticipates the change from employed *to* retired *months or years before it occurs.*

There is a tendency to glamorize both the work role of the past and the former role of the family, while deprecating the present status of both. This may well be a function more of nostalgia than of accurate memory. We have no studies about how many people in 1910 or in 1930 would have wanted to work until their very old age, assuming that a minimally adequate income was available, but I would personally hazard the estimate that it would be very few.

On the other hand, we do have some information about how many people retire because they are forced to by arbitrary retirement regulations, and the number is surprisingly small. Most elderly retire either because their health does not permit them to work or because they prefer not to work. Of course, this fact should not be used to ignore the thousands of persons who are, indeed, forced into a retirement that they do not want and need not, by virtue of health, accept.

The entire issue of changing roles in the later years—work roles, family roles (see Chapter Seven), community roles—is a major one in social gerontology. Some investigators have even characterized old age as being a "roleless role."

"Retirement in health, honor, dignity—after years of contribution to the economy." This statement, taken from the declaration of objectives of

*Edited from "New Roles and Activities for Retirement," by G. Streib. This material originally appeared in George L. Maddox (Ed.), *The Future of Aging and the Aged*, a book in the Southern Newspaper Publishers Association Foundation Seminar Series published in 1971 and distributed by the Duke University Center for the Study of Aging and Human Development. Reprinted by permission of the SNPA Foundation and The Duke University Center for the Study of Aging and Human Development.

the Older Americans Act of 1965, provides a general goal with which Americans of all ages can agree. But how can this commendable ideal be translated into specific expectations and actions that will enrich the lives of individuals, or into policies and programs that will directly affect people? A clarification of this broad objective can occur only by a closer examination of the many roles available to older citizens, once they have left the work roles and child-rearing roles which perhaps absorbed the greatest part of their attention in the young and middle years. These two role losses, combined with declining physical health and reduced economic resources, constitute the broad framework of the disengagement process which is regarded with apprehension and anxiety by many people as they approach their later years.

Society must be aware of this role loss and the necessity for role realignment and the need for new role opportunities. There must be a clearer understanding that goals based only on power and acquisitiveness that were compelling at an earlier phase of life are no longer appropriate. New ways must be found to use time and to enhance satisfaction and self-realization. It is to these problems that this paper is directed—a discussion of the need for a flexibility of life style—one that changes to take advantage of the increasingly abundant time which one has in later years, and also permits one to engage in new roles which he may not have been able to pursue in earlier years. There must be a new realization of the many different roles that older citizens can fulfill to maintain a sense of personal growth, to enrich their social contacts and to retain mental alertness.

Within our broad discussion of roles in retirement, there is another guiding principle which has been fundamental in dealing with the problems of America's older citizens. We quote the tenth objective of the Older Americans Act: "Freedom, independence and the free exercise of individual initiative in planning and managing their own lives."

I

There are four main sources of need for role realignment in later life. First, for many there has been a loss of work role which may have been the major focus of attention and activity throughout the person's life. The loss of gainful employment affects not only the man but also his wife, who must adapt to a lower economic situation, and also a changed domestic situation.

The second is closely related to the loss of work role—namely, the loss of income. This means that the ability to engage in certain subsidiary roles which demand an expenditure of money may be curtailed.

Third, retirement in many cases is the result of declining health. However, many persons are automatically retired while they are in good health. In either case, most older people find that as they age, their physical condition declines, and this may necessitate the dropping of certain roles, and the need to realign or re-examine their roles.

Fourth, the changes in the family cycle, many of which have started in late middle age are also a major source of need for role realignment. As children grow up and leave home, there is a shift in role behavior and expectation for both the father and mother. By the time retirement has occurred, help and assistance patterns may change, with aid flowing from the child to the parents instead of the former pattern of parent to child. Death of a spouse and severe illness of a spouse also cause severe adjustment in the other partner's role.

The need for role realignment varies considerably in different segments of American life, for there are urban-rural differences, ethnic differences, variations in patterns because of poverty or affluence, and widely varying life styles. Because of these factors, combined with the vast complexity of American social structure, there is confusion in the minds of gerontologists and others as to the optimum role for the aged. There is a tendency to lump all older Americans into one monolithic category and to search for one clearly defined, ideal role. This simplistic approach is factually incorrect, and unless this notion is altered, it can only lead to confusion and misunderstanding, with many older people feeling that they are not "measuring up" to what is expected of them. Instead, there must be recognition of the important factors of different values, different capacities, different personalities, and different life styles. Thus there is not one ideal role for the aged but literally dozens of roles. The problem of role needs in retirement is further complicated by a philosophical issue which determines how retirement is viewed. On the one hand, there are many groups and individuals who are committed to the position that retirement is the period of life in which a person "can take it easy," the pressures and demands of work are relaxed, and it should be a period of leisure earned by one's lifetime work activity. On the other hand, there are those who subscribe to the position that a person should work as long as he can. If he is retired by one employer or from an occupation, he should seek other full-time work. This point of view takes the position that gainful employment is one of the most important roles a person ever enacts, and thus he should maintain the work role as long as possible. They feel his skills are valued only if he is paid for them.

Between these two extremes, there are people who advocate gradual realignment of roles, by advocating part-time employment so that the older person is slowly phased out of the work role. They also suggest the need for new kinds of paid employment in the retirement period.

II

The long range goals pertaining to roles in later life have been set forth at various times by the work of aging conferences, state commissions, Congressional recommendations and Presidential reports. For example, the first national conference on aging in 1951, sponsored by the Federal Security

Agency, listed six major goals (*Man and His Years,* 1951, pp. 227–228). Those which are most pertinent are: "(1) Obtaining income and achieving economic security through socially useful and personally satisfying means. This goal requires solution of economic problems associated with employment, vocational readjustment, and income to replace or supplement wages or salaries. (2) Spending leisure time constructively. To this end, emphasis must be placed on assuring the development of personal resources within the aged themselves, recreation centers and opportunities within the community, and more adequate knowledge of the interests and capacities of older persons on the part of those who work with them. (3) Achieving and maintaining positive and well-integrated social relations within the family and community. This result will require reorientation of the attitudes of the young toward the aged and of the aged toward themselves and toward the social group."

These statements are still as pertinent today as when they were written. In the decade following, these long range goals provided the focus for many new programs and agencies to deal with America's older population. In 1961 the White House Conference on Aging restated these goals in slightly different form (*The Nation and Its Older People,* 1961, p. 285). One of the new emphases of the conference was an awareness of the problems of the late middle-aged person—that cohort of the population which in due time would become retirees. There was a realization that older citizens should begin to anticipate their retirement and to give some attention to the new roles that they will enact. One of the declarations of policy for the 1961 White House Conference specified the goal of "assisting middle-aged and older persons to make the preparation, develop skills and interests, and find social contacts which will make the gift of added years of life a period of reward and satisfaction and avoid unnecessary social costs of premature deterioration and disability."

In the ensuing years, the statements of the goals were refined further. Robert J. Havighurst stated: "The individual's goal in an automated society is the achievement of a *flexible life style*-one that changes to meet new demands and to take advantage of new opportunities. The goal, for a society responsible to its citizens, is to help the individual maintain a sense of personal growth by establishing and maintaining economic and social arrangements to provide possibilities for growth" (Havighurst, 1969, p. 17).

The increasing awareness that older citizens need help in realizing their full potential in their new roles is expressed in a statement of President Nixon's Task Force of 1970: "Even if the income, health, and shelter problems of older persons were resolved, or at least ameliorated, the Task Force believes that significant barriers would still exist to the involvement of the elderly in the life of the community. Additional measures are needed. . . . A common thread which runs through all of the recommendations contained in this chapter is that their successful implementation depends on the extent to which either business or voluntary organizations, or both, take part. The Task Force expects the Federal Government to take the lead in encouraging the growth of such a partnership" (p. 42).

III

The basic notion of the concept of role, as employed here, is focused on descriptive real life roles such as parent, spouse, worker, retiree, widow, sick person, etc. Involved in these roles and many others which older persons enact are three basic conceptual distinctions: the normative, the behavioral, the interactional.

A role is always associated with a position in a social structure, organization or group. These positions are normatively defined and these norms establish expectations for what is appropriate behavior to the role.

A second major dimension is the behavioral or performance aspect. This component is what a person does in enacting a certain role or set of roles.

Almost all roles are interactional—that is, they involve some kind of social exchange with other persons who are in complementary or conflicting roles with the person carrying out his role—i.e., parent, child, spouse, worker, supervisor.

The problem of analyzing roles at any stage of the life cycle is complicated by the fact that the person has a number of intersecting and overlapping roles which he must carry out—sometimes simultaneously and sometimes sequentially, according to expectations held by himself and others in the particular situation in which he finds himself.

There has been much talk in recent years about the role of the aged in American society. The lumping together of all persons of a chronological age—60 and over, or 70 and over—is a meaningless categorization. Certainly for administrative purposes, chronological age is an arbitrary, but useful, way of categorizing persons. For example, one votes at 21 (or 18) years of age and can collect social security at 65. But once we move beyond the broad administrative demands and take account of the factual social realities of older persons, we must be more precise and specific as to role definitions and expectations. The specifications by sex, by ethnicity, by race, by health condition, by socio-economic status and by educational level are more significant in their social and social-psychological importance than crude age categorizations. Moreover, specification by particular membership and reference groups—kin, neighborhood, religions, labor unions— enlarge our knowledge of older people and begin to focus attention on the more crucial aspect of social life.

The older person has a distinctive role set which includes a complement of roles and role relationships such as: worker, husband, father, grandfather, neighbor, church member. The increased specification of the position-role concepts also includes a dynamic or processual aspect—status sequence—which refers to a series of positions a person occupies over a period of time and role sequence which refers to role performance in successive time periods.

In the role set of a hypothetical man before retirement, he does not have merely one role, but a variety of roles: family and kin, homeowner, friend, citizen, church member and of course, worker. The latter role occupies a larger area of "role space" because in the preretirement phase, the worker role is such an important component of a man's role set. For a woman, the role of homemaker might occupy the largest area in the role set. On the other hand, a woman who works outside the home would have a worker role, and in addition a homemaker role.

In a hypothetical role set of a retired person, the worker role has disappeared, but the other roles have expanded to fill up the role space formerly occupied by the work role. Activities related to what we might call the leisure role have expanded, and so has kinship. Similarly there has been expansion of role activities in other spheres. There is an opportunity, if one wishes, to expand the role in the citizenship-service area, for the person may not have had the time or strength to pursue such activities while he was working. This is a hypothetical kind of role enlargement, and will vary considerably because many older persons have great role flexibility. The point to be emphasized is that in retirement, persons do not have to endure a "roleless role" as so many persons have claimed. Old age can be a period of role realignment in which the person, in keeping with his interests, his tastes, his resources, sets new goals. He does not need to remain chained to the goals of former periods of his life, such as making money, wielding power, emphasizing the collecting of consumer goods, etc.

It should be stressed that the older person has a distinctive role set, and it is shaped by broad norms and expectations linked to age. Our knowledge is limited in this area. One of the few studies of this problem was carried out at the University of Chicago. These investigators stated the issue in these words: "There exists what might be called a prescriptive time-table for the ordering of major life events: a time in the life span when men and women are expected to marry, a time to raise children, a time to retire. This normative pattern is adhered to, more or less consistently, by most persons in the society" (Neugarten, Moore, and Lowe, 1965, p. 711).

The preceding discussion has focused on a person's role set at one point in time. It is important that we understand the processual nature of social roles and the fact that certain roles are of long duration (such as the role of spouse) while other roles are brief (such as the role of student). Many roles may occupy one person's life. Obviously each person would have somewhat different time schedules for his personal roles. Roles also undergo change throughout life—some are of short duration and some are retained longer . . . .

VII

In considering present knowledge of the roles and activities of the aged, it is pertinent to discuss how these findings bear on two theories of optimum aging—the "activity theory" and disengagement theory.

The basic premise of "activity theory" is that: "The older person who ages optimally is the person who stays active and who manages to resist the shrinkage of his social world. He maintains the activities of middle age as long as possible and then finds substitutes for those activities he is forced to relinquish" (Havighurst, Neugarten, Tobin, 1968, p. 161).

Disengagement theory, as originally formulated by Cumming and Henry (1961) stated: "In our theory, aging is an inevitable mutual withdrawal or disengagement, resulting in decreased interaction between the aging person and others in the social systems he belongs to. The process may be initiated by the individual or by others in the situation. The aging person may withdraw more markedly from some classes of people while remaining relatively close to others. His withdrawal may be accompanied from the outset by an increased preoccupation with himself; certain institutions in society may make this withdrawal easy for him. When the aging process is complete, the equilibrium which existed in middle life between the individual and his society has given way to a new equilibrium characterized by a greater distance and an altered type of relationship" (p. 14).

Damianopoulos (1961, pp. 210–218), who restated disengagement theory in propositions, said: "Because the abandonment of life's central roles—work for men, marriage and family for women—results in a dramatically reduced social life space, it will result in crisis and loss of morale unless different roles, appropriate to the disengaged state, are available" (Damianopoulos, 1961, p. 215). There are several issues in this proposition which require qualification and re-examination. While it is true that work and family are central roles for men and women respectively, the assertion that retirement, in the case of men, results in a sharp decline in social life space is not tenable for persons in many occupations. The disengagement theorist and the activity theorist incorrectly assume that work for many people is an interesting and stimulating social experience, but this may not be the case for many persons. They may tolerate the social side of work with their associates, but the social aspects of work may be unimportant in the long run. One has little, if any, choice in the selection of work-mates, and one's fellow employees are usually selected for other reasons than social compatibility. Damianopoulos referred to a "crisis" after retirement. The findings of the Cornell Study of Occupational Retirement show that most people do not undergo any crisis or loss of morale following retirement (Streib & Schneider, 1971).

A broad view of the facts concerning the roles and activities of older citizens seems to suggest that neither theory is adequate. While disengagement ultimately comes to all, people vary greatly in the degree to which they retrench. In contrast, while it is generally agreed that activity has a salubrious effect on health and morale at any stage of life, it is hardly advisable to urge older people to keep up a frenetic whirlwind of activity for its own sake—whether it is meaningful or not. Certainly this misses some of the richness of later years, for it seems to adapt the goals of the middle years—power, accomplishment, acquisitiveness, aggressiveness—instead of seeking new criteria for fulfillment.

Instead, we would propose that "differential disengagement" is more reasonable as a model—that people should and do disengage according to their own life experience, personality, health and energy status. There is no "ideal role" to which everyone should aspire.

VIII

As people age, in general they enact fewer social roles and consequently there is a reduction in the number and variety of their contacts with other persons and with their environment in general (Riley et al., 1968, p. 413). This is based on a study of 200 healthy men and women from 50 to 80 in Kansas City. Similar findings have been reported by others in later analysis of additional information on these same respondents (Havighurst et al., 1968). In broad terms, role activity is associated with general life satisfaction and a feeling of meaningfulness, a positive self image, and general optimistic attitudes.

Despite this broad generalization, there are wide differences in the mode of adjustment according to one's style of life and personality. Both passive and active behavior can lead to satisfaction in retirement and old age. Williams and Wirths have found that in the Kansas City sample, there were persons who were isolated and yet adjusted satisfactorily to aging. In describing one person with minimum involvement, they state, "He was in fair balance with his social system but at a very low level of involvement. Disengagement was no problem for him. . . . It is possible to be somewhat anomic, alienated, and isolated and yet cope very well, if one's style is one of Minimal Involvement" (Williams & Wirths, 1965, p. 279).

In this connection it is pertinent to discuss the research of Reichard on how different personality types react to the aging process. Reichard and her colleagues delineated five types of retired men: the "mature," the "rocking chair," the "armored," the "angry men" and the "self-haters" and described as a "well-integrated person (one) with some self-awareness, neither impulsive nor over-controlled. Freedom from neurotic inhibitions permitted him to enjoy life. His capacity for enjoyment was reflected in the warmth of his personal relationships. He readily assumed family responsibilities and was an affectionate husband and father, who also enjoyed seeing friends and valued retirement for the chance to spend more time with them" (Reichard et al., 1962, p. 115). She adds that such personality types took growing old for granted and were not shaken in their basic self esteem (Reichard et al., 1962, p. 127).

The "rocking chair" men also adjusted easily to retirement. They were described as a passive-dependent group who were unambitious, found little satisfaction in work and were glad to take it easy when retirement came. Reichard said, "Why did these men adjust well to aging? Because they welcomed the chance provided by old age and retirement to take it easy. Society grants, in old age, permission to indulge needs for passivity and dependence that it does not grant young people. Thus they were free to be more truly themselves" (Reichard et al., 1962, p. 130).

In contrast, the "armored type" had good adjustment to aging through a smoothly functioning system of defenses. They tended to have stable work histories and to participate actively in organizations. "The armed counteracted their fear of growing old by remaining active. Afraid of physical and mental deterioration associated with aging, they were happy and adjusted as long as they could keep busy. . ." (Reichard et al., 1962, p. 137).

Thus we see that an understanding of the variety of personality types reflected in role behavior is essential for those who work with the aged, for they must realize that successful adaptation and role realignment for one person is not necessarily to be recommended for another . . . .

X

The reduction in role activity as worker and as parent, combined with declining health and usually reduced income, constitute the realistic framework within which most older persons enact their many roles in later life. Many persons—old, young, persons of influence, and the man in the street—must be aware of the role losses and the necessary role realignments which are an integral part of later life. There must be, however, a clear recognition that old age can be a period of new role opportunities. Public and private organizations can aid in reaching broad goals of spending the new leisure time of later life constructively, and achieving positive and well-integrated roles within the family, the community and in a broad spectrum of groups and organizations.

Roles involve social norms and expectations, performance in the defined position and usually some kind of social exchange with other persons. The older person has a distinctive *role set* which includes a complement of roles and relationships. The older person does not have to enact a "roleless role." Both the old and the young occupy role space in which they have considerable latitude in deciding what roles to carry out and what roles should receive time and priority. It is possible—given health, some social supports, and personal motivation—for older persons to alter their role sets in later maturity. Because we are concerned with life as an on-going process one must be aware of the changing nature of these roles in later life resulting from health changes, familial rearrangements, and the important shift from worker to retiree.

The Normal Dependencies
of Aging*

Margaret Blenkner

Social workers meet those old people who need social services; physicians and nurses meet those old people who need health services; both groups tend to see a highly selected sample of older persons and, further, see them under a restricted set of circumstances. My point is that neither social workers nor health caretakers meet many normal older people under normal circumstances. As a result, they sometimes develop a distorted picture of the needs of the greater proportion of American and Canadian elderly.

Although author Blenkner focuses on the dependencies of the elderly, she has a keen eye for their strengths.

This paper is addressed to dependency as a state of being, not a state of mind; a state of being in which to be old—as to be young—is to be dependent. Such dependency is not pathological, it is not wrong; it is, in fact, a right of the old recognized by most if not all societies. It cannot be cured and the only way to forestall it is to die young. In short, it is the normal dependency or dependencies of old age that are the focus of what follows. These normal dependencies may be reduced to four basic categories:

1. Economic dependency stems from having crossed over from the productive to the consumer status in the economy. No longer a wage earner, or the spouse of a wage earner, and not having been able to accumulate sufficient savings to support himself through 15–25 years of retirement, the older person typically finds himself dependent on income transfers from the currently working generation, provided primarily through taxes but also in contributions from children and other younger relatives (Kreps, 1965).

2. Physical dependency arises from the simple fact that in the process of aging, muscle strength inevitably diminishes, sensory acuity decreases, reflexes are slower, coordination is poorer, and the general level of energy is lower. The ordinary chores of living—personal self-care and grooming, keeping up one's living quarters, preparing or securing food, transporting oneself from place to place, shopping, participating in social functions, etc.—become increasingly difficult, strenuous, and eventually impossible to perform entirely without aid.

3. Mental dependency arises from a decline in the power of mentation paralleling the decline in physical power, but occurring more slowly or not

*Edited from "The Normal Dependencies of Aging," by M. Blenkner. In R. A. Kalish (Ed.), *The Dependencies of Old People* (Occasional Papers in Gerontology, #6, 27–38). Copyright 1969 by the Institute of Gerontology, University of Michigan—Wayne State University. Reprinted by permission.

reaching such magnitude as to be seen as a source of dependency until quite advanced old age. At that time, when deterioration or change in the central nervous system produces marked deficits in memory, orientation, comprehension and judgment, the old person, quite literally, no longer can use his head to solve his problems and direct his affairs; he must rely on the cognitive functions of others (Donahue, 1965).

4. Social dependency develops out of a complex of factors and losses. As the individual ages, he loses persons who are important objects and sources of affection, stimulation, and assistance. He loses roles that are the basis of status and power, and avenues to social participation. He loses contemporaneity as his knowledge, values, and expectations become obsolete in a fast changing society. He becomes without volition a progressively isolated and disengaged nonparticipant in the surrounding social world, increasingly dependent on bureaucratized substitutes for missing kith, kin, and agents of former days, increasingly dependent on recognition by others of his rights rather than his power. He becomes dependent on the social conscience of the generation in positions of authority, those who currently have all that he has lost in the way of vitality and performance. In other words, in old age, without the powers of one's prime—economic, physical, mental, and social—one is dependent on the ethical responses of his fellow man (Rosow, 1962).

That these dependencies of the aged are intermixed and interacting hardly needs mention. The fact that they occur simultaneously, though at differing rates of development and force of impact at any given time, reduces considerably the possibility of defensive counteraction or substitutive maneuvers.

I have not included emotional dependency here, because emotional dependency, in the sense of depending on others for love and emotional response, is part of the human condition. We are social animals. It is in our genes, whatever our stage of development or generational status. If disengagement theory and certain libidinal theories are to be believed, the need for intense emotional involvement with others may be less for the old than for the young and middle-aged.

There are three sources of help or types of solution for the normal dependencies of aging:

1. Self-Solution, whereby the older person himself seeks to modify his behavior or circumstances. For example, he balances his budget by restricting consumption; he conserves his energy by restricting his activities; he bolsters his failing memory by writing notes to himself; he counters his social losses by social disengagement. This is the first line of defense. Such maneuvers are sensible and valid ways of coping, up to a point; beyond that point, they become increasingly pathological and dangerous until, in an extreme form, they may jeopardize the sanity and survival of the individual (Clark, 1967).

2. The Kinship Solution, the most common type among those of advanced years, requires the existence and proximity of children or other relatives. For the aged who are fortunate enough to have concerned and

capable kin, most of their dependent needs can be and usually are met by the care-giving services of such kin.

Typically, the old person remains in his own abode as long as he is capable of personal self-care. However, children or other relatives increasingly take on or assist with the heavier tasks of housekeeping and home maintenance, provide transportation and escort, manage his financial affairs, supervise his health care, nurse him in time of illness, and in general watch over him, substituting their strength, mobility, and judgment for his declining abilities. As he becomes more frail he is likely to move into the home of a relative where more personal care and protective supervision can be given. Only a small minority are institutionalized, and then only when the demand for intensive and skilled care rises beyond the capacity of family members (Stehouwer, 1968).

These too are sensible and valid solutions up to a point; but if carried too far they become destructive to both the old and their kin. An excessive burden of care can so overwhelm a family as to actually endanger its members' physical, emotional, and social stability, or else result in a complete and irreversible rejection of the old person, with all the accompanying guilt and suffering.

3. The Societal Solution consists of arrangements or programs through which society assists its members to cope with needs and problems beyond the resources of the individual or his primary group. It assigns consumer rights to goods and services by nonmarket criteria. Social insurance, public housing, and rent supplementation are good examples of such solutions.

Under the impact of modern living conditions (urbanization, increasing technology, mobility of population, disappearance of the three-generation household, extension of the retirement years), there is a tremendous need to develop and expand imaginative and inventive societal solutions to the normal dependencies of aging. Commenting on the "pressing requirements of a fast-growing aged population," Robert Morris in 1965 asserted that "No organization, no agency, no community is yet ready to organize itself on a mass basis that will be sufficient to ensure all the necessary services for all the elderly whenever they may require such services" (Morris, 1965). That statement is as true now as it was then.

Despite the woeful inadequacies of our present income maintenance system, we are further along the road to solution in the economic sphere than any other. We know the answer; the question is, do we have the generosity? The obvious answer to economic dependency among persons no longer in the labor market is either to supply them with money, or to pay their bills. This in effect is what we have done in the United States for the older person; but we have done it penuriously and, for too many, we have done it demeaningly.

Building on our present social insurance system, we could take care of this particular dependency by instituting universal coverage of all retired or disabled persons 60 years and over, and making the minimum benefit sufficient to secure a modest but adequate standard of living. We could remove the questionable co-insurance and deductible provisions from Medicare, add some provisions for "preventicare," and thus insure that all—not just part—of the elderly's medical bills will be paid. We could, once and for all insofar as the aged are concerned, get rid of the means test approach to economic dependency. Presently, neither old age insurance nor old age assistance is meeting the economic need of our older citizens. If they were, the old would not comprise one-fourth to one-third of the poor we talk so much about today.

Generously meeting the economic dependency of the aged will do much to solve or forestall the rise of problems in other areas. In fact, satisfactory solutions to dependency needs in other areas hinge on first satisfactorily and adequately solving the problem of economic dependency. Failure thus far to solve this problem is a major source of failure and confusion in our efforts in other dependency areas, as will be seen later.

Problems of physical dependency may be met by various congregate and protective living arrangements of an institutional or semi-institutional character, or by services delivered to the old in their own homes or those of relatives or friends. In the United States, despite lip-service to the slogan "keep the old in their own homes," most money and manpower directed specifically toward services and facilities for the aged segment of the population are designed to remove the old from their own homes.

With public funds and through public policy, we have subsidized the development and expansion of the proprietary nursing home into a major industry (Blenkner, 1968). Private philanthropic money for the aged is nearly all concentrated in congregate care facilities of one sort or another, as is professional personnel employed by the voluntary agencies to serve the aged. The one program that could put action into the slogan of keeping the old in their homes—an extensive system of home help services (visiting housekeepers or home aides, home handymen and maintenance aides, transport and escort aides, etc.) is grossly underdeveloped in the United States in contrast to other advanced industrialized societies (Townsend, 1968). Even worse, under the impact of Medicare legislation, such service as has been developed is now being distorted and sidetracked into a restricted type of health care. It is available only on prescription and limited to part-time, intermittent, personal care services, instead of being developed in its own right as a major societal solution to the normal physical, mental and social losses incurred in old age (Harris, 1968).

A program that should be available as a social utility on user initiative, to any older citizen who wishes to use it, generally is available only in package deals and tie-in sales with professional services (Kahn, 1965). The old person should not have to be sick or disturbed and under treatment by a physician, nurse, or social worker to receive home aide services. Age itself should constitute an entitlement. Fees should be charged that reflect the amount of service received, but it is no more practical to charge individuals the full cost of such service than it is to expect younger individuals to pay the full cost of their education. Heavy but by no means complete subsidization is necessary; devices analogous to tuition scholarships for the educationally indigent should be invented for persons unable to pay even nominal costs. However, the number of such persons will be considerably reduced if and when our income maintenance system catches up with present-day realities.

Solutions to social dependency have become confused with solutions to mental dependency. This is evident on the social welfare scene in the newly developing programs of protective service. Although directed toward the aged person whose behavior is such as to render his mental competence suspect, a review of services usually included under the "protective service" rubric reveals that many of them may be needed by any old person at one time or another, especially if he is without accessible relatives, friends, or personal agents to help him manage.

The social characteristic of being "without anyone reliable, ready, willing, and able to act on his behalf" is sufficient to identify a public assistance recipient as "one who needs protective services." There is danger in such confusion of social and mental characteristics. Although done with the best intentions, i.e. to make scarce services available to the largest number of older persons, it tends to cast an aura of marginal mentality and civil status over all older persons seeking social services. It reinforces an already existing tendency to deny self-determination to persons in the client/patient role to assume that the professional always knows best.

No one has yet demonstrated that the average client cannot do just as good a job as the average caseworker in deciding what his major problem is, and what service would be most effective in solving or ameliorating it. With old people who in the past have managed their lives and filled their social roles adequately, this is a particularly tenable hypothesis. Some of our touted procedures of study and diagnosis that characterize practice in the "best" agencies look a bit ridiculous from the client's side of the desk.

I'll never forget an old man who applied for admission to an apartment house for older people, operated by a social agency for which I was then directing a study of a model program of services to the aging. We gave him the works in the way of study and diagnosis. The caseworker interviewed him, a public health nurse visited him, a physician examined him, he made a trial visit to the apartment house, he met and talked with house staff and residents, we held innumerable staff conferences about him. I can't recall whether we had a psychiatric consultation, but we probably did. Altogether it was a glorious interdisciplinary experience in psychobiosocial diagnosis for all—except the old man. After several weeks we concluded our deliberations and decided that he was a proper candidate for residence in the house. He was called in and the service director, exuding the warmth of the professional offering a tangible reward for good client performance, informed him of our decision. Puzzled by his somewhat flat response, she asked "Aren't you pleased?"

The old man sighed: "I guess so." Then, with rising inflection: "But that was a hell of a lot to go through just to rent a room!"

My enthusiasm for professional procedures has been somewhat tempered ever since.

Solutions to social dependency may also be confused with economic solutions, as witness the development of programs to put old people to work in hospitals, clinics, schools, social or recreational agencies, and beautification efforts. Are these programs promulgated because they provide meaningful roles to the old whose life has lost meaning, or because they provide needed cash income to those who work in the programs, or because they promise a source of cheap labor to a segment of our economy where unionization and minimum wage legislation are rapidly raising labor costs? Does the activation of such programs meet a basic social need for a considerable number of the aged, or does it serve primarily to distract us from the larger issue of inadequate Social Security benefits? How many of the old would choose to work, if they had adequate retirement incomes?

These are nasty questions, but I think we must ask them as long as retirement is synonymous with poverty for large numbers of older Americans.

Confusions and contradictions such as these reflect the difficulty we in the social and behavioral sciences, and the applied fields of social welfare and mental health, have encountered in coming to grips with normal old-age dependency as a development that must be planned and provided for, and is unlikely to be cured, treated, rehabilitated, or exorcised away.

The Elderly Confront Death*

Richard A. Kalish

There was a time, just a decade ago, when the topics of death and dying were virtually never considered appropriate for public airing. No more. Since the publication of Elisabeth Kubler-Ross' excellent discussion of the dying process (Kubler-Ross, 1969), death and dying have become familiar topics in books, articles, educational films and television, workshops, and college and high school courses.

DEATH AND AGING

The relationship between age and death has altered greatly over the centuries. During prehistoric times, the life expectancy was probably around 18; this increased to about 20 in the Greco-Roman period, then to 35

*Edited from "Death and Dying in a Social Context," by R. A. Kalish. In R. Binstock and E. Shanas (Eds.), *Handbook of Aging and the Social Sciences*. Copyright © 1976 by Litton Educational Publishing, Inc. Reprinted by permission of Van Nostrand Reinhold Company.

by the Middle Ages (Dublin, 1965). Turn-of-the-century Americans could anticipate living for nearly 50 years. Even allowing for the substantial contribution to these low life expectancies of high rates of infant mortality, only a small proportion of the population survived into their sixties or seventies.

Death is now highly predictable as a function of age; moreover, in much of the Western world and Japan, it is the old who die. Although the old have always died, the dying have not always been old. It is only in very recent decades that death has become primarily the province of the elderly, rather than an event scattered erratically across the life span.

If death is highly distressing, a supposition not contradicted by the observation that life for some is so painful that death is actively sought, and if the elderly are—with obvious exceptions—those who are going to die, then being old is in itself frightening, not only to those who are old but to those who work with or live with the elderly. Indeed, it may well be more frightening to the non-elderly, for whom experience with death is limited and who perceive themselves as having more to lose by dying. Therefore, because of the close association between old age and death in modern industrial societies, the individual and social issues relating to death are in many ways individual and social issues of aging. We may certainly hypothesize that one of the significant reasons that the old are avoided and isolated is their proximity to death.

THE MEANING OF FACING DEATH

Whether an individual faces a death that is imminent or whether he is facing a demise presumably much later in time, this death has many different meanings. These meanings obviously vary as a function of age, for several reasons. First, with increasing age, the anticipated life span is normally foreshortened, requiring constant readjustment in the allocation of time, effort, and other resources. Second, older persons tend to be perceived—and often perceive themselves—as not having sufficient futurity to deserve a major investment of the resources of others: the state, the family, the community, the work organization, and so forth. Third, older persons receive more reminders of impending death through signals from within their bodies and through the responses of other individuals and social institutions, as well as through the deaths of their age peers.

All these factors tend to encourage the process of disengagement, both psychological and social (Havighurst, Neugarten, & Tobin, 1968). Much of the present controversy regarding the adequacy of the disengagement model dissolves when applied to persons facing their own death. Kubler-Ross (1969) considers the final stage of dying, *acceptance*, as highly adaptive. She describes this stage as pertaining to a dying person who is well advanced in reducing his attachments to people, groups, material possessions, and ideas, a course of action that permits him to focus his remaining energies on only those attachments that are most vital to him. The dying individual's sense of loss diminishes as his attachments diminish in importance. That this stage closely resembles the concept of disengagement is not generally recognized (Kalish, 1972).

Apparently the pressures for disengagement that so often confront the elderly individual also confront the dying person at any age. These pressures encourage a turning inward, contemplation of meaning of the past through reminiscence, concern for the meaning of the present and the future, and pulling back from the emotional pain that occurs when attachments are lost or broken. When an elderly person enters the terminal phase, he has presumably already begun to disengage as a function of being old, and the additional detachment that is apparently induced by an imminent death encounter may be easier for him to cope with than for a younger person facing the same circumstance. Therefore we might hypothesize that the death of an older person would be less stressful than the death of an individual whose disengagement only began in response to the dying itself. Such a hypothesis is in need of empirical testing.

Two meanings of death with particular significance for the elderly are suggested by the previous discussion. First, death is an organizer of time and old people are known to have limited time. Second, death is loss and old people are known to have suffered many death-imposed losses, as well as other losses that are often associated with the dying process. A third meaning is also important: death as punishment. Since death and dying are normally perceived as intensely negative occurrences, and since negative occurrences are readily seen as punishments for transgressions, then logically death might be considered a punishment. Further, since it is old people who die, then the elderly may be thought of as victims—perhaps deserving victims—of punishment. These three meanings of death will be explored in the following discussion.

Death as an Organizer of Time

The meaning of anything, whether it is a physical object or a feeling or a human relationship, is defined in part by its boundaries. Our life is similarly defined and understood, in part, by conception, birth, and death, and we organize our lives in terms of these boundaries, even though we rarely know with more than moderate certainty where the boundary of death is. Nonetheless, we do know with complete certainty *that* it will be, and this knowledge influences our planning.

The end of life serves to organize life in two ways. First, the awareness that life will end makes all possessions, all experiences, all of everything transient. If all is recognized as transient and if detachment occurs appropriately, then more can be experienced without emotional disruption. If life were infinite, we might not need to withdraw our affect from people and things, since we might not need to experience their loss.

Second, the finitude of life alters the meaning of the way in which we use time. If time were infinite, we could have time to do many things and we would not need to establish priorities or to give up desirable options. To the elderly, death is a clearly perceived parameter that directly limits their personal futurity. Older persons were found to project themselves into a much more limited time futurity than younger persons, when asked to report coming important events in their lives and the timing of these events (Kastenbaum, 1966a). There was, however, no difference in their ability to use the concept of time to organize and interpret experience in general.

Many people have noted that retrospective time seems to pass with increasing rapidity as they age, while on-going experienced time varies not so much with age as with the nature of the experience, mood, fatigue, and anticipation. A graphic illustration of this was an 80-year-old man in a geriatric institution who made the following two comments within the same interview: "When you're as old as me, you'll learn that time devours you." ". . . nothing I could do with the time" (Kastenbaum, 1966b).

Thus, on the one hand, the coming of death speeds up the feeling of being "devoured" by time when contemplated retrospectively in weeks and months; on the other hand, death makes the moments and minutes creep by because there is nothing to do, i.e. nothing *meaningful* to do, because whatever is attempted will be transient or unfinished, a situation that renders a person helpless to achieve what he feels is important.

Back (1965) reports on a study with elderly residents of rural communities in the West. When they were asked what they would do if they knew they were to die in 30 days, they were less likely than younger respondents to indicate that their activities would change at all. A more recent study of 434 respondents in the Greater Los Angeles area, divided approximately equally into three age groups (20–39, 40–59, 60+) supported and expanded Back's figures. Given a similar situation, except that the duration was six months instead of 30 days, more of the older group would not change

Figure 1. Responses of 434 residents of Los Angeles County to the question: If you were told that you had a terminal disease and six months to live, how would you want to spend your time until you died? (Kalish & Reynolds, 1976).*

	Age		
	20–39	40–59	60+
Marked change in life style, self-related (travel, sex, experiences, etc.)	24%	15%	9%
Inner-life centered (read, contemplate, pray)	14%	14%	37%
Focus concern on other, be with loved ones	29%	25%	12%
Attempt to complete projects, tie up loose ends	11%	10%	3%
No change in life style	17%	29%	31%
Other	5%	6%	8%

*From *Death and Ethnicity: A Psychocultural Study*, by R. A. Kalish and D. K. Reynolds. Copyright 1976 University of Southern California Press. Reprinted by permission.

their life style at all, and nearly three times as many older persons as younger would spend their remaining time in prayer, reading, contemplation, or other activities that reflect inner life, spiritual needs, or withdrawal (Kalish & Reynolds, 1976). How much these results reflect physical and health-related changes, how much is due to the pressures of disengagement, and how much results from a preference for inward-directed rather than interpersonal involvements is not known.

Death as Loss

An elderly person, in contemplating his own death, is likely to be aware that he will suffer a variety of losses. He will lose self, which includes his body, all forms of sensory awareness, his roles, and his opportunities to have experiences: he will also lose others and he may be able to empathize with the grief others will feel in losing him.

Diggory and Rothman (1961) developed a list of seven values that they stated were lost through death: (1) loss of ability to have experiences, (2) loss of ability to predict subsequent events (for example, life after death), (3) loss of body (and fear of what will happen to the body), (4) loss of ability to care for dependents, (5) loss suffered by friends and family (for example, causing grief to others), (6) loss of opportunity to continue plans and projects, and (7) loss of being in a relatively painless state.

Kalish and Reynolds (1976) modified the statements slightly for their study of 434 people in four ethnoracial communities in Los Angeles, and asked that they be responded to in terms of importance. Caring for dependents and causing grief to friends and relatives were found to be less important to the older respondents than to the younger, a finding that might well arise from their having fewer dependents and their awareness of their reduced impact on others. That older persons felt less reluctant to give up experiencing is readily explained, since the potential for satisfying future experiencing for the elderly is often less, both quantitatively and qualitatively, than for other age groups.

Other kinds of losses are associated with the dying process and death. One of these is loss of control, which takes place in a variety of ways. People are well aware today that dying often occurs in a milieu where the dying individual himself has little control over what is put into or taken out of his body. Decisions are made by family members, hospital personnel, and physicians with little or no input by the dying person, although these decisions are presumably made for his welfare. The ascribed role of the dying patient is certainly one that would re-arouse any anxieties connected with loss of mastery. Caution is required in applying the global concept of loss to the great diversity of specific kinds of losses discussed above. While the notion of loss as a generic construct has heuristic value, it is necessary to remember that the meaning to an older person—or, indeed, to anyone—of loss of his physical body is vastly different than the meaning to him of the loss of loved ones (resulting from his own death) or the loss of ability to retain control of the self.

Death as a Punishment

Death is often seen as a punishment for "sins," although this tends to be the case more with the death of a younger person than with the death of an elderly person. A large proportion of people in our society maintain the implicit assumption that the actions of an individual will be rewarded or punished by what happens to him during his lifetime. Therefore, in order to make sense of what is seen as a premature death, one alternative is to seek some wrongful mode of behaving in the functioning of that individual that—in this magical thinking—"caused" him to die. For older people, the comment is made, "Well, their time has come," implying that their death was not out of sequence, was not a punishment. This belief lies deep in our history, since Western theology ascribes the advent of death itself as having arisen from human transgressions.

Kalish and Reynolds (1976) included two relevant questions in their survey, asking for agreement or disagreement with the following statements: "Accidental deaths show the hand of God working among men." "Most people who live to be 90 years old or older must have been morally good people." Nearly two-thirds of those who responded agreed with the former statement, while only slightly more than one-third agreed with the latter. However, significantly more older people than younger people agreed that the morally good live longer, while no age differences were found concerning the punishment by God through accidents. The results suggest that nearly twice as many people believe in death as a divine retribution as believe in long life as a divine reward. In some instances, when the process of living has become too painful—whether the suffering of a terminal patient or the despair of a presumably healthy person—death is seen as a welcome relief rather than a punishment. This mood often affects the survivors of an elderly individual, especially if they have observed him suffer physical pain, emotional stress, or cognitive confusion. His death is perceived as his release from a terrible existence—and, more covertly, as *their* release from the agonies of involvement in his dying process.

Aging and the Fear of Death

That fear of death exists is undebatable. The basis for such fear is much less certain. Becker (1973) posits two alternative stances. The first, which he terms the "healthy-minded" argument, contends that reactions to death are learned and that, therefore, fear of death is not natural. With proper early learning, with appropriate human relationships, the meaning of death, whether perceived as annihilation or as a rite of passage to another existence, can be assimilated as a natural process that need not be feared. Those who try to introduce death education into school curricula and elsewhere most likely accept this view implicitly.

The alternative, the "morbidly-minded" argument, insists that "the fear of death is natural and is present in everyone, that it is the basic fear that influences all others, a fear from which no one is immune, no matter how disguised it may be" (p. 15). This view does not exclude the role of early learning and lifetime experiences as influencing fear and anxiety, but essentially stipulates that fear of death is part of the human condition.

Becker himself opts for the morbidly minded position. Because the fear of death is so powerful, people have developed belief systems and rituals to cope with their terror. The success of these beliefs and rituals varies from society to society and also from individual to individual within societies. The apparent calmness with which certain people meet death is a tribute to the effectiveness of their beliefs, but does not rule out the universality of the terror.

Attitude surveys do not support Becker's position. When people were asked directly, they placed fear of their own death fairly far down on their list of fears, indicating the fear of the loss of others through death as their primary concern (Geer, 1965). Similar results are found in other studies. Depending on the wording of the items, the population studied, and the setting, the actual percentages vary, but the general conclusions remain the same: in response to direct questions, relatively few people indicate a fear of death. About one-fourth of a multi-ethnic sample indicated such fear (Kalish & Reynolds, 1976); 16% of a reasonably alert, institutionalized geriatric group stated their fear (Kimsey, Roberts, & Logan, 1972); only 10% of a group of 260 older community volunteers directly admitted fear of death, although another 31% indicated mixed feelings or ambivalence (Jeffers, Nichols, & Eisdorfer, 1961). These are typical of the many related studies.

Several studies have compared death attitudes of the elderly with those of other age groups. These show, with fair consistency, that the elderly think and talk more about death, whether they were asked to respond in terms of the frequency with which they contemplated death (Kalish & Reynolds, 1976; Riley, 1970) or in terms of having had such a thought during the previous five minutes (Cameron, Stewart, & Biber, 1973). Nonetheless, death appears less frightening for those who are older; this has been found in a variety of groups and using a variety of instruments and procedures (e.g., Feifel & Branscomb, 1973; Kalish & Johnson, 1972; Kogan & Wallach, 1961; Martin & Wrightsman, 1965). A study in India found not only highly significant differences in death fear between young and retired persons, but a still significant difference between respondents 55–60 years old and those who were 61 years old or older (Sharma & Jain, 1969). Not all studies, however, are in agreement; Templer, Ruff, & Frank (1971) obtained no age trends at all.

Initially it might seem contradictory that the old, for whom death is more imminent and who admit to finding it more salient, are still less fearful, yet the data make sense. Three reasons may be proposed:

1. In old age, there is a diminished social value of life; that is, the elderly person places less value on his own life, and others in his environment tend to share his evaluation (Glaser, 1966). The older person recognizes his limited futurity; he is likely beset by health problems and economic restrictions; earlier roles, once very satisfying, are often closed to

him. At the same time, our future-oriented social value system emphasizes the need to expend its energies on the producers of tomorrow rather than on those of yesterday. As is sometimes said of the elderly, their future is behind them.

2. People in industrialized nations can anticipate a life span of 65 to 75 years, women a few years longer, men a few years less. Perhaps this life expectancy becomes incorporated as a given in the thinking of many people. When they face their own deaths in advance of that time, they feel deprived; when they outlive their own expectations, they feel they have received their entitlement or even more.

3. As people become older, they are socialized to their own death. The rehearsal for widowhood is well-known and begins at a fairly early age (Kalish, 1971). As older family members and, eventually, age peers begin to die in larger numbers, each death must be worked through in some fashion. By the time an elderly person faces his own death, he has dealt with death sufficiently often, perhaps even rehearsing his own death, that he has been socialized to death. However, this does not in any way mean he is inured to death.

The latter point may also help explain why older people think and talk more about death. Not only is their death more imminent and, therefore, more on their minds, but they have experienced the deaths of others more frequently and have more death-related experiences to recall (Kastenbaum, 1969, pp. 28–54). Supporting data come from a British study of the be-reaved: the proportion of bereaved who visited physicians, required medicine for shock or anxiety, or reported sleeplessness decreased with age (Cartright, Hockey, & Anderson, 1973). These are presumably indications of less fear of death among the elderly, which the authors interpret much as has been done here.

Sexual Behavior
in the Later Years*

Elliott M. Feigenbaum

Some people are aghast at the thought of sexual relations between an elderly man and an elderly woman; others think it is cute. Neither attitude is likely to bring about an effective understanding of the tensions that lead to sexual problems in the later years or of the tensions that arise from these problems. In recent years, greater permissiveness regarding all sexual behavior has come to include such behavior in the elderly. Even now, however, the issue is still one that can upset professionals and laymen alike. And many people who can accept heterosexual relationships between two older people find that homosexual relationships or sexual relationships between old and young are very distressing.

Even in this time of openness regarding sex, there persists a mutual reluctance by physicians and older patients to discuss sex and sexual problems. Sex continues to be a physiological function that is the subject of jokes, myths, superstitions, and guilt. Often the guilt and anxiety lead to neurotic behavior, organic complaints, and aggravation of preexisting medical problems. The current rapid increase in our population in actual numbers as well as in percentages of people over the age of 50 means that there will be even more persons in this older age group. Therefore, it is imperative that we begin to look at the subject of sex objectively and with intelligent understanding.

Although it is true that a greater proportion of men over the age of 50 are impotent than in similar groups below that age, impotence is not necessarily a product of age. As Kinsey et al. (1948) have pointed out in their book *Sexual Behavior in the Human Male*, "The most important generalization to be drawn from the older groups is that they carry on directly the pattern of gradually diminishing activity which started with 16-year-olds." Even among the people we now refer to as the "old-old," there is no rapid drop-off of any substantial number of persons from sexual activity. Each man apparently may reach a point at which he becomes physically unable to perform sexually, and he then loses interest in sexual activity. The rate at which this occurs in later years, however, is no greater than the rate at which it occurs in earlier age groups. Kinsey emphasizes that this "seems astounding, for it is quite contrary to general conceptions of aging processes in sex."

---

*Edited from "Sex after Sixty," paper presented at the symposium, "There Is a Life after Work," sponsored by the faculty Program Center, San Francisco State University, 1971. This is the first publication of this article.

The rates of coitus for married couples, however, do drop from a peak of about 4.8 per week among the young, to 1.8 per week at age 50, and 1.3 per week at age 60. It must be noted that these figures are based on responses from married men and women, and, of all factors that influence coital rates, an available partner is the most important. Thus, whereas the frequency of coitus decreases gradually with age, 70% of all married men are still sexually active at age 70, and 50% are active at age 75. It has been shown that the sexual practices developed during the early part of one's life are those that continue through middle and older ages, so an early active sex life usually leads to relatively high activity in the middle and later years.

Studies regarding older women are very few in the literature. However, a report by Christenson and Gagnon (1965) points out that this paucity of information may be based on the lack of interest in the sexual life of old people, particularly of older women. Christenson, who worked with the Kinsey group in the preparation of *Sexual Behavior in the Human Female* (Kinsey et al., 1953), joined with Gagnon to study women over the age of 50 in terms of the information that the Kinsey people had gathered in 1953.

Again, marital status is the one important factor that predicts the coital activity of middle-aged and older women. At age 60 only 12% of postmarital women (widows and divorcees) were engaging in sexual intercourse, compared to 70% of a comparable group of married women. However, among the postmarital women, masturbatory activity was almost double that for the marital group. The postmarital group also reported more dreams with overt sexual content than did comparable married subjects.

Studies of male sexuality have demonstrated that impotence at any age may be based on physiological and psychological changes. Because the emotional life of any individual does not remain static but changes constantly, there is no reason to suppose that psychological elements have no role in the sexual activity of an elderly male. In fact, he is faced with a variety of stresses that he has not had to face before, including retirement, loss of loved ones, impending death, and, often decreased physical ability. Frequently age is used as an excuse for partners who have had longstanding unresolved conflicts to give up sexual relationships that were never satisfactory.

The termination of the reproductive life of the male is more gradual than that of women and is rarely, if ever, associated with any specific symptomatology. In women, however, sexual aging with respect to reproductive life has a very specific and definite end-point. The menopause occurs when the ovaries no longer release ova for possible fertilization. The inability to conceive, however, is not associated with any decrease in sexual interest, which appears to maintain itself quite steadily until the later years. Men, on the other hand, evidence a constant decline in sexual interest throughout middle and later years. Kinsey suggests that even in the late 50s and 60s, lower frequency of intercourse for women is "not based so much on the woman's loss of desire, but it is more a product of the older man to whom she is married."

This disparity in the aging processes of husbands and wives may create a number of problems. In the early stages of many marriages, the husband is very desirous of sexual contact, whereas the responses of the wife may still be undeveloped. Over the years, however, the female becomes less inhibited and more eager for sexual intercourse. As Kinsey indicates, by this time, the responses of the typical man may have diminished so much that his interest in intercourse, particularly in intercourse with his wife, who has had a history of objecting to his frequent requests, may well have decreased substantially. Many of the husbands in Kinsey's study stated that they had wanted intercourse more often than their wives during the early part of their marriage, whereas the women indicated that they would have been satisfied with less sexual involvement than their husbands desired. Later in marriage, this shifts, with increasing numbers of women expressing the desire for intercourse more often than their husbands then appeared willing to provide. Perhaps this shift has changed since Kinsey's study, but we have no good evidence one way or the other.

Following menopause, physical changes take place. Fatty deposits become reduced, which usually causes the breasts to sag. The tissues of the vulva become thinner and lose their erectility, which leads to a reduction in the size of the vulva, a loss of elasticity, and a decrease in moisture. Furthermore, the vaginal labia become smaller and thinner, and genital secretions, which are important for lubrication during intercourse, become scanty. In some instances the dryness may cause enough pain during intercourse to discourage the desire for sexual relations. With time, the uterus and the ovaries shrink, but these processes have no influence on sexual interest.

With advancing age, degenerative changes or disease states often require surgical correction or medical treatment. In men, traumatization of the pelvic nerves in the course of prostatic surgery can prevent ejaculation, although at times it may not prevent erection. Vaginal surgery in women can certainly narrow the introitus so that sexual intercourse becomes impossible. Diabetes in males also can cause sexual disturbances and, at times, it is because of the sexual disturbances that the diabetes is discovered. Medical treatment with such drugs as barbiturates and tranquilizers can produce impotence. It is important to note also that alcohol consumption is a primary cause of impotence. The issue of coronary artery disease is one that is open to question, because it can be argued that the psychological stresses of enforced celibacy may predispose the individual to more anginal pain than would the physical exertion of intercourse or masturbation. What is more alarming is that approximately one-third of patients who have had heart attacks are over the age of 50, and among these, two-thirds have received no advice regarding sexual activity from their physicians, and the other one-third report that the advice was vague or nonspecific.

There are other surgical procedures that can lead to sexual problems in the elderly. Among these are rectal and colon surgery, especially in those cases that require a colostomy, often the source of great embarrassment and fear. The greatest difficulty for individuals with colostomies is anxiety that the appliance may slip during intercourse or that somehow sexual intercourse will cause damage to the incision or to the colostomy itself.

Breast surgery in women may seriously affect self-image and lead to an unwillingness to expose themselves to their husbands. Furthermore, frequent concomitants to surgery for cancer of the breast are ovariectomy and adrenalectomy. Although removal of the ovaries does not affect sexual impulses, the woman may feel that she has been castrated and, therefore, no longer should have sexual intercourse. The adrenal gland, however, produces some testosterone, the hormone that has the greatest influence on sexual impulses. The lack of testosterone following adrenalectomy may indeed be responsible for a diminution or a complete loss of female sexual impulses.

Psychologically, older people are faced with the stress of having to see themselves in a less favorable light. They have lost many of their physical capabilities, and in addition, especially in men, they generally lose the role of breadwinner, and that further amplifies their lowered self-esteem. Without substitute methods of maintaining self-esteem, the elderly often become depressed, and with depression comes the lack of desire for, or even an inability to participate in, sexual activity. Depression then sets up a vicious cycle in which an episode of impotence is followed by a fear that it is permanent, followed by withdrawal from any attempt at sexual involvement and a further reduction in self-esteem.

The greater degree of sexual interest among older women relative to men of the same age group may be based on the fact that women do not experience as great a change in general life role during the later years. In some instances, however, a woman may feel that her husband's impotence is a response to her aging, and so her depressive cycle may derive from her husband's impotence.

Low self-esteem among the elderly is usually associated with a great deal of anger at a society that dictates that youth shall prevail. This anger is often turned inward, however, and leads to deepening depression and extreme frustration.

Functional impotence may result from sheer boredom. By the time a couple has been married 30 or 40 years, they have reached some sort of a well-worn groove of relationship with each other. This, of course, has certain advantages, but, psychologically, the same stimulus repeated over and over again loses its power. Many studies emphasize the importance of variety in maintaining a pleasurable sex life in later years. If the marriage partners, like most in our society, have restricted themselves to a mechanical and repetitious sex life without variety or novelty, boredom is inevitable. This situation is often reflected in the behavior of men who congregate to exchange risqué stories and jokes. To compensate for their less-than-dynamic sexual experiences, they express their interest and also share with others in the same plight. In such a group, men often seem better able to face the situation with some degree of humor. Obviously, however, they seek to stimulate the otherwise dull sexual aspect of their lives.

A few years ago I worked with the Geriatric Research Program in San Francisco. As part of our study, we asked our respondents (600 people over the age of 60 who had never had any psychiatric hospitalization) the question: "How much sex do you think a person of your age ought to have?" (1) "I can't answer. Know only my own feelings. No, I'm not past the age. When tired of looking at women, you're ready for the box. Asked doctor about it. He agreed with me." (2) "Nothing. Rosary beads and go to church. Shame. Foolish." (3) "At least once a week. That will keep you young not only physically, but also mentally. It's good for a person. It's healthy." (4) "Almost once a week, I guess, if they are physically able." (5) "Hard for me because I've been cut up and sewed too much." (6) "That's the darndest question. As far as I'm concerned, I'm not interested. Holy Moses, how do I know? That depends on whether they are happily married. Vitamin E has a great deal to do with it." (7) "Depends on glandular conditions, on food. Once or twice a week. Maybe if he can eat enough and has the urge. Lots of beefsteak and eggs." (8) "Depends on individual. I asked my internist if masturbation once or twice a week would be harmful. He said it was a good idea." (9) "I don't know anything about that. I think that would be a doctor's field, don't you?" (10) "Some, but I don't know . . . depends on health and compatibility. It takes two to have it." (11) "I've never talked about sex. I had one man and that's all. I don't understand about sex. I was raised very religiously." (12) Long pause. "Well, try weekly." Interviewer noted last two words and said "How are you spelling that?" Response: "I gave an answer. Now it's up to you." (13) "Are you crazy? I'm 95!" Note that a number of the respondents indicated that their doctors were the source of their opinions about whether sex was good for them, normal at their age, or something to be ashamed of.

Two clinical examples from my case files are also interesting and informative. An 82-year-old woman I've been seeing every other week for chronic depression usually has an increase in her difficulties around Thanksgiving and Christmas. She is a widow who also lost her only child, a son, during World War II. Last year she was so inhibited by her depression that I was seriously considering hospitalization and possibly a course of shock treatments. When things were darkest, I made a house visit during which time she began to cry and apologize to me, confessing that she had sexual feelings for me and was concerned that she would be responsible for breaking up my family. She feared that I would no longer be able to see her because I would lose respect for her. This was an obvious projection of her feelings toward herself onto me. I was able to reassure her that my continued concern for her had not been injured by her thoughts and feelings. Within a matter of one day she was a changed person and was able to resume a healthy state of functioning.

This year (1975), she started her downward slide around Thanksgiving but has not become incapacitated, and her state of depression is far milder than that of previous years.

A 77-year-old man has also been chronically depressed for seven years since the death of his wife, who at that time was 52. He was seeking young women for companionship. This interest in younger women relates to a long-harbored concern over a homosexual act in which he was involved at age 21. He had not married until he was in his mid-forties but had been a Don Juan in an attempt to prove his heterosexuality. When I first saw him (about four years ago) he was unable to achieve erection because of arteriosclerosis. Slowly, after two years of treatment, he was able to tell me that he realized that some of his preoccupation with sexual thoughts was not a sign that something was wrong. More recently, while he was quite depressed, he confessed that he was able to get an erection by using a vibrator. My response to this "shocking" information was essentially "So what's new?" The next meeting we had showed him to be markedly less depressed and back to his previous active life.

In conclusion, I think it's important for me to point out that I am not suggesting that every older person is able to indulge in a youthful, vigorous, active sexual life. What I am saying is that people in their later years do have interest in sexual matters and that they are not necessarily barred from the enjoyment of it merely by reason of their age. There are many factors that have their influence, but age, in and of itself, is not necessarily one of them. In our present state of understanding, it is impossible to know what the full potential of sexuality in the later years is, because we're dealing with people who grew up in a "neurotically conditioned culture." There is evidence that this same culture exists today, and perhaps part of the role of those of us who work with the elderly is to do something about this earlier learning of sexual attitudes.

In what may have been the first book encouraging sex behavior for the elderly, Rubin (1965) addresses physicians about their potential role in aiding older persons. I would like to paraphrase his statements for a more general audience.

At present, the role of professionals working with the elderly is crucial because of the authority with which they are invested by many older persons. Professionals in the field, especially (but not only) physicians, can bring about successful change not so much by the information they convey as by their attitudes and the persuasive effects of their personalities. If they are personally uncomfortable discussing sexual matters, or if they themselves are not convinced of the psychological importance of sexual functioning in the later years, they can do irreparable harm to the elderly with whom they work.

Therefore, gerontologists and geriatricians, in health care and in social service, must not only come to terms with their own sexual attitudes, but must be keenly aware of the extent to which these attitudes affect their relationships with the elderly. This is true for professionals who work with persons of any age, but it is particularly true for those relating to the elderly, for whom sexuality is greatly complicated by anxiety.

It is far from my desire to turn every worker in this field into a consultant on sex. Indeed, that would be a gross error. Great damage could be done by well-meaning people who intrude into this arena, where often the sensitivity of the topic requires the kind of relationship that exists only with a physician, a psychotherapist, or a highly skilled and experienced (and knowledgeable) professional. Nonetheless, the same general principles of maintaining an open, non-judgmental attitude, neither encouraging nor discouraging any particular form of sexual behavior and not overstepping the bounds of one's role and knowledge apply to all people who work with the elderly.

Chapter 3

Money In, Money Out

Money isn't everything, but getting along when there's none to be had is certainly an immensely difficult problem. No one knows this better than the elderly. Not only are many living on reduced (often substantially reduced) incomes, but the usual avenue to increased earnings, working, and the means of establishing credit often are closed to people of advancing age.

To some extent, older people are distressed by the lack of money, because income often symbolizes worth. If you have money, you are worth something; if what you are doing is rewarded with money, then what you are doing is worth something. But the symbolic value of money for those who have very little often pales before the practical value of money. Without money, goods and services are normally unavailable, and the elderly need and want as much in the way of goods and services as the nonelderly.

Not all elderly people are poor, by any means. A few are wealthy, and many are quite comfortable. Some who might seem poor to outside observers consider themselves moderately well off, perhaps because they have learned to function successfully on a limited income; perhaps because they never have had more than a modest amount of money.

A little history may be worth considering at this point. In times past, older people retained power over money and jobs by means that generally don't exist today. In many families, the elderly father (or his widow) had control of the family income, which was very likely to be substantially greater than the incomes of the young adult children. He owned whatever land was owned by the family; he owned the family store.

Often, the father was also the gatekeeper to work for his children. Because he owned the land or the store, and because the children (at least one or two of the sons) needed access to the family farm or business for a livelihood, they had to be responsive to the demands of the parental generation. In other instances, the father worked in the mines, was a member of a craft union, or was employed by large or small business. Young men who wished to follow in their father's footsteps often benefited greatly from the father's knowledge and reputation. Today this work pattern has all but disappeared. Rarely do sons learn their father's trade or assume responsibilities in their father's business. Rather, they go to college or technical school, and they enter their chosen fields on their own merits. Often at age 30 or 35 sons are earning more money than their 55- or 60-year-old fathers. I have focused on fathers and sons in this discussion, because it is extremely rare that daughters use their father's connections to get jobs, and mothers seldom have the power to serve as gatekeepers to work for their children. The changing role of working women may lead to changes in the gatekeeping function, but just what those changes may be is difficult to project, for, as I said earlier, the father's role in bringing his children into the work force has all but vanished. An employee of General Motors, or the local Department of Public Welfare, or Sears Roebuck has little influence in getting his children jobs. Furthermore, the educational level of children exceeds—sometimes far exceeds—that of their parents, and the children often have the option of seeking jobs that pay more and have higher status than those to which their parents have access. The tradition of passing jobs from parent to child ceases when the father works in a Pennsylvania coal mine or manages a "mom-and-pop" liquor store in Texas, and the son has a degree in engineering and the daughter is studying to become an accountant.

The changing work-financial picture in our society not only reduces parental influence on the children's choice of work, it also reduces the demands on children to care for elderly parents. Social Security payments and private pensions provide the older person with some sources of retirement income, and health insurance and Medicare/Medicaid cover substantial proportions of medical needs. As financial security becomes more dependent on work and work-related retirement income and as society provides increasing support for the elderly, each generation becomes more independent of the other. This permits the generations greater autonomy, but it simultaneously eliminates financial dependency, formerly a powerful factor in maintaining family closeness.

*The Economic Status of the Aged**

Y. P. Chen

What is the economic status of the older person in the United States? In Canada? Elsewhere in the world? We can answer the question in terms of average income, of the average accumulated wealth, of the average total net worth, or of some combination of these and other figures. As computers have been developed with increasing sophistication, economists can pour in a lot of data and get out a lot of answers in a short time.

The limitations are not in the calculations but in two factors that affect the input. First, valid data are not always available. We don't have accurate, up-to-date figures on the total income of older people. To obtain such figures, we must include gifts from family members; we must determine the financial value of one month spent living with a married daughter or son; and we must consider discounts often available on public transportation, in movie theatres, or on property taxes.

More important is the inherent danger in talking about "the older person." Try to recall your high school graduating class and think about what it

*Edited from *Income*, White House Conference on Aging Background and Issues. Washington, D.C.: U.S. Government Printing Office, 1971.

would mean to describe the entire class in terms of the average level of verbal fluency or mathematical ability. Would the grade-point average of all students provide you with useful information? Probably so in a crude fashion. If you wanted to compare your high school with other high schools or to chart a trend over a period of years, it might be useful, but how helpful would it be in giving a picture of what the students at your school were like? I suspect that your answer would be "Not very helpful." Or, to become more personal, how would you feel if your friends viewed your abilities strictly as if you were average for your class, regardless of what your actual abilities were? Or if a potential employer learned the average grade-point for your senior class and assigned that grade-point to you, regardless of what your actual grades were?

It is widely recognized that income is one of the most powerful forces affecting the life of a person or of a family. In order to achieve a sense of economic and psychological well-being, a certain adequate level of income as well as the assurance that such income will continue are of fundamental concern to everyone. In short, adequacy and security of income are among the basic preconditions of a person's or a family's welfare. This is not to say that income is the overriding issue in a person's life, for it is not. But it is a prime mover in the marketplace, a force that affects the young and old alike. Moreover, the collective welfare of a society would be enhanced if adequate and secure income were available to all its members, for there would be increased harmony among people through reduction of discontent, fear, alienation, and antisocial behavior. Society at large could also be enhanced by a reduced incidence of mental and physical illness, which probably would result from improved conditions of life.

INCOME, POVERTY, AND SECURITY

Many needs of the elderly and much of their isolation and unhappiness may be traced to the inadequacy and insecurity of income. Even when hardships are not caused directly by a lack of income, insufficient financial resources certainly aggravate the discomfort and misery that are visited upon the old. Adequate and secure retirement income may well be a very significant preventive or at least ameliorative factor.

When income is secure and adequate, any person, young or old, may compete in the marketplace for food, shelter, and clothing; for medical and educational attention, and the like. The satisfaction of such basic human wants indeed depends on the command of dollar votes. Furthermore, when such income is available, there is less need for public policy to provide alternate markets through which special prices and free services and facilities are made available. In a society that is making progress toward reducing economic poverty (as opposed to cultural, moral, spiritual "poverty"), a strategy to bolster the income of the poor would be strengthened if it were to include efforts to improve the availability and quality of public and private services. Such improvements would enable the underprivileged to gain better information and skill and better access to the basic amenities of life. Even though income inadequacy is defined as poverty, it does not necessarily follow that all problems associated with inadequate income can be solved simply by giving people more money. It is debatable, for example, whether increases in income without improvements in the availability and quality of health care, housing, transportation, and other public and private services would permit the elderly to participate fully in family and community life. The supplementary role of services and facilities is particularly significant in the short run.

Whereas there is little dispute that income adequacy and income security are universally desirable, there is no consensus on what level of income is adequate and what degree of protection is secure. A solution to the income problem involves a host of issues, including the various demands on income. Income need is a relative, not an absolute, concept; there is no single level of income that may be regarded as fulfilling all the monetary needs of every person. Even the subsistence-income level differs according to the country or community in which a person lives. Of course, statistically, it may not be too difficult to suggest several income levels that meet the basic needs in life. For example, poverty-level "threshold" incomes have been computed in accordance with age, family size, and other reference factors. Although consumer budgets have been estimated for one purpose or another, they can be used only as general reference points. Where consumption patterns and expectation levels are concerned, substantial variations exist among individuals. Not only do standard budget figures vary among different places of residence (North or South, metropolitan or nonmetropolitan, for example), but also wide differences are observed between standard figures and actual expenditures by persons and by families. Medical care expenditures, for example, can be variable among families as well as within the same family over time—so variable, in fact, as to render budget allowances unrealistic.

Estimates of adequacy of income based on poverty, near-poverty, or any other standard of living may be misleading from yet another point of view. For the aged, such estimates may fall far short of the standard of living to which they were accustomed prior to retirement. And unless they are psychologically prepared to accept a lower (sometimes much lower) standard, a serious loss of morale will ensue. Thus, although a budget may cover the physical requirements of a person, it may not provide much psychological sustenance. Of course, not everyone is necessarily entitled to obtain what he "expects." It seems appropriate, however, to suggest that financial and other mechanisms be made available so that those persons who choose to do so may have a chance to realize their expectations.

There is no intention here of questioning the importance of estimating budgets for various standards of living. In any attempt to abolish poverty— for example, through a program providing cash income to the poor—clearly there is a need for an estimate, albeit a rough one, of what the contemporary standards are. Rather, the intention here is to suggest that in considering income adequacy in old age, close attention should be paid to the relationship between preretirement and postretirement income levels. In an economic system in which personal incentive and responsibility generally are rewarded differentially according to individual contributions, it follows that the preservation of equivalent differentials in retirement income is desirable.

Another important issue that affects retirement income also deserves close attention. An annual income that is adequate at the time of retirement may become inadequate with time. This unfavorable development may occur for three major reasons. First, the progressive decline in purchasing power brought about by price inflation depletes a relatively fixed income. Second, although improvement in the living standard of the working population is to be expected, the living standard of the retired will remain at the fixed level. Over time, the buying power of the elderly will fall behind that of the working population to the extent that the aged will experience feelings of relative deprivation and insecurity. Third, to the extent that assets are drawn upon for supplementation, interest, dividend, and rental incomes will diminish as well.

There is little doubt that the United States and Canada have the material resources to abolish poverty or eliminate absolute deprivation, especially if that goal is to be achieved within a reasonable period (say, by the end of this decade). The need to devise mechanisms that sustain personal initiative and motivation during the working years, however, cannot be overemphasized. The goal of maintaining both individual initiative and collective effectiveness concerns income differentials above the minimum poverty-threshold level. That is, in order to sustain productivity as well as morale, it would seem necessary that postretirement income hold a *reasonable relationship* to preretirement income. If income declines severely for a large number of people at retirement, this will affect the spirit of the aged, who will then feel deprivation or insecurity relative to the larger society. An extreme differential in preretirement and postretirement income also might affect the incentive of the young, who face such uninviting prospects. Some may argue that the young do not really think ahead toward retirement or that the young may give some thought to retirement but do not care about what might happen in the distant future. It is possible also that there is a great diversity in personal opinion in the matter of retirement income needs.

THE PRESENT FINANCIAL STATUS
OF THE ELDERLY

Any attempt to portray the current financial status of the elderly runs an obvious hazard. Because of the time it takes to collect, compile, and publish the data, the specific numbers often become obsolete. Therefore, as you read this section—or, indeed any material regarding income, costs, and so forth—take careful note of the year in which the statistics were collected, and then try to account for whatever changes have taken place. With this in mind, let's look at some of the data that describe the economics of aging.

In 1973, all persons aged 65 and over (including their spouses, regardless of age) received a total of $95 billion. That total obviously is higher today, and it certainly represents an immense amount of money in the aggregate, although it doesn't look particularly high when it is divided by the more than 22 million people to whom it belongs.

Perhaps the first question to ask is "What exactly is income?" Obviously, personal earnings are income, and in 1967 30% of the total amount received by persons 65 and older derived from such earnings. Social Security payments (26%) and public and private pension funds (11%) are also included in the total. Earnings from such sources as bank interest, rental income or other monies derived from property owned, and stock dividends accounted for another 25% of the 1967 total. The remaining 8% derived from other sources, including veteran's benefits and public assistance, with only a minute proportion coming from gifts made by family members (Schulz, 1976). Unfortunately, these percentages from 1967 may not be totally accurate, since there are well-known tendencies among people to distort certain sources of income either by underreporting or by nonreporting. Personal earnings and income from assets may be underestimated to avoid taxes, to remain eligible for certain programs with income ceilings (public housing, nutrition programs), or to remain eligible for full Social Security payments. (After a certain amount of money is earned, one dollar of Social Security is deducted for every two dollars earned.) Also, gifts from family members may not be mentioned simply because such gifts often are not perceived as income. In one family, the elderly parents are given an income supplement of $200 per month by their children, and they probably do not perceive this as income. The three adult children of one elderly man take turns paying his rent; an older woman spends about three months a year with her daughter in Arizona and about six weeks with her son in Michigan. Neither of these people considers these benefits as income.

What happens to the level of income from all sources after retirement? Most obviously, it drops. Thus, in 1974, the median income of all men over age 65 was $4535, and the median income of all women in that age group was $2375 (mean incomes were higher).[1] These figures represent less than half the income of younger persons. Furthermore, heads of households over age 65 had substantially higher incomes than those living alone. Thus the elderly woman who lives alone has, on the average, a very low income; it is even lower if she is Black.*

Discussing any group as large as the elderly in terms of averages can be extremely misleading. In 1974, for example, 15% of all men over age 65, but less than 4% of all women in that group, received more than $10,000 per year, with 2.4% of the men and 0.2% of the women having annual incomes in

---

[1]The median income of a group of persons is that amount earned by 50% of the group members. That is, half of all men over 65 earn the indicated amount. The mean income is the total amount of money earned by all group members divided by the number of members.

*These and subsequent data are from the U.S. Bureau of Census, *Consumer Income, Current Population Report Series P-60,* No. 99, 1975.

excess of $25,000. Obviously, a small proportion of the elderly are extremely well off financially, and a modest proportion are quite comfortable. At the other end of the continuum, 27% of older men and 65% of older women receive less than $3000 in annual income, percentages that increase substantially for unrelated persons (that is, those who do not live with a relative in a household). Older heads of household are less likely to have so little money, but often they must support two or more persons on the income they receive. It quickly becomes apparent that the number of elderly living at very low income levels is much greater than the number living in wealth or moderate comfort.

Sex and marital status are not the only factors affecting income of the elderly, of course. Race is a major determinant. As might be expected, Black elderly receive considerably less than White elderly in all categories. In 1973, nearly 32% of White married couples received $10,000 a year or more in income, whereas just 13% of Black couples received that amount; the ratio was 6 to 1 for unmarried persons.

Perhaps the statistics for women, both among Blacks and among Whites, are confusing. There seem to be so many more poor elderly women. Part of the explanation resides in what happens at the death of a spouse. If the wife dies, the income of the widower remains virtually the same; if the husband dies, the amount received by the widow is likely to drop, especially if Social Security and private pensions are providing the major portion of retirement income, which normally is the case. Inevitably, the incidence of widowhood increases with advancing age. Therefore, the higher numbers of elderly widows and of low-income elderly Blacks demonstrate that the truly poor among the elderly are Black women.

So far we've looked at the income for older people, but what about the expenditures? In some ways, the financial demands on the elderly are reduced. For example, they normally do not need to be involved in supporting dependent children; their space needs are reduced, because there are usually only two (or one) in the family unit; and portions of their medical expenses are covered by Medicare and Medicaid programs. Furthermore, those who are no longer in the job market often can reduce automobile and other transportation expenses, clothing budgets, and other job-related expenses (tools or uniforms, for example). Similarly, there are a few financial benefits in being over 65—added income-tax deductions, low-cost public transportation (in some communities), and reduced property taxes (in some states and communities). Rarely, however, do changing needs and added benefits compensate fully for the substantial reduction in income following retirement.

INCOME ADEQUACY

One of the first important questions is what level of income may be considered as providing *minimum or absolute adequacy*. There appears to be wide agreement that a poverty-level income is inconsistent with the so-called American standard of living, judging from public and private discussions and programs designed to lift people out of poverty. Differences among people in their views of the world include varying opinions about what the poverty level of income really is.

Although it is fairly easy to suggest a minimum adequacy of income that might eliminate *absolute deprivation*, it is difficult to suggest what level of income provides psychological sustenance beyond the minimum necessary for physical subsistence—a level of income necessary to avoid the *relative deprivation* discussed earlier. It has been suggested that a reasonable relationship between preretirement income and postretirement income and a reasonable relationship between the living standard of retired persons and that of the working population are two criteria that might be applied. What is *reasonable*, however, is not capable of objective, quantifiable measurement, and a subjective notion of reasonableness reminds us once again that one person's reasonable relationship may be another person's unreasonable relationship.

The *relative adequacy* level of income is highly variable and debatable. It depends on the preferences of individuals with respect to their lifetime allocation of income and consumption. Some prefer to consume more when they are young and less when they become old, whereas others want to moderate their consumption in early stages of life in preparation for more income in retirement. In a society in which there is a strong belief in personal preferences and a heavy reliance on individual initiative, it may be argued that choices about distribution of income and expenditures over a life-cycle should be left to the individual. However, the ideal of maintaining as much freedom of choice as possible in the management of one's financial and other matters may never become a reality for some people, either because they miscalculate or because they fall victim to forces beyond their control. A compromise approach to spending or saving early in life may provide a life-long standard of living that is acceptable to society at large.

Such an approach might call for a compulsory public retirement program to provide income *up to a level*. Beyond that, individuals would be expected to provide for their own retirement. This is, in fact, the system of divided responsibility for providing retirement income that exists today in this country. However, a crucial question remains: What level of income is a compulsory public retirement program designed to provide? Is it the *minimum adequacy* designed for avoidance of poverty? Surely a level of income below the poverty line is contradictory to the American standard of living, but does the American standard merely call for the abolition of poverty?

It seems equally clear that the American standard of living cannot be based on what the most fortunate members of society may attain (maximum adequacy). Thus, the objective of assuring provision of "an adequate and secure retirement income in accordance with the American standard of living" may imply a system of retirement income provision under which the retired will be assured of (1) *minimum adequacy* of income to be guaranteed by society, (2) a *relative adequacy* of income to be generated from group plans (both government and nongovernment), and (3) a *maximum adequacy* of income to be determined by and planned for the individual himself or herself.

HOUSING ANNUITY PLAN

Many elderly people have one asset that is certainly helpful. Over three-fourths of all older couples own their own homes, and more than 60% have fully paid their mortgages (1967 data). Even though the average value of these homes is not especially great, the people who own them can live in reasonable accommodations at a relatively low cost. Unfortunately, the key word here is *relatively*. These homes may be in deteriorated neighborhoods where theft and vandalism are daily problems. Furthermore, property taxes, the cost of home repairs, and insurance premiums continue to rise annually. Frequently the home owned by an elderly couple was purchased for a family with children, so there are more rooms than are needed in later years. Yet, if the elderly homeowner tries to sell his house, invest what he receives, and use the earnings from his investment to rent a small house or apartment, he usually will find himself having to accept a significant drop in his standard of housing. Inevitably, if he draws on the invested principal derived from the sale of his home, the income from that investment (interest or dividends) will diminish proportionally. In today's inflationary economy, the cost of renting is going up, whereas the return on investments has remained fairly stable or even dropped. Therefore, at least for the decade prior to 1976, most people who sold their homes ended up with inferior housing.

In order to help older people out of their dilemma, the Housing Annuity Plan (HAP) has been proposed (Chen, 1970). This plan enables elderly homeowners to trade their equity in the residential property for spendable cash, without requiring outright sale of their home. Under HAP, the homeowner and a surviving spouse would be guaranteed the right to lifetime occupancy of the house itself. Through a trust set up with a bank, life insurance company, savings and loan association, pension fund, or perhaps a governmental agency, the homeowner would agree to have the deed of title given to the institution at the time both husband and wife were dead. In exchange, the couple could live in the house as long as they wished, with a regular monthly income in addition.

The amount of income the homeowner received under HAP would depend on a number of factors: the age of husband and wife, the rate of appreciation of property value, the rate of depreciation of the home, the condition of the home, the net value of the home, and the expenses incurred in completing the various transactions. Thus, a widow in her eighties would receive a great deal more than a couple in their late sixties, because the actuarial tables indicate that her death (and, therefore, the transfer of the property to the institution) would occur much sooner. In such circumstances, an agreement might also be arranged so that her heirs would receive an additional amount of money if her death were to occur within a specified period of time.

Two problems immediately become obvious. First, with land and property values increasing so rapidly, a couple in their late sixties might be reluctant to make arrangements today since their property value might be much higher in five or ten years. Second, some older people lack the money or the ability to take proper care of their homes, and the house itself might depreciate. Therefore, these arrangements might be required to come up for review after a period of time, and the institution that purchased the deed to the property might be given the right to inspect the house and to make necessary repairs.

Another difficulty emerges if the homeowners later wish to sell the house. In this event, they might sell it directly to the institution that holds the trust, but if they could receive a better price elsewhere, or if they wished to give the home to their children, there would have to be a method by which they could buy back the contract and regain full title to the property.

The advantages of the proposed HAP program are great. First, and probably foremost, older people would know that they could remain in their homes as long as they wished. Although they would no longer be able to will the home to their heirs, many, probably most, children would be only too happy to give their parents this security; furthermore, the children would be much less likely to be called on to supplement their parents' income, because HAP payments would provide another source of income. Second, by waiting until death to "sell" their home, the owners could avoid the capital-gains tax imposed on profits derived from the sale of a house that has risen substantially in value since its purchase. Third, the owners would have a steady and dependable source of income at a time in life when income is normally reduced.

In essence, HAP is the opposite of the process of purchasing a home. When you buy a house, the purchase is made gradually. When you sell a house under HAP, the sale is made gradually. Thus, HAP can be viewed this way: When young people seek to build equity in a home, they mortgage future income to acquire that asset. Under HAP, older people with equity in their home could mortgage the asset to acquire a steady income.

A Brief Look at
Social Security*

When I was a young boy and Social Security had just begun, a joke was making the rounds. One person, usually under the age of 10, would approach someone and ask "What did one duck say to another duck?" The person questioned would usually become puzzled and then say "Well, I don't know." "Social Security," the answer would come back. "I don't get it," the still puzzled individual would respond. "You will when you're 65." Followed by gales of laughter.

I knew the joke well before I knew anything about Social Security. The fact that I haven't heard it for at least 20 years is a compliment to today's 10-year-olds, whose sense of humor need not seek such levels. People on the whole, of course, were not laughing at Social Security 40 years ago, and they are not laughing today. The system has grown from a simple retirement program into a health, disability, survivor insurance, and retirement program. It has become more complex, more confusing, and more the object of political attack.

The next selection comes from two brief government pamphlets that outline what Social Security is and how supplemental security income works. Keep in mind that the actual dollar amounts distributed do change over time as new legislation is passed and as cost-of-living rises.

YOUR SOCIAL SECURITY

Today, social security is the Nation's basic method of providing a continuing income when family earnings are reduced or stop because of retirement, disability, or death.

—Nine out of 10 workers in the United States are earning protection under social security.

—Nearly 1 out of every 7 persons in this country receives monthly social security checks.

—About 21.9 million people 65 and over, nearly all of the Nation's aged population, have health insurance under Medicare. Another 2 million disabled people under 65 also have Medicare.

Nearly every family, then, has a stake in social security.

Through the years since social security was enacted in 1935, there have been many changes to improve the protection it gives to workers and their families. At first, social security covered only the worker when he

---

*Edited from *Your Social Security* and *Helping the Aged, Blind, and Disabled in California*, U.S. Department of Health, Education, and Welfare. Washington, D.C.: U.S. Government Printing Office, 1975.

retired; but in 1939, the law was changed to pay his survivors if he died, as well as certain dependents when he retired.

Social security also covered only workers in industry and commerce when the program began. But in the 1950's, coverage was extended to include most self-employed persons, most State and local employees, household and farm employees, members of the Armed Forces, and clergymen. Today, almost all jobs in the United States are covered by social security.

Disability insurance was added in 1954 to give workers protection against loss of earnings due to total disability.

The social security program was expanded again in 1965 with the enactment of Medicare which assured hospital and medical insurance protection to people 65 and over. Since July 1, 1973, Medicare coverage has been available to people under 65 who have been entitled to disability checks for 2 or more consecutive years and to people with severe kidney disease who need dialysis or kidney transplants.

As a result of legislation enacted in 1972, social security benefits will increase automatically in the future as the cost of living goes up.

WHO GETS CHECKS?

Who gets a monthly social security check? The question can be answered in one word. People. All kinds of people. Young people, old people, poor people, rich people. Men, women, and children.

Monthly social security checks may go to workers and their dependents when the worker retires, becomes severely disabled, or dies. Then, there's Medicare, which helps pay the cost of health care for eligible people who are 65 or over or disabled.

Monthly benefits social security pays include:

Retirement checks—When you retire, you can start getting retirement checks as early as 62.

Disability checks—A worker who becomes severely disabled before 65 can get disability checks.

Under social security, you're considered disabled if you have a severe physical or mental condition which: Prevents you from working, and is expected to last (or has lasted) for at least 12 months, or is expected to result in death.

Your checks can start for the 6th full month of your disability. Once checks start, they'll continue as long as you are disabled. If you are severely disabled, you could get benefits even though you manage to work a little.

Survivors checks—If the worker dies, survivors checks can go to certain members of the worker's family. A lump-sum payment also can be made when a worker dies. This payment usually goes to the widow or widower.

Checks for a Worker's Family

Monthly social security checks also are paid to certain dependents of a worker who has retired, become disabled, or who has died.

Retirement or disability—Monthly payments can be made to a retired or disabled worker's:

—Unmarried children under 18 (or 22 if full-time students).

—Unmarried children 18 or over who were severely disabled before 22 and who continue to be disabled.

—Wife or dependent husband 62 or over.

—Wife under 62 if she's caring for worker's child under 18 (or disabled) who's getting a benefit based on the retired or disabled worker's earnings.

Survivors—Monthly payments can be made to a deceased worker's:

—Unmarried children under 18 (or 22 if full-time students).

—Unmarried son or daughter 18 or over who was severely disabled before 22 and who continues to be disabled

—Widow or dependent widower 60 or older.

—Widow, widowed father, or surviving divorced mother if caring for worker's child under 18 (or disabled) who is getting a benefit based on the earnings of the deceased worker.

—Widow or dependent widower 50 or older who becomes disabled not later than 7 years after worker's death, or in case of a widow, within 7 years after she stops getting checks as a widow caring for worker's children

—Dependent parents 62 or older.

Checks also can go to a divorced wife at 62 or over, or a surviving divorced wife at 60, or to a disabled surviving divorced wife 50 or older if the marriage lasted 20 years or more. Children may be eligible for social security benefits based on a grandparent's earnings under certain conditions.

Generally, a marriage must have lasted at least 1 year before dependents of a retired or disabled worker can get monthly benefits; survivors can get benefits in most cases if the marriage lasted at least 9 months.

BUILDING PROTECTION

Monthly Cash Benefits

Before you or your family can get monthly cash benefits, you must have credit for a certain amount of work under social security. The exact amount of work credit depends on your age.

For each 3-month calendar quarter that you work under social security and are paid wages of $50 or more, you get one social security quarter of coverage. If you work a whole calendar year, you get four quarters of coverage, one for each quarter you worked.

If you're self-employed, you receive four quarters of coverage for a year when you have self-employment net profit of $400 or more.

More than 9 out of 10 jobs in paid employment and self-employment in the United States are covered by social security.

If you stop working under social security before you've earned enough credit, you can't get benefits later. But the credit you've already earned will stay on your record and you can add to it if you return to work under social security.

Having enough credit means only that you or your family can get checks. The amount of your check depends on your average earnings over a period of years.

Under a special rule, cash payments can be made to a worker's children and their mother or father even though the worker dies with fewer credits than shown, provided she or he has worked under social security 1½ years in the 3 years before death.

WHAT IS IT WORTH?

Amount of Monthly Checks

Social security checks usually are based on your average earnings under social security over a period of years. The amount of your benefits to your dependents or survivors also depends on your average earnings. In addition, social security benefits will increase automatically in future years as the cost of living rises. Each year, living costs will be compared with those of the year before. If living costs have increased 3 percent or more, benefits will be increased by the same amount and will be included in checks issued the following July, unless Congress has already acted to raise benefits. The first automatic increase is payable in July 1975.

While you are working, social security contributions are taken out of your wages. You will pay social security contributions on all wages up to $14,100 in 1975. This amount will increase automatically in years to come to keep up with changes in average covered income levels. This means that a worker paying increased social security contributions can be sure of higher benefits later because his benefits will be based on a higher level of earnings.

Social security checks are not subject to Federal income tax.

If you qualify for checks on the record of more than one worker (for example, on your own record and your husband's), you'll get the larger of the two amounts.

The lump-sum payment made at a worker's death is $255.

Reduced Benefits

You can retire as early as 62, but your retirement check will be reduced permanently. Payment amounts are also reduced if a wife, dependent husband, widow, or dependent widower starts getting payments before 65.

The amount of reduction depends on the number of months you get checks before you reach 65. If you start your checks early, you'll get about the same value in total benefits over the years, but in smaller installments to take account of the longer period you'll get them.

Bigger Checks by Additional Work

If you return to work after you start getting retirement checks, your added earnings will often result in higher benefits. Social security will automatically refigure your benefit after the additional earnings are credited to your record.

In addition, a worker who doesn't get any benefits before 65 and delays retirement past 65 will get a special credit that can mean a larger benefit. The credit adds to a worker's benefit 1 percent for each year ($1/12$ of one percent for each month) from age 65 to age 72 for which he did not get benefits because of work. The credit applies only with respect to months after December 1970. This increase also applies only to the worker's check and not to those of dependents or survivors.

Special Minimum Benefit

There is a special minimum benefit at retirement for some people who worked under social security at least 20 years. This helps people who had low earnings (but still above a specified level) in their working years. The amount of the special minimum depends on the number of years of coverage. For a worker retiring at 65 with 25 years of coverage, the minimum would be $135 a month; with 30 or more years of coverage, the minimum would be $180. Most people who have worked 20 years or more under social security already receive benefits higher than the special minimum.

Years of coverage from 1937 to 1950 are determined by dividing the total wages for those years by $900, with a maximum of 14 years of coverage counted for that period. After 1950, a year of coverage is any year a person has earnings of at least 25 percent of the maximum covered by social security.

The automatic cost-of-living benefit increase does not apply to the special minimum benefit amounts.

WHY PAYMENTS STOP

If You Work after Payments Start

After you start getting social security checks, they will continue to arrive each month unless your circumstances change and cause payments to stop.

If you go back to work and are under 72, your earnings may affect your social security benefits. You don't have to stop working completely, though, to get social security benefits. Beginning with 1975, you can earn as much as $2,520 in a year without having any benefits withheld. If your annual earnings go above $2,520, we withhold $1 in benefits for each $2 in earnings above $2,520. No matter how much you earn a year, you can get full benefits for any month in 1975 in which you do not earn more than $210 in wages and you don't perform substantial services in self-employment. The decision as to whether you are performing substantial services in self-employment depends on the time you devote to your business, the kind of services you perform, how your services compare with those you performed in past years, and other circumstances of your particular case.

The amount you can earn without having any benefits withheld will increase automatically in future years as the level of average wages rises.

(*Note:* Different rules apply to work performed by people getting benefits because they are disabled. For more information, ask for a copy of the leaflet, *If You Become Disabled*, at any social security office.)

If you are getting retirement checks, your earnings may affect your dependent's checks as well as your own. If you get checks as a dependent or survivor, your earnings can affect only your own check.

Income That Counts

When figuring what income may affect your social security checks, you must count earnings from work of any kind, whether or not it's covered by social security, except tips amounting to less than $20 in a month with one employer. Total wages, not just take-home pay, and all net self-employment earnings must be added together.

However, income from savings, investments, pensions, insurance, or royalties won't affect your checks.

Your earnings for the entire year in which your checks start or stop count when we figure the amount of benefits that can be paid for that year. But earnings after you reach 72 won't affect your checks.

FINANCING

The Basic Idea

The basic idea of social security is a simple one: During working years employees, their employers, and self-employed people pay social security contributions into special trust funds. When earnings stop or are reduced because the worker retires, becomes disabled, or dies, monthly cash benefits are paid to replace part of the earnings the family has lost.

Part of the contributions made go into a separate hospital insurance trust fund so workers and their dependents will have help in paying their hospital bills when they become eligible for Medicare. The medical insurance part of Medicare is financed by premiums paid by the people who have enrolled for this protection and amounts contributed by the Federal Government.

Contribution Rates

If you're employed, you and your employer each pay an equal share of social security contributions. If you're self-employed, you pay contributions for retirement, survivors, and disability insurance at a somewhat lower rate than the combined rate for an employee and his employer. The hospital insurance contribution rate is the same for the employer, the employee, and the self-employed person.

As long as you have earnings that are covered by the law, you continue to pay contributions regardless of your age and even if you are receiving social security benefits.

Through 1977 employees and employers each pay 5.85 percent on the employee's wages. The total rate for self-employed people is 7.90 percent. The rates include .90 percent for hospital insurance under Medicare. The maximum amount of earnings that can count for social security purposes and on which you pay social security contributions is $14,100 in 1975.

Future rate increases are scheduled. In 1978 the employee and employer will each pay 6.05 percent. The rate for each will go to 6.30 percent in 1981 and 6.45 percent in 1986. The self-employed rate goes to 8.10 percent in 1978; to 8.35 percent in 1981; and to 8.50 percent in 1986. The hospital insurance part of the rate will be 1.10 percent in 1978; 1.35 percent in 1981; and 1.50 percent in 1986.

Funds not required for current benefit payments and expenses are invested in interest-bearing U.S. Government securities.

The Government's share of the cost for supplementary medical insurance and certain other social security costs come from general revenues of the U.S. Treasury, not from social security contributions.

How Contributions Are Paid

If you're employed, your contribution is deducted from your wages each payday. Your employer matches your payment and sends the combined amount to the Internal Revenue Service.

If you're self-employed and your net earnings are $400 or more in a year, you must report your earnings and pay your self-employment contribution each year when you file your individual income tax return. This is true even if you owe no income tax.

Your wages and self-employment income are entered on your social security record throughout your working years. This record of your earnings will be used to determine your eligibility for benefits and the amount of cash benefits you and your dependents will receive.

Future Increases Are Automatic

The maximum amount of annual earnings that count for social security will rise automatically in the future as earnings levels rise. This will mean higher benefits later because a greater portion of a worker's earnings will be counted towards social security. Every year, starting with 1975, the increase in average covered wages will be determined, and if wage levels have increased since the base was set last, the base will be raised—but only if there is an automatic benefit increase the same year.

SUPPLEMENTAL SECURITY INCOME

Helping the Aged, Blind, and Disabled

People in financial need who are 65 or older or who are blind or disabled, including blind or disabled children, may be eligible for monthly cash payments from the Federal Government. The payments are called supplemental security income (SSI).

The payments come to eligible people in a check from the Federal Government every month. The check includes money provided by the states as a supplement to the Federal payment (see Table 1).

People may be eligible for payments if they have little or no regular cash income and don't own much in the way of assets that can be turned into cash.

To qualify for SSI payments because of blindness, a person must have central visual acuity of 20/200 or less in the better eye with the use of a corrective lens, or visual field restriction of 20 degrees or less.

SSI payments for disability may be made if an individual is unable to engage in substantial gainful activity because of a physical or mental impairment which can be expected to result in death or which has lasted (or is expected to last) for 12 months or longer.

Table 1.   Schedule of Maximum Monthly Payments for Aged, Blind, and Disabled (payments may be lower than the maximum amounts if recipient has other income).

Category of Eligibility	Independent Living Arrangement*	Residing in the Household of Another and Receiving Room and Board in Kind	Nonmedical Board and Care†
Individuals			
Aged	$259	$206.44	$306
Disabled	259	206.44	306
Blind	292	239.44	306
Couples			
Aged person and aged spouse	488	409.14	612
Disabled person and disabled spouse	488	409.14	612
Blind person and blind spouse	584	505.14	612
Aged person and disabled spouse	488	409.14	612
Aged person and blind spouse	550	471.14	612
Blind person and disabled spouse	550	471.14	612

*Payment may be increased by $29 for aged or disabled people who do not have a place to cook and store food at home.

†Protective living arrangement outside a person's home. Benefit level includes allowance for the board, room, personal care, and supervision provided, as well as an allowance to be spent by the recipient for personal and incidental needs.

The basic Federal payment can be as much as $157.70 to an eligible individual, or $236.60 to an eligible couple. Payments go up automatically once a year to keep up with increases in the cost of living.

Things You Own

If you are single (or married but not living with your spouse), you can have assets—things you own—worth up to $1,500 and still get payments. The amount for a couple is $2,250. This includes savings accounts, stocks, bonds, jewelry, and other valuables.

Not everything owned counts as an asset. A home with a market value of $25,000 or less doesn't count. (If you are eligible and own a home valued above $25,000, you may receive payments from your local county welfare office but not from the Federal Government.)

Personal effects or household goods don't count if their total market value is $1,500 or less. Insurance policies are not counted either if their total face value on any one person is $1,500 or less. If the total face value is more than $1,500, only the cash surrender value counts.

If you own a car, only the portion of the retail value which exceeds $1,200 is counted. A car isn't counted at all if it is used for transportation to a job or to a place for regular treatment of a specific medical problem.

Income You Have

You can have some money coming in *and* still get supplemental security income. The first $20 a month in income generally won't affect the payment.

In addition, if you work, the first $65 in earnings in a month won't count against the payment; and only half of any additional earnings will be deducted from the monthly payment.

Apart from earnings, any other income above the first $20 a month generally will reduce the payment amount. This includes social security checks, veterans compensation, workmen's compensation, pensions, annuities, gifts, and other income.

Also, for eligible people who live in someone else's household—a son's or daughter's home, for example—the payment may be reduced.

Not Social Security

Even though the Social Security Administration runs the program, supplemental security income is not the same as social security. Money for supplemental security income payments comes from general funds of the U.S. Treasury. Social security benefits are paid from contributions of workers, employers, and self-employed people. There are no limits on the amount of money or property you can have and still get your social security payments. Social security funds are not used to make supplemental security income payments.

You can get social security and supplemental security income, too, if you are eligible for both.

How To Apply

If you believe you may be eligible for supplemental security income payments, you may apply at any social security office. When you apply you should bring along:

—Proof of age, unless you are already receiving social security checks.
—Your latest tax bill or assessment notice if you own real property.
—Names of any persons who help with your support and the amount of money provided.
—Bank books, stock certificates, and bonds.
—Motor vehicle registration.
—Proof of pensions and annuities.
—A copy of your most recent tax return if you are presently self-employed.
—If blind or disabled, a list of medical sources (doctors, hospitals, or clinics) where you have received treatment.

You have the right to appeal if you disagree with the decision on your application.

If you want more information about the supplemental security income program, call any social security office.

Smoothing
the Humps and Valleys*

Juanita M. Kreps

Now that you have read what the Social Security pamphlets say, you may wish to know more about how economists view the program and, more important, the entire issue of intergenerational transfers, that is, the transfer of money from one generation (in this instance, the nonelderly worker) to another generation (in this instance, the elderly nonworker). The media contain so much discussion of the potential bankruptcy of the Social Security system that many people are fearful that the income they have counted on for retirement won't be there when the time comes. A careful and sober analysis

*Edited from "Social Security in the Coming Decade: Questions for a Mature System," *Social Security Bulletin*, *39*, 21–29, Social Security Administration. Washington, D.C., U.S. Government Printing Office, 1975.

of some of the problems is difficult to find. In the selection that follows, Dr. Kreps explains how some of the stresses have come about and what kind of changes in demographic patterns, in retirement age, and in the work involvement of women may influence what Social Security will be like when you are ready to retire.

Some time ago Ida Merriam (1966) noted that "Earnings . . . have a very poor fit over time to the individual's changing consumption needs" (p. 167). The problem of smoothing out the "humps and valleys," handled through individual savings and family care in simpler societies, now falls to social institutions that are able to develop procedures for universal coverage. Having such institutions in place, however, the society also has to decide the level of income to be maintained in old age, compared with the level of earnings or, in brief, the extent to which income is to be made even between generations.

Transfers of income between generations may be viewed differently by different age groups, as James Morgan (1975) points out. We have, he says, a social contract,

> where each generation helps to pay for increased benefits of the previous generation on an implicit promise that the next generation will do the same for them. From this point of view, the system looks like a bargain in retrospect to each older generation and like a rip-off in prospect to each young cohort if they ignore the probable future increase in benefits [p. 3].

The need for a support pattern between generations has grown during social security's lifetime; financial arrangements previously made within the family are now met largely through fiscal measures. What appears in the social accounts as a huge increase in the income allocated to old people obscures the fact that in the absence of the payroll or other taxes, workers would need to support their aged parents directly. Or alternatively, persons at work would have to save enough to support themselves in their own retirement. The difficulties of the latter method are emphasized in a recent paper by A. J. Jaffe (1975) who shows that a worker would need to save about one-third of his earnings throughout worklife in order to pay for his retirement.

Although few people would challenge the need for income transfers from workers to nonworkers, including retirees along with the unemployed, the disabled, dependent children, and handicapped adults, the question of the size of the transfer is constantly under debate. As retirement benefit levels have improved, payroll taxes have increased, and the amount of income shifted from young and middle-aged workers to retirees has grown.

Professor Robert Clark (1975), making certain assumptions, estimates that the intergenerational transfer in the social security program grew from about 2.1 percent of a young worker's income in 1950 to approximately 9.0 percent in 1970. Although the replacement ratio—that is, the benefit paid to a retiree as a proportion of his preretirement earnings—has not increased significantly, the increase in tax receipts made it possible to extend coverage, raise minimum benefits, and lower the retirement age.

Clark then asks whether this 9.0 percent is likely to increase under conditions of zero population growth. On the assumption that the fertility rate moves to the replacement level of 2.11 immediately and remains there (and assuming a constant rate of income growth and a constant replacement ratio), he shows that the ensuing changes in age structure will necessitate an increase in the tax rate. Specifically, the 1970 tax rate would have to be increased by 50 percent by the year 2050, when stable population is reached, assuming that retirement age and age of entry into the labor force remain constant. Noting that retirement age has been falling steadily during recent decades, however, he speculates on the effect of a continuation of this trend. If the age of exit from work has fallen to 60 by 2050, for example, more than a twofold increase in taxes will be required; if it has fallen to 55, more than a threefold increase would ensue. To the extent that age of entry into the work force is rising, the tax rate would need to be even higher.

The fairly low proportion of earnings maintained under the social security system, compared with the replacement ratios in certain other nations, raises the question of whether the level of pensions should not be improved in the future. To do so, Clark points out, the cost would have to be offset by an equal increase in tax receipts. Hence, in order to raise the present pension level from a replacement ratio of 40 percent to a ratio of 60 percent, it would be necessary to raise taxes by 50 percent.

Our position would not seem to give cause for alarm, even with the probable growth in tax liability as the social security system matures. Concern over the change in demographic profile may also appear premature, since a reduction in the number of workers relative to retirees will not occur until after the turn of the century. But if retirement age is lowered without an off-setting rise in the labor-force participation of others in the working-age population, tax rates could rise quite sharply.

RATIO OF WORKERS TO RETIREES

Ultimately, serious problems could emerge as a result of a decline in the proportion of the population of working age and the consequent necessity for transferring a larger percentage of a worker's income to retirees. To the extent that levels of living in old age are raised, these problems will be intensified.

The central question of the relationship between a population's age composition and the economic security of the nation's elderly was reexamined recently by Joseph J. Spengler (1975). He points out that the ratio of working age to total population is at or near maximum when population growth is zero. Whether this maximum is achieved depends on whether the labor-force participation rates in the years before age 65 remain high or, as in recent years in the United States, the work-force rates are declining. He notes that "Continuous increases in the relative number of older persons, together with decline in work-life expectancy, could contribute to financial problems in a country in which payments to retired persons from such programs as social security rest essentially on a pay-as-you-go basis." Early retirement, he concludes, is particularly unfavorable in a stationary population. Removing those aged 55–66 from jobs would reduce the ratio of workers to retirees by 20 percent and increase the number of older dependents by 46 percent.

Earlier or Later Retirement?

The notion of retiring workers as early as age 55 appears farfetched. Indeed, there is discussion, for the first time, of arrangements for later retirement (and incentives to encourage a postponement of withdrawal from work beyond age 65) that would encourage longer worklife in order to offset the aging of the population.

The condition that led first to fixing the age of eligibility for social security benefits at age 65 and subsequently to encouraging even younger work-force withdrawals was one of a seeming excess of workers. Unemployment was massive when the Act was passed and quite severe when the decision was made to allow men to retire at age 62 with a reduced benefit. Not only Government policy but industry-union bargains as well now make it possible for workers to leave the work force at least 3 years earlier than was initially envisioned. In response to the availability of early pensions and in the face of job shortages, many men have come to view early retirement as a desirable option, provided benefits and other retirement income sources are thought to be adequate (Barfield and Morgan, 1969).

The level of unemployment declined somewhat after the initial arrangements allowing for early retirement, but it is now higher than at any time since the depression of the nineteen-thirties. Labor-market conditions would therefore indicate a possible further lowering of retirement age, on the assumption that a reduced labor-force size would help to assure jobs to those still actively seeking work. In the absence of greater flexibility in wage rates or working schedules, the allocation of jobs among jobseekers may well be achieved by a reduction in labor-force participation rates for men at both the beginning and the end of worklife—a process that has been underway since the early nineteen-hundreds, and particularly since the end of the Second World War.

Pressure for early retirements appears to be likely if unemployment continues. But offsetting this pressure is the overall need to lengthen worklife in order to maintain a favorable ratio of workers to nonworkers. As the social security system matures and the numbers of beneficiaries grow relative to the size of the labor force, appropriate policy for the system would seem to be one that encourages persons to work through their late sixties, perhaps by offering some increment to beneficiaries who retire after age 65. Were this movement to occur, a number of gains could accrue to the individual worker: Increased income, both before and after retirement; reduced dissatisfaction, perhaps, with mandatory retirement; and greater flexibility in varying work-leisure arrangements to match individual preferences.

Retirement Age and Rising
Labor-Force Activity of Women

Women's labor-force activity rates were of course much lower at the time of the social security legislation, and there is no evidence that the framers of the Act expected the sharp rise in these rates that began only a few years later. Much of the current concern with unequal treatment of men and women under the law emerges from provisions designed to meet income needs in an era when most married women were not engaged in market work but relied instead on their husbands' earnings during worklife and their retirement income thereafter.

But what was not foreseen or planned for has nevertheless come to be one of this century's major social developments. Married women have supplied most of the increase in the work force during recent decades; the worklives of single women, which have traditionally resembled those of men, have continued in much the same pattern. In more than half of all husband-wife families of the age group 25–64, both members are now at work. An important effect of women's entrance into market jobs has been the addition of female workers in sufficient numbers to offset the male workers' withdrawal, leaving the percentage of adults engaged in market work relatively stable during the past half a century.

For purposes of anticipating the future ratio of workers to retirees it is necessary to make explicit one's assumption regarding the labor-force activity of women in the decades ahead. Will the decline in work rates for men, occasioned by their longer periods of schooling and retirement, continue to be offset by women's higher levels of market activity, or will one change faster than the other?

Projections are difficult to make because of the number of factors affecting both the supply and the demand sides of labor. Women have been drawn into the labor market by the availability of jobs and rising wage scales. In the past, they have sometimes dropped out of the work force for childbearing and childrearing and also when they were discouraged by poor job prospects. But there is increasing evidence that young women now in the labor force have much stronger attachments to the labor force than was true of earlier cohorts and that they are less likely to return to fulltime home work either to meet family responsibilities or because the job market is unfavorable.

If the expectations of these women are borne out, their participation in the labor force will have greater continuity through worklife and their numbers will surely swell the proportion of the adult population seeking work. Whether men will experience further reductions in the length of their worklives, thereby continuing the secular decline in the labor-force activity of men, depends in large measure on the rate of economic growth and the availability of jobs. What both sexes might reasonably demand is shorter workweeks—or work interspersed with longer vacations, sabbaticals, education, and training. This pattern would be especially helpful if men and women come to share more evenly the home work, as they are now sharing the market work.

The net effect could be to produce a favorable ratio of workers to re-tirees and possibly to retard the downward drift of retirement age for men. By contrast, slower economic growth and heavy unemployment in the last quarter of this century could lead to some discouragement of workers and probably to a continued pressure for postponed entry to and early retirement from the work force. The impact of a reduction in worklife on the con-siderations before the Social Security Administration is critical, whether such reduction is a result of the population's age structure or an outgrowth of shrinking job opportunities.

To change the ratio of workers to nonworkers is not impossible, how-ever. Indeed, such a change can be accomplished fairly easily in a period of economic expansion. It would be feasible, for example, to extend working age from 65 to 68 and thereby keep a more favorable ratio, when jobs are available for both the middle-aged and the older worker. Moreover, the proportion of women in the job market would be greatly increased if a strong demand for their services pushed up their wages. In view of women's greater life expectancy, an extension of worklife could be particularly beneficial to them. The Social Security Advisory Council suggests that retirement age might be extended by 2 months a year, beginning in the year 2005 and ending in 2023. The result would be to lower payroll taxes as shown below (Advisory Council on Social Security, 1975).

	Tax Rate	
Calendar Year	*Scheduled*	*With 68 as Retirement Age by 2023*
2005–2014	12.3	12.1
2015–2024	14.2	13.5
2025–2050	16.1	14.6

A later retirement age is appealing for individual as well as societal reasons: Personal preferences can be accommodated; earnings can be ex-tended later into the lifespan; the worker's sense of self-worth is enhanced. But the probability that social policy will move toward a lengthened work-life is low in an era characterized by job shortages and high unemployment, as we noted earlier. The reverse movement toward earlier retirement has been occurring, with departure from the work force before age 65 becoming the norm. Hence, an extension of working years in later life would seem unlikely unless the rate of growth is accelerated.

CONCLUSIONS

Current public preoccupation with the future of social security is perhaps a good sign. It may signify an interest in one's own retirement, admittedly, rather than a concern for the general welfare. Still, recognition of the need to provide income for the future forces a wage earner to confront the costs of retirement benefits and the problems inherent in offsetting any demographic shifts along the way. It has been suggested that eventually it may become necessary to change the retirement age to 68 or even to 70 in order to maintain a work force large enough to support the Social Security system. The birth rate is down, and without a dramatic rise there soon will be only two workers to every retiree. With that ratio, the workers, who pay Social Security taxes, would bear a tremendous financial burden. Therefore, although compulsory retirement is efficient and it allows younger workers to move up the job scale, it may be a luxury that coming generations simply cannot afford until the later ages. It is nevertheless important to call attention to a possible reversal of the downward drift of retirement age and to the basic explanation for the existence of a younger or later age. General acceptance of extended worklife or higher taxes for the support of retirement benefits is essential to the further growth of the system, and such growth is more difficult to achieve in the wake of frequent warnings that the fund is depleted.

The problems facing a mature system need to be addressed, with perhaps more attention to public sentiment than has been necessary in the past. The costs of substantial increases in the level of benefits, the growing proportion of the population to be supported, new questions on the manner of funding, and the possible impact of social insurance on private saving— these are the issues that lie ahead. The more clearly these issues are stated, the greater the chances of developing a consensus that the gains of the system far outweigh its costs.

It is an error to play down the costs of adequate retirement benefits, as Harvey Shapiro (1975) argues. Coupled with increased longevity and lower birth rates, he notes, retirement benefits are bound to be expensive. The question before the public is not whether the clock can be turned back four decades to a time when a tax of 2 percent of the first $3,000 of earnings covered a small number of retirees, and those only meagerly. The debate turns, instead, on the proportion of earnings we wish now and in the future to maintain in retirement, and how we wish to finance that benefit. There can be no doubt that the costs will be high, even if we merely hold to the present replacement ratio. For when the retirement stage of life extends to one-third the length of worklife, the transfer of earnings is necessarily large, even when the humps and valleys are only partially smoothed.

Chapter 4

After Work: Then What?

Few issues in the field of social gerontology stir up as much emotion, as many disagreements, and as strong a sense of injustice as the topic of retirement. On the one hand, compulsory retirement is seen as an abridgement of the rights of individuals. When someone is required to leave his or her job, give up what is often a meaningful and important role, and accept a much lower income, all because the magical 65th birthday has taken place, it is obviously unfair. In such instances, the retired person is categorized as a member of an age group, then treated like all other members of that group, regardless of individual abilities. Federal laws that outlaw age discrimination do not protect people who are 65 or older.

On the other hand, the opportunity to retire is eagerly sought by many, perhaps most, persons in the work force. Work is something they tolerate in order to earn income, have social status, meet people, and feel a part of what is going on in the world. If the option to retire were removed, they would become furious.

Furthermore, the assumed needs of industry and business, of unions and younger employees, are often supportive of retirement. Whether the older person is doing a good job or not, there are others waiting for him to retire. In a society in which there are more jobs than potential workers, a compulsory retirement age would probably not be found; in a society like ours, with more people who wish to work than there are jobs available, forcing some workers out through retirement is one method of assuring more jobs for younger people. Equally important is the opportunity for middle-aged workers to feel that they can move up to higher status and into higher-paying positions now held by older persons.

There are alternative systems, of course. For example, we could evaluate every person over age 60 or 65 every year, perhaps using some combination of work evaluation and testing program, to determine whether another year of employment should be offered. Or we could increase retirement income sufficiently that it would not make financial sense to continue to work, that is, to offer an individual 50% of his base income at age 62, then increase that figure by 5% every year.

Both these suggestions have a major inherent limitation—immense financial cost. Also, the first alternative would produce undesirable high anxiety among workers subject to repeat evaluation. As it is, there is little likelihood that the arbitrary retirement rules will be relaxed as long as there is an abundance of labor.

One aspect of work that is often emphasized is its ability to bring meaning to the otherwise empty lives of older people. I recognize that this is often true, but I also suspect that it is not nearly so widespread as many people assume. Also, this raises the question What is it that makes the job meaningful? The work that is being performed? The opportunity to provide a role in developing goods or services for others? The relationship to co-workers? The ability to refer to oneself in terms of vocational role? The feeling that getting paid for something makes that something worthwhile?

And related questions arise. Can people find equivalent meaning in creative opportunities through the arts? That is, can older people gain as much satisfaction from painting, ceramics, or playing a musical instrument as they did from their jobs? How about bridge or poker? Shuffleboard or backpacking? Cooking or gardening? Or just having fun?

Another issue is more probing: Why is there so much concern with being meaningful? Have the elderly—or, for that matter, other age groups—always desired to feel meaningful? Is this a concern that represents all elderly people, most of them, or only a few? Can people find leisure as satisfying as work? Can they find it even more satisfying?

Thus the topics of retirement and of leisure generate a variety of social, political, economic, psychological, and philosophic issues. And these issues are not restricted to the elderly, since the meaning of work, the feelings experienced by unemployed persons, and the ability to enjoy leisure time are all salient factors affecting people of all ages.

*The Meaning of Retirement**

Carl Eisdorfer

Although most of us associate retirement with the elderly, this is not necessarily the case. Many nonelderly persons have retired, either permanently or temporarily. Sometimes the cause is health-related or the consequence of motherhood; sometimes an individual has enough money for his or her needs and decides not to work for a time. In other instances, workers will retire with a pension after only 20 or 25 years on the job (for example, the military, some federal or other governmental agencies, some police and fire departments) and remain out of work for a time before they reenter the job market.

Regardless of the age at which a person retires, there are many adjustments to be made involving time, finances, friendships, and sometimes health, among other matters. Some people never adapt, but others make the adjustments very easily.

*Edited from "Adaptation to Loss of Work," by C. Eisdorfer. In F. Carp (Ed.), *Retirement.* Copyright 1972 by Human Sciences Press (formerly Behavioral Publications). Reprinted by permission.

Work—as an activity in its own right, as a system for obtaining a variety of rewards to fill more or less essential needs, and as a basis for establishing major parameters of one's style of life including the status and number of roles played—would appear to be crucial in determining personal adjustment. Then loss of work must precipitate a new phase of adaptation.

Given an open market, older workers hold a vulnerable position in the labor force. Kreps (1963) demonstrates that they tend to be among the first to be fired during times of economic hardship and the last to be hired. Whether or not aged persons are employed is a function of the labor supply and the economic condition at a given point in time: in periods of high employment and scarce labor supply, older persons work; when labor is abundant, they are not hired or retained. In view of increases in individual work productivity, Kreps predicts that in the immediate future a decreased labor force will be needed. This should lead to greater unemployment of the aged and the heightened probability of retirement from the labor force at an earlier age. In addition to these economic facts and predictions, there are projections of population growth which indicate an increase in the number and proportion of persons aged 65 and over in the near future.

Such information about the population and the labor force lends urgency to the need to analyze retirement in terms of its implications for human adaptation. This section identifies and discusses variables which appear to have major significance for response to loss of work and which consequently may be relevant to the design of investigations into retirement as an adaptational process.

The pattern of preprogramming termination of job at a particular age, although related in a general way to deficits found in the aged, seems to have developed independently of any empirically derived understanding of the effects of age. The work-related problems found among the aged can only be said to interact with advancing years. As a consequence of the paucity of accurate information, retirement has been associated with several sets of conjectures. These assumptions, as summarized by Kent (1965), include the construct that there are predictable, negative effects upon aged persons who retire, and that such effects may be seen in physical or social deterioration or both in the immediate post-retirement period. In view of the complexity and scope of the issues involved, it seems appropriate to discuss the relationships of retirement with health, social interactions, work status, finances, and feelings of self-worth.

HEALTH

The relationship between retirement and health or physical pathology is complex. The work of Thompson and Streib (1958) suggests that poor health frequently leads to retirement, particularly among "blue collar" workers, and that there may be a post-retirement improvement in health in many individuals. For many years, however, it has been conjectured that retirement and its attendant interpersonal difficulties led to a poorer level of health.

Ellison (1968), in fact, proposes that the sick role may be adopted as an alternative to the retired role. He suggests that while retirement is identified with hopelessness and helplessness, the expectation for the sick is improvement and return to health. In addition, the sick role is more consistent with the dependency status in which some retirees perceive themselves. Thus, the worker may turn to sickness as a way of legitimately exempting himself from social responsibilities.

As Martin and Doran (1966) have pointed out, however, the evidence concerning the relationship between health and retirement is equivocal at best. Their survey data on men over the age of 55 show a steadily increasing incidence of illness requiring medical intervention, which drops from 50% to 30% immediately after retirement. All of the evidence, they feel, points to a drop in illness with retirement.

A confounding issue in these investigations is the measurement of health as reflected in the relationship between self-health ratings and other indexes of health. It has been reported that, despite chronic illness, a great majority of the aged do not identify themselves as seriously limited (Suchman, Streib, & Phillips, 1958). Ostfeld (1968, pp. 83–96) suggested that his sample of older persons in an urban area had considerably greater physical impairment than they recognized or reported. His subjects, all welfare recipients, were examined by physicians, and more than half were found to have symptoms reflecting moderate to severe illness. Yet a significant proportion of this group of physically ill individuals had accepted their symptoms as the limitations of normal old age. Most of Ostfeld's subjects, in fact, had not sought medical help for their ailments. It is not surprising, then, that in the sample of community volunteers who visited the Duke Center for two days of examination, about a third of the aged significantly misjudged their physical condition (Busse, 1967).

In assessing the relevance of failure to recognize poor health, it should be recognized that self-perception of health may be less accurate during a static period, when the individual is at rest, than it is during a period when the individual is involved in sustained physical activity such as work. The early or milder forms of many chronic diseases are rarely observable until the victim exerts himself. Cardiovascular illness and emphysema, which are common disorders among the aged, may manifest themselves initially only as shortness of breath upon exertion. This complaint is subjectively interpretable as being out of condition due to lack of exercise or "old age creeping up," and the individual may report that he is physically fit for his age.

In a similar vein, the positive value of retirement to individuals with subtle and minor physical problems may not readily be identified, despite the relevance of poor health as an etiologic factor. The findings of Ryser and Sheldon (1969) on 500 aged retirees in Massachusetts do, in fact, indicate that while over 10% indicated poorer health post-retirement, nearly one-quarter of the sample reported improved health. Overall, 85% of the subjects (ages 60 to 70) indicated good or very good health, although 32% indicated some limitations imposed by the state of their health. Reported visits to physicians was the only objective criterion of health reported in this study. It is impressive that, despite their reports of good health, 40% had made more than routine visits to a doctor.

In his discussion of these issues, Eisdorfer (1968, pp. 97–104) identified the pitfalls of using self-estimate of health as a criterion for making judgments about the physical status of subjects. Health, particularly as it involves the problems of functional capacity (Lawton, 1967) and the separation of "illness" from age, needs to be better delineated. The remarkably high proportion of older persons suffering from chronic diseases makes this variable an essential one in attempts to study any behavioral function among the aged.

INTERPERSONAL RELATIONS

Cumming and Henry (1961) stress the adaptive function of progressive social withdrawal in their disengagement concept. Remarkably little is known, however, about the relationship of subclinical or poorly identified illness to this process. Withdrawal from social situations, as described in the context of disengagement theory, implies an active movement away from interpersonal contacts by the aging individual. In reality, of course, there is an important admixture of involuntary withdrawal. The amputation of extensive as well as intensive social interactions through death, retirement, or removal from home and neighborhood may cause a pattern of multiple crises resulting in personality changes which we have yet to understand fully. In their investigation, Cumming and Henry focused primarily upon the extent of interpersonal involvements, and gave scant attention to the intensity of relationships. The possibility that a limited number of very intense relationships may act as a buffer against loss of extensive role relationships of a more superficial kind should not be overlooked.

It is reasonable to assume that retirement results in a decrease in the number of automatic social contacts. In their observations regarding their own person-to-person contacts during the first few years after retirement, Pressey and Pressey (1966) imply that in order for the aged retiree to sustain a high number of contacts, he is required to "work at it" by appropriately restructuring his environment.

Rosow (1967) observed that social homogeneity as well as residential proximity is important in forming and sustaining friendships, and that the social contacts of the manual worker may be relatively more vulnerable to changes in his immediate neighborhood than are those of the middle-class or upper-class individual. It seems probable, too, that the neighborhoods surrounding the residences of manual workers are more vulnerable to change, adding to the impact of loss of job-related contacts. In this regard, workers in our lower socioeconomic classes may have more difficulties. If there is a differential life expectancy related to income level, then the aged poor may stand a relatively greater chance of losing their friends through death.

The impact of loss of any intensive relationship, such as that with a spouse or life-long friend, is difficult to assess in the absence of information concerning other contacts, and the life style and mobility of the aged retiree. Such interpersonal losses, however, should constitute an important focus for study in attempting to understand the difficulties of aging individuals. It may be helpful to contrast this stage of life and its attendant losses with the events of youth, which typically involve increasing numbers of interpersonal contacts as well as greater mastery over the environment.

Perhaps the greatest problem presented by retirement is the loss of automatic, job-defined roles. The ex-president of a corporation or former government official has some status without his previous power, but too often he may prefer to fall back upon his self-perceived old status rather than redefine his relationship to others.

Interpersonal relationships, then, represent a second crucial area of concern for the retiree and for the investigator hoping to assess adaptation to loss of work. There may be quite significant differences between the loss of certain types of job-related relationships, those relationships seen as transcending the employment status, and those with varying degrees of interpersonal intensity. Simple quantitative analyses of number of contacts, group memberships, and the like may reveal little about adaptation, in the absence of knowledge about the intensity and perceived desirability of such relationships.

WORK STATUS

Simpson, Back, and McKinney (1966) have indicated that response to loss of work is in part a function of the kind of work performed prior to retirement. They propose that upper-status workers (for example, executives and professionals) have the highest degree of job satisfaction. This includes feelings of job autonomy, recognition of performance, and receipt of higher wages. Middle-status workers, by definition, have less autonomy. They are usually identified with the results of their work to a lesser degree, and they vary significantly in the extent to which they share values with other workers. The workers in such middle-status jobs report some job satisfaction. Semi-skilled work seems to involve the least job satisfaction and is associated with limited development of skills and low work autonomy. It involves some norms related to the work situation, but few occupational norms.

In view of these differences, lower status workers would seem to have less to lose upon retirement in terms of job-related satisfaction. Simpson, Back, and McKinney do, in fact, report that upper white-collar retirees were most likely to be involved with retirement concerns prior to retirement, semi-skilled retirees were least likely to be so involved, and middle-status retirees were in their customary intermediate position. It is important to note, however, that following their retirement, the sample of upper-status retirees experienced the greatest loss of involvement, the middle-status the least, and the semi-skilled an intermediate amount. The survey data from this panel of subjects suggest that while the upper-status retirees did experience a loss of self-esteem from retirement, the extent of their loss was less than among retirees of lower status.

It seems clear, too, that while the upper-status retirees lost a larger percentage of specifically work-related interests, overall they lost fewer interests. Reduction in income appeared to be a more important influence than the intensity of involvement with job deprivation among the semi-skilled retirees, while work involvement was as influential as income in predicting the effects of job deprivation among middle-status workers. Orderliness of work history, even apart from job status, seems to reduce the likelihood that pre-retirement involvement will be lost. A pattern of status and orderliness seems to emerge as inversely related to feelings of job deprivation and directly related to morale.

Among the middle-status retirees, involvement in a variety of activities is as important as a high ratio of pre- to post-retirement income in lessening job deprivation. In contrast, among the lower-status workers, the post-retirement changes seem intimately related to the sharp drop in income which accompanies their exit from work. These data are similar to the results obtained by Thompson, Streib, and Kosa (1960), and support the hypothesis that the effects of job deprivation differ by economic strata as well as by the variety of other variables which operate in the work situation.

A variety of issues related to work status, then, lend themselves to the investigation of personal adaptation to retirement. Not only could socioeconomic status and the relative importance of job-related income be better understood, particularly in real dollar terms, but also self-perception of success-failure might well be explored. This can be studied, not only directly at the time of retirement, but perhaps also in the middle years when it becomes clear to the individual what the probability for his self-fulfillment on the job is to be. A withdrawal or heightened involvement with the job, many years pre-retirement, on the part of a middle-management executive may be an important factor in appreciating his response to anticipated retirement.

FINANCES

It may be useful to note that the aged must live at income levels approximately half those of younger workers. Thus, data describing the social contacts and interaction patterns of the aged might well be reexamined in terms of the economics of social participation. Membership dues for clubs, church contributions, and travel costs may impose limitations on participation because of the marginal or submarginal income of the retiree. Even visits to the family may involve economic hardship for the aged individual with a low income, since transportation costs and gifts for grandchildren are among the hidden expenses which make such visits relatively costly. The oft-voiced contention that retirees do not need money because their children are grown is a disturbing misconception. The potential cyclic effects of social withdrawal, secondary to economic privation, can be significant. The aged person who may have constricted his activities involuntarily is no longer considered a prospective participant in the social unit, and therefore contacts with him are reduced. The aged individual counters what he may perceive as a new rejection by further increasing his active withdrawal (disengagement?).

From the studies of Thompson and Streib (1958), it has been suggested that aged blue-collar employees do not look negatively upon retirement and that, in fact, they may look forward to giving up full-time employment with positive feelings, particularly when retirement income is adequate and when there is a health-related difficulty. Ash (1966) has reported that for blue-collar workers in Great Britain, the closer an employee is to the age of retirement, the more likely he is to say that he does not want to retire. However, a particularly interesting aspect of this study is that, in contrast to a similar survey performed a decade before, 10% more of the employees were accepting of their imminent retirement. At the time of the second study (1966), fewer felt it to be the worst thing that could happen to a person. This seems also to be reflected in the finding that while a decade before more than half (56%) viewed retirement relatively passively, only 20% so regarded it in 1966. The number who regarded retirement as a reward went from 30% to 45% in ten years. The employees of the prior decade were more likely to see retirement as based on physical disability, while the employees of 1966 were more likely to regard it as a reward for services rendered. This shift on the part of the retiree in the direction of a more positive attitude toward retirement is an important development.

The worker's attitude that his retirement income was earned through his own efforts and was not merely a charitable act by the government may be a significant variable in determining his acceptance of retirement. It is reasonable to assume that income should be viewed not only in terms of its direct effect on purchasing power but also in terms of the attitude of the receiver. While financial status is related to self-worth, identification of income as charity is perhaps not as supportive to the integrity of the ego as the same income perceived as earnings. This may be another example of the need to feel autonomous and the master of one's own fate. Retirement income as deferred wages earned through work, and not as a "hand-out," implies independence and adds to self-esteem.

Ash's data indicate, too, that positive attitudes and better adjustment in retirement are both related to the extent to which the employee anticipates and makes plans for this major change in his activity pattern. Thus, of those employees 60 years of age and older who had made retirement plans, 81% wanted to retire. Of those who had made no retirement plans, only 38% expressed an interest in retirement. In the follow-up of persons retired more than three years, previous planning appeared to make a striking difference. Among those who had made plans for retirement, only 8% expressed the feeling of having nothing to do, in contrast to 22% of the group that had made no plans.

In interpreting such results, the selective bias of the subjects becomes a central issue. While a positive relationship was found between planning for retirement and favorable attitude toward retirement, it may only demonstrate that persons with favorable attitudes toward an event are more likely to think about and to provide for that event. The value of pre-retirement planning and counseling, while widely heralded, needs to be the subject of investigation, particularly with regard to the client's age and the period in employment history when such planning is most meaningful. It would hardly be surprising to discover that pre-retirement counseling initiated with a group of sixty-year-old workers who have denied their impending retirement, and who have insufficient time remaining at work to plan effectively even for their financial needs, might result in more negative than positive effects.

The notion that money is important to adaptation could hardly be ranked as a major insight. Despite the obvious character of this relationship, there has been relatively little investigation into adjustment to poverty or near poverty, and perhaps even less into the effects of replacement of income. Combined economic, social, and psychological studies are sorely needed for understanding this critical problem.

Retirement:
Continuity or Crisis?*

Robert C. Atchley

Retirement has never been a crisis before because, until the past few decades, people did not retire unless they were very wealthy or their health required it. Is retirement a crisis now? If so, for whom? I would personally hypothesize that retirement is perceived as a crisis by middle-aged and younger people who write about retirement. They enjoy their work and they are capable of finding jobs that provide challenge, growth, status, and good income.

But almost everything I might say either was said in the last section or will be said in the next section, so I will not attempt to elaborate on the points that are made.

*Edited from "Retirement and Leisure Participation: Continuity or Crisis?" by R.C. Atchley, *The Gerontologist*, 1971, *11*, 13–17. Reprinted by permission of the Gerontological Society.

Recreation and leisure are institutions that are different yet closely related. *Recreation* refers to activities such as sports, games, the vacation, hobbies, and the like that aim to renew mind and body by either relieving them of tension or delivering them from boredom. Recreation is thus primarily a reaction to some state of body or mind. *Leisure* activities, on the other hand,' are pursued as ends in themselves. They are unplanned and unrequired. Leisure is primarily *action*, directed generally toward self-development.

Leisure and recreation share one prime characteristic: both are reserved for time periods not already set aside for working at a job, sleeping, performing domestic tasks, or meeting family obligations.

Recreation and leisure aim primarily at relaxation, entertainment, and personal development. As such, they are institutions that are oriented around the needs of individuals, particularly the needs for tension management, enhancement of self-esteem, and identity (Atchley, 1970).

For simplicity we will lump recreation and leisure together under the general label of leisure.

Information about patterns of leisure among older people is essential in examining the nature of growing old. People gradually expand the time they spend in leisure roles as age increases (Riley et al., 1968). Upon retirement, leisure pursuits occupy a great deal of the individual's time, and there is a question as to whether leisure roles can fill the void left by work. There is little doubt that leisure can fill the *time* formerly occupied by work, but the problem is whether leisure is capable of giving the individual the kind of *self-respect* and identity that he got from the job.

THE IDENTITY CRISIS THEORY

Perhaps the most articulate and repeatedly quoted spokesman on the negative side is Miller (1965) who has taken the following position:

1. Retirement is basically degrading because although there is an implication that retirement is a right that is earned through life-long labor, there is also a tacit understanding that this reward is given primarily to coax the individual from a role he is no longer able to play.

2. Occupational identity invades all of the other areas of the person's life. Accordingly, the father and head of household roles, the friend role, and even leisure roles are mediated by the individual's occupational identity.

3. The identity that comes from work is related to deeply ingrained values as to which roles can give a legitimate identity.

4. Leisure role cannot replace work as a source of self-respect and identity because it is not supported by norms that would make this legitimate. That is, the retired person does not *feel justified* in deriving self-respect from leisure. Leisure is simply not defined as a legitimate source of self-respect by the general population.

5. Beyond the simple need to be doing something there is a need to be engaged in something that is defined by most people as utilitarian or gainful

in some way. Thus, the stamp collector must emphasize the financial re-wards, paintings are offered for sale, or woodworking is confined to im-mediately "useful" objectives. In short, the only kinds of leisure that can provide identity are work-substitutes.

6. There is a stigma of "implied inability to perform" that is associated with retirement and carried over into all of the individual's remaining roles and that results in an identity breakdown.

7. Identity breakdown involves a process whereby the individual's former claims to prestige or status are invalidated by the implied inability to perform, and this proves embarrassing for the stigmatized person. Miller calls this result "the portent of embarrassment."

8. Embarrassment leads to the individual's withdrawal from the situ-ation or prevents him from participating to begin with.

9. The answer lies not in inventing new roles for the aging, but rather in "determining what roles presently exist in the social system . . . offering vicarious satisfactions, that can reduce the socially debilitating loss accom-panying occupational retirement."

10. Miller implies that creating an ethic which would make full-time leisure an acceptable activity for a worthwhile person is a possible way to resolve the dilemma of the retired leisure participant.

Miller's analysis of the situation is an insightful one. Nevertheless, it rests on the assumption that prior to retirement the individual derived his identity primarily from his job. Also implied in Miller's identity crisis theory is the assumption that most people want to stay on the job, since this is their main identity, and that therefore most retirement is involuntary. This is no doubt related to the fact Miller leaves out of his discussion those who retired voluntarily. Miller also implies that he subscribes to the activ-ity theory of adjustment to aging since he assumes that lost roles need to be replaced (Havighurst, 1963).

EVIDENCE CONCERNING IDENTITY CRISIS

There are several sets of questions which thus emerge from an exami-nation of the identity crisis theory presented by Miller. First, is his por-trayal of the relationship between involuntary retirement and leisure an accurate one? Second, is the pattern, even if accurate, typical of most older leisure participants? Third, what is the pattern among those who are volun-tarily retired? Data from recent studies of retired people can shed some light on these questions.

1. Retirement has been found to result in a loss of a sense of involve-ment, *but this was unrelated to other self-concept variables of optimism and autonomy* (Back & Guptill, 1966).

Disengagement theory tells us to expect some withdrawal from in-volvement, and it is noteworthy that this loss of involvement does not ap-pear to have adverse results for other aspects of the self-concept. This leads to skepticism concerning Miller's "portent of embarrassment."

2. Strong work-orientation *is* frequently found among retired people, but this is *not* accompanied by anxiety, depression, dislike of retirement, or withdrawal from activity (Cottrell & Atchley, 1969).

Our findings indicate that a strong positive orientation toward work "*exists* apart from the job itself but . . . has no *import for the individual* apart from the job itself." In terms of adjustment, there was apparently *no* negative result from carrying a positive orientation toward work into retirement.

3. When men retired from upper-white-collar, middle-status, and semi-skilled jobs were compared, it was found that the upper-white-collar people had internalized occupationally oriented norms. Middle-status workers were oriented toward specific tasks and situations often resulting in the acquisition of skills that were transferable to leisure situations. Semi-skilled workers were engaged mainly in activities oriented about things (Simpson, Back & McKinney, 1966a).

Of these occupational strata, the upper-white-collar stratum comes closest to Miller's model of the retired person. These are work-oriented people. However, neither of the other two strata fits the work-oriented model. Middle-status people develop skills on the job that carry over into other roles. Thus, the salesman may carry his smooth-talking style over into his leisure roles. Semi-skilled people are oriented around the job, but not necessarily because they have any deep abiding commitment to the job. For them it may be purely a matter of not having been trained for anything *other than* a job.

4. The *style* of work activities tends to remain dominant in retirement.

Simpson et al. (1966a) found that upper-white-collar jobs were oriented about *symbols*, middle-status jobs were oriented around *people*, and semi-skilled jobs were oriented around *things*. The middle-status people showed the greatest continuity in style from pre- to post-retirement. This suggests that retirement, and leisure roles in particular, offers greater opportunities for practicing interpersonal skills than for practicing skills oriented around symbols or things.

The implication of this finding is that it is not so much the *ethic* learned on the job that interferes with successful pursuit of leisure in retirement but rather the skills. Those who learn job-skills that cannot be readily used in leisure pursuits have a hard time adjusting to an increase in leisure unless they have had the opportunity to learn these skills elsewhere. This concept is reinforced by the finding that in terms of retirement activities middle-status people who had thing-oriented jobs resembled the semi-skilled more than they did their middle-status peers.

5. In addition, data from retired railroaders indicate that there are continuities in the situations people face that minimize the impact of retirement (Cottrell, 1970). Family, friends, church, and other roles continue despite retirement. Cottrell's data suggest that the portent of embarrassment and loss of identity is minimized by the tendency to select friends on the job from among those of one's own age. The end result of this process is to create *retirement cohorts* of people who have known each other on the job and who retire together. In the Scripps Foundation studies of retirement

this phenomenon has been observed among those retired from occupations as diverse as teacher, railroader, and telephone operator (Atchley, 1967; Cottrell, 1970; Cottrell & Atchley, 1969). It results in a group of retired friends who have known each other for years and whose concepts of each other involve a great deal more than the mere playing of an occupational role. Nevertheless, this group is also capable of sustaining the prestige gained on the job because they know all about how this prestige was generated.

To the extent that older people are geographically mobile, they might tend to lose these continuities, but most retired people, particularly the semi- or unskilled, do not move away from their place of long-term residence (Riley et al., 1968).

6. Cottrell's data (1970) also indicate that as the concept of retirement is incorporated into the culture, the tendency to look upon work as a temporary part of life increases.

The implication here is that if work is not a permanent part of life, then one puts greater emphasis on other parts of life that are more permanent. For example, if a man knows the day he begins working that he will work 25 years and then quit, he is very likely to avoid letting work become an all-consuming part of his life.

7. In terms of ethic, it is not at all clear whether most people regard work as a necessary prerequisite for making leisure legitimate or simply as a necessary economic function which interferes with the pursuit of leisure. It *is* quite clear that our heritage has always included those who did not work because they could afford not to. Accordingly, legitimacy of leisure may rest not so much on work as on the idea that the money used to sustain leisure came from a legitimate source, that is, it was either earned by working or inherited. In the Scripps Foundation studies of retirement many middle-income retired people have shown not the slightest reluctance to embrace leisure roles, given the fact that their income was secure (Atchley, 1967; Cottrell & Atchley, 1969). Perhaps if most retired people were not pauperized by retirement the "portent of embarrassment" mentioned by Miller would fade away.

8. Nearly two-thirds of retired men retired as a result of their own decision. *Less than 1 in 5* was retired involuntarily as a result of reaching retirement age (Cottrell & Atchley, 1969; Riley et al., 1968).

By leaving out those in poor health and those who voluntarily retired, Miller (1965) effectively limited the group he was talking about to less than a third of the retired men and an even smaller proportion of the retired women.

IDENTITY CONTINUITY THEORY

It may seem that we have dwelt too long and too deeply with the relation between leisure and retirement. Nevertheless, if we are to understand the nature of leisure among older people, it must be put in its proper context. Miller's position is a very common one and is constantly being used as a basis for decisions that influence older people's lives. Our detailed examination of this approach has shown it to be at least questionable and very possibly false.

To begin with, there is evidence in the Scripps Foundation studies and elsewhere that the adjustment problems sometimes associated with retirement are *not* the result of the loss of work and the identity it provides. In fact, a highly positive orientation toward work had little influence on retirement adjustment. There is no indication that highly work-oriented people are unable to take up leisure roles; in fact, just the opposite. We could find no concrete evidence that retirement in and of itself negatively influences the *quality* of one's family life, friendships, or associations.

Accordingly, an alternative to Miller's identity crisis theory of the relationship between retirement and leisure might contain the following points.

Many people are never highly work-oriented and thus they may very well provide a model for others concerning what it would be like to derive self-satisfaction from leisure. In addition, the ethic of the system allows this as long as the money used to lead a life of leisure is legitimately earned.

Self-respect *can* be gained from leisure pursuits in retirement if (a) the individual has enough money, and (b) he has a cohort of retired friends who will accept his full-time leisure as legitimate and help him to negate the stigma of implied inability to perform, if such a stigma exists. As retirement becomes more and more an expected part of the life-cycle, this orientation should spread beyond the cohort of friends. In any event, the retired individual will continue to see *himself* as a railroader, teacher, etc. even though he no longer plays the role. Thus, the crux of this alternative theory is *identity continuity*.

Wide occupational differences exist in the concept of the usefulness of an activity. There are many people for whom interpersonal interaction *was* their occupational skill and it is this *activity* that is useful rather than some abstract goal. In this sense, then, leisure can act as a work-substitute where it needs to and provide identity continuity.

Very few people rest their entire identity on a single role. The only thing that makes failure bearable is that we seldom fail in all our roles at once.

Each person generally has several roles that he stakes his identity on. Work may be at or near the top, but not necessarily so. There simply is not the kind of homogeneous consensus on the value of work that would keep it at the top for everyone. In fact, the many systems of competing values in a complex society *insure* that there will be a wide variety of self-values. Thus, the probability that retirement will lead to a complete identity breakdown is slight, and there may be just as many people who rely on leisure pursuits for self-respect as there are who rely on work, particularly among those with unsatisfying jobs.

Some decline of involvement may be natural as the individual adjusts to declining energy, but most people expand their leisure involvement when they retire. Nevertheless, this change is not regarded negatively by most retired people. In fact, most people voluntarily retire, and many of these volunteers cite a preference for leisure as their reason for retiring.

CONCLUSION

There is no doubt that there are some people for whom Miller's identity crisis pattern is a grim reality, but it does not appear to be a typical pattern, even among the minority of older people who are forced to retire. Among voluntary retirees, a third retired to devote more time to leisure. The ethical issue may be difficult for some to resolve, but not for the majority, even among the highly work-oriented.

The identity continuity theory and the data which give rise to it suggest that leisure can have a great deal of positive value as a bridge between pre- and post-retirement life and that this value will increase in the future.

Between the two of them, the identity continuity and crisis theories probably account for the majority of cases. Nevertheless, to settle the inevitable question as to the proportions of retired people who fit each model, studies are needed that are broader in scope and wider in range than any thus far brought to bear on the question. One of the intriguing but often infuriating aspects of studying aging in the United States is the sometimes overpowering geographic, social, and psychological diversity of the older population. Perhaps further probing will uncover still other patterns of relationship between retirement and leisure participation.

While the research that has been done seems to support the identity continuity model more than Miller's identity crisis model, there is still a great deal of work that needs to be done before either model can be used with a high degree of confidence.

*Attitudes toward Retirement**

Mark H. Ingraham

College and university faculty members are hardly representative of all individuals who hold jobs; similarly, retired college and university personnel are hardly representative of all individuals who have retired. Since the following section is based on questionnaires sent only to retired faculty mem-

*Edited from *My Purpose Holds*, by M.H. Ingraham. Copyright 1974 by the Teachers Insurance and Annuity Association of America—College Retirement Equities Fund. Reprinted by permission.

bers, it must be understood as descriptive only of retired persons who have better-than-average financial resources and more-than-average options in retirement.

In social gerontology, as in many fields of social endeavor, however, we tend to focus our attention on those persons most in need of help. Whereas from the point of view of services, this makes a certain amount of sense, it also provides us with an uneven perspective. There is considerable value in knowing what happens to those whose chances for success are great. After all, when we know what they have achieved, we have a standard for what others might accomplish.

The variety of points of view brought to retirement is fascinating. Even if one's attitudes are in large part internally generated, they often also reflect circumstances of finances, health, family, activity, etc. . . . There were those among the respondents who totally rejected retirement, even condemning those who enjoy it. "I do not know of any aspect of retirement that is likeable, if one has enjoyed his work and has been busy for years. Those who enjoy retirement are the ones who have never liked to work in any case." By contrast, "retirement is the best thing to happen since the invention of the wheel," or, in the same vein, "I would rank retirement second only to the wheel." The writers of these last two statements were very different, one describing herself as "a semi-administrative female employee who was bumping her head on the promotion ceiling"; while the other liked the fact that he was "Free to be one's self; free to say 'no'; free to say 'To hell with it' (or 'with you') and walk away; free from the telephone; free to be as selfish or as selfless as I like."

Of course most of the respondents were neither resentful nor ecstatic, but registered milder degrees of discontent or, much more often, of pleasure with their current lives. The usual picture given by more detailed analysis was of a person with at least adequate means but fearing inflation or overwhelming medical expenses; active, but wondering how long he can keep up the pace; healthy, but realizing that a period of poor health may be in store; pleased with the persons he knows, especially children and grandchildren, but rather put out with those under sixty—and even more with those under thirty—whom he does not know.

For many, contentment with retirement derives from satisfaction with new or continued activities, under less-pressured conditions than formerly, as in the case of the woman, who, though no longer rising at 5:30 A.M. declared, "I really love retirement although I have become involved in so many different activities that I am attending meetings all the time." Others care more for the life of appreciation, delightfully typified by the woman of 70 years who quoted Stevenson's *A Child's Garden of Verses*, "The world is so full of a number of things,/I'm sure we should all be as happy as kings."

There were a number who welcomed a new and stimulating period of life, sometimes even termed "career." But one man in a more ironic mood welcomed "the transition from organized confusion to disorganized chaos."

My rather extensive acquaintance with the elderly should have, but had not, prepared me for the general euphoria of the replies. Depending on your temperament and momentary mood, you might say that the spirit of the retirees was an inspiration or that they were "disgustingly cheerful." The attitudes of a few may have been bravado and lack of realism, but I believe that far more frequently the elderly had acquired serenity based upon a mature philosophy of life, and courage often strengthened by religious faith. They knew that their energy was lessening and that the major portion of their work was done, yet they had tasted life and the sweetness of its savour had not departed. Sometimes, however, the courage and philosophy were being severely tested.

Most of those who had lost their husbands or wives had made, if the losses were not recent, reasonably good adjustments, but still lived with an undercurrent of sadness—more with resignation than with zest.

For some perhaps the greatest struggle had been to attain a more relaxed conscience which could tolerate unused moments and the receipt of unreciprocated kindnesses.

Of course there were some who were unhappy because of ill health or because they found retirement an emotional catastrophe, but the latter were exceptions.

In spite of the fact that the general tenor of the replies was remarkably happy, retirement isn't all fulfillment or all "beer and skittles." Between religion and a well-developed philosophy of life, many retired persons lead lives of serenity, but I believe that only a minority prefer retirement to their former lives. Of course, the greatest curse is not retirement itself, but decreased energy and the illnesses which come with increasing years. These arrive earlier for some than for others; and there are a fortunate few who retain their vigor and their clarity of mind into very advanced years and then die with little or no warning except from the calendar.

Perhaps loneliness, loss of status, and lack of routine, coupled with boredom, are mentioned more often than other unpleasant circumstances; but there are other complaints, ranging from those that are rather general to those which might be labeled "pet peeves."

LONELINESS

A large proportion of those who wrote of their loneliness had lost a husband or wife, some other close relative, or a friend who had been a constant companion. Mealtime may be especially poignant as more than one widow attested. Like least: "Eating alone since husband's death. Companionship of husband and intellectual stimulation greatly missed." The ability to recover from such a bereavement differs greatly from person to person and is less in the aged than in the young.

A second cause of loneliness is moving away from the community where there are many friends to a place where there are few. Such a move does not always, perhaps not usually, result in loneliness as many respondents bore witness. The consequences of a move depend on the type of community to which one goes and upon one's temperament. Moreover, the effect may be different upon the husband than upon the wife. Even without a move, the daily association with colleagues can be sorely missed.

Loneliness was mentioned more often by women than by men; perhaps this is because among the respondents there were more single women than single men. Moreover, because the wives, on the average, are younger than their husbands and more long-lived, there are more widows in the general population than widowers.

CHANGE OF STATUS

Loneliness is hard to bear but usually not blamed on others, whereas frequently, but not always, a change of status—real or imaginary—is resented as caused by the inconsiderate, the patronizing, or the unwise attitudes of past colleagues, new acquaintances, or that catch-all of all evil, the "young." Sometimes a sense of uselessness is not the result of the opinion of others but of the feeling of guilt, or at least of uneasiness, in oneself. This was complained of particularly by the recently retired, and some described how this complex had either faded away or been mastered through the development of a more mature philosophy or through finding activities interesting in themselves and valuable to others. One of the "pet peeves" related to status is the euphemistic, often patronizing, language used concerning retired people. The phrases "senior citizen," "golden years," and their ilk appear to be particularly obnoxious. To me, they are trivially disgusting. But it is well to remember that the words "senior citizens" have become big business. Another source of anguish is the surprise retired persons encounter that they are still around or even alive.

FREEDOM AND BOREDOM

It takes a great deal of self-discipline not to be bored by freedom. If it is a relief not to work so hard and to have a reasonable amount of free time, it is difficult to find an interesting or rewarding occupation. The result can be an uncomfortable lack of direction and boredom. It is sometimes difficult to distinguish between those who feel the loss of status when they lose the job and those who miss the work for its own sake. During most of my life when bored, it has been chiefly either by inactivity or by certain kinds of people. I am surprised to find how few reported the second of these causes. It, perhaps, is not surprising that boredom, especially immediately after retiring, was more frequently reported by the obviously energetic than by those whose physical condition precluded much activity. A man, age 72, wrote concerning retirement, "If you are lazy, it's good. If not, Blooey."

WHEN TO RETIRE

"Among my former colleagues, those who retired as early as possible seem to regret not having worked longer before retirement, while those who continued their regular employment to the latest possible time regret not having retired much earlier."

As the above quotation indicates, one of the matters on which there is greater diversity of opinion than consensus is "when to retire." This diversity is shown in institutional policies and also in personal opinions. Some institutions have a single mandatory retirement age; others have a normal retirement age, a later mandatory age and between, a limbo subject to administrative decisions. Individual beliefs as to what is desirable vary greatly. For instance, one woman advises "retire as soon as possible" (she retired at 63), while one man, age 76, said "being in good health and in good teaching performance, my retirement, even at the age of 72, was too early."

The optimum retirement age is a subject often discussed by administrators, and it is notable how much their perceptions of human abilities conform to institutional stresses. In a time of expansion, maturity, judgment, experience, even mellowness (which in fruit foreruns decay) is praised, while currently, with limited budgets and stable or shrinking student bodies, it is time for the old fogies to move along and young people with new ideas (and lower salaries) to come in. Changing circumstances can justify altered decisions, but a certain continuity of viewpoint concerning one's fellowmen is desirable.

There are many persons who believe that retirement should be gradual, with perhaps part-time work for a number of years. In fact, it often is gradual, considering how frequently assignments and chores become lighter as a person nears retirement. Sometimes special part-time appointments are given. Of course there are those whose post-retirement activities form a buffer that provides for a gradual slowdown.

There were many statements as to the undesirability of a mandatory retirement age, especially one as low as 65. Some of these deal with the variability in persons, declaring that retirement should be based on "capacity and ability"; others with the waste of talent; and still others with the impact of formal retirement on an active individual. Moreover, some people resented being told that they must retire, even to such an extent that they chose to retire a year early in order that it might be voluntary.

Life-Style
and Leisure Patterns*

Robert J. Havighurst

What do people do when they retire? Some take on another paying job, perhaps fewer hours a week or less-demanding work, but it is not unusual for retirement jobs to require as much time and effort as previous jobs–or even more. Other retired persons turn toward hobbies, spectator sports, participant sports, card-playing, volunteer work, gardening, and the ever-present television set. Sitting on the park bench and watching the passing parade is also familiar; so is getting actively involved in supporting a political candidate or party or espousing a social cause.

The variety of possibilities is limited by such practical concerns as money, transportation, and physical health. It can also be limited, although probably not as frequently as many nonelderly assume, by shyness, fear and anxiety, and low self-esteem. The evidence is certainly not all in, but there is good reason to believe that when an elderly person in reasonable health and with modest finances is an isolate, he may well have been an isolate earlier in life.

I am not contending that all elderly are now participating in leisure and recreational activities as much as they wish or that additional services would not be welcome. Rather, I am trying to make the point, as I have elsewhere in this book, that older people often are more competent than others give them credit for being. When they don't participate, it is often because lack of funds, health, or transportation keeps them away—and many do an amazing job of overcoming even these limitations, when they wish to.

One of the major changes that confronts retired people is that work no longer structures their lives. Work, or in earlier years school, is often the base upon which we plan and structure our hours, days, weeks, months, and years. When there is no work or school, we no longer have to wake up in the morning; Saturday becomes much the same as Tuesday (except for other people's schedules and the television programming); October is as good a time for a vacation (often better) as July. In retirement, you rise in the morning with 16 hours ahead in which you can do essentially whatever you wish, assuming that you have the personal and practical resources necessary.

How is this time spent? At one end of the continuum are those retired persons who pursue activities to fill all their waking hours; sometimes their pace appears frantic, although at other times there seems to be a comfortable rhythm. At the other end of the continuum are those who never quite get organized, and the hours, days, months, and years slide through their fin-

---

*Edited from "Life Styles and Leisure Patterns: Their Evolution Through the Life Cycle," by R. J. Havighurst. In J. A. Huet (Ed.), *Leisure and the Third Age.* Copyright 1972 by the International Center of Social Gerontology. Reprinted by permission.

gers; some of these people thoroughly enjoy this way of spending time, but others resent the lack of accomplishments. Our society tends to approve of activity and accomplishment more than reflection and relationship, but the elderly are more likely to emphasize the latter functions.

Which brings up the very practical question—practical at least to those who work directly with the elderly or who establish policy—do you, as a person in the field of aging, encourage the elderly to fill their time as they please, or do you encourage them to do "what's good for them"? Do you let them play poker all day long if they wish, or watch television, or sit and reminisce? Or do you try to get them to discussion groups, art classes, or nature walks? One senior center director asked her members where they would like to go for a weekend trip. The group voted for the Nevada side of Lake Tahoe, where they could spend two full days gambling. The center director would have preferred a more physically and psychologically stimulating environment, especially since the trip was subsidized by city government funds. (They went to Tahoe, and most of them ended up losing money; almost none paid any attention to the beauty of the area, but they all enjoyed their stay there.)

The following excerpt helps to set the stage for further consideration of some of the questions posed in the previous paragraphs. Author Havighurst draws on his own research and that of others in an effort to define the meaning of leisure for older persons.

Some years ago the Paris Le Matin conducted an essay contest around the subject, "What is the best ten years of a man's life, and why?" The winner wrote that the decade of 50 to 60 was the best, for the following reasons:

1. Daughters, if any, are married and their dowries paid.
2. Inherited wealth, if any, has come.
3. Competitors in business are too old to be effective, or too young to be experienced.
4. A man can really enjoy his interests.

The contemporary man of the post-industrial society might argue for the age period 60–70 on much the same grounds. More and more people are able with regard to their money income to "really enjoy their interests" as they pass the 50 or 55 or 60-year milestone of life. They may be able to make these the best years of their lives.

The expansion of leisure in post-industrial society is due partly to increased productivity and partly to increased longevity. A country with ten percent or more of its population over 65, as is the case in most post-industrial societies, has a much larger leisured population than a country with five percent or less of its population over 65, which is characteristic of most of the less developed parts of the world.

I have made a crude estimate of the numbers of people aged 65 and over who are living today, and I came up with the figure, 150 million, or about 5 percent of the world's population. Then I estimated the numbers of people who have reached the age of 65 in the 2000 years since the beginning of the present era, and I came up with an estimate of 450 million. That is, one third of the people who have reached the age of 65 in the last 2000 years are alive today. And relatively few of them are employed in the labor market, even on a part-time basis.

Thus we can see that there is a very much larger amount of leisure, or time for unpaid free activity, than ever before in human history, in the high productivity and also in the low productivity countries.

LEISURE AND WORK

Last summer I visited the St. Johannis Grabhof (cemetery) in the middle of the old city of Nuremberg. Many of the headstones date back to the 16th century, the period when Luther and the Reformation were coming into the value-consciousness of the Europeans. One headstone, dated about 1550, read as follows:

> *Ruhe sanft, die Ihr so*
> *treu gewirkt im Leben,*
> *Eurer Liebe Lohn*
> *wird Gott Euch geben.*

Translated crudely, this is:

> Rest quietly, thou who has
> worked so faithfully in this life,
> God will reward you.

This reminder of the "Protestant ethic" is still valid today. Work is still, for most people, the most important value of their adult lives. The ethics of work still dominate the practical ethical codes of most people in the post-industrial societies.

But work is losing some of its ethical significance. As people devote less of their time and energy to work, they are likely to respect it less as a principal source of value. At the same time, leisure is acquiring an ethical significance. Any activity to which people devote as much as a quarter of their waking time is almost sure to take on a moral flavor. People are likely to judge this activity in terms of good or bad, better or worse.

The time has arrived when it is useful to speak of an ethics of leisure. People will be judged partly by their use of free time, as well as by the quality of their work.

In any study of the social roles of adults, we always pay great attention to the worker role, along with family roles and community roles. Now we can begin to speak of a leisure role. A social role is defined by the social scientist as a set of behaviors that is judged to be appropriate and desirable for a person who occupies a certain position or status in a society—such as a worker, or a parent, or spouse, or child, or friend, or neighbor, or church member, or citizen. A social role has an external and an internal aspect. That is, the society around a person expects him to behave in certain ways when he is in this role, and he expects this kind of behavior of himself.

The leisure role does not yet possess the well-defined expectations— societal and personal—that adhere to a true social role, but it is gaining a set of expectations and norms for free-time activity. An ethics of leisure is evolving to parallel the ethics of work and of family which have dominated Western society during the past hundred years.

EQUIVALENCE OF WORK AND PLAY

In a series of studies made by the writer and his students (Friedmann and Havighurst, 1954; Donald and Havighurst, 1959) the significance or meanings of work and of play have been examined by asking people what values they find in their work, and in their leisure or free-time activity. It turns out that these meanings are parallel, after one makes an exception of work as a means of earning money. There are six other broad social-psychological meanings of work, which are also meanings of leisure activity. These are:

1. A basis for sense of worth, or self-respect.
2. A locus of social participation. One makes and finds his friends at work and at play.
3. A source of prestige. One gets status or recognition from others through the quality of one's work, and also through the quality of one's leisure activity.
4. New experience; a chance to be creative and to achieve. Many people find their leisure more productive of this value than their work.
5. A chance to be of service to others. Many people give service and friendship to others in a variety of formal and informal noneconomic activity.
6. A way of making time pass. Both work and play help people to get through the day or the week without boredom.

What play does for people. Play, or leisure activity, is sometimes thought of as only expressive, never instrumental. This is a mistaken view, and it needs some analysis. An expressive activity is something that is done for itself, not for what it produces. A person expresses himself, we say, or he does his thing. He does this thing for what it gives him at that moment. If it also serves as a means to an end beyond the act, then it is instrumental, but this is not the essential thing about play. Yet a certain activity may be both expressive and instrumental. For example, playing a card game may be expressive (just fun) for one person, and a means of making money for another. Or, studying mathematics may be instrumental for the student who plans to become an engineer, and an expressive or joy-providing activity for a person who likes to "play with numbers."

As a matter of fact, there is probably no human activity which is purely expressive or purely instrumental. Thus, work is a joy to some people, and some forms of play may be no more than a performance of an obligation to some people.

Yet, leisure activity, in the sense of activity for which one is not paid in money or material goods, is generally clearly distinctive from work. But leisure activity can be expressive or it can be instrumental. In a society which has more and more time for leisure activity, it is likely that people will spend more time with various forms of non-paid service (instrumental), as well as with play (expressive).

Play does the following things for people:

1. It gives ecstasy, or pure enjoyment.
2. It prepares one for the future, by enabling him to try himself out or to play-act in certain situations that he expects to arise in the future. It enables him to experiment with roles that he will take on later (in earnest). Children and adolescents do much of this anticipatory role-taking in their play.
3. It gives one lee-way for living. It extends the customary limits of one's behavior. Thus it enriches human experience with additional space (*Spielraum*, in German), beyond that provided by the customary roles which one has learned and which actually tend to limit or contain one's behavior.

Leisure Patterns

A pilot cross-national study of role behavior was made by a team of researchers in eight different countries (Havighurst, Munnichs, Neugarten, and Thomae, 1969). They studied samples of retired male teachers and workers in heavy industry, aged 70–75, from large city and industrial areas as follows: Chicago, Vienna, Warsaw, Milan, Bonn and the Ruhr in West Germany, Nijmegen in South Holland, London and Paris. They used an intensive open-ended interview with small but random samples of 25 men in each occupational category, though only teachers were involved in the London and Paris samples. Thus they could compare the social-class factor with the factor of nationality, although the "nationality" dimension was more nearly that of certain large metropolitan areas than of nations or countries. For instance, Vienna may not be representative of rural Austria, and Chicago may not be representative of the United States.

Using data from this study, combined with a factor analysis of the leisure activities of a sample of people aged 40–70 in the Kansas City Study of Adult Life (Havighurst, 1961, pp. 309–344) they found the following patterns of free-time activity (Havighurst and de Vries, 1969).

1. Challenging new experiences. The respondent does things for his own interest and pleasure, and does them with such energy that they bring him in touch with new people. For instance, a teacher in Milan works mathematical problems for fun, constructs mechanical toys for children, reads a good deal of history, and watches a variety of sports. He is known in his neighborhood as a man with a variety of active interests. Another example is a London teacher who has written two books on music since his retirement ("They are not moneymakers.") and plays the cello two hours a day ("Schubert is my main interest.").

II. Instrumental service. When a person gives a large portion of his free time and energy to doing something useful for the family, the church, the community, or his occupational group, he is performing according to Pattern II. Among retired people, service to the church is very frequent. Thus a retired Dutch teacher spends two afternoons a week calling on about 40 families of the church, and attends meetings on church business two nights a week. A Chicago teacher is Chairman of the Finance Committee of his church, and spends two mornings a week in the church office, filing materials for the pastor. Another Chicago teacher is a precinct captain for his political party, has run for public office, and works vigorously for a reform of the state constitution. A London retired teacher is vice-president of a local association for assistance to the blind, a committee member of the Anglican church council, and treasurer of the Old Students Association of his teacher-training college.

III. Expressive pleasure. In a way this is the opposite of Pattern II. The individual uses his free time for sheer pleasure, and not as a means to the improvement of society or himself. While all people do some things "just for fun," this pattern is present when a person is quite energetic and autonomous in his search for pleasure. For instance, a Viennese teacher has season tickets for two theaters and the opera; still plays the piano for his own pleasure; reads many journals and books; and always goes with his wife to the Tyrol for a month in the summer. A Warsaw teacher (a widower), who still teaches 8 hours per week, goes one night a week to the theater or cinema, spends at least one evening a week with male or female friends, plays his violin one and a half hours à day, and reads widely. A Chicago steelworker has a room full of canaries in his basement, and a shop where he makes articles for his home; likes to grow flowers in his garden; watches baseball and football regularly on television; and plans to go to California next summer.

IV. Mildly active time filling. This pattern consists of a routine leisure activity which takes 2 or 3 hours a day and requires some degree of initiative. The man may go to a park or tavern regularly every morning to play cards and talk with friends. This is a common pattern for the Milanese steelworkers in this study, who have a recreation center maintained by the company that formerly employed them. Another rather common example of this pattern is the 1 to 2 hour daily walk frequently found in the German, Dutch and Viennese retired teachers. One German teacher visited all the new constructions in his neighborhood every week-day afternoon, as a kind of "side-walk superintendent." Another took a long walk in the wooded park known as the Venusberg which he said he knew "like the pockets in my jacket."

V. Ordinary routines expanded to fill the day and week. In this pattern the person exercises little or no initiative and does nothing outside the ordinary routines. The ordinary social roles expand to fill his day or his week, as his energy and tempo of action are reduced. For example, a 72-year-old steelworker goes to the market every morning with his wife. He says, "By the time you shop and come home and put your purchases away it seems to be a day's work." Another Chicago steelworker comments, "You take three hours for breakfast and the newspaper. Then you fuss around in the basement or the garden. They're building a garage in back of us. The man next door is retired; the man over there is retired; we all three go over and supervise the job; I don't know whether it's leisure or wasted time; after all, I guess it's all leisure time if you have nothing to do."

VI. Apathetic. The person with this pattern has had no new interests for some time and does not initiate anything. Thus, a 74-year-old Chicago steelworker who is not well said, "All my time is free, but I can't do much with it." Another steelworker goes to 6 o'clock mass every morning with his wife. When the interviewer asked him what he does the remainder of the day he said, "Just what I was doing when you came here, sitting in that chair; and I sleep 2 hours every afternoon."

VII. Literally has no free time. This is uncommon, but a few men who are still working have so much role-activity that they have little time or energy for non-constrained free-time activity. For example, a Chicago teacher works as an accountant and income tax consultant. He still cares for a large garden and lawn. He belongs to a Country Club, but has no time to use his membership. A retired teacher in Milan works part time as inspector of schools for handicapped children. In the afternoon he takes a nap, reads or helps grandchildren with their studies. Though he has a stamp collection, he does not have much time for it.

Conclusion: Leisure in a Changing Society

What can we predict about the nature of leisure activity through the life cycle over the next 30 years? Concerning the situation in which adults find themselves, we may make an optimistic prediction. With increasing economic productivity, people in the high-productive countries will have greater incomes and more free time. More countries will become highly productive. Also, people will have as good health and vigor through their adult years as they have today. Thus the external situation will favor more leisure activity.

There will be an increase of expressive activity, or play, due to the pervasive change of values which is coming to post-industrial societies. That is, a cohort of people born in 1940 will be more play-oriented and less work-oriented than a cohort born in 1910.

The importance of free-time activity and the nature of free-time activity for a particular person are functions of his personality. This proposition has some face validity, but has not been subjected to a rigorous empirical test. A few studies have been made of personality and personality change during adulthood, but they have not singled out leisure activity as a personality characteristic to be investigated explicitly. There are some suggestions in the studies by Reichard et al. (1962) and by Neugarten (1964) that patterns of leisure activity are systematically related to personality patterns.

It is still an open question whether the pattern of leisure activity that we see in a 70-year-old person could have been predicted by observing this person at the age of 30 or 40. The stability of leisure pattern is probably related to stability of personality and of life-style. Our information on these matters is limited by the scarcity of longitudinal data concerning personality through the adult years. Cross-sectional studies show a low or insignificant correlation of personality and leisure patterns with age between 40 and 70 (Havighurst, 1957), thus indicating that such patterns do not change their incidence in a study group in relation to age. Maddox (1968) found life-style to be stable in the Duke University longitudinal study among elderly people over a period of seven years.

In general, the evidence indicates that personality organization and structure is rather stable through the adult years, and therefore life-style, including leisure style, may be expected to be stable. However, the personality must deal with the various contingencies in life, such as health, family events, political and economic events, and these may force some adaptation of his life and leisure styles.

Leisure activity and leisure patterns will probably become more significant for life satisfaction of the individual and more salient as determiners of the quality of a society in the years ahead.

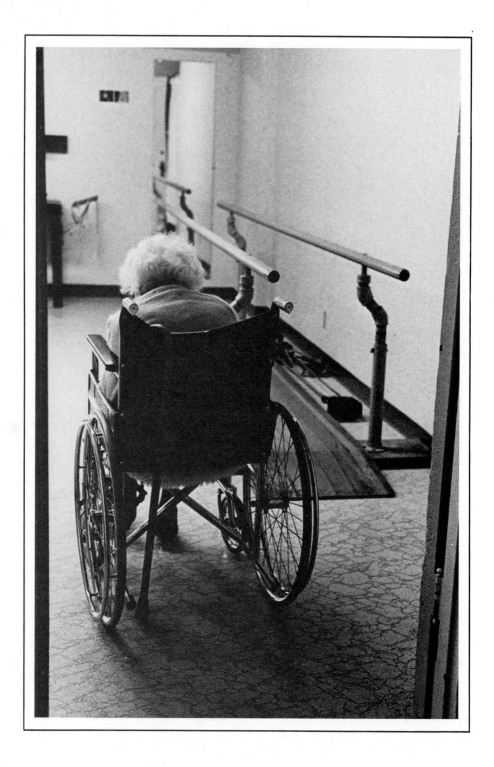

Chapter 5

Health and Illness

In the National Council on the Aging (NCOA) survey (1975), most older people stated that poor health was the worst thing about being over age 65. In fact, three times as many respondents cited the *health factor* as the greatest single problem of aging as cited *loneliness*, which ranked second. And these figures hold for men and for women, for Whites and for Blacks, for people of low income/limited education and for those of high income/high education. Furthermore, when the same people were asked to explain the basis on which they defined "old," they cited physical changes as their primary criteria. When they were asked what they personally experienced as problems of aging, 50% of those over 65 listed poor health as "very serious" or "somewhat serious," again ranking it first. (When the data analysis was limited to the response "very serious," the problem of *health* was second to *fear of crime.*)

So there is little doubt that health looms large as a problem for the elderly, both among those who are over the age of 65 and among those who are younger. But many, probably most, of the older people have accommodated themselves to health difficulties, and they function with—or in spite of—whatever limitations poor health imposes.

A decline in health has many effects on individuals of any age. It may result in limitations on one's ability to get around, unhappiness over loss of competence, and considerable cost in time and in money. But there is an element in poor health that affects the elderly that generally does not affect the nonelderly: with advancing age, the recuperation process slows down, and complete recovery may never occur. The idea that an illness a person has may lead to a downhill path from which there is no return is obviously distressing.

In distinction to these fears is the essential optimism of the elderly. Although most people over the age of 65 cite declining health as a major problem, they also appear to be able to get on with the task of living. Perhaps because they use their own age peers as a reference group, or perhaps because they have seen illnesses much more serious than their own and many deaths, most older people state that they are in pretty good health. "Not as good as 40 years ago, maybe, but not bad. I get by."

So there is a dual nature to the health of the elderly. The objective reality, as described by data and biomedicine, indicates declining health, eventuating in death. And the subjective reality, as perceived by large numbers of elderly, is "Oh, yes, I do have problems—mild diabetes, 20% loss of hearing, some glaucoma, one moderate coronary behind me, some arthritis—but I'm really fine." And they mean that whatever discomfort they have, it is worth it to be alive.

Health, of course, is not something attributable to an isolated physical organism. Interest in holistic medicine, a health-care approach that takes into account personal attitudes, feelings, self-esteem, family and friendship relationships, and cognitive stimulation, is rapidly growing. When people feel depressed, angry with themselves, or helpless and hopeless, they are more likely to perform overtly self-destructive acts. Perhaps they also become self-destructive by losing the will-to-live or by developing the will-to-die. The practice of psychosomatic medicine has been developed to examine possible interrelationships between mental attitudes and physical symptoms. Whether psychological orientation affects the body directly has not been established, but many health-care professionals believe it does. It has been observed that negative attitudes and even a sense of resignation may decrease an individual's willingness to follow prescribed health-care procedures; that is, a person may ignore medications, not eat properly, become careless, or get insufficient exercise. Mental attitudes also might affect such body processes as digestion, respiration, and cardiovascular function. Also, and again we must say "perhaps," resistance to the progress of disease may be influenced by psychological factors. We know that body chemistry is altered by emotions and that people have the ability, through a feedback system, to exert some control over both voluntary and involuntary body functions. It seems possible that this ability *might* also be exerted to forestall the growth of cancer cells or to help increase the effectiveness of the blood flow.

If negative attitudes do affect physical well-being, the elderly are particularly at risk, since their resistance is already lower, and it would take less change in their immunological functioning to permit a disease to become more serious or even to lead to death. This is very speculative, but we do need to keep in mind the possibility that the psychological and social treatment of the elderly can be assumed to have direct effects on physiological health.

Health Factors in Aging*

C. J. Tupper

Health is so important to all of us, and since for the elderly it seems to be a major—perhaps the *major—concern, it is valuable to examine what we know about health conditions in the later years. We actually know quite a bit about geriatric health problems, but we don't know how to make them go away. In the section that follows, Dr. Tupper shows both clinical insight and personal understanding of the elderly patient. Although he writes of disease entities, it is easy to see his sensitivity to the human beings who are afflicted with the medical conditions. At the same time, he continues to emphasize that aging is a process, not a sudden happening, and that conditions first noted in old age have their origins in youth.*

The medical knowledge we possess about the phenomenon of aging is generally considered to be collected under the title "Geriatrics." In my opinion, however, geriatrics is not a clearly defined medical specialty; rather, it is a philosophy. Geriatric medicine involves a specialized approach to the health of the aging, as well as the aged, and the aging process begins with conception and ends at death. Health in old age is predicated on health in youth and throughout maturity, and thus the practitioner of geriatric medicine must have an attitude of anticipation as he or she observes the physiologic, structural, and immunologic changes that occur throughout the human life-cycle.

The process of aging is not symmetrical in the human race or in the individual. We all know people who are very old at the age of 50 and people of 80 who are very young. Likewise, in the individual, various parts of the anatomy age at different rates. I find it difficult to accept the idea that we can select a particular age as the point at which geriatrics begins. In my opinion, the practice of geriatric medicine should begin in the mid-thirties and early forties. Every experience we have, whether physical, mental, biochemical, or immunologic, leaves its traces, so each of us is largely a product of our yesteryears.

A research team at the Washington University School of Medicine, St. Louis, studied 200 human sternoclavicular joints at autopsy. The investigators chose the joint between the collarbone and the breastbone because it does not bear weight and therefore is relatively free of the influences of a lifetime of shifting weight. They noted that age changes in this joint began as early as the third decade and progressed with age. The lesions of osteoarthritis also appeared early and became progressively more severe with age. Over 90 percent of the individuals studied were affected with varying degrees of osteoarthritis of the sternoclavicular joints. The increase in severity of disease was steady up to the age of 80. Men were more susceptible than women; Blacks more than Whites; obese more than nonobese; and diabetic more than nondiabetic.

It is clear, however, that there are changes seen so frequently in aging in the usual sense that we have come to look upon them as normal (physiologic) rather than abnormal (pathologic). It may well be that some conditions that we accept as natural concomitants of aging will be redefined in the future. Science, however, must work within the limits of knowledge.

One key feature of aging is a generalized loss of elasticity. This occurs throughout the system, but the most familiar changes are in skin and hair, bones and teeth, and eyes and ears. The effects of reduced elasticity in the blood vessels and the lungs are not so apparent, but certainly they are equivalent to the changes in other body systems.

THE NERVOUS SYSTEM

With advancing age, the nervous system—that complex set of electronic wiring and gear that helps make man so magnificent—begins to slow down. With this change, lengthened reaction time is apparent, hand tremors may occur, and the onset of fatigue comes earlier and with less exertion. Though tasks may be performed more slowly, the quality level of performance seldom is diminished.

The incidence of cerebrovascular accidents (strokes) also increases with age. These episodes often are characterized by periods of unconsciousness and varying degrees of paralysis. A stroke may be caused by hemorrhage from a broken blood vessel, by thrombosis (a clot blocking a blood vessel), or by embolism (transport of a clot formed in another part of the circulatory system to a blood vessel of the brain, where it lodges and obstructs blood flow). Many strokes are not fatal; some are transient, with no apparent damage; others cause varying degrees of temporary or permanent functional impairment or paralysis. For the patient who has suffered even a mild stroke, active and vigorous rehabilitation is indicated, and careful attention should be paid to the total health of the individual.

THE EYES

The eyes, an extension of the central nervous system, specifically the brain, show characteristic changes with age. Such changes generally appear in the late thirties or early forties, with the development of *presbyopia,* or aging eye. The human eye has an infinite number of distances at which it can focus, thanks to the flexibility of the crystalline lens. As this flexibility becomes reduced, near vision is impaired, and the fine print in the telephone book or the classified ads is difficult to see at close range. To compensate for this difficulty, people often hold what they are reading at arm's length; a more convenient solution is corrective lenses. Another eye problem associated with age is cataract, or clouding of the lens. This condition can be surgically corrected. Glaucoma, or an increased pressure within the eye, which may lead to blindness, can be detected by measuring the eye pressure with an instrument called a *tonometer*. In most cases, progression of glaucoma can be prevented.

THE EARS

The reduction in hearing acuity associated with age is termed *presbyacusis*. Some, but not all, people with hearing loss can be helped with a hearing aid.

THE DIGESTIVE SYSTEM

The Teeth

The teeth play an important role in general nutrition and physical appearance, so good oral health is important. We should never forget that digestion begins in the mouth, where the enzymes in saliva begin the breakdown of starches. In dentistry, we have moved gradually away from the DMF (decayed, missing, and filled) philosophy to a positive approach that gives much more attention to diseases of the gums and supporting structures of the teeth. Gum disease, formerly referred to as *pyorrhea* and now called *periodontitis*, begins to show its effects in people in their thirties and forties. Good dental care throughout these years can help to preserve natural teeth. If dentures do become necessary, it is important that they fit properly.

The Digestive Tract

The changes of senescence are in part consequences of cellular malnourishment. Nutrition includes the ingestion of food and its digestion, but these functions are merely preliminaries to the absorption, transport, and utilization of nutrients at the cellular level. Malnutrition may be caused by factors operating inside the body or by factors in the environment; it may include excesses as well as deficiencies in diet. Diet can be adjusted to compensate in part for internal changes associated with age.

With age, levels of normal gastric acidity become reduced. In fact, approximately 20 percent of men over the age of 65 have no free acid in their stomachs. Gall bladder disease is also common among the elderly. More women are affected than men, and gall bladder disease is found in association with obesity more often than not. Constipation in older people is usually a problem that is related to an inadequate intake of water and roughage in the diet, together with inadequate exercise. With aging, oxygen needs and caloric requirements decrease as activity levels become reduced. Even if people do the same things, they do them more slowly. Therefore, even if caloric intake is not increased, the older individual will gain weight. It is interesting to note that as we grow older, our needs for protein increase and yet our desires for it tend to decrease. If protein intake is inadequate over time, such changes as tissue wastage, bone atrophy, anemia, and, finally, swelling or edema occur. Also with age, the ability of the cells to absorb calcium tends to decline. Calcium loss may lead to a lightening of the bone structure called *osteoporosis* and an increased vulnerability to bone fractures. The fractured hip seen in the elderly as a result of a fall is frequently related to osteoporosis.

THE MUSCULOSKELETAL STRUCTURE

Arthritis and rheumatism are common concomitants of aging. In older people, osteoarthritis, or degenerative arthritis, is the most common type. Where wear and tear on the bones and joints has been accelerated, as in the hands of the farmer or the sailor or the knees of the professional football player, the knobby hands and stiff knees that we see in other people at older ages make their appearance earlier. Rheumatoid arthritis, a crippling disease, generally affects the young, with improvement occurring by the age of 40. In some cases, however, joint inflammation continues into old age. Some older people also suffer the residual deformities from rheumatoid arthritis with which they were afflicted earlier in life. Physical medicine has much to offer these people, and there are many devices that improve their joint function and enhance their level of activity.

THE CARDIOVASCULAR SYSTEM

The primary effect of aging on the heart and blood vessels is the loss of elasticity. Two terms are utilized in this regard: *arteriosclerosis* and *atherosclerosis*. The arteries are made up of three layers, a lining, a middle muscular layer, and an outer layer. In arteriosclerosis, progressive deposition of calcium in the middle muscular layer causes the arteries to become increasingly rigid. As a result, when the heart contracts and forces blood through the aorta to the arteries, the blood pressure becomes abnormally elevated (*hypertension*). With relaxation of the heart, the arteries are relieved of their workload, and the blood pressure returns to a more normal level immediately preceding the next contraction. Other factors influence blood pressure, but regardless of cause, it appears to be better tolerated by women than by men. In most cases, drug therapy is effective in controlling blood pressure levels. Atherosclerosis, however, has different consequences. It, too, is a progressive disease in which fatty deposits collect between the lining layer and the middle layer of the blood vessel. Sometimes these deposits break through to the inside of an artery and create rough spots on which blood may clot. As clotting develops, the internal diameter of the vessel is narrowed, and blood flow is therefore reduced. When this happens in the coronary arteries, which supply the heart muscle itself with blood, heart function may become impaired. Because the blood carries oxygen and essential nutrients throughout the body, when blood flow to any area is reduced or cut off, that area is deprived of necessary oxygen and sustenance. In the case of the heart, when the oxygen supply to cardiac muscle is reduced, the tissue is, in a sense, strangled, and struggles to get more oxygen. When this occurs, the chest pains known as *angina pectoris* develop. If the blood supply to any area of the heart muscle is cut off completely, that portion cannot survive. This condition, *coronary occlusion with myocardial infarction*, is commonly known as a heart attack. There are three major coronary arteries, so occlusion of one does not necessarily lead to death. In fact, only 12 percent of those affected die following a first heart attack. The risk, however, increases with succeeding attacks. People with coronary atherosclerosis can be assisted in reducing the risk of a first or subsequent heart attack with drug therapy and with adjustments in diet and life-style.

Another heart ailment that affects many older people is *congestive heart failure*. The most common symptoms of this condition are shortness of breath, severe discomfort when lying flat, and swelling of the ankles. Here again, medical management can be most helpful, but patterns of living may need to be changed, and even the matter of appropriate living quarters on one floor, without steps, may be extremely important.

As I said earlier, when the capacity of an artery to transmit blood is reduced to the point that inadequate oxygen is delivered to the tissues, then pain such as angina pectoris results. When such a reduction in blood flow involves the lower part of the aorta or the arteries leading to the legs, the condition known as intermittent claudication (an episode of lameness and pain) can develop. Such pain develops with walking and usually is relieved by rest. Individuals who experience any of the symptoms suggestive of obstructive atherosclerosis should be evaluated medically. There are many forms of treatment, including operations in which obstructed arteries may be repaired or bypassed.

THE PULMONARY SYSTEM

The chest and lungs demonstrate further that a loss of tissue elasticity is a physiologic concomitant of aging. Emphysema occurs with increasing incidence in our population. It involves an overexpansion of the lungs, which causes the chest to become bigger, but air is moved in and out of the lungs much less efficiently. This causes shortness of breath and also predisposes to such respiratory tract diseases as chronic bronchitis. The patient who has been asthmatic is inclined to develop emphysema at an early age. Other major diseases which affect the lungs are tuberculosis and cancer, both of which occur frequently and without respect for age.

THE GENITOURINARY SYSTEM

The cessation of menstruation is a normal feature of aging for the women in our society, and there appears to be a gradual increase in the age at which the menopause occurs. Today, it is not unusual for women to continue menstruating through their late forties and early fifties, whereas in years gone by, the onset of the menopause was expected to occur in the late thirties or early forties. The fact that menses have ceased does not in any way decrease the need for an annual pelvic examination.

Infections of the urinary tract, particularly of the bladder, are common among older people, but they are frequently difficult to detect because they have few symptoms. Once a urinary tract infection is diagnosed, however, effective treatment may be easily accomplished.

Men characteristically experience progressive enlargement of the prostate gland as they age. The urethra, the canal through which urine is passed externally from the bladder, passes through the center of the prostate gland. With outward enlargement of the prostate, the urethra becomes constricted. Consequently, men with this condition note an increased frequency of urination during their waking hours, and at night as well. Prostate enlargement may eventually cause complete obstruction of the urethra.

This condition can be remedied surgically, and it is surprising how very well men in their seventies and eighties tolerate this surgical procedure and recover without difficulty.

THE ENDOCRINE SYSTEM

The pituitary is the master gland of the body. It controls the function of other glands and is itself responsible for production of the growth hormone. Most older people have essentially normal pituitary activity. Imbalances in the thyroid gland, however, are quite common and lead either to hyper-metabolism with overactivity and weight loss, or more frequently in the elderly, to diminished function, with obesity, intolerance to cold, somnolence, and lassitude. The decrease in thyroid function, termed *hypothyroidism*, can be corrected with the administration of thyroid hormone. Inadequate iodine in the diet may give rise to an enlargement of the thyroid gland termed *goiter*.

The pancreas gland is responsible for carbohydrate metabolism, or the assimilation of sugars and starches into the body tissues. When it does its job inadequately, sugar diabetes (*diabetes mellitus*) is the result. Among diabetics, some 80 percent are obese at the onset of the disease. Diabetes most often begins late in life, in which cases it often can be controlled with adjustments in diet and the oral administration of insulin. Because older people generally show a reduction in carbohydrate assimilation, the diagnostic criteria for diabetes in older people are currently being revised.

The parathyroid glands are responsible for calcium metabolism. With reduced calcium intake, the secretions from these glands mobilize calcium from the bone tissue in order to maintain the proper calcium level in the blood. In time, the depletion of the calcium deposited in the bones leads to osteoporosis, which as I have mentioned, lightens the bone structure.

The adrenal glands, which are located on top of either kidney, are very important because they supply the body with hydrocortisone, the source of support in times of stress. In Addison's disease the adrenal glands become relatively inactive, and the afflicted individual has very poor responses to stress, so replacement treatment is necessary.

The hormonal functions of testes and ovaries also show a decrease as aging proceeds. The production of female sex hormones, however, continues long after the menopause has occurred, and estrogen production is thought to delay progressive atherosclerosis. For example, a man and a woman at thirty years of age are strikingly different in their susceptibility to coronary artery disease. The man is 20 times more likely to have a heart attack than the woman. With age, the odds lessen, but it is not until the age of 70 that the female has an equal chance of suffering a heart attack. The decrease in function of both the ovaries and the testes with age is reflected in a decrease in calcium absorption and some changes in blood fat content. Here again, the tendency of the elderly to continue previous dietary habits may result in changes in health status that are not immediately apparent.

The aging skin is more susceptible to the development of such skin cancers as *epithelioma, squamous cell carcinoma,* and *basal cell carcinoma.* Other skin lesions called *senile keratoses* are quite benign but are frequent in the aging individual. Generally speaking, any skin defect, particularly one that is raised, pearly white, or appears as a sore that does not heal, should be evaluated medically, because with treatment, skin cancers can generally be completely cured.

The use of the word cancer brings us to the question, "Are degenerative and malignant diseases a normal expectancy of aging?" My answer to that question must be a qualified "no." As I have indicated, some of those things currently considered to be physiologic aging may actually represent the consequences of cellular malnourishment. This means that we must pay more attention to preventive nutrition, as well as to preventive health; that we must eliminate from our environment those agents that are now known to be carcinogenic (cancer-causing); and that we must continue the intensive research effort currently under way to elucidate the causes of cancer.

I think the outlook for the future, where health is concerned, is a very optimistic one. It is important, however, for us to concern ourselves not only with increasing the human life span, but also with enhancing the quality of life so that as people live longer they will also be content in their later years.

*Life Expectancy and Major Causes of Death**

The previous section offered a humane discussion of the most common medical problems of the elderly. The next section is a straight statistical presentation of the numbers of persons affected by health problems. You will need to use some imagination to consider the numbers in terms of people who are suffering varying degrees of pain, discomfort, and reduced functional ability—and in some instances, people who are faced with imminent death. If you put the two sections together—the nature of the health condition and the numbers of people who are its victims—you can better understand the immense impact of health concerns on the spirit of the elderly. If you can go a step further and imagine yourself a 70-year-old person with arthritis, limited hearing, a cardiovascular condition, or perhaps all three (and that is not unusual), then you may come a bit closer to understanding what the elderly confront, often with great personal strength.

The National Center for Health Statistics prepared the text and the tables that follow. Some data are a few years old, but the changes in numbers

---

*From *Health in the Later Years of Life: Selected Data From the National Center for Health Statistics*. Washington, D.C.: U.S. Government Printing Office, 1971.

have not been substantial.[1] *Most statistics in the report are based on the noninstitutionalized elderly, or 95 percent of the U.S. population over the age of 65. The remaining 5 percent, who live in nursing homes, mental hospitals, and other institutions, obviously are in poorer health, on the whole, than the 95 percent living in the community. Had the institutionalized elderly been included in the statistical analysis, many rates would have been slightly higher.*

LIFE EXPECTANCY

Average length of life is a traditional measure of the health status of people of all ages. By this standard, the health status of older Americans of the 1970's is markedly better than that of earlier generations. People who are 45, for example, have already lived almost as long as the average person born in 1900 could have expected to live, and, today, they have about 30 more years of life remaining.

In only a few countries in the world does the life expectancy of women ages 45 and 65 exceed that of American women. However, there are many countries in which older men have a longer life expectancy than do American men. (See Figure 1.)

In the United States, there are significant differences in average expectation of life by sex and by race. Older women have a longer life expectancy than do older men, and, in general, white people will live longer than non-white people (see Table 1).

Average life expectancy reflects the death rate at various ages. Generally speaking, the lower the death rate, the higher the life expectancy, and vice versa. The death rate has long been used as an important measure of a people's health status. After a steady decline from the late 19th century, the death rate in the United States has remained roughly the same since about 1955. There has been little further decrease in the rates for older men and only slightly more for older women. Even so, it is not until age 65 and over that the death rate exceeds the high rate for children in the first year of life.

A most striking change in recent mortality trends is the widening gap between the death rates for men and women at the older ages. For example, among white men at ages 55–64, the death rate in 1940 was about 50 percent higher than for white women. In 1950, it was about 80 percent higher, and by 1974 it was more than double the rate for women. A similar but narrower divergence characterizes the rates for non-white men and women.

Differences in mortality by occupation, income, education, and other characteristics provide further insight into such trends. Many special studies indicate that these factors do substantially affect mortality levels. For example, socioeconomic characteristics seem to account for a large part of the differences between death rates for white and non-white persons.

[1]Updated statistics are from the *Statistical Abstract of the U.S.*, October 1976, prepared by the U.S. Bureau of the Census.

Figure 1.   Life expectancy for men and women over age 65 in 14 countries of the world. (From United Nations 1969, Demographic Yearbook. Copyright, United Nations, 1969. Reprinted by permission.)

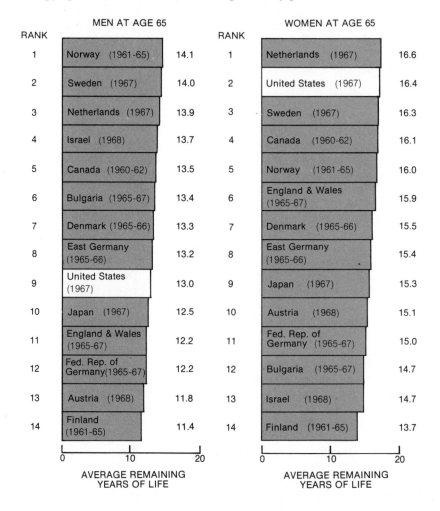

RANK	MEN AT AGE 65		RANK	WOMEN AT AGE 65	
1	Norway (1961-65)	14.1	1	Netherlands (1967)	16.6
2	Sweden (1967)	14.0	2	United States (1967)	16.4
3	Netherlands (1967)	13.9	3	Sweden (1967)	16.3
4	Israel (1968)	13.7	4	Canada (1960-62)	16.1
5	Canada (1960-62)	13.5	5	Norway (1961-65)	16.0
6	Bulgaria (1965-67)	13.4	6	England & Wales (1965-67)	15.9
7	Denmark (1965-66)	13.3	7	Denmark (1965-66)	15.5
8	East Germany (1965-66)	13.2	8	East Germany (1965-66)	15.4
9	United States (1967)	13.0	9	Japan (1967)	15.3
10	Japan (1967)	12.5	10	Austria (1968)	15.1
11	England & Wales (1965-67)	12.2	11	Fed. Rep. of Germany (1965-67)	15.0
12	Fed. Rep. of Germany(1965-67)	12.2	12	Bulgaria (1965-67)	14.7
13	Austria (1968)	11.8	13	Israel (1968)	14.7
14	Finland (1961-65)	11.4	14	Finland (1961-65)	13.7

AVERAGE REMAINING
YEARS OF LIFE

AVERAGE REMAINING
YEARS OF LIFE

MAJOR CAUSES OF DEATH

Diseases of the heart, malignant neoplasms (cancer), and cerebrovascular diseases (mainly stroke) are the major causes of death for older Americans. Together these three conditions accounted for nearly 70% of the 1.7 million deaths of people aged 45 and over in 1968. Heart disease is by far the leader, causing over 40% of the deaths. These conditions contributed 75% of the causes of death to persons 65 years of age and over in the same year.

Accidents rank fourth among the causes of death for the middle aged (45–64 years); influenza and pneumonia hold this rank for the older group.

Table 1.   Average remaining years of life at ages 45, 65, and 75, by sex and color: United States, 1974

Sex and Color	Average Remaining Years of Life		
	At Age 45	*At Age 65*	*At Age 75*
WHITE			
Men	28.1	13.4	8.3
Women	34.3	17.6	10.7
NON-WHITE			
Men	25.5	13.4	9.6
Women	31.1	16.7	11.8

Other major causes of death for those in the later years of life include bronchitis, emphysema, and asthma; arteriosclerosis; diabetes; and cirrhosis of the liver.

CHRONIC DISEASES AND ACUTE CONDITIONS

The lives of millions of older Americans are affected daily by illnesses or impairments, for chronic health problems increase sharply with advancing age. Indeed, chronic diseases might well be called "companions of the aged." The statistics are striking: 85 percent of those 65 and over living outside of institutions have at least one chronic condition, and about half of these individuals suffer some limitation of activity because of chronic conditions. Information on these health problems has been gathered from two surveys conducted by the National Center for Health Statistics—health examinations and household interviews, both excluding persons living in institutions. The data from the health examinations provide estimates of the prevalence of selected diseases and impairments, while those from the household interviews indicate the extent to which illnesses of all types interfere with normal activities.

Heart disease, hypertension, diabetes, and arthritis—four of the major chronic diseases studied by the Health Examination Survey—occur more frequently as aging progresses, and all four are more common among women than among men. Heart disease and hypertension affect roughly the same proportions of the older population. At ages 45–64 nearly one-sixth of white men and women have definite heart disease, while over one-third of the black men and women have this condition. For the older age group, the percentages increase sharply. Both heart disease and hypertension are much more prevalent among the black population than among the white; the higher frequency for blacks 45–64 years of age is particularly notable (see Figure 2).

Arthritis, one of man's oldest known ailments, frequently causes permanent joint deformities and chronic invalidism. Of its two major forms,

Figure 2.   Prevalence of heart disease at ages 45–64 and 65–79, by sex and race: United States, 1960–1962.

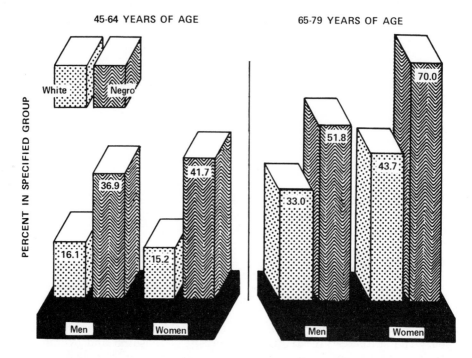

osteoarthritis (degenerative joint disease) occurs far more frequently than rheumatoid arthritis. Both forms most often affect the hands and feet. Over 50 percent of middle-aged men and women and about 80 percent of the older group have some degree of osteoarthritis.

Diabetes is rarely reported for young people; in fact, the disease is about ten times more frequent after age 65. The proportions of older people with known diabetes are relatively small in comparison with heart disease, hypertension, and arthritis. However, many additional persons were suspected of being diabetic on the basis of limited glucose tolerance test results and urine analyses, but their conditions had not been diagnosed by physicians prior to the examinations.

As part of the Health Examination Survey, participants were asked to fill out a Medical History Questionnaire. They answered a number of questions about their experience with symptoms of psychological distress or nervous breakdown. At ages 45–64 years, about 4 percent of both white and black men reported having had what they considered a nervous breakdown. More women in this age group reported affirmatively; 9 percent of white women and 14 percent of black women. The percentages are generally slightly higher at ages 65–79.

Dental problems, primarily loss of teeth and periodontal disease, also increase with age. Over one-fourth of the middle-aged people have lost all their teeth; about half of the older age group are also toothless (edentulous). Fortunately, a good majority of these edentulous people have satisfactory artificial dentures. A very high proportion of older Americans have periodontal disease—an inflammatory disease of the tissues surrounding and supporting the teeth and a leading cause of tooth loss. At ages 45–64, about 85 percent of the men and 76 percent of the women with any natural teeth have periodontal disease; at 65–79 years, the percentages are even higher.

Poor vision becomes much more common after age 45, particularly among women. Moderate to severely defective visual acuity is about twice as prevalent among older persons as among the middle-aged (see Figure 3).

Figure 3.   Visual acuity, uncorrected, at ages 45–64 and 65–79, by sex: United States, 1960–1962.

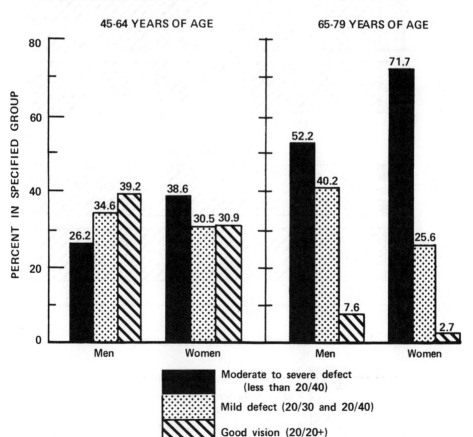

As would be expected, the use of corrective lenses also increases with age; even with their usual correction, about 5 percent of those in the middle-aged group have severe or moderately severe impairment of vision, and these percentages more than triple for the elderly. Among men and women in both age classes, the proportion with severely defective vision, with their usual correction, is substantially higher in the lower income groups.

The rise in hearing impairment with advancing age is quite dramatic—the rate of impaired hearing for persons 65–79 is about 40 times that for those between 18 and 24 (see Figure 4). The percentages of people

Figure 4.   Hearing impairment at ages 45–64 and 65–79, by sex: United States, 1960–1962. (Impairment is limited to frequencies essential for speech—500, 1000, and 2000 hertz.)

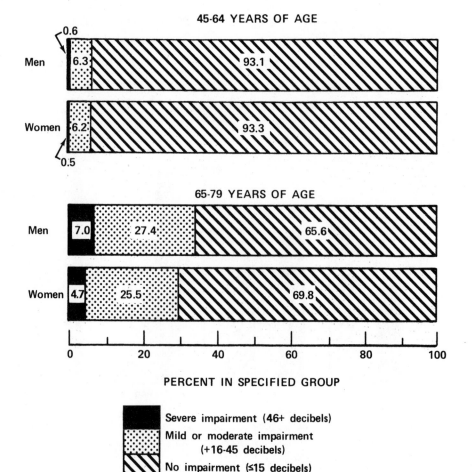

with some hearing impairment range from about 7 percent for the middle-aged group to 30 percent or more for the older group. Many cases of hearing impairment can be improved by a hearing aid. Among those 45 years and over with a hearing loss in both ears, about one in five uses a hearing aid, according to data from the household interviews.

Orthopedic defects—impairment of limbs, back, and trunk—are another chronic health problem particularly affecting older Americans. Data from household interviews reveal that about 16 orthopedic defects (not counting absence of limbs or paralysis) occur per 100 persons over age 45. The principal cause of these impairments is injury.

Even though chronic conditions are the most frequent health problems among the aged, older people do experience a large number of acute conditions—some 70 million in a recent year—involving activity restriction or medical attendance. Each person over 45 averages at least one such episode during a year, according to the household interviews. The most common acute conditions are respiratory diseases and injuries (Table 2).

Enforced limitation or prevention of normal activities is a principal consequence of chronic health problems among our older population. About two-fifths of persons 65 years and over suffer some limitation of activity (including ability to work, to keep house, to participate in recreational or civic pursuits) because of chronic conditions—a high rate indeed when com-

Table 2. Incidence of Acute Conditions* at Ages 45–64 and 65 and Over: United States, 1969

	Incidence of Acute Conditions			
	45–64 Years of Age	*65 Years and Over*	*45–64 Years of Age*	*65 Years and Over*
Condition Group	(Number in thousands)		(Number per 100 population in specified group)	
All Acute Conditions*	52,619	17,697	129.2	94.8
Infective and parasitic diseases	4,006	815	9.8	4.4
Respiratory conditions	29,385	8,675	72.1	46.5
Upper respiratory conditions	15,354	3,805	37.7	20.4
Influenza	12,942	4,188	31.8	22.4
Other respiratory conditions	1,089	**	2.7	**
Digestive system conditions	2,656	1,346	6.5	7.2
Injuries	8,712	3,069	21.4	16.4
All other acute conditions	7,859	3,792	19.3	20.3

*Includes only medically attended conditions or those involving restricted activity. Conditions are categorized according to the Eighth Revision, International Classification of Diseases, Adapted for Use in the United States, 1965, with certain modifications.

**Figure does not meet standards of reliability or precision.

pared with those under 17 years of age, of whom only 2 percent are limited in activity. In the middle-aged group, 7 percent of men and about 2 percent of women are in the most severely limited category, that is, unable to carry on their major activities. At the older ages, the proportion of people in this severely limited category is three to four times greater. There is a clear racial differential in the proportion of people unable to work or keep house; the percentages for non-whites are almost twice as high as those for the white group.

There are, of course, many other health conditions that affect the elderly, but this overview has provided a sampling of the most important among them.

The Dying Process*

Richard A. Kalish

The first section in this chapter focused on disease entities; the second section was concerned with health statistics. The third selection looks at the feelings and thoughts of the individual in poor health, particularly one who is seriously ill and believes he or she is dying.

Death certainly is not selective for age. In our time, however, most people who survive to maturity will live into old age. In times past, death occurred almost randomly across the life span, striking infants and children, women during childbearing, men at war, and general populations through epidemics, poor medical care, unsterile hospitals, and unclean living conditions. Today, although conditions could still be greatly improved, most people in the developed nations die in old age.

Some people never learn that they are dying. They are homicide or accident victims; they die from an initial massive coronary; they die from a progressive disease that has been misdiagnosed, or they have been sufficiently sheltered from knowledge of their real condition that death is not anticipated. We can only estimate how many die in this fashion. More and more evidence has accumulated to suggest that the dying person is much more likely to be aware that he is dying than we have previously believed. However, the dying person is frequently unwilling or unable to share his knowledge with others, even though he recognizes that the others have

*Edited from "The Onset of the Dying Process," by R. A. Kalish, *Omega*, 1970, *1*, 57–59. Reprinted by permission of Greenwood Periodicals, Inc.

access to the same knowledge. There is a mutual pretense situation (Glaser & Strauss, 1965).

Most often the fatally ill person has some recognition of his circumstances. To gain this awareness, there must be some sort of informational input. Such input may be categorized in several ways.

First, it may be explicit in varying degrees. The physician who informs his patient point blank of a terminal condition is providing highly explicit information. Data, however, indicate that relatively few physicians will take this frontal approach. More commonly only hints are given. In many instances, the physician conspires with a family member, while the dying person himself is told nothing; nonetheless, he learns—from overhearing conversations, from comparing symptoms to those of people he has known, from the bedside stage whispers of physicians, nurses, relatives, friends, and others, from worried looks on faces, from questions about wills and funerals. The clues are too numerous to mention. One dying woman went so far as to tell her son, her one confidant, that "Everyone must think I'm either stupid or deaf—they stand at the foot of the bed and talk about when I'm going to die, then they come up to the head of the bed and smile and tell me how well I'm looking and how quickly I'll be out of here." Since explicit information is frequently lacking, the terminal person must put together the available information like a puzzle.

Second, the input may be complete or incomplete. There might be the kind of information that permits the person to know, without doubt, that his condition is fatal. Or there might be enough to make a judgment, but without knowing for sure. Completeness and explicitness are related, but are far from identical. A physician might very explicitly tell a patient that his condition is serious, but not give enough information for the patient to determine whether the illness is fatal. An explicit but incomplete statement might be "You have a malignant tumor in your stomach, but it is possible that an operation would remove it completely." An example of a non-explicit and incomplete statement would be "You seem to have something seriously wrong with you, but we'll do some more tests and see if it isn't something we can take care of." Explicit and complete: "Your tests show that you have a malignancy that is—as far as I can now determine—inoperable." By definition, a complete but non-explicit statement would be impossible. However, the patient may obtain complete information without ever hearing an explicit statement, merely by putting together a variety of vague comments, behavioral nuances, and other clues into a coherent picture.

A third way of categorizing informational input is according to the source of information. The patient may learn from any one or combination of the following ways:

1. A direct statement from the physician. Inevitably, this may occur in a variety of ways, ranging from gentle to abrupt, from lengthy to brief, from encouraging questions and other responses to shutting off discussion.

2. Overheard comments made by the physician to others. Patients are frequently discussed in their presence as though they were inanimate ob-

jects. Stage whispers at the foot of the bed, explanations from physician to nurses, and so forth, may be informative.

3. Direct statements from other health care personnel, particularly nurses. This would normally occur only in response to direct questioning on the part of the patient, although occasionally a nurse will feel that the physician has shirked his responsibility and she will find some method of eliciting the direct question so that she must answer it. This is a rare circumstance, however.

4. Overheard comments made by other health care personnel. This parallels the statements of physicians.

5. Direct statements by others involved, such as a family member, a social worker, a clergyman, or the family lawyer. This occurrence is also unusual, since for a variety of reasons, the physician is normally the individual to take the responsibility for direct comments.

6. Overheard comments by others involved. Again, this is similar to comments overheard from the physician.

7. Changes in behavior of others. In some instances, the visits of the attending physician drop off after a terminal diagnosis is made. The interactions with nurses and other staff members become more abrupt. Friends and relatives who visit may exhibit additional strain through unduly forced cheerfulness, through sudden wires and telephone calls to out-of-town family who soon appear on the scene (after all, what would prompt a brother living 2000 miles away to drop by for a casual visit?), through poorly masked tears, through tense admonitions that everything will be all right. Hushed voices or false joviality become more frequent, from both family and professional staff.

8. Changes in medical care procedures. Different medication is now given. Exploratory surgery produces neither report nor follow-up. The patient is given narcotics and other painkillers more readily.

9. Changes in physical placement. The patient is moved to another room or another ward. He is sent home or there is talk of sending him home. The physical location has great significance in terms of the progress of his illness.

10. Self-diagnosis. Many patients learn a great deal about their own conditions and the conditions of others. Mixed in with confusion, ignorance, and distortion is a fair amount of truth. Through reading magazine and newspaper articles, through a careful search at the local library, through listening to the fatal symptoms of others, a reasonably valid self-diagnosis can often be made. Even if the diagnosis is incorrect, the degree to which the person accepts it and acts accordingly is extremely important. Sick people will frequently find a source of information describing their own symptoms.

11. The signals from within the body. As pain and discomfort increase, as curative and ameliorative efforts become progressively less successful, as sedation becomes more necessary, the fatally ill person often senses the changes within his own body and understands that his future is brief.

12. Altered responses to personal futurity. Discussion of the future suddenly takes a new tack. Visitors and hospital staff become reluctant to

talk about future plans. Queries about funerals, burial, wills, and so forth enter the conversation surreptitiously—or else are aggressively avoided. Slips of the tongue are made and corrected with great embarrassment.

A person can respond to the informational input in many ways. He may be able to absorb the information immediately and completely, even though it is totally unexpected. Or he may accept one clue, live with it a while, and learn to deal with the entering wedge of probability of impending death, then return to consider another clue. Or he may vacillate, move back and forth between acceptance and denial, or accept and deny simultaneously. He may overtly express his knowledge that he will die, while not emotionally accepting it. Conversely, he may be able to accept his own dying, but be unwilling to verbalize his feelings and knowledge. And he may deny his circumstances completely. Many physicians have reported making a direct, explicit statement to a patient concerning his medical condition, only to have the patient deny ever having heard such a statement a month later. The patient, of course, can distort the information by seizing upon the thread of hope the physician holds out, by seeking other medical opinions or treatment, by visiting faith healers and those who offer pseudo-medical help, by redefining the probability of survival, by denying the existence of a particular symptom, and in other ways.

The patient also may misinterpret clues and assume he is dying, when in actual fact he is not at all likely to die. In this context also, the family mutual pretense situation will prevent the patient from establishing an effective two-way communication system. He does not know how—or is unwilling—to send out the kind of signal that would elicit the feedback needed to give him appropriate answers. Knowing that the dying person is not told the truth (indeed, he has probably participated in the deception of others), the non-dying patient may ignore all the clues that may be interpreted as suggesting a fatal illness. After all, it is very easy to re-interpret a sincere smile into a forced smile, a valid word of encouragement into an attempt to reduce anxieties, a conversation between doctor and nurse as to the outcome of the football pool into a conversation on a forthcoming rapid decline.

For the dying person—and equally for the person who suspects that he is dying—vague and otherwise meaningless events suddenly become Rorschach cards into which he projects his fears and hopes. If the psychological set is that dying is likely, the interpretation of the environment will reinforce the set. The more his circumstances, his past history, his symptoms, etcetera resemble his concept of a fatal illness, the more likely he is to interpret whatever feedback occurs as signifying dying.

Tasks of the Dying Person

As the fatally ill person copes with the process of learning about his own coming death, he also undertakes a variety of added tasks. Until his acceptance of his own fatal condition is complete, his need to accomplish the related tasks may not be sufficient to produce action or at least to produce sustained action. As an example: a dying person might need to consider the financial circumstances of his survivors and plan for them. However, a non-dying person either is required to make other plans or is able to postpone the entire concern of planning. As the ill person is increasingly convinced that he is dying, he may be increasingly motivated (assuming physical and intellectual functioning is appropriate) to plan for the family. Very possibly he will pass through periods when dying seems impossible or improbable. At any given point in time, denial may be struggling with reality so that he simultaneously feels that he (a) must and (b) need not take immediate steps in this regard.

This may serve as the first example of a task of the dying person: he must contemplate arranging a variety of affairs. Inevitably he does not have to do anything concrete—but it is doubtful if he can avoid contemplation. Thus, he may wish to verify, alter, or initiate a will; he wants to have back debts paid off; he may have messages for friends, neighbors, relatives, co-workers. He wants to discuss funerals, burial, autopsy, tissue donation. There are undoubtedly other arrangements, including, of course, those that involve inter-personal relationships.

These comments presuppose, of course, that the dying person is sufficiently intact mentally and physically to make the arrangements. Often pain and discomfort, fear and anxiety, or confusion and disability prevent the dying person from taking such a direct role in arranging his affairs. Of course, if denial has caused him to reject the possibility of dying, he may refuse to make such arrangements because he would feel they were unnecessary.

In addition, if the dying person has received misleading input, he may make inappropriate decisions. Often the family is able to take over most decision-making functions while the ill person merely signs the papers. Why should a sick person, intellectually intact and led to believe that his condition is reversible, suddenly add a codicil to his will, bring together his life insurance policies, and decide whether he wants to donate his eyes to an eye bank?

What occurs is obvious: either the person receives enough input to provide a reasonably clear picture of what is taking place, or else some tasks may be left undone. A mutual pretense situation does not permit the freedom to discuss the dying process, and those in his environment are unable or unwilling to provide the required information. In order to arrange his affairs properly, the dying person must have a reasonably accurate perception of his prognosis. This means that three things must have occurred: first, he must have received sufficiently explicit information, or have been able to bring together information from various sources into an explicit understanding, so that he can recognize the extent of his potential for death; second, he must have received sufficiently complete information to enable him to be fully aware of his condition; third, he must be psychologically able to deal with the clues he receives without resorting to extreme denial or repression or other mechanisms that would permit him to turn aside the implications of the informational input.

The second task is that of dealing with loss, both the loss of the survivors and the loss of the dying person himself. The dying person is often deeply concerned with what his death will mean to his survivors in ways other than legal and financial. He will frequently consider their feelings, their grief, their vulnerability, their isolation, their coming need to establish replacement relationships. Mutual pretense prevents any discussion of these feelings; open awareness permits such discussion, at least in some instances. One woman commented that during her last year of marriage, when her husband was terminal, the mutual deceit placed so much stress on top of an already stressful situation that the year was robbed of the potential it did have for closeness and intimacy.

Similarly, the dying person must accommodate himself to his own loss, i.e. that he is going to lose the entire world that he has known and —at least temporarily—all the people in it. Dealing with impending loss is one of the most difficult tasks for the dying person. In the final analysis, his tears are probably a combination of his own personal sorrow and his capacity to empathize with the sorrow of others.

Task number three is arranging for future medical and other care needs. Often this task can be left to others, but the fatally ill person may wish to take an active role in the way in which he dies. He may wish to consider alternate care arrangements: nursing home, versus own home, versus hospital; hiring a nurse, versus utilizing family members; using narcotics or other painkillers, versus retaining as much self-awareness as possible. It is not that the individual must make final decisions, but that he may wish to participate in the decision-making process.

The fourth task is that of planning his future and allocating whatever time, energy, and financial resources are available. The knowledge that death is imminent changes the meaning of time and futurity. Is this the time to take a trip? To go on an orgy of eating and drinking and other hedonistic activities or an orgy of reading and listening to music? Are walks in the woods more important? Is there one final *beau geste* to be made? Does he want to give away his money while still alive, so that he sees it being enjoyed?

Fifth, the fatally ill person might have to anticipate future pain and discomfort. Additionally, he might be faced with various forms of motor, sensory, and cognitive decrements in performance. None of these prospects is pleasant, and, fortunately, most terminal patients can avoid severe physical pain and extensive changes in functional effectiveness. Again, the realities of the situation are less important than the anticipations and the anxieties. We have learned a little about how to communicate with the dying person to reduce his fears.

The fear of loss of performance capability is extremely great also. The reaction of horror many people express upon seeing an elderly relative or friend reduced to a semi-coherent, shuffling, forgetful figure is common. "I would rather be dead than end up that way" is a frequent statement. Yet, by the time the condition is far enough advanced to be serious, the person is no longer capable of influencing his own destiny.

Other physical changes can occur with equally disruptive effects. Fatal illnesses often produce changes in appearance that are very difficult for either the sick person or those in his environment to accept. Similarly, unpleasant odors can also occur. Accident victims and burn victims are particularly dramatic examples, but cancer and other diseases can have similar impact.

The loss of physical function, the fear of regression, the recognition of loss of control over physical and cognitive capacities, the coming destruction of the body, all these suggest a loss of self or a loss of identity. If the body is shortly to exist no longer, who is he? (Or, more cogently, who are you when your body ceases to function?) Is it sufficient to be a name in the record books, a memory among your friends, a statistic in the Bureau of the Census? We associate ourselves so completely with our physical body that it is difficult to conceptualize our existence apart from the body.

The sixth task is closely related to the fifth: the dying person needs to cope effectively with his own death encounter. I have already mentioned that he must contend with his feelings of loss. Similarly, he must account for his fear of a *rite de passage* from which no one has returned with descriptions of the demands of the new role; he has to deal with the possibility of permanent extinction; he must consider becoming a non-person, a forgotten person, a person whose continuation resides only in memories, official documents, and a few temporary results of work and human relationships.

Seventh, the dying person faces the task of making a decision: to the extent that it is in his power, should he attempt to slow down or to speed up the dying process. The will-to-live is far from established as an effective determinant of life and health; yet, in spite of the inadequacy of research literature, clinical literature and personal reports are filled with examples of the importance of the will-to-live. But the patient's attitude extends beyond the will-to-live. It affects his willingness to follow medical orders, to take medication, to restrict certain eating or drinking or smoking or other activities. It is doubtful whether many patients state to themselves that they want to die sooner or later than the physician has predicted and then set about doing something about it. However, the speeding up or slowing down of the dying process is undoubtedly part of a pervasive pattern of response to the entire sickness–dying role.

The last task to be discussed consists of dealing with the numerous psycho-social problems that might beset a dying person. For example, our society condemns dependency, but the dying person must often anticipate a future of increasing dependency. He is going to be a burden upon his family, regardless of whether he wants to or whether his family accepts him willingly. He may need financial help, personal care, housing, and emotional support. The dying person frequently loses mastery over his environment and, thereby, loses one of the major supports of an adequate self-concept. He must make some adjustment to the sick role or the dying role. In so doing, he must accept the idea that others are going to do for him many things that his own selfhood required he do for himself.

A related matter: our society rewards the person who contributes to it, but causes to feel guilty the person who extracts from it. The dying person, with few exceptions, is not going to make any additional contribution to the community or to his family and friends. He will only remove resources from the society. His lack of productivity may be distressing to himself, and he is likely to reject himself to some degree because of it.

When the professional faces the needs of the dying person to accomplish the handful of tasks previously described, the problem becomes more difficult. Let me return to those tasks in this context.

First. Making arrangements, particularly financial arrangements. Someone is likely to have to help the dying person do this. One of the most persuasive reasons for an open-awareness context is to enable the individual to realize the urgency that he make necessary arrangements. We may underestimate the importance of tying up the loose ends, of arranging for family finances, of feeling assured that things are in order and that the survivors will be able to carry on without him. This offers the dying person mastery over himself and over a portion of his phenomenal field, at least for the time being. It is his arrangements that will be executed, not those of subsequent advisors.

But it is just at this time that people are least likely to discuss such matters openly. Fear of being seen as greedy or insensitive may impede such discussion. It is sometimes better for the topic to be opened by a person not closely involved with the family, e.g. the physician, the social worker, the minister.

Second. Arranging for nonfinancial concerns of survivors and dealing with personal loss. In being effectively humanistic, we need to learn a lot more about how to help the dying person and his survivors to cope with the loss, both when impending and when past history. However, it is not necessary to wait for additional research in order to put into effect what we already know.

Third. Arranging for future medical and other care needs. Here again we need to learn about what kinds of decisions what kinds of patients can make with what degree of effectiveness. It is his death—he should have as much to say about it as possible, even if it distresses the family, irritates the physician, and inconveniences the charge nurse. When a person is terminal, we are inclined to read him off as a non-person and do our planning in terms of those he leaves behind. It is his life as long as he has it, and it is his body after his earthly existence ceases.

Fourth. Allocating time, energy, and financial resources. Dr. Avery Weisman advocates that professionals working with the dying focus upon the time and opportunities that remain, rather than upon those that are lost. What can be done in such limited time? What can be done with a given organic condition? Planning for the future is part and parcel of middle-class America: just because the future is sharply reduced does not mean that planning should cease. To attempt to bring this idea home more forcefully, everyone of us is going to die, so any medical condition we alleviate merely postpones the inevitable day. The only difference between you and the patient dying of lung cancer is that there is a very high statistical probability that you will outlive him. The probability is not, however, 1.00.

We all have a future, no matter how brief or how bleak. That future deserves attention. To draw an analogy: At what point do you stop repairing your house? A week before you expect to sell it? A month? A year? A decade? You will never be in that house permanently, so you might argue that any improvement is temporary and should not be worth bothering with. Now change your set and assume that this is the last house you will ever live in—now how do you feel about it? Your decisions probably waver—you are no longer so certain. Perhaps this will help you empathize with the dying person.

Fifth. Anticipation of future pain and performance decrement. As mentioned before, we should try to learn how important this is and to whom. Professionals can do a great deal to help in this regard. Sometimes the dissemination of accurate information is sufficient. In other instances, a good listener to attend to expressions of fear of pain is requisite.

Sixth. Dealing with the death encounter. The task here is similar to that outlined briefly above, except that the task may be more complex and difficult, partly because of the feelings of the professional.

Seventh. The decision to affect the rate of decline. The complexities of this concern are too great to deal with here.

Eighth. Psychosocial problems, including loss of independence, loss of mastery, and loss of productive roles. What does the dying person really fear he will miss most? If we can learn what types of role change and capacity change are really the most destructive to the individual dying person, we might be able to structure his environment to make these losses less important. Again, we do not need to wait for more research before beginning—we have ample information to launch our efforts.

Pattison (1969) describes six ways in which practitioners and others in the phenomenal world of the dying person can assist in creating an appropriate death:

1. Sharing the responsibility for the crisis of dying . . . so that he has help in dealing with the first impact of anxiety and bewilderment.
2. Clarifying and redefining the realities of the day-to-day existence which can be dealt with by the patient.
3. Making continued human contact available and rewarding.
4. Assisting in the separation from and grief over the realistic losses of family, body image, and self control, while retaining communica-

tion and meaningful relationships with those who will be lost.
5. Assuming necessary body and ego functions for the person without incurring shame or deprecation, maintaining respect for the person, and helping him maintain his self respect.
6. Encouraging the person to work out an acceptance of his life situation with dignity and integrity so that gradual regression may occur without conflict or guilt.

Accidents and the Elderly*

Allen Bernard
(based on materials by
Manuel Rodstein)

Many age-related changes make older people more susceptible to accidents, and the rates, especially for accidents from falls and from vehicles, rise greatly in the later years.

Persons age 65 and over have the highest accidental death rate in the United States, according to Dr. Manuel Rodstein. Although they comprise only 9.4 percent of our total population, the aged account for more than one-fourth of all deaths of this type. Accidents are the fifth leading cause of mortality in the 65–74 group, and the sixth leading cause in the 75-plus group, exceeding deaths from diabetes.

"In addition, it is estimated that over 3 million aged individuals annually suffer accidental injuries, of whom 200,000 are hospitalized and 800,000 are bedridden, resulting in about 100 million days of restricted activity."

The accident rate among the hospitalized aged is particularly revealing. It is five times as great as among younger persons, reaching the staggering total of 62 accidents per thousand admissions in patients between 70 and 80 years old.

The excessive incidence of accidents in the older age groups may be attributed in large part to aging changes in the body. These bring about loss of visual and auditory acuity; decrease in muscle strength, endurance, and coordination; impairment of sense of balance; and slowing of reactions. Gait changes such as the tendency to drag the feet, bowleggedness, and waddling are a contributing factor. The bones become thinner and more brittle; in

*Edited from "Accidents and the Elderly " (based on materials by Manuel Rodstein), by A. Bernard, *Geriatric Focus*, 1969, *8*(10), 1; 3; 5. Reprinted by permission of Knoll Pharmaceutical Company.

women, even minor stress such as sneezing or opening a window may result in collapse of the vertebrae.

Memory deteriorates, concentration becomes difficult, awareness of environmental hazards declines. Sudden changes in body position may decrease blood flow to the brain, leading to dizziness and faintness. Getting up too fast to answer the phone or doorbell, for example, the aged individual may become dizzy and fall, or trip over the edge of a rug or an extension cord.

Older people have lower tolerance for drugs. Tranquilizers may make them drowsy, or cause a fall of blood pressure on standing; the barbiturates may confuse or overexcite them; digitalis may cause rapid, irregular heart rate and decrease of blood supply to the brain.

Chronic illness adds to age-induced weakness, sense of detachment from the environment, lessened alertness, and consequent predisposition to accidents. An accident may also be the first manifestation of acute disease, or occur shortly after its onset. Since appreciation of pain generally diminishes with aging, and fever due to infection decreases or is entirely absent, older people frequently keep walking about with pneumonia, fractured hips, and acute coronary occlusions.

In a previous study of 147 consecutive accidents at the Jewish Home and Hospital for Aged in New York City, Dr. Rodstein found that nearly one-third of them occurred in conjunction with chronic conditions such as mental disorders, heart disease, hypertension, cancer, anemia, and Parkinson's disease. More than one-fourth of the accidents were associated with the onset of acute disease such as cardiac or cerebral insufficiency, sudden elevation of blood pressure, epileptic seizure, pneumonia, asthma, gastroenteritis, and rectal bleeding.

"All accidents in the aged should be reported and thoroughly investigated," he observed. "Early acute and chronic illness frequently will be detected. A series of minor accidents with little or no damage often precedes a major accident in the same person, leading to invalidism or death."

Psychologists have found that emotional strain makes people more vulnerable to accident. So does boredom, loneliness, anxiety, aggressive feelings, frustration, fear, and excitement. All these are common among the aged. "Often they feel isolated, unwanted, and lonely; or they are relegated to institutions where they lead regimented lives and share their quarters with strangers."

Simple preventive measures could greatly reduce the excessive toll of accidental deaths among the aged.

Falls. Persons 65 and over were victims in 73 percent of all deaths from falls in 1967. Some 3,000 fatal falls per year occur in various institutions for the aged. They frequently take place on staircases, due to missing the last step or steps. Top and bottom steps and risers should be painted in highly visible colors, non-skid treads used, landings brightly illuminated.

A detached rail on both sides of the stairs is essential, according to Dr. Rodstein. Handrails now in use often are too broad and close to the wall for effective reflex grabbing at the start of a fall. They should be distinctively shaped at the top and bottom of the stairs. "The hand should not reach this shape until the feet have left the staircase, thus preventing accidents due to missing a step, or looking for one that isn't there."

Slippery surfaces are another important cause of accidental falls. Small mats, sliding rugs, and slippery linoleum are common hazards. Preventive measures are obvious: the use of rubber-backed non-skid rugs or wall-to-wall carpeting, non-skid floor waxes, and corrugated shoe soles; tacking down the rugs, removing thresholds, etc.

Many falls in the aged are attributed to "drop attack"—a sudden and unexpected fall without loss of consciousness but with complete loss of muscular power in the legs and body. These attacks may be due to degeneration of the nervous system. A similar phenomenon may occur when the head is suddenly turned, compressing the carotid arteries that frequently are narrowed and kinked by aging. Therefore the aged should be warned against climbing on ladders to change light bulbs, adjust drapes, or paint, and against working with the arms above the head. "Any sudden movement of the head in space is dangerous to the aged, because of deterioration of the balancing mechanism in the inner ear."

Falls from bed are common in older patients. They can be prevented by use of a high-low bed that is kept in the low position at all times, except when treatment is administered. Side rails merely provide a higher point of departure for the fall of a disturbed or mentally confused patient; they should not be used without adequate nursing supervision, and orientation of the patient as to their purpose and use.

Fire and burns associated with fire. Some 28 percent of all fire-associated deaths in 1967 were in the over-65 age group. Fires are a significant problem in nursing homes and homes for the aged, but severe or mortal burns and scalds often are incurred by the aged due to poor memory and inattention. The hot water is turned on and forgotten, loose clothing is caught in the flames of a gas jet, hot kettles are touched or dropped, severe scalding in the bathtub is frequent.

Automobile accidents. Older persons were the victims in 12 percent of all driver deaths, and 28 percent of all pedestrian deaths due to autos in 1967, Dr. Rodstein stated.

The aged driver is more vulnerable to accidents because of poor night vision, lower tolerance of glare, diminished field of vision, and lessened visual acuity, as well as slower reflexes. Arthritis of the spine and neck may make it difficult for him to turn his head when backing his car, medication may make him drowsy and confused.

"The physician should explain to the aged patient limitations imposed on his driving activities by his ailments, and the various drugs he takes. Frequency of driving should be regulated, driving at night or in bad weather and the use of high-speed freeways curtailed. Finally, the question as to when the older individual should give up driving entirely must be faced."

Aged pedestrians pose another type of problem. The proportion of death and of injuries incurred while crossing at an intersection (47.6 percent) is higher in the elderly than in the younger age groups. Smaller numbers are hit while "jay-walking" (30.4 percent), walking in the roadway (7.6 percent), and getting in or out of vehicles (1.5 percent).

"We need special crossings for the elderly, with ramps rather than high curbs on which they may trip or fall, and longer spacing of traffic signals. A single green light often does not give them adequate time to cross city streets, particularly broad one-way avenues."

Accidental injury of the aged formerly condemned many of them to invalidism and death, Dr. Rodstein concluded. "Skilled rehabilitation procedures and good medical care, adequate nutrition, and treatment of their psychological problems in an atmosphere of hope, not despair, now often yields remarkable results in the restoration of function and enjoyment of life, even after a major accident.

"However, the avoidance of needless accidents is a more positive contribution. For the most part it demands only common sense."

Sociological Factors in Nutrition for the Elderly*

Allen Bernard
(based on materials by
Sylvia Sherwood)

As gerontologists, we haven't the slightest idea of the proportion of older people who eat some of their meals while standing in front of the refrigerator door and spooning food out of half-finished cans. Nor do we know much about how older people prepare their food, how many overcook much of what they eat, how much food ages so much that the nutritive values are lost, or how much food gets thrown away.

Based on what we do know, however, there is little doubt that improved nutrition is one of the greatest needs of the elderly, especially the low-income and the isolated elderly. The federal government has, in recent years, applied a large proportion of the funds for aging to nutritional programs. At the present, much of this money is going to congregate feeding; that is, programs

*Edited from "Sociological Factors in Nutrition for the Elderly " (based on materials by Sylvia Sherwood), by A. Bernard, *Geriatric Focus,* 1969, *8*(12), 1; 3; 5. Reprinted by permission of Knoll Pharmaceutical Company.

*that provide meals in a church or school or other central facility. Such pro-
grams encourage older people to come together not only to eat, but also to talk
and sometimes to participate in other activities.*

Though nutritional status in the elderly has become a matter of some
concern, little is known on a systematic basis about the extent to which the
maintenance of proper diet is an age-associated problem, or even a major
problem in the current generation of the elderly, Dr. Sylvia Sherwood stated
at a meeting of the Gerontological Society. According to Dr. Sherwood: "This
in part is due to problems of measuring nutritional status itself, and in part
to lack of adequate research. At present we have no accumulation of long-
term longitudinal data required for conclusions concerning the aging process, nor do we have representative short-term studies of the current generation of elderly needed for conclusions concerning the magnitude of their
nutritional problems."

Nevertheless, some data on sociological variables in nutrition do exist.
These may be analyzed and hypotheses relevant to gerontology formulated.

Dr. Sherwood believes that it is very likely that inculcated norms
governing food preferences and eating patterns affect the dietary intake of
the aged in much the same way as they do the general population. The
elderly tend to follow the dietary pattern of the community, rather than any
special pattern of old age. There is one important qualification. Food habits
are determined early in life, and old people tend to follow the eating pattern
of the years when their habits were formed.

"This in itself may account for more malnutrition in older people than
in the rest of the community, who profit more from advances in nutritional
knowledge," one observer at the meeting pointed out.

These findings indicate some of the difficulties that may be anticipated in setting up ideal diets for the aged, Dr. Sherwood remarked. "They
suggest that a program for improving dietary intake would do well to
focus on already accepted foods, using well established eating patterns to
best advantage."

Within the lifetime of a single generation there has been a dramatic
shift from malnutrition to overnutrition as a major danger to national
health. Clinical observations, surveys of aged populations, and studies of
older patients in hospitals reveal that obesity now is a much more pervasive
problem in the elderly population in this country than is undernutrition.

In a study of 605 white married couples with a husband 60–64 years of
age, it was found that 60 percent of the subjects were overweight, and "more
than one of every 4 could be identified as obese." Obesity was found to be
related to certain social variables: sex, religion, ethnicity, and to some extent socioeconomic status. Women were more likely to be obese than men;
Italian Catholics, than other religious and ethnic groups. Subjects of higher
socioeconomic status were *less* likely to be obese than those of lower status.
However, upper-class females were more likely to be overweight than either
medium or low socioeconomic females.

A study of 200 elderly persons in the nutrition clinic at Ohio State University also found obesity a major health problem. It stressed the need for dietary control, particularly in the light of the statistical association between obesity and various diseases related to aging such as diabetes, congestive heart failure, biliary tract disease, and arthritis.

These findings are somewhat paradoxical, in view of the fact that studies generally show decrease in weight and caloric intake in the 70-and-over age groups, Dr. Sherwood observed. The possibility has been advanced that reduction in caloric intake in advanced age is a response to decreased activity. "Presumably a lessening of caloric need would be accompanied by a lessening of hunger."

Another hypothesis is that age-related reduction in caloric intake can be accounted for in terms of survival rate, obese individuals being more vulnerable to death from diabetes, arteriosclerosis, and other cardiovascular diseases.

Though overshadowed by overnutrition, undernutrition remains a health problem in the U.S. A larger proportion of older people have chronic diseases that promote malnutrition, either indirectly by limiting the choice of foods, or more directly by disrupting physiological processes and thus reducing the nutrient supply to the tissues. Social isolation inhibits shopping for and preparing food, particularly in times of illness; the most extreme cases of malnutrition, in many communities, are found among elderly recluses.

Various surveys have demonstrated the relationship between low income and undernutrition among the aged. Insufficient funds may result in a reduction of food expenditures on the "protective" foods (meats, dairy products, fresh vegetables and fruits) and their replacement by cheaper items such as bread, potatoes, and sweets.

Some studies suggest that educational level may be even more significant in diet adequacy. Elderly persons of higher education apparently are more able to recognize advances in nutritional knowledge, and incorporate them into their daily pattern of living.

In any event, nutritional studies of the general population indicate that the elderly are relatively uninformed about good nutritional practices as compared with other age groups. The need for educational programs directed to the aged as a group has been pointed out by many nutritionists. However, there is no evidence that such programs are likely to have any effect, particularly in view of the evidence that early food attitudes and practices persist even when other behavior patterns change.

Another variable found to be related to diet and nutrition is social interaction. A study of 130 subjects at the Age Center of New England revealed that the 10 persons with the best nutrient intake were among those rated as "most gregarious," whereas the 10 rated as lowest in nutrition adequacy were among the most isolated. In another study it was found that 36 percent of persons who ate alone were rated as having good diets, as compared with 46 percent of those who usually had company at their meals.

Several investigators have found that elderly persons living alone tend to neglect nutrient value in favor of foods easily available and easy to prepare.

"To the extent that high morale and feelings are related positively to digestive processes, it can be hypothesized that social interaction is functionally related to nutritional status," Dr. Sherwood said.

Emotional stress and tension have been shown to have a critical effect on metabolism—notably nitrogen and calcium balance, and cholesterol levels. "Should they be found to hold, such findings have important implications for malnutrition in the elderly, since old age in our society often is a time of stress and frustration."

A number of other societal variables may affect the nutritional status of the elderly and are worth investigating. These include frequency of dietary intake; variety of foods eaten; the accumulation of food contaminants (insecticides, chemical fertilizers, atomic fallout, etc.); enrichment of food; fluoridation of the water supply, etc.

Data from an experiment on the effects of a 6-month semi-starvation diet on the behavior of 32 normal young men may have profound implications for the elderly. These men showed "anxiety and feelings of insecurity, irritation, lack of emotional control, moodiness, depression, apathy, boredom, lack of interest in the ideas or activities of others, and inability to make decisions."

These same symptoms are descriptive of many elderly patients. A question might be raised as to the extent they are related to undiagnosed malnutrition in the aged.

"If these manifestations are not considered symptoms of nonhealth, but are accepted merely as signs of 'growing old,' pathologic conditions related to nutritional deficiency may be overlooked. It is possible that such conditions start out as potentially reversible, but eventually result in permanent damage. This in part may be true of some symptoms of senility. It can be hypothesized that nutrient deficiency of thiamine, for example, accounts for decreased learning performance in the aged. Instead of pursuing the possibility that this is a reversible condition, it may be assumed that the patient has brain damage and is entering into 'unchangeable' senescence. Obviously such assumptions are likely to have enormous consequences for both the mental and social life of the elderly."

Chapter 6

Aging, Politics, and the Law

When people wield power in a society, they do so through control of its institutions: political, legal, educational, religious, family, and communications (in addition to work/financial institutions and the military). In this and the next chapter, these social institutions will be discussed.

As people grow older, they gain power within each of these kinds of social institutions . . . until they reach the magic age of 62 or 65 or, occasionally, 70. At that point, power and influence usually diminish suddenly; society perceives its institutions as entities that should provide services for the elderly, rather than ones in which the aging members maintain control.

If I had written this book in 1970, I would have said that none of the legal or political institutions of our society had much concern for the elderly. True, politicians had voted for Medicare, lawyers helped older people make out wills, police were kind to old women; but, by and large, little was happening that enhanced the lives of people over the age of 65.

This is no longer true. Politicians are now very much aware that older people not only vote, but that they vote in large numbers. Political activism among the elderly, represented by groups like the Gray Panthers and the National Council of Senior Citizens, is bringing pressure to bear on the political front. The National Senior Citizens Law Center, based in Los Angeles, has a staff that is sensitive to the needs of older persons. It provides education, research, consultation, and other informational services to the elderly and to the legal profession. Police services to the elderly have also improved. Many law-enforcement departments in the United States and Canada are setting up programs to enable older persons to avoid being victimized by criminals.

Indeed, awareness that older persons are particularly vulnerable to criminal victimization, although always well-known, did not provoke much action from law-enforcement decision-makers until very recently. Police departments are developing a greater concern for the victims of crime throughout their work, and the elderly will profit from this change in approach. Of course the legal problems of the elderly are not limited to purse-snatching and mugging but include everything from consumer fraud to questions of guardianship for people no longer competent to carry out their responsibilities.

Aging and American Politics*

Robert H. Binstock

In the United States Congress and in many state legislatures, regulations and traditions permit power to be accumulated by the people who have been around the longest. These are the people who chair the committees, who know everyone by first name, who have the greatest power in determining who receives appointive positions. They are often so well-known in their home districts that they don't have to run very strenuous campaigns, and they are virtually assured of the nomination, since they are in charge of their party's local decision-making apparatus. They are also courted by statewide and national candidates and lobbyists, because they have power, they know how to reach others who have power or money or both, and they understand how to get things done.

Since it can take many years for someone to develop this degree of influence and knowledge, you might assume that many of the most powerful legislators would be elderly; you might therefore logically assume that the prerogatives of the elderly in general must be well-protected in the U.S. Congress and in state legislatures. Your first surmise would be correct, but your second would fall wide of the mark. Relatively few older people see themselves as members of an age group; rather, they see themselves in terms of ethnicity, present or previous vocation, neighborhood, religious denomination, and social class or income group. Legislators seem even less likely to classify themselves as older persons. Many attempt to display a "young image" when they run for office, and therefore, political support for the elderly is just as likely (I often think more likely) to come from a young candidate or officeholder as it is from one who is technically eligible for retirement.

Several contemporary trends suggest a dramatic increase during the next few decades in the number and proportions of Americans who will be regarded, by society and by themselves, as aged. Because of these trends, journalists and scholars have begun to consider the implications of aging for the future of American national politics. The possibilities discussed have ranged from gains in so-called senior power to the emergence of gerontocracy—literally, rule by the aged.

While the terms senior power and gerontocracy are provocative, they do little to focus a serious discussion of the aging in American politics. To consider how much political power the aging are likely to have in the future—or even to assess the contemporary extent of senior power—requires some specification of referents. In short, one must ask: power for what?

*Edited from "Aging and the Future of American Politics," by R. H. Binstock, *The Annals of the American Academy of Political and Social Science,* 1974, *415,* 199–212. Reprinted by permission.

Since discussions of senior power have been generated by the possibility of substantial increases in the proportion of aging citizens, the most immediate issues for attention should center on those political activities—voting and interest group politics—which have their bases in large categories of citizens. The issues implicit in discussions of senior power and gerontocracy would seem to be: (1) does and will "the aging vote" determine the outcome of elections and (2) do or will organizations based on the existence of millions of aging members, consumers, and clients have significant power in the conflicts and accommodations that take place in American interest group politics? To focus on electoral and interest group politics is to emphasize selected sources of power in the American political system at the expense of others. Nonetheless, these are the most relevant political dynamics to consider when analyzing the prospects for mass-based power.

THE PRESENT AND FUTURE AGING

... In 1974 about 10 percent of the American population is 65 years and older. These persons constitute approximately 15 percent of those who are old enough to vote, and they do, in fact, cast about 15 percent of the votes in national elections.[1]

Stimulated by these figures, many observers of the political scene feel that senior citizens are, or at least could be, a powerful force in contemporary American politics. In building up this case, they assume not only that numbers is an important source of power in American politics, but also that masses of citizens can be led to cohesive political behavior on age-based interests.

Trends of two different types suggest possibilities that the current proportions of aging citizens and voters may increase substantially in the years ahead. Demographic trends could lead to a greater percentage of persons who are chronologically aged—65 years and older. Trends in retirement from the work force at earlier ages could lead a great many Americans younger than 65 to confront the social and economic problems that are commonly faced by the chronologically aged. Consequently, many retirees as young as 55 or so may come to regard themselves, and to be regarded by society, as within the category of "the aging."

The percentage of Americans who are chronologically aged could grow considerably by the year 2000 or beyond. Until then it will remain approximately the same as it is now. All of the people who will be old enough to vote between now and the early 1990's have already been born; plausible assumptions about declining mortality rates due to biomedical advances do not change the picture substantially. Whether the age structure of the American population will be significantly altered by the year 2000 or some

---

[1]These percentages are calculated from tables appearing in U.S. Department of Commerce, *Statistical Abstract of the United States,* 1973 (Washington, D.C.: Government Printing Office, 1973), pp. 31, 379.

more remote decennial marker depends primarily on fertility rates in the years ahead. Zero or sub-zero population growth rates over the next several decades could result in a dramatic increase in the proportion of persons 65 and older in the 21st century. Or by then, a currently implausible biomedical discovery for prolonging life may have been identified and widely implemented for a period of time sufficient enough to alter drastically our current rate of mortality. While low fertility rates in the past few years indicate that a substantial increase in the proportion of the chronologically aged is possible by the year 2000, this trend would need to continue for some time for such a change in age structure to be reliably projected. The trend may well continue, but an increase in the percentage of chronologically aged is currently a matter for conjecture, not prediction.

Trends increasing the proportion of younger "retired-aging" persons seem more reliable (Jaffe, 1971), though not susceptible to quantitative projection. Many workers are now opting for early retirement when they anticipate a comfortable retirement income. Others seem to retire early because of pressures generated by various factors in labor force activity. Some of these factors are: the relatively high rate of technological obsolescence among workers in their 50's and early 60's; increasing relocation of major firms; cyclical unemployment; and stagnation of certain sectors of the economy. While the extent of retirement at ages younger than 65 has not been quantitatively projected for the future, it is probably safe to assume that the phenomenon will continue and increase.

With the trends toward early retirement, millions of persons in their 50's may face problems now associated with the chronologically aged, such as the economic dependency that comes from living on a reduced, fixed income in an inflationary economy. Inadequate housing, lack of access to transportation, and other problems stemming from inadequate purchasing power may emerge. If they choose to re-enter the labor force they may find it extremely difficult to obtain employment. And they will no longer have the social roles and the various forms of status that work provides. At the same time, the retirement status of these younger retirees may lead the rest of society to assign to them the stereotypes of aging. For along with images of physical aging and the infirmities associated with old age, retirement status is one of the chief means of identifying the aging in American society.

A future in which young retirees perceive themselves, and are perceived by society, as being in a category with the chronologically aged is not at all implausible. Such a future is especially possible in the contexts of economic and social aging. It may, in turn, have political implications if the younger retired-aging and the chronologically aged come to share economic and social aspirations and problems.

. . . If there is no dramatic increase in the proportion of aging citizens, there will be no political implications. But if we assume that the proportion of the aging—in one sense or another—will increase dramatically, what differences will it make for American politics? On the basis of contemporary data regarding the political participation of persons in their 50's and older, we can assume that—whatever their number—at some future date they will be highly active.[2] Will this change existing patterns of electoral and interest group power in national politics?[3]

CONTEMPORARY ELECTORAL POLITICS

The most important general assertion to be made about the contemporary electoral power of the aged is that there is no "aging vote" (e.g., Campbell, 1971). The political attitudes and partisan attachments of the aged are diverse and notable for their stability. To be sure, one can identify instances in which the percentage of older persons voting for a party or a particular candidate has switched markedly from one election to the next. But in such instances the switches have been paralleled by comparable shifts among middle-aged and younger voters; age is not an important variable for explaining voting swings. In short, there is no evidence to indicate that aging-based interest appeals can swing a bloc of older persons' votes from one party or candidate to another.

That presumed old-age interests do not form the basis for a cohesive voting bloc should not be at all surprising. Even to the extent that older persons identify as aging, it is a relatively new identity, negative in effect; and only one among many (usually stronger) competing identities.

Various studies suggest that a substantial proportion of older persons, ranging from 40 to 65 percent, do not perceive themselves as old or aged. Data suggest that most of these persons are relatively well-off, ranking high in socio-economic status and health. . . . To the extent that they are concerned with problems and grievances linked to old age, some fragmentary evidence suggests that they do not perceive these problems as stemming from the fact that they are aged.

Even comparatively disadvantaged older persons, who are most likely to identify as aged, do not tend to see their income, health, housing, safety, and transportation problems as primarily aging problems. No systematic studies dealing directly with this question exist. Nonetheless, general scholarship in the field of developmental psychology as well as political science indicates that even if the disadvantaged aged see their problems as age-related problems, they see them in other contexts as well. A full life cycle of socialization, experiences and attachments—family, schooling, ethnicity, occupation, income, residence, peer and other associations—presents a multitude of sources for group identification and perceptions of special interest. It would not be unreasonable to infer that many of those who identify as aged—even those responsive to the special needs of the

---

[2]For a summary of literature on political participation and aging, see Matilda White Riley and Anne Foner, *Aging and Society* (New York: Russell Sage Foundation, 1968), Vol. 1, pp. 463–479.

[3]Here, the discussion is necessarily confined to national politics for reasons of space. It can be generally asserted that the electoral behavior of the aging in state and local politics is approximately the same as in national elections, although aging voters seem to respond more homogeneously than usual to certain municipal referenda propositions.

disadvantaged aged—would have stronger competing identifications and interests. Presumably these competing factors substantially dilute a response to attempts to mobilize a cohesive voting bloc, even of the disadvantaged aged, based on their special interests.

FUTURE ELECTORAL POLITICS

For these reasons it should be clear that even a 100 percent increase in the proportion of chronologically aged voters during the next several decades would not likely, in itself, engender a cohesive aging vote that could determine the outcome of elections. In some remote future, beyond the year 2020, the generational cohorts who enter the ranks of the chronologically aged may be sufficiently homogeneous in their political attitudes and attachments to respond to aging-based interest appeals by voting cohesively. But all of the generational cohorts that will reach 65 years of age between now and then have displayed already their political heterogeneity. As Campbell (1971) has expressed it: "Because each age cohort includes people who differ profoundly in many important conditions of life it is not likely that any age group will be very homogeneous in its attitudes. The evidence which national surveys provide us does in fact demonstrate that attitudinal differences between age groups are far less impressive than those within age groups." (p. 117). . .

While the emergence of the younger retired-aging would not be likely to provide the basis for a decisive aging vote bloc, it could engender greater electoral cohesion based on aging interests. One can speculate that passage into retirement status, with its attendant problems and interests, at a comparatively early stage in the life cycle could lead to the development of an aging identity that takes on political strength and meaning through the reinforcement of time and experience. But to suggest that such a development could provide the basis for an aging vote that would determine the outcomes of elections is to go beyond the bounds of reasonable conjecture.

If one considers that a person retiring at 50 spends almost as much of his life in retirement as he does at work, it is reasonable to expect that retirement status can play as significant a role in the formation of his political orientation as does his occupational identity. Moreover, the distribution of occupations within any age cohort is highly diverse. The status of retirement, in contrast, is relatively uniform despite variations in other characteristics of retirees. Thus, while occupational identities lend heterogeneity to political orientations, retirement identity developed through a substantial number of years might well engender homogeneity. The common experiences of retirement could be a cohering factor in the electoral behavior of the younger retired-aging.

Lest such speculation be regarded as wholly fanciful, it should be stated that nothing that is known about political socialization through the life cycle precludes such a development. While it is often assumed that the political orientation of adults is largely determined by childhood political

socialization, the evidence available contradicts this. The research literature indicates that there are no bases for saying: (1) whether childhood
learning of political attitudes endures throughout life, or basic orientations
acquired during childhood structure the later learning of specific issue beliefs; (2) whether adult socialization mediates or even replaces childhood
learning of issue beliefs, even acknowledging that socialization takes place
throughout the life cycle; (3) under which circumstances political socialization affects political attitudes and behavior; or (4) under which circumstances, if any, planned efforts at socialization can be effective.

To the extent that retirement status may provide some measure of
commonality in the political orientation of persons under 65, translation of
this latent group bond may be accelerated by broader politicizing forces.
Heightened public controversy over governmental policies that distribute
resources among Americans in relation to age and work force status, could
bring to the surface any tendencies that the younger retired-aging—and
perhaps the chronologically aged—may have for perceiving their political
self-interest in terms of conflict between old and young. Some precedence for
this can be found in the nationwide Townsend Movement of the 1930's and
the California Ham and Eggs movement, which began in the Depression
and extended into the 1950's.

Signs that public policy issues may be debated increasingly in age-
distribution terms are already evident. Perhaps the most notable example is
the contemporary spate of magazine and newspaper articles that identify
Social Security payroll deductions as regressive taxes and not—as was
widely accepted for many years—premium payments into an old-age insurance program (e.g., Miller, 1974). That Social Security is not an actuarially
viable insurance program has been clear to economists and other professional analysts for at least two decades; for some time they have technically
categorized the program as an income transfer from the productive to the
unproductive. Even the Secretary of Health, Education, and Welfare proposed to Congress in 1972 that the Social Security trust fund be fully expended since it has no use as an ongoing resource for making benefit payments. But it has been in 1974, when the impact of inflation on middle class
and working class pocketbooks has become a popular concern, that syndicated columnists have begun to politicize the program by writing about "the
Social Security rip-off."

Continuing politization of age-distributive programs would not in itself lead to more cohesive electoral behavior. Whether aging-based political
orientations might result in greater senior power depends upon the presence
or emergence of leadership to cohere any existing potential for electoral
power, or for other forms of political influence based on a large category of
citizens.

Organizations built on aging-based interests are currently active in
national politics. What kind of power do they have, and what do they use it
for? Will trends in the aging population change the power and goals of these
interest groups? Will new aging-based organizations with different objectives emerge in the decades ahead?

CONTEMPORARY INTEREST GROUP POLITICS

While literally hundreds of organizations participate in the politics of national decisions affecting the aging, only ten are more or less exclusively preoccupied with issues related to aging (Binstock, 1972). The power of these organizations is derived from the existence of more than 20 million older Americans. Three of the organizations . . . are mass-membership associations. The other seven deal with the aging as consumers, clients, and as subjects for study. Four of these are trade associations, another is a professional society. Still another is a loose confederation of social welfare agencies, and a coalition of individual professionals, activated just several years ago, is attempting to bring special attention to the plight of black older persons.

The bases provided by millions of older members, consumers, clients and subjects provide these interest groups with sufficient credentials to participate in most formal and informal national policy processes. Indeed, in the classic pattern of American interest group politics, public officials and other politicians feel it incumbent upon them to invite these groups to participate in most policy activities related to aging. Because of this legitimacy they have essentially three forms of power available to them.

First, they have ready, informal access to public officials—to Congressmen and their staffs, to career bureaucrats, to agency and department heads and occasionally to the White House. Consequently, they can put forth their own proposals and work to block the proposals of others. To be sure, their audiences or targets may often be unresponsive, but access provides some measure of opportunity.

Second, their legitimacy as aging interest groups enables them to obtain public platforms in the national media, in Congressional hearings, and at pseudo-events such as the 1971 White House Conference on Aging. From these platforms they can exercise power by initiating and framing issues for public debate. They can bring attention to conditions in nursing homes, point up the double-jeopardy to which black older persons are exposed or ask whether biomedical breakthroughs in the prolongation of human life are desirable, given the qualitative problems of existence for the aging in the United States. And, of course, they can use such platforms to register public support or opposition on any issues that have already been framed.

A third form of power available to these groups, particularly the mass-membership organizations, might be termed the electoral bluff. As indicated earlier, the votes of aging persons cannot be swung in a cohesive bloc through an aging-based interest appeal. Most politicians—certainly national politicians—recognize this and do not develop special appeals to the aged as the central issues of their electoral campaigns. Nonetheless, they wish to avoid offending the aged and therefore are disposed to favor proposals for providing incremental benefits to older persons. The interest groups, with their access to politicians and their platforms for framing issues, are in a key position to interpret the interests of millions of aging voters whom politicians do not wish to offend. By virtue of their symbolic role in representing millions of aging citizens, the mass-membership organizations are particularly credible in interpreting the interests of the aging. Whether the interpretations are accurate is never tested politically. Within moderate limits, public officials are responsive to the interpretations of the interest groups; and the interest groups keep their interpretations within these moderate limits, never putting forth radical proposals that might force politicians to call the bluff of the aging vote.

Given these forms of power, what do the interest groups do with it? The activities of the aging organizations in national politics are hardly militant or radical. They do articulate and support many demands favorable to the interests of elderly persons. But their efforts do not reflect a vigorous pursuit of major policies that could bring about substantial changes in the fundamental status of the aged in American society. . . .

. . . While they probably would not have sufficient power to achieve such goals even if they sought them, the very incentive systems that create and sustain their organizational viability—interests of their members and the pursuit of their trades and professions—preclude them from testing the extent of their power to achieve fundamental changes for the aging. In short, these organizations are similar to those in many other arenas of interest group activity that have been examined by students of American politics.

FUTURE INTEREST GROUP POLITICS

If the next several decades bring substantial increases in the proportions of chronologically aged and younger retired-aged citizens, will aging-based interest groups have more power, and will they exercise what power they have for different purposes than they do now? Will new types of aging interest groups emerge? Will they have different political objectives?

An increase in the proportion of chronologically aged persons would probably have little effect upon interest group politics. The legitimacy provided by greater numbers of members, consumers, clients and subjects would probably enhance the capacity of the interest groups to gain access to public officials and to obtain platforms for framing public policy issues. The size of the electoral bluff would be more impressive. The contemporary interest groups and any new ones that join them would have more security in their efforts at organizational maintenance. They would probably succeed in establishing a larger domain of funds and authority to divide among themselves through conflict and accommodation. But unless the political orientations of the chronologically aged undergo considerable change, there is no reason to expect that aging interest groups would vary significantly the nature of their objectives. . . .

The development of a younger retired-aging constituency, even with political orientations based on a stronger aging identity, is only somewhat more likely to change the activities of aging-based interest groups. A common aspiration among them to find new social roles and identities may well give rise to additional organizations based on constituencies of aging members, consumers, and clients. But as Bernice Neugarten (1974) points out . . . , the "young-old" are likely to desire a wide range of options and opportunities. Therefore, organizations developing in response to this common need for meaningful activities will probably be numerous, but diverse in nature and unlikely to have a shared basis for working alliances. Their political relevance would probably be negligible.

To the extent that there is group cohesion focusing on the problems of economic dependency in retirement and its attendant difficulties, the aging-based interest groups—particularly the membership organizations—may be forced to put forth stronger age-redistributive policy proposals in order to maintain their legitimacy and to avoid the threats of new organizational competition. If their proposals do not seem too radical to the politicians of the day, the latter may continue to acquiesce to the bluff of the aging vote. In the unlikely event that the proposals are so radical that the politicians feel forced to call the electoral bluff, the subsequent power of the aging-based interest groups will decrease or increase sharply, depending on whether a decisive aging vote materializes on that critical election day in the future. More likely, as indicated by our consideration of electoral behavior, there would be no pivotal bloc of aging voters on that day; the power of the aging-based interest groups would subsequently decline.

THE PROSPECTS FOR SENIOR POWER

. . . Before touching on other political dynamics that could have implications for aging and the future of American politics, what can one conclude about the possible consequences of an increased aging population for senior electoral power and senior interest group power?

The aging do not vote cohesively to determine the outcome of contemporary elections. Are they likely to do so in the future? Although a number of possibilities have been raised, there is no sound reason to expect that in the immediate or remote future the aging will wield decisive power in determining the outcomes of national elections. Even if the proportion of aging Americans were to double, the most powerful consequence one can reasonably imagine is that politicians might woo the aging vote as assiduously as they now woo the vote of organized labor. But even this is most unlikely. The organizational structure of unions provides a far stronger—though hardly reliable—mechanism for swinging votes than any aging-based interest group is likely to develop.

The aging-based interest groups have some power by virtue of their ready access to public officials and other politicians, their opportunities to obtain public platforms for framing policy issues and their discreet exercise of an electoral bluff. They use this power to support incremental benefits for the aging and to carve out and divide among themselves the middleman's share in government programs which provide services and facilities for the aging. If there is a substantial increase in the number of members, consumers, clients, and study subjects that form the bases for these organizations' power, what is likely to happen?

The most powerful consequence that one might realistically suggest is that the aging-based interest groups will have credentials to participate in a broader range of interest group political arenas. Currently they are only legitimated for invitation and access to arenas that are clearly labeled as relevant to the aging or to some category of disabled adults. But with substantial increases in the numbers of citizens they symbolically represent, these groups may find the doors of more general policy forums thrown open to them. Even as the 1971 White House Conference on Aging could not be conducted without prominent representation of business and labor interest groups, the aging-based interest groups may become welcome and sought-after guests at major forums dealing with issues central to business and labor.

To suggest these possibilities is to intimate that a substantial increase in the proportion of aging will have little impact on the basic nature of American politics. To be sure, some roles in the system will have changed if aging voters are wooed a bit more than some other category of voters, and if aging-based groups take some other interest's seat at the many bargaining tables of interest group politics. Some aging citizens as well as the aging organizations will achieve incremental gains in the playing out of what Theodore Lowi (1969) has characterized as interest-group liberalism.

If one looks briefly to forms of power other than voting and interest groups, are there alternatives for increased senior power in national politics? No, not very strong ones, unless there are sweeping changes in the nature of American society. While government and corporate elites are comparatively advanced in age and may well continue to be, they do not wield their power on behalf of aging-based interests. Ad hoc protest groups of the aging have demonstrated some capacity to influence the outcome of minor decisions in local politics, such as the reduction of public transit fares for senior citizens. Like most groups mobilized around ad hoc purposes, they have not provided the base for longer-lived protest organizations. One can never exclude the possibility that a nationally-focused ad hoc protest—a march on Washington by senior citizens—might be successful. But given the obstacles of logistics, economics, and group cohesion, the odds of any success seem formidable.

A less conservative approach to prediction than the rather rudimentary modes of projection implicit in this discussion can yield a variety of futuristic scenarios involving the aging in American politics. For instance, one can posit the emergence of the so-called no-growth economy, which has been the focus of fashionable intellectual speculation in the past several years, and find that cleavage between the economically productive and the nonproductive is the central political conflict of the day. Surely the political behavior of the chronologically aged and the younger retired-aged would be exceptionally cohesive in such a setting. To consider whether that cohesion would provide a basis for power in the no-growth society would be to lead oneself through an endless series of fanciful speculations.

Of all the imaginable political implications of growth in the numbers and proportions of aging citizens, the most serious can be found in the impact that their presence will likely have on the need for public services and facilities. The needs of the contemporary population of aging citizens—in physical and mental health care, social services, educational opportunities, recreational and community activities, appropriately designed housing—far outstrip the available personnel and facilities . . . to meet them. Yet it is already established policy of the American government to undertake responsibility for meeting these needs (U.S. Senate, 1973). With millions of additional aging citizens, the gap between government's official policy and its capacity to implement that policy will be enormous. As this situation emerges, the politics of federal resource allocation may lead to retrenchment in, or abrogation of, policies committing government to help meet all these needs. If government responds positively to the challenge of expanding services and facilities, it will be because of pervasive ideological considerations and not because it is pushed to do so by senior power.

The Necessity for Legal Services*

Paul S. Nathanson

Older people are, first, last, and always, people. This truism is easily forgotten when we begin to look at them as problems or as people who need help or, for that matter, as them. They are us, albeit at a different stage in life in some ways. This is most certainly true when we consider the legal concerns of older persons. Regardless of their age, people need to cope with both the possibility that they might break the law and that they might be victimized by someone else who is breaking the law. They also need to have enough knowledge of the law to provide for their families if they should die, to complete tax forms, to understand the legal implications of divorce, to know what their rights are when they are denied employment or when automobile repairs aren't done properly—the list goes on and on.

For older people, the nature of legal problems remains much the same, but the emphasis changes. For the elderly, consumer issues more often revolve around hearing aids and funerals than around razor blades and auto repairs. Family law issues focus on wills and estates rather than divorce and child care. Age discrimination, rather than ethnic, sex, or religious discrimi-

*Edited from "Research Needs in the Field of Law and Aging," by P. S. Nathanson. This is the first publication of this article. All rights reserved. Permission to reprint must be obtained from the publisher.

nation, may prevent the older person from working. But consumer protection, family relationships, and discrimination are still the themes.

THE NEED

Perhaps more than any other group, the elderly rely upon complex public and private institutions for their daily subsistence. Therefore, their legal problems frequently relate to the policies and actions of governmental agencies and private corporations, both of which often present undecipherable bureaucratic mazes which even very well-educated and sophisticated persons find difficult to manage.

Superimposed upon the lives of the low-income elderly is a vast array of complex statutory, regulatory, and decisional law. Their shelter may be provided or secured under federal and state public and subsidized housing laws, relocation laws, environmental protection laws, and zoning laws. Their health is often dependent upon Medicare, Medicaid, laws regulating nursing homes, and laws relating to the advertisement of prescription drugs. Their nutrition is often secured by the Food Stamp Program and nutrition programs established by other federal laws. The source of their income may be Social Security, Supplemental Security Income (SSI) under Title XVI of the Social Security Act, or private pensions. The dignity of personal freedom and control of property is subject to the vagaries of the law of guardianship, conservatorship, and involuntary commitment.

Unlike younger people, who have been forced from birth to live under governmental programs and large bureaucracies, today's elderly have not learned to "work the system." The elderly are, on the one hand, confronted with a vast complex of crucial legal issues, bureaucracies, and forms with which to deal; and on the other hand, they have no real place to turn for adequate and effective assistance.

The unmet need for legal services has been recognized by many entities of the federal government considering the needs of the elderly. Joint hearings held by the Senate Committee on Aging and the Judiciary Subcommittee on Representation of Citizen Interests on June 14, 1974, clearly indicate that the nation's elderly in many important spheres lack adequate legal representation and, therefore, access to the judicial process. Statistics indicate that the low-income elderly comprise approximately six per cent of the client load of the average Office of Economic Opportunity (now Legal Services Corporation) Legal Services Office, although the elderly comprise over twenty per cent of the nation's poor. The 1971 White House Conference on Aging recommended: "The Federal Government (through the Office of Economic Opportunity, any successor Legal Service Agency, or other agency) should establish a special center concerning legal rights of the elderly. . . ."* Three of the 18 major recommendations of the Federal Council

---

*White House Conference on Aging, Protective and Social Support: Report of the Special Concerns Sessions 29–30, 1971.

on Aging made on September 10 and 11, 1974, relate to the provision of legal services to the elderly.

THE LAWYER'S ROLE

Title III of the Older Americans Act outlines social services which are to be delivered to older persons in a comprehensive and coordinated manner. These social services include health services, continuing education, welfare services, counseling, services to assist older people to obtain adequate housing, services to assist older people to avoid institutionalization, and any other services necessary for the general welfare of older persons. An examination of lawyers' activities on behalf of older persons demonstrates that providing legal services not only accomplishes these Title III services frequently, but often acts to coordinate their comprehensive delivery.

Lawyers basically provide older persons three types of services which coordinate with the Older Americans Act and other legislation designed to benefit older Americans.

Information and Referral

First, lawyers act as information and referral services in terms of the Older Americans Act and Title XX of the Social Security Act. A high percentage of the problems which bring an older person to an attorney significantly affect the older person's daily life, but do not result in a specific legal response or in the framing of a legal question which might ultimately lead to litigation or drafting of a legal document. As discussed above, the older person's life is affected by a maze of federal, state, and private bureaucracies. A lawyer with expertise in programs such as food stamps, SSI, Medicare, or Social Security often provides substantial legal service to an older person by informing the older person of government benefits program eligibility requirements, by assisting in the completion of appropriate forms, by explaining rights under government benefits programs, and by calling the appropriate administrative offices when the older person encounters problems in attempting to obtain government benefits to which the older person is legally entitled. Thus, legal services for the elderly often is more akin to Information and Referral than traditional litigation.

A final aspect of this first basic service provided by lawyers serving the elderly is the preparation of educational materials informing elderly clients of their rights under the various programs or laws affecting their lives. This educative function activates the senior community, and makes it aware of community resources available for protecting rights of older persons.

Routine Litigation

A second basic service provided by lawyers to their elderly clients is routine litigation. For example, lawyers can defend their elderly clients against evictions, suits to enforce unfair consumer contracts, or repossessions of goods bought on credit. Lawyers will often bring affirmative suits or appear at administrative hearings to establish their elderly client's eligibility for government benefits including food stamps, SSI, Social Security, Medicare, or Medicaid. Lawyers can also contest involuntary commitment of elderly persons to mental hospitals when those persons are not dangerous, or the appointment of guardians or conservators to manage the property of allegedly incompetent elderly persons. In this context, the lawyer's role is particularly vivid, and dovetails perfectly with the Title III goal of helping older people avoid institutionalization. A recent study by the National Senior Citizens Law Center indicated that, in Los Angeles, less than three per cent of 1,010 guardianship and conservatorship cases sampled in a one-year period involved an attorney acting on behalf of the proposed ward. Consider the Los Angeles figures in light of a recent Ohio study (Wenger & Fletcher, 1969), which showed an extremely high relationship "between the presence of legal counsel and the decision not to hospitalize the patient." The lawyer's role on behalf of the elderly, and the need of the elderly for legal services, could not be more graphically illustrated.

A variation of this second basic service is providing routine legal assistance to senior groups. For example, a group of elderly people might want to become a nonprofit organization or form a co-op. If so, they have to incorporate and obtain tax exemptions. Lawyers are aware of the various federal programs that provide loans, mortgages, and special housing grants, and they can thus help groups package a program for the local community.

Law Reform Activity

The third basic service provided by lawyers to their elderly clients is law reform activity, which seeks to affect the rights of broad groups of people. Attorneys engaged in law reform activity on behalf of the elderly generally have as their primary goal a full and effective participation by their clients in legislative programs designed and instituted to benefit their clients. These attorneys perform the watch-dog function of seeing that such programs are carried out as intended by their legislative drafters. Law reform activity can take the form of either test case litigation on behalf of a class of elderly people, or legislative or regulatory reform. Examples of test case litigation and legislative reform are set forth below:

a. In the nursing home field, cases have recently been filed challenging nursing home conditions as a deprivation of civil and constitutional rights, and seeking state and federal enforcement of nursing home standards. One case seeks damages against the nursing home on behalf of the named plaintiff and each of the class members.

b. In the area of utilities, the enactment of a city ordinance restructuring water and sewage rates to favor the elderly was recently accomplished by attorneys representing a group of elderly persons in Toledo, Ohio. By restructuring the rates to allow lower rates for less than minimum usage, these attorneys effectively put money in the pockets of the city's elderly utility users.

c. In the food stamp field, the elderly component of Milwaukee Legal Services, which was created only in March, 1975, has obtained the reinstatement of SSI recipients in the Wisconsin Food Stamp Program. The reinstatement is the result of a preliminary injunction in a lawsuit filed by the elderly component on behalf of a statewide class of 54,000 elderly and disabled SSI recipients. This preliminary injunction thus restores to each class member's SSI budget the amount previously used to compensate for the loss of food stamps under the challenged state policy.

d. In the Social Security area, a lawsuit is pending which would enable divorced husbands to apply and be awarded Social Security benefits in their own right. Current law precludes divorced husbands from obtaining such benefits if their ex-wives receive such benefits. Further, a possible lawsuit would prohibit the Social Security Administration from obtaining waivers from inadvertently overpaid Social Security and SSI recipients of their rights to contest the Social Security Administration's recoupment of over-payments made through government error and relied on by the recipient. Such successful resolution of either case clearly would confer substantial economic benefits on the elderly class members.

e. In the SSI field, cases are pending which would require the Social Security Administration to observe reasonable time limits in the application and appeals process. A favorable resolution of these cases would obviously have beneficial impact on elderly persons across the nation.

f. In the pension area, successful challenges to term of service and break-in-service rules will provide additional financial resources to retirees. One suit seeks to reduce the term of service necessary to qualify for pension eligibility from 15 to 10 years. A second suit seeks to abolish a break-in-service rule as to all retired employees unaware of the rule so as to qualify such persons for pensions otherwise denied them pursuant to the break-in-service rule.

g. In addition, lawsuits have been brought challenging: lack of procedural due process under the Medicare and Medicaid programs; sex discrimination in the Social Security Act; mandatory retirement; and involuntary commitment or the declaration of guardianship without adequate representation at, or notice of, the hearing.

Such major litigation works hand in hand with legislative and administrative advocacy. The elderly's daily lives are concerned with the government and various governmental enactments, regulations and legislation. It is crucial that attorneys (who can often understand and interpret those enactments in the best interests of the elderly) are involved in the drafting of legislation and regulations on behalf of the elderly, and in monitoring the administrative actions of agencies concerned with administering programs for the elderly.

Obviously, the elderly's main needs relate to inadequate income, housing, health care, and nutrition. As can be seen from the foregoing, legal services can do much to alleviate those admittedly basic problems on a scale and with efficiency not within the reach of the average social service office.

LEGAL SERVICES AS A TOOL FOR ADVOCACY ON BEHALF OF THE ELDERLY

The concept of advocacy on behalf of elderly persons is pivotal to the Older Americans Act's philosophical underpinnings. State and Area Agencies on Aging must themselves advocate the interests of the elderly, and must provide for social services which will advocate those interests. Webster's defines the verb advocate as "to plead in favor of." The noun advocate is defined, "one that pleads the cause of another; specifically, one that pleads the cause of another before a tribunal or judicial court." Lawyers are by instinct and training advocates, and the essence of their profession is advancing and securing the position they have undertaken to support.

Specifically on behalf of the elderly this general advocacy may take the form of attempting to convince public and private agencies not specifically concerned with the elderly to devote their resources to the elderly, and to ensure that private and governmental agencies specifically concerned with the elderly, or with programs designed to benefit the elderly, are doing their best for the intended beneficiaries. These refined types of advocacy are natural outgrowths of delivering legal services to the elderly.

The first type of advocacy, convincing agencies not specifically concerned with the elderly to devote their resources to the elderly, is a major thrust of the Older Americans Act. This type of advocacy helps draw down and make available to the elderly additional resources previously not available. The concept pivotal to the Area Agency on Aging is that the small amount of funds allotted to the Area Agency should be used not to provide direct services, but to initiate and instigate the use of other agencies' funds for the elderly. Thus, the Area Agency on Aging may use its grant as "seed money" to induce other agencies to spend equal or greater amounts in projects coordinated on behalf of the elderly. This first type of advocacy also involves getting the special needs of the elderly into the consciousness and sensitivity of various state agencies, and working with the legislative branches affecting the elderly in order to apprise the legislators of special programs needed by the elderly. Attorneys can be especially useful in this type of advocacy by analyzing existing and proposed legislation to determine its effect on the elderly and the State or Area Agency. As developed above, attorneys independent of the state bureaucracy can also draft and have introduced legislation to enhance the position of the elderly.

The usefulness of legal services as a tool for advocacy on behalf of the elderly is obvious under the second type of advocacy, which involves ensuring that agencies devoted to the elderly are doing their job. Since attorneys invariably draft the legislation and regulations implemented by the state and federal governments, attorneys dedicated to the elderly are invaluable in analyzing those statutes and regulations affecting the elderly to determine, pursuant to this type of advocacy, whether agencies created by those statutes and regulations dealing with the elderly are fulfilling the requirements of the law. On those occasions when violations of statutory or regulatory precepts are discovered, the mere threat of a lawsuit can provide immense assistance in negotiations with agencies which are not doing their utmost as is required by their enabling legislation or regulations; and successful lawsuits against recalcitrant agencies provide impetus on a national scale for other offending agencies to comply with their legislative mandates. To be most effective as an advocacy tool, the attorneys providing these services should not be part of the governmental units involved, as are the State and Area Agencies on Aging, but rather should be specifically funded Legal Services programs acting as advocates for the elderly.

The recently enacted Amendments to the Older Americans Act emphasizing legal services for the elderly as distinct from other social services under the Act, provide State and Area Agencies on Aging a most effective tool for advocacy on behalf of older people. Further, Title IV-A as amended provides money to trial lawyers and paralegals as advocates to address the elderly's legal needs. Not only may such money be used to train lawyers and paralegals to provide legal and counseling services to the elderly, but also to:

> ... monitor the administration of any program ... designed to provide assistance or services to older persons, including nursing home programs ... ; and ... (to) identify legal problems affecting older persons, develop solutions for such problems, and mobilize the resources of the community to respond to the legal needs of older persons.

It would indeed be a disservice to the elderly people State and Area Agencies are meant to serve if the unique advocacy tool afforded by the Older Americans Act were not utilized fully.

*The Older Person as Victim**

Evelle J. Younger

Older people, like all other people, commit crimes and are victims of crimes, but as you might expect, the nature of both their criminal behavior and their victim roles differ from those of younger people. There is evidence that older people actually suffer less from criminal acts than adults of other ages, but whatever the statistical reality may be, the personal reality is that

*Edited from "The California Experience: Prevention of Criminal Victimization of the Elderly," by E. J. Younger, *The Police Chief,* 1976, *43,* 28–30ff. Reprinted by permission.

*the elderly fear being victimized more than other age groups (Clemente &
Kleiman, 1976). Although the elderly have long been afraid of crime, it is
only recently that gerontologists have begun to pay it heed. This article is
from one of the first publications, perhaps the first, that have given significant
attention to crime and the elderly.*

Law enforcement must direct its efforts in a major thrust to develop
the field of crime prevention. Everything that has happened in recent years
reinforces that conclusion. We have witnessed consistently escalating rates
of crime and must honestly confess that reliance upon the traditional police
approach of apprehension, prosecution, and incarceration has failed to stem
the tide.

Evidence is increasing that a substantial proportion of crimes are
never reported to police agencies. Of those crimes reported, a very low percentage result in apprehension of suspects; the proportion of eventual con-
victions of such suspects is still a smaller percentage; and despite continual
efforts at rehabilitation in penal institutions, recidivism rates are still dis-
couragingly high.

The conclusion seems inescapable that while we must vigorously continue our efforts to improve the effectiveness of traditional approaches, we
cannot rely upon such efforts. And even if in the future we should become
vastly more successful in dealing after the fact with criminal offenders, and
were to reap the presumed consequent benefits of improved deterrence, the
devastating impact upon the victim of crime still remains. This impact in
terms of physical, psychological, and financial loss cannot be redressed
through apprehension and punishment of offenders.

We in the California Attorney General's office became convinced in
1971, at the time when the White House Conference on Aging reported
crime to be a major concern, that criminal victimization of the elderly had
been largely ignored. Research done by our crime prevention unit staff
revealed that there was almost no attention being given nationally or in
California to the problem of crimes against the elderly, and that there was
almost no hard data extant on the incidence of such victimization.

In view of the traditional focus of police agencies on the criminal act
rather than on the victim, the question arises whether it is justified to
utilize law enforcement resources for the particular benefit of a segment of
the population. Dr. Jack Goldsmith (1975) has addressed this concern as
follows:

> The sifting out of the older segment of the population for purposes of
> crime prevention is important in two ways: it highlights the differential
> impact of these crimes and it considers the special characteristics of the
> older victim. It should be noted that there are other segments of society
> that have been singled out for special consideration by law enforce-
> ment—most notably, children, public officials, and celebrities—because
> of either differential impact or special victim characteristics. Unlike
> these groups, however, the elderly have a great potential for segmental
> crime prevention.

The principle of specialized treatment for older persons is becoming a well established part of public policy in several areas including property tax relief and reduced rate public transportation. There has also been a movement for special legislation providing greater protection and greater criminal penalties for crimes committed against persons over 60 in some states . . . (pp. 18–19).

The special vulnerability of senior citizens to criminal victimization results generally from: physical deterioration attendant upon the process of aging, economic factors resulting in severe financial deprivation for the elderly population so that economic loss from crime has a considerably heavier impact upon the elderly than the rest of the population, and the highly traumatic psychological impact of crime upon senior citizens.

While the data both nationwide and in California are still somewhat minimal, the data developed over the years of our experience, plus recent research in California, coincide with some national research on elderly vulnerability. A recent poll, while showing that the general public thought the elderly were more victimized than the seniors did themselves, still showed that seniors listed "fear of crime" ahead of all other concerns as a "very serious problem" (NCOA, 1974).

The only extensive and in-depth study extant, conducted by the Midwest Research Institute in Kansas City, demonstrated a special vulnerability of elderly victims. The study involved research over 18 months on 1,800 victims of crimes who were 60 years or over. It found that elderly persons living in high crime areas of Kansas City were victimized in 1973 by burglary and robbery at a rate frequently 3 to 4 times higher than that of the city's overall population. Of the more serious crimes against the elderly, vulnerability occurred in the following order: burglary, robbery, grand larceny, auto theft, non-violent purse snatch, assaults, rapes, sexual molestation, and homicide (Midwest Research Institute, 1975).

The increasing fear of crime among the elderly has become almost epidemic, and we must alleviate this fear by convincing them that they are not powerless to prevent victimization and that law enforcement is concerned and prepared to support and assist them.

Crimes against the Elderly

Both experience and recent research reveal the special vulnerability of California's elderly to certain crimes—crimes of force, buncos and confidence games, medical quackery, and consumer fraud—crimes of the marketplace.

Crimes of force. The crimes of force to which California elderly are most vulnerable appear to be street crimes—particularly the purse snatch directed toward senior women and burglary. While statistics generally reveal that seniors are not victimized by criminal assault against person as frequently as are young males, for example, the special vulnerability of elderly to assault lies in the fact that the impact upon them is much more traumatic physically, financially, and psychologically than upon younger age groups.

A statistical picture of the incidence of crimes of force upon elderly in Los Angeles is revealed by a recent U.S. Census Bureau survey. Of those surveyed who were over 65 years of age, 1 in 56 seniors had suffered a theft (burglary or auto theft); 1 in 73 had been assaulted; 1 in 188 was a victim of purse snatch; 1 in 204 was a victim of robbery; and 1 in 440 was a victim of attempted robbery.

In working with seniors, the California Attorney General's office crime prevention unit has developed methods of prevention to minimize the likelihood of victimization by these crimes. Detailed information on residential target hardening teaches inexpensive methods of improving resistance to forceful entry through windows and doors, the importance of thinning and lowering shrubbery for visual survey, and other methods of discouraging entry. We encourage self-help projects such as neighborhood watch, Operation I.D., organized security checks, and partnership with local law enforcement in these and other deterrent strategies.

With respect to purse snatch, there is simple instruction given on carrying money and credit cards in inside pockets of clothing instead of in a purse, methods of carrying purses for quick release to minimize physical injury, and avoidance factors related to place and time.

Seniors are also trained in techniques of avoiding assault, including when and where to walk, carrying whistles or sirens for deterrence, and the use of the buddy system.

Giving emphasis to the positive aspect of prevention efforts minimizes the pervasive climate of fear among seniors, who often fear crimes of personal violence considerably out of proportion to the actual likelihood of incidence. We need to combat fear by the demonstration of law enforcement's concern and by presenting concrete evidence of successes in prevention programs involving both law enforcement and self-help and mutual aid efforts. It is image bolstering to seniors, for example, for law enforcement to recognize their special availability and usefulness for neighborhood or block-watch strategies.

Bunco and confidence games. While California seniors are experiencing increased incidence and fear of crimes of force, the fact of the matter is that they are even more vulnerable to certain nonviolent crimes. Crimes of a bunco and confidence nature are almost exclusively directed toward the senior citizen. The San Francisco and Los Angeles police departments report that more than 90 percent of the bunco victims are over 65 years of age and are mainly women. In California, the predominant bunco schemes victimizing elderly citizens are the "Bank Examiner" scheme; the "Pigeon Drop" scheme; and welfare, social security, and pension check frauds. In one six-month period in the Los Angeles Police Department's jurisdiction, almost twice as much money was lost by seniors through the bank examiner and pigeon drop con games as was lost by banks through robberies. Recently, evidence is surfacing that efforts of the attorney general's office and those of local law enforcement are reducing bunco incidents. This evidence comes from participants in our crime prevention programs and from reports of the Division of Law Enforcement in the State Department of Justice. In the San Francisco Bay area, an intensive media campaign on bunco methods of operation was undertaken; and in the period of January to June 1975, the San Francisco Police Department recorded 24 bank examiner attempts and only one loss ($4,000).

The vulnerability of seniors to buncos and con games results from their isolation, their economic distress, and the fact that their life savings are usually readily accessible in bank or savings and loan accounts. Bunco prevention consists of teaching them to recognize current bunco schemes and frequent reinforcement of a few simple rules:

  —Never discuss your personal finances with strangers.
  —Don't expect to get something for nothing.
  —Never draw cash out of a bank or savings account at the suggestion of a
    stranger.
  —Always check on anyone who claims to be an FBI agent, bank official,
    official inspector, or representative of any public agency.
  —Do call the police and report any bunco approaches.

We also train personnel of California banking and saving institutions on bunco methods of operation and victimization patterns, and enlist their cooperation in public education programs at various bank branches.

In an effort to improve bunco prevention methodology for local law enforcement, our department's division of law enforcement through the crime patterns analysis section of the organized crime and criminal intelligence branch, develops special investigative training materials and information-sharing procedures for local law enforcement personnel. In the past, crime reporting by law enforcement relating to bunco schemes has not been uniform. In an attempt to correlate cases and identify problem areas, we are training law enforcement investigators throughout the state in the use of standard crime report forms for these schemes.

Medical quackery. In California, where quackery is estimated to be about a $50 million business, common "get well quick" schemes include cures for cancer, arthritis, baldness, obesity, loss of youthful vigor, and, yes, even the common cold! Economic loss is substantial, and delay in receiving proper medical treatment while dealing with the quack may lead to more serious problems and even death.

The primary target of the medical quack is the senior citizen. Vulnerability arises out of the obvious fact that as the aging process unfolds, concomitant deterioration of physical condition and increase of health problems occur. Further, the more serious the health problem, and the less susceptible to cure or amelioration by legitimate medical services, the more desperate the sufferer becomes and the more likely he or she is to resort to miracle cures.

Seniors are the victims in approximately 7 in every 10 cases of medical quackery fraud coming to the attention of the criminal justice system. We inform seniors of details of specific current schemes and instruct them in methods of identifying the medical quack:

—Any person who guarantees to be able to cure a disease is suspect.
—Statements along the line that the practitioner has a secret formula or a special treatment known only to him should arouse suspicion.
—Responding to an advertisement will often lead to exposure to quackery.
—Great success by quacks is achieved through direct mailing.
—Some food faddism and false nutritional therapy are special types of quackery.

Emphasis is placed on checking the legitimacy and qualifications of anyone offering medical help and in the case of such devices as hearing aids, checking whether a provider is appropriately licensed by the state.

Consumer frauds—crimes of the marketplace. Experience in California, in addition to recent research surveying district attorneys' consumer fraud units, the State Department of Consumer Affairs, local law enforcement, and local senior committees, indicates the particular consumer crimes to which seniors are the most subject. Additionally, seniors are more vulnerable to consumer fraud in general due to their condition of substantial economic deprivation. The loss of $5 in a consumer transaction has a financial impact upon seniors which is substantially greater than a similar loss by members of the working population.

In training seniors to detect crimes in the marketplace, we take a twofold approach: we deal in depth with special areas of consumer crime, and we discuss general guidelines to follow to avoid consumer frauds common in the marketplace.

Consumer crimes most frequently victimizing the elderly begin with supplementary health insurance and medical plans. Because of their unique health problems, the elderly are particularly vulnerable to so-called suede shoe salespersons peddling these plans door-to-door. Training includes: (1) refraining from impulse buying with respect to health plans, (2) recognizing that oral commitments have no validity unless included in a written contract, (3) consulting with public authorities as to the licensing and reputation of corporations selling health plans, and (4) consulting for translation of legal and small-print terminology regarding benefits into understandable terms.

Seniors are also particularly victimized by mail order frauds. The mail order business is a hazardous area since post office boxes may be taken out under false names of businesses that do not exist. One approach of the mail order fraud operator is to insert ads in magazines and newspapers and give a post office box for return of monies. However, the media do not attempt to check the validity of such ads. Frauds also operate through use of bulk mailings, using the telephone book and addressing their ads to "resident" or "occupant."

· In connection with mail order frauds, the California Attorney General's office works closely with the U.S. postal inspector in the state as well as provides ongoing education on current victimization schemes. Schemes currently most common in California involve work-at-home offers, since seniors are desperately anxious to supplement their incomes. Perhaps the most common of such frauds involves offering work in addressing and stuffing envelopes. Seniors sending in their money to secure work may not in return receive work, but simply get a sheet of instructions on how to search for such work. Other common mail order schemes include offers to make products in the home, franchise schemes such as the purchase of vending machines, pyramid sales, chain letter schemes, "estate searches," phony puzzle contests, and free offers.

Other areas of consumer crime to which seniors are vulnerable include auto repairs, home repairs, mobile homes, and door-to-door sales. We train the elderly in the provisions of the consumer law in general, covering areas regarding contracts, retail instalment buying, and credit problems. Seniors are taught to recognize various deceptive sales practices, including bait and switch, deceptive pricing, fear-sell techniques, false descriptions of goods or services, referral selling, unordered merchandise, collection practices, and the law with respect to garnishment.

In consumer fraud education, we outline the role of the various public legal offices in the enforcement of California consumer law.

Conclusion

Experience in California has demonstrated that segmental crime prevention efforts provide concrete results, prove the effectiveness of mobilizing interagency resources in the community, and validate the benefits of partnership between seniors and law enforcement.

One training tool we have developed is a bi-monthly "Senior Crime Preventer's Bulletin," which alerts seniors to current crimes and schemes against them throughout California, presents in-depth education in the areas of crime to which they are susceptible, and provides action models. The bulletin is received by all seniors who participate in our crime prevention seminars in local communities, and is used as a training tool by law enforcement and senior citizen agencies of local governments. Local agencies frequently duplicate the training materials and regularly circulate them.

After nearly four years of leadership, we see an increasing disposition among local law enforcement agencies in California to undertake segmental crime prevention programs in their local jurisdictions toward the prevention of elderly victimization. It is our hope that the criminal justice system throughout the nation, especially local law enforcement and public legal offices, will recognize the special problems and needs of elderly citizens and undertake concerted strategies to respond to those needs.

Chapter 7

Social Institutions and the Elderly

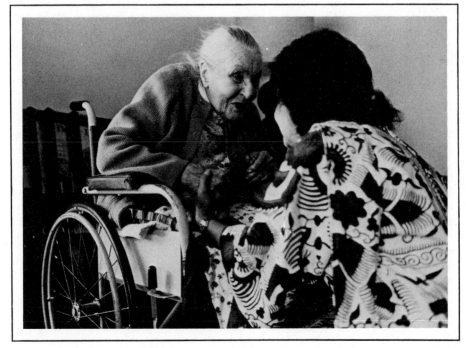

The family, the school, the church, and the media are institutions that are every bit as powerful and influential as politics, law, and the criminal-justice system. Indeed, it would not be difficult to justify the statement that the family is the most powerful of all institutions, in spite of many predictions of its imminent demise.

A great deal is heard about the loss of status of the older person within the family. This may be true, but the evidence is shaky. The first section of this chapter will touch on the matter, but I would like to develop another kind of idea. When the older parent controlled the land or the job that the children needed in order to live, that older person had immense power and could readily gain respect. When the disapproval from the community was so great that adult children dared not ignore their elderly parents, respect was also shown. But the world is different today. Children do not depend on their parents for access to farmland or jobs, and communities are not so punitive of those who ignore their parents. Therefore, we have reached a point at which parents are not likely to have gained the respect of their children through economic power; rather, they earn respect by developing positive relationships with their children.

It may be harsh to say, but I believe many parents do not deserve the respect of their children; similarly, many children do not deserve the love of their parents. Ironically, most adult children do respect their aging parents, even when the parents have not done much to earn it, just as many parents do love their children, even when the children have not done much to earn it. My point is that *respect* and *love* no longer are questions of social sanction; they develop within a relationship, or they don't develop at all. In our society, people are free to select their own spouses, their own living arrangements, their own jobs, and their own forms and levels of education. They are also free to pursue or reject parent-child relationships. This point is debatable, I realize, and you may wish to give it further thought.

The other institutions discussed in this chapter—the school, the church, and the media—function differently from the family. Each of these social institutions has virtually ignored the older adult until very recently. Now, as one aspect of the swell in interest toward the aging segment of the population, each of these institutions has turned its attention to the elderly.

Many church congregations have learned that while they were working diligently to bring young people into the church, their older members were being ignored. Similarly, colleges and universities preached the importance of developing a lifelong interest in learning, but they did little to encourage it in any active sense. And the media seemed satisfied with putting an old lady on the seat of a motorcycle in a television commercial—the height of tokenism. Now churches, schools, and the media are all establishing programs for older persons, and there is every reason to believe that these will increase in the coming years.

Older People in a Family Context*

Gordon F. Streib

A great deal of nostalgia about how strong and cohesive the American family used to be and how disrupted it is today has become a pervasive social issue. The extent of change in the role of the family, however, is difficult to assess. There is no doubt that the divorce rate has zoomed upwards in recent years, with substantial increases occurring at all age levels, but there is still a question about how cohesive the American family actually was in the past.

For example, large numbers of today's elderly came to the United States from other countries when they were young, not infrequently when they were children. We don't have good data, but I would surmise that relatively few North Americans over the age of 60 had long-term relationships with their grandparents. Not only did people of that generation die at much younger ages (not infrequently in childbirth), but also, many remained in the countries of their birth. So, when today's elderly reminisce about the respect and love given to their grandparents' generation, they may be thinking of a past situation in which they themselves did not actually participate. Nevertheless, it is probably true that families were more cohesive when today's older generation was young. There were no Social Security benefits and few homes for the elderly; medical care was a private responsibility, and whatever nursing care was given usually was provided by the family. And, as I have said before, children were much more dependent on family business connections for entrance into the work force.

The cohesiveness and security of strong family ties appear to have been exchanged for autonomy and freedom. There is good evidence, however, that today's elderly are closer to their children and other family members than popular publications suggest. There is also evidence that the youthful relationships of today's elderly to their parents and grandparents have been glorified beyond reality.

There is a tendency in the popular literature to paint a bleak and pathetic picture of all the aged as being rejected, lonely and isolated— forgotten by their children and relatives. This picture is inaccurate and misleading, judging from the increasing amount of research evidence available. There are, of course, cases where a person has never married, or has never had children, or has outlived his kin. There are also cases in which parent-child relations have been strained for a lifetime and it is perhaps

*Edited from "New Roles and Activities for Retirement," by G. Streib. This chapter originally appeared in George L. Maddox (Ed.), *The Future of Aging and the Aged,* a book in the Southern Newspaper Publishers Association Foundation Seminar Series published in 1971 and distributed by The Duke University Center for the Study of Aging and Human Development. Reprinted by permission of the SNPA Foundation and The Duke University Center for the Study of Aging and Human Development.

unrealistic to expect a reconciliation when the parent is aged and needs help.

A major distinction which must be emphasized is that between the residential family or the kind of family in which one lives, and the modified extended family or kin network to which a person belongs.

When we examine the kinds of residence patterns of households which one finds among 65-year-olds and older, we note that five household types encompass the most frequent living arrangements. The two most frequent kinds of household type in old age are the married couple and the widowed person living alone. These two kinds account for about two-thirds of all families having persons over 65 years of age. Thus in specifying the family in old age, we see that there is a substantial proportion of "single-person families." Many of these older "families," while they maintain separate residences from their children or relatives, keep in close contact through frequent visiting or telephoning.

The specific data gathered by Townsend, Wedderburn, Henning, Milhoj, and Stehouwer (1968) of the distribution of the five household types are indicative. These authors found that in three industrialized societies household types were represented as follows: (1) living alone and never married, 4–8%; (2) married couples, 35–45%; (3) married couple living with one or more children, 7–14%; (4) widow(er)ed, divorced, or separated (primarily the former) and living alone, 22–28%; (5) widow(er)ed, divorced, or separated and living with one or more children, 9–20%.

The two major family structures—the residential family and the extended family, as described above, are essentially static views—a snapshot taken at one point in time. What is more interesting, more important, and much more difficult to study is the dynamics of the family and their effects on the kinship networks. When we examine families with members over the age of 65, we must be concerned with the fact that the distribution of various kinds of kin structures and living arrangements are changing. This dynamic quality is striking. For example, the modal pattern of living arrangements in the period beyond age 65 declines tremendously from what it was about 20 years earlier. Census data for the United States show that almost 80 percent of males 45–54 years of age and slightly more than 70 percent of the females in the 45–54 age category live with a spouse in their own household. There is a steady decline in this kind of living arrangement with a drop at about age 65. There is an increasing differential over time between men and women so that at age 75 and over, more than 40 percent of all men are still living with a spouse in their own household in contrast to less than 15 percent of the women.

These demographic facts are the underlying base for understanding the familial roles of older people and the role changes and role realignments which are an integral part of the family cycle.

The basic family unit in old age is the marital pair, for among persons 65 and older, 53 percent are married couples (Riley et al., 1968, p. 159). A broad picture of all persons over age 65 in the U.S. shows that 71 percent live in families with other persons to whom they are related and 22 percent of older married couples live with their children (Riley et al., 1968, p. 168). Intimacy at a distance continues to be preferred by both old and young as the optimum living arrangement for older persons, as married older couples prefer to live separately from their children.

One of the fundamental observations concerning family roles is the clear-cut differentiation according to sex. Men have certain tasks and activities and women have theirs (Zelditch, 1968). Although there may be some variation in the nuclear family system of the United States and other highly industrialized societies, the modal pattern is for the man to "provide" for his family, and for the mother to be primarily engaged in expressive roles: housewife, mother, teacher. There is a broad range of role activities for older women and millions of married women work even when they have small children at home. For the male the primary role in the family is his occupational role as the breadwinner. He is expected to be responsible and support his family. The American family probably has a more flexible system of role allocation within the family than is true of other societies, and this pattern is probably more characteristic of the middle income strata than the lower strata. American fathers over the years have assumed a number of tasks which traditionally have been considered to be maternal. Fathers may help with the dishes, perform certain "heavy" household chores such as window washing, supervise the children, help with the shopping. This growing shift in role activities is probably a salutary pattern, leading to easier role adaptation in the latter part of life.

Perhaps the major change in roles which the male must face is that of stopping work and retiring. The act and process of retiring can have major consequences for husband-wife roles. Kerckhoff has found, for example, that men who take more part in familial activities upon retirement tend to be better adjusted than those who do not (Kerckhoff, 1966a, p. 184).

Another major role change which affects husband-wife relations is the death of a spouse. The role of widow is much more likely to occur than the role of widower, and so from the standpoint of family roles wives are more likely to have to cope with bereavement and role realignment resulting from death than the husbands. As persons age, a much larger percentage of women than men are widows living alone or widows living with children.

Another aspect of changing family roles is the trend toward more retirement marriages. Most of these second marriages result from widowhood and not from divorce. But whatever the cause, marriage in later life poses problems of role change and role realignment.

McKain carried out a study of 100 retirement marriages, and he offered a series of factors or conditions which tend to be associated with marriages which are more successful. He found that persons who know each other well, who have the approval of children and friends, who have been able to cope with disengagement, and who have a stable income, particularly home owners, are more likely to have successful retirement marriages. As in marriage at younger ages, McKain found that personality factors are important in predicting success in retirement marriages. Satisfaction, stability and adaptability are crucial. McKain wrote:

If the older person is experiencing difficulty in arranging his life to meet the reduction in his social roles, the added adjustment created when he remarries may prove too much for him. Failing health, the loss of a job, or a withdrawal from active participation in the social life complicates the process. On the other hand, if he is well adjusted to the retirement years he usually can take a retirement marriage in stride [McKain, 1969, p. 128].

McKain reported that the attitude of adult children may be a serious deterrent to retirement marriages. Rigidity of expectations concerning family roles is not only found among older persons. He stated that some children were shocked when they learned that parents were planning to marry. In some cases the core of the problem was related to the inheritance of property. In others it was considered an "insult" to the memory of the deceased parent. Indeed he asserted that "a negative attitude on the part of the children probably has prevented a large number of retirement marriages which otherwise would have taken place" (McKain, 1969, p. 116).

Contrary to some of the stereotypes about the rejected old person, there is considerable contact between old parents and their adult children. Even though the residential family may consist of only one person, the modified extended family remains an important part of the older person's life (Sussman, 1965).

In the study of three industrialized societies (Shanas et al., 1968, p. 174), it was reported that most older parents (over three-fifths) had seen at least one child the same day of the interview or the previous day and another fifth had seen a child within the previous week. The percentage of older persons who had not seen a married child in the previous year was very small (3 percent). The existence of an extended kin network in which parents and children are in regular and frequent contact with one another is a fundamental part of intergenerational relations in industrialized societies. The assertion by some theorists that the isolated nuclear family is the modal pattern is not supported by a variety of studies in the contemporary situation.

Adult children and their parents maintain a viable kin network involving mutual patterns of assistance. Small services are rendered reciprocally by each generation. More than half of the older persons in the United States sample reported that they helped their children (Shanas et al., 1968, pp. 204–205). Moreover the aged are independent of regular monetary aid from their children (Streib, 1958). In a nationwide study in the United States, only 4 percent report receiving regular financial aid.

The reciprocity of help—shopping, housework, babysitting, home repairs, etc.—as a form of kin assistance is an important characteristic of family role relations.

The post-parental period is not a traumatic and negative experience for most families, in spite of the gloomy reports of the "empty nest" syndrome. Deutscher, in a survey in an urban middle class neighborhood in Kansas City, found that 22 out of 49 older couples evaluated the post-parental period as "better" than preceding phases of life; 15 said it was as good as preceding phases, seven said changes were not clear, two said it was "as bad" as preceding phases, and only three said it was worse. Those who said it was better mentioned a sense of freedom—freedom from financial responsibilities, freedom to travel, freedom from housework and other chores, and finally freedom to be one's self for the first time since the children came along (Deutscher, 1964).

With increasing longevity and earlier retirement plans, there are a growing number of instances in which an older person must face the problem of taking care of an octogenarian parent, just when he is ready to enjoy his own retirement. In these instances, somewhat small in number but sometimes pathetic in their import, the retiree role involves assuming the "parental role" *vis-à-vis* an older parent or other older relative. Perhaps some type of day care or overnight facilities should be developed so the retired person may enjoy some of his retirement free from this new kind of "parental" role.

Religion and the Institutional Church*

David O. Moberg

Definitions of religion and religiousness are many, ranging from whatever a person's ultimate values are to attendance at church services. "The spiritual is variously interpreted as the realm of faith, revelation, illumination, and insight, in contrast to the realm of phenomena which are empirically observable by man through his senses" (Moberg, 1971, p. 2). There can be religion where there is no physical structure such as a church or a shrine, and there can be churches and shrines without religion being about. Often the two come together, however, since spiritual feelings frequently cause people to wish to express their devotion through creating a visible structure.

One useful differentiation in the study of religious values is between intrinsic and extrinsic religiousness. The former refers to having spiritual feelings and acting upon them, whereas the latter refers to participating in rituals and ceremonies—adhering to the forms of religion. Again, one can be intrinsically religious without being extrinsically religious, and vice versa, although the two are often found together.

Another important kind of differentiation was presented in the sociological literature a number of years ago. Here the dimensions of religiousness are defined as (1) adhering to religious practice, (2) maintaining religious be-

*Edited from "Spiritual Well-Being," by D. O. Moberg. White House Conference on Aging, Background and Issues. Washington, D.C.: U.S. Government Printing Office, 1971.

liefs, (3) having knowledge of religious matters, (4) having had religious experiences, and (5) living according to religious values (Glock & Stark, 1965). Early in this section, we will look at what is known about the elderly in terms of these five dimensions of religiousness; later we will consider some of the church-related programs for the elderly. (When a specific citation is not given, the information provided was taken from one of the following sources: Gray and Moberg, 1962; Maves, 1960; Moberg, 1965; Riley et al., 1968).

SOME BIBLICAL TEACHINGS

Some of the oldest wisdom of mankind pertinent to the aging is found in the Bible:

> You shall rise up before the hoary head, and honor the face of an old man, and you shall fear your God: I am the Lord [Leviticus 19:32].

The young clergyman, Timothy, was instructed by Saint Paul to deal respectfully with older people:

> Do not rebuke an older man but exhort him as you would a father; treat younger men like brothers, older women like mothers .... Honor widows who are real widows. If a widow has children or grandchildren, let them first learn their religious duty to their own family and make some return to their parents; for this is acceptable in the sight of God [I Timothy 5:1-4].

Then, as now, some of the elderly prayed, "Do not cast me off in the time of old age; forsake me not when my strength is spent" (Psalm 71:9). The assurance was given that old age could be productive, the righteous still bringing forth "fruit in old age" (Psalm 92:12-15). "The Preacher" admonished his hearers to remember their Creator in the days of their youth before "the evil days" of old age come (Ecclesiastes 12:1-8).

Consistently throughout the Bible are doctrines of man that provide a framework for action pertinent to the aging (as well as all other age groups).

RELIGIOUS PRACTICES

Church Attendance, Memberships, and Social Participation

Such attendance is generally maintained at a high level in the later years of life, although, with advancing age in the late sixties or early seventies and above, the rate of attendance gradually declines, presumably as a result of increasing rates of disability, problems of mobility, and financial limitations. In one study of urban Catholic old people in relatively good health, attendance rates of people past their seventy-fifth birthdays were higher than those of persons aged 65 to 74 (O'Reilly, 1957). As in other age groups, the attendance rates of older women are higher than those of men in each equivalent age category.

More of the memberships and formal social participation of senior citizens is in churches and their auxiliary associations than in all other types of social organizations combined. There are variations, however, by type of community (those in rural areas participating proportionately more heavily in church groups (Pihlblad & Rosencranz, 1969), by social class (the working class having few formal group activities besides those related to their churches, and the upper class having many, most of which are outside of religious groups, with the middle class falling between those extremes), and presumably by ethnic identification and religious faith.

Radio and Television

Substantial proportions of older people listen to church services and other religious programs on radio and television. As church attendance among the religiously oriented decreases, use of the mass media as substitutes for it increases. This helps to explain why many "radio pastors" slant their programs deliberately to try to meet spiritual needs of homebound people.

Personal Devotional Activities

Activities like Bible reading, praying, and meditating, increase steadily with age during the adult years. To what extent the increases among the age groups are indicative of actual increases among the same individuals as they age and to what extent they represent generational differences in which successively younger age cohorts are inherently less religious is not completely clear, but it is likely that some elements of both factors are involved.

RELIGIOUS BELIEFS

Belief in God and Immortality

Belief in God reaches its highest levels and is held with the greatest certainty in the later years of life. For example, in the 1966 Catholic Digest Survey, 86 percent of the respondents aged 65 and over were "absolutely certain" that there is a God, compared to declining percentages with each successively younger age category to ages 18–24 at which 71 percent were "absolutely certain." Correspondingly, only three percent of those aged 65 and over but eight percent of the youngest group either were not at all sure there is a God or did not believe or know it (Riley et al., 1968).

Belief in life after death is expressed by over three-fourths of the national samples of population aged 50 to 55 and over, compared to smaller proportions of younger age groups (Riley et al., 1968; cf. Gallup & Davies,)

1969). In their interviews with adults from four ethnic groups in Los Angeles, Kalish and Reynolds (1976) found an increase in belief in life after death from 48% of those 20–39 to 64% of those 60 and over.

Belief in the Importance of Religion

A belief in the importance of religion is held by a larger proportion (about six-sevenths) of people past age 65 than by younger adults. Several studies indicate that more people say religion has become more helpful and of increasing meaning with advancing age than the opposite. This is also true among Southern Negroes and white welfare recipients (McNevin & Rosencranz, 1967). Yet it is possible that religion is perceived as less salient than are family, relatives, and friends, for in a national sample survey the latter were mentioned more often as a source of satisfaction and comfort in the lives of the elderly "today" than religion (Barron, 1961).

Conservative Religious Beliefs

Conservative religious beliefs about the deity of Jesus, Biblical miracles, the devil, and other traditional Christian doctrines are more common among elderly than among young and middle-aged adults (Stark, 1968; Fukuyama, 1961).

Religious Knowledge

Intellectual or cognitive differences between older persons and others have not been investigated thoroughly with respect to religion, and the research findings to date are somewhat inconsistent. A poll in 1950 revealed that the elderly are more likely to name selected books of the Bible correctly (Erskine, 1963). Yet there was a decline in religious knowledge among the elderly on a score of religious information in a large study of urban Congregational Church members (Fukuyama, 1961).

Davidson's (1969) study of Methodist and Baptist church members in two Indiana cities, however, found that knowledge of church history and teachings was greater among adults aged 51 to 60 than among younger adults, and it was greatest of all among those over 60. On the other hand, members past fifty also revealed

> a marked decline in their willingness to rationally examine, doubt, or question church teachings. In short, church members gained in religious knowledge after fifty, but were less disposed to a rational-critical approach to religious issues [Davidson, 1969, p. 39].

When age comparisons are made holding years of education constant, it is wise to recall that the general rise in educational level in the nation may mean that "people who are now old [may be] of higher mental ability than the young people with the same amount of education," for "the rising average level of education may well have led to a decline in average mental ability at some if not all educational levels" (Glenn, 1969, p. 22). Lower test scores may reflect variations in test-taking experiences, speed of response (if that is a factor in grading), and other variables besides intellectual ability and knowledge.

RELIGIOUS EXPERIENCES

Many older people experience religious feelings, emotions, thoughts, visions, and dreams and share them with clergymen, relatives, and friends, even though they do not often talk with their physicians about them. Although the evidence is not decisive, partly because both expressive and instrumental components are involved in most activities, there apparently is a desire on the part of the aged to turn from instrumental activities, in which people

> are expected to achieve, to produce, to withhold emotions, to restrict their range of obligations . . . [to] expressive relationships and activities— diffuse endeavors in which they can spontaneously "express" themselves, in which their actions are ends in themselves rather than instruments to the accomplishment of other ends [Hammond, 1969, p. 303].

This may be part of the reason why they are more inclined to seek comfort than challenge through their church involvements (Glock, Ringer, & Babbie, 1967).

From his study of responses to items in the Minnesota Multiphasic Personality Inventory by 50,000 patients at the Mayo Clinic, Swenson (1967) reported that the highest proportion of persons saying they had experienced some "very unusual religious experiences" was among those aged 70 and over, and the same is true of those agreeing that "I am very religious (more than most people)." Belief that "Evil spirits possess me at times" was low in all categories except those under 20, but it was lowest of all among the eldest.

Davidson's (1969) Indiana Baptists and Methodists generally scored highest on the experiential dimension of religion in the youngest and oldest categories. They were "increasingly inclined to desire and report having had personal experiences with the supernatural" from age 50 on.

CONSEQUENCES OF RELIGION
ON PERSONAL AND SOCIAL LIFE

Other Social Relationships

Participation in religious groups is associated with other social relationships. Church members are more likely than nonmembers to be active in community associations, clubs, and other organizations, although the rates of voluntary association membership are lower among the oldest than among middle age categories. While this undoubtedly is partly due to other factors that are mutual influences on both types of participation,

> it is not unreasonable to think that association with people in church-related activities and organizations contributes to knowledge of other voluntary organizations; friendships in the church with persons who are members of other groups may lead to social participation in them [Moberg, 1965, p. 83].

Self-Images and Personality

Self-images and personality apparently are influenced by religious orientations. A higher proportion of elderly than of younger adults say they are "a religious person." The teachings of Judaism and Christianity affirm the dignity and worth of the individual, and apparently this has a wholesome impact upon a substantial proportion of believers. Although some other doctrines also have negative consequences, such as accentuating feelings of guilt, religious beliefs and faith in God have helped disorganized geriatric patients overcome grief and cope with lonesomeness, unhappiness, and despondency (Wolff, 1959).

Attitudes toward Death

Attitudes toward death are influenced by religion. A sense of serenity and decreased fear of death tend to accompany conservative religious beliefs, possibly because death is viewed as a portal to immortality. Yet the affirmation that one is not afraid of death could be an expression of a neurotic personality which disguises death and pretends that it is not a basic condition of all life (Fulton, 1961) or of a need to control strong anxieties concerning death (Feifel, 1956).

> A convinced belief in a future life by no means eradicates anxiety over death. . . . Religious belief is obviously relevant to dying people. . . . Those who had firm religious faith and attended their church weekly or frequently were most free of anxiety, only a fifth were apprehensive. The next most confident group, in which only a quarter were anxious, were those who had frankly said they had practically no faith. The tepid believers, who professed faith but made little outward observance of it, were more anxious to a significant extent [Hinton, 1967, pp. 38; 83].

Cultural efforts to deny death in contemporary funeral and burial practices and mourning customs accentuate the problems of dying and bereavement. This may be why there apparently is greater fear of the process of dying than of death itself among a majority of the aging (Kubler-Ross, 1969). Fears also are associated more with what is left behind at death, the problems of survivors, and discontinuance of life on earth, especially if there is a feeling that life's responsibilities have not been fulfilled, than with death itself (Feaver & Boyd, 1970). The greatest fear of all is of social isolation—desertion by friends, relatives, and other visitors, which has been referred to as the "bereavement of the dying" (Hinton, 1967). Even the differences in attitudes toward death of the religiously faithful from those of nonreligious people may be due to a considerable extent to variations in their social integration (Treanton, 1961). The nonreligious are less likely to have a reference group that gives them social support and security.

Personal and Social Adjustment, Happiness, Morale, Feelings of Satisfaction

These feelings and adjustments are associated with religious attitudes and behavior. (The contradictory evidence on this subject apparently is due to divergent definitions of "the religious factor" and different indicators of its presence or absence.) Experimental designs controlling other factors linked with personal adjustment have revealed that church membership as such is not a primary variable but only a derivative of religious beliefs and participation in church activities which happen to be correlated with membership (Moberg, 1953). Contrary evidence from Barron's (1961) New York City study may be a result of the manner in which the evidence was obtained (asking what provided the most satisfaction and comfort in life) or the sample, of which approximately three-fourths were Jews, in contrast to the predominance of Protestants and Catholics in most other studies.

It is possible that good personal adjustment is more a cause of conventional religious beliefs and activities than a result of them. This is not to say, however, that old age is seen by the elderly as the most satisfying time of life. On the contrary, it is seen by most as the least happy, with the one exception of finding it the most satisfactory for religious activity (Bromley, 1966).

Humanitarian Programs, Service Activities, and Welfare Institutions

Religious motivations have contributed to humanitarian programs, service activities, and welfare institutions which serve the aging. The spiritual motivation of love that compels action to meet the numerous needs of the aging is greatly needed today.

NEGATIVE AND DYSFUNCTIONAL CONSEQUENCES OF RELIGION

Problems in and Related to the Church

Older people often experience problems in and related to the church. A sense of guilt may develop when they wish to die because of long training that such wishes are sinful (Kramer & Kramer, 1967). In the natural process of succession of leadership from one generation to the next, they may

feel that they are being pushed aside by younger members, no longer respected and wanted for their wisdom, experience, and abilities. They may
feel they ought not to participate if their financial resources prohibit them
from making significant contributions or from dressing well. They may feel
slighted and ignored. Many have difficulty attending religious services because of physical limitations or transportation costs. Some are unhappy
with changes in the church and feel their opinions are ignored. These dis-
satisfactions may sometimes result from other problems of adjustment, but
they certainly contribute to maladjustment for substantial numbers of
people (Gray & Moberg, 1962).

In churches, as in other organizations and programs,

> is it not possible that in our attempts to provide "busy time" for the
> elderly we are saying: "'Poor soul' nothing to do; come play and pray with
> us." And in so doing we dramatize and institutionalize the very condition
> abhorred by the elderly, the condition of idleness and/or nonproductivity
> [Oakes, 1969, p. 220].

The expectation by the elderly that they will be visited by a clergyman
or other church representative when shut in or committed to a nursing home
or hospital can have highly negative results if the expectation is not fulfilled. In a British study of the socially isolated, only 5.4 percent had seen
their religious minister or vicar during the last week, and the majority of
these were seen at a religious service or other church activity. There was
little indication that the clergy detected need among old people and alerted
the social services to the needs (Tunstall, 1966). The frequent complaints by
the elderly that they are ignored by the church do not always coincide with
the actual situation, but the complaints are more often justifiable than not.

In the process of providing pastoral care for the elderly or the dying,
the clergy are less likely to avoid the issue of impending death or other
problems or to reveal hostility and displaced anger themselves than are
other members of the helping professions. Yet Dr. Kubler-Ross (1969) indicates in recounting experiences in helping people minister to the needs of
the dying:

> What amazed me . . . was the number of clergy who felt quite comfort-
> able using a prayer book or a chapter out of the Bible as the sole com-
> munication between them and the patients, thus avoiding listening to
> their needs and being exposed to questions they might be unable or
> unwilling to answer [pp. 226–227].

CHURCH PROGRAMS FOR THE AGING

The resources of religious institutions for meeting spiritual needs of
the aging are great. Theological and spiritual assets include doctrines which
pertain to man's fate in this life and the next, an ethical commitment to
serving others, an orienting perspective that puts all things and events into

a meaningful frame of reference, and traditions of ministering to the needs of mankind. The physical buildings and equipment of churches provide a meeting place and locale that can be used to serve the aging without interfering with services to other age groups. Church personnel are oriented toward serving other people more than toward taking from them. Pastors and rabbis already are serving in the capacity of a central referral agent who can easily and quickly become informed of available services to meet the needs of the aging and can refer old people to these services in a manner acceptable to both clients and agencies (Robb, 1968).

Conventional activities and services of religious bodies have contributed directly to the promotion of man's spiritual well-being. Worship, rituals, symbolism, socialization opportunities, religious education, and perhaps most of all, pastoral care (counseling, confession, prayer, referrals to community agencies, moral support, etc.) have served this need. Older people participate more in church life than in all other types of social organizations together. They turn to their minister, priest, or rabbi for counsel and support in times of major crises related to illness and developmental turning points in the life cycle. The majority even of those who lack active membership in a church are culturally conditioned to turn to a clergyman for funeral services when they have been bereaved. The traditional religious orientation that a long life is a sign of God's favor and scriptural admonitions to honor the aged are a part of the current heritage of America's religious faiths. Nevertheless, in their conventionalized activities to meet man's needs for spiritual well-being, most churches have done little specifically to confront the unique needs of the aging except as these are covered by other generalized activities.

Providing ministries of these kinds is commonly interpreted as adequate service to meet the needs of the aging. As a result, the unique needs of old people tend to be overlooked in the typical church. In addition, biases on the part of the professional and lay leaders in religious bodies reflect their personal fears of aging, stereotyped ideas about the nature and characteristics of the aged, and false assumptions about the needs of older people. These biases interfere with the establishment and fulfillment of plans to meet the relatively specialized needs of people in their later maturity.

Despite the fact that many churches tend to ignore the special needs of the aging and devote more attention to young adults, youth, and children, numerous specialized programs and projects have been initiated. These can be viewed as demonstrations of potentialities for service that are worthy of consideration by all religious bodies. Some of them are most appropriately sponsored on the denominational or diocesan level and others on an interdenominational or ecumenical community basis. But the majority of these programs are pertinent primarily on the congregational or parish level. When the older person thinks of "church" or "religion," he most often thinks in terms of the local agency of his religious faith more than of larger and more remote organizational units of it, so it is there that the greatest opportunity and need resides.

Religious organizations have helped to establish and maintain specialized agencies and institutions to serve the aging. These include: (1) retirement homes; (2) hospitals; (3) convalescent and nursing-care homes; (4) retirement centers or "villages"; (5) senior citizen centers; (6) housing programs; (7) sheltered workshops. Most service projects of these types have been sponsored by groups larger than a local parish or congregation, either within a denomination, or cutting across denominational lines in cooperative interfaith programs.

Within the normal operations of parishes and congregations are numerous service programs for the aging, including the following types: (1) weekly religious education programs to study the Bible, church history, the relevance of faith to daily life, and other subjects; (2) specialized continuing education programs; (3) clubs or centers with regular creative and social activities for the aging; (4) counseling, guidance, and referral services; (5) summer camping programs and other retreats.

Volunteer service projects both serve and give an opportunity to many older people to be of service to others. Examples of the kinds of services provided by church groups, frequently in cooperation with others in the community and sometimes with a paid or part-time staff, are the following: (1) friendly visiting of homebound, hospitalized, other institutionalized, and isolated people; (2) telephone reassurance programs; (3) homemaker, home aide, or home health services; (4) meals-on-wheels; (5) bringing religious services to the homebound by tape recordings or direct telephone line; (6) transportation services, including dial-a-ride pools; (7) programs by gospel teams, musical ensembles, choirs, and other groups for institutionalized elderly; (8) comprehensive volunteer services in hospitals and other institutions; (9) adopt-a-grandparent programs.

Churches can give older members opportunities for service. When they are given adequate leadership, screening for assignments, and suitable preparation, churches can help to provide volunteer services of the kinds mentioned above for the aging and other people. Such services would maintain church properties, assist with clerical work, work with children's and youth groups, serve on a "telephone brigade" when special announcements are needed, take care of the church library, represent the church in community programs and inter-church projects, and fulfill numerous other responsibilities related to the church and its programs (Gray & Moberg, 1962).

The church also can cooperate with or encourage enlisting in volunteer service programs of other agencies and institutions. Examples of these are VISTA, the Peace Corps, Foster Grandparents, Head Start, Late Start, Operation Green Thumb, home health aides, Senior Service Corps, International Executive Service Corps, SERVE, Second Careers Institute, Medicare Alert, and Project Find. The volunteer service programs of SERVE (Serve and Enrich Retirement by Volunteer Service) demonstrate that it is possible to get older people to volunteer for programs that provide valuable services ("SERVE's Success Invites Imitation," 1968; SERVE's Volunteers Help the Mentally Ill, 1970).

Religious bodies can offer educational programs for their own staffs and for others in the communities they serve. Their regular religious education programs for people of all ages can and ought to include corrections of stereotypes about the aged, development of wholesome perspectives toward aging, preparation for retirement (a process that begins very early in life), provision of a wholesome outlook on life and the future among the elderly, and cultivation of attitudes at all ages that will help to bridge the generation gap (cf. Gray & Moberg, 1962).

Too often, education of the clergy overlooks the special needs of the aging and elderly. Unless attention is given to this subject, it is assumed that there are no differences between them and other adults. In the ultimate sense that is true, but on a more practical and immediate level it can be pointed out that a large proportion of the pastoral ministries of the average clergyman is devoted to the aged and problems pertaining to them. Many older people are facing crises more severe than any with which they have been confronted since adolescence and early adulthood. Misleading folklore about the aged and the aging process needs to be corrected and its subtle influence on the clergyman himself overcome. The fulfillment of Judeo-Christian ethics demands attention to aging in theological education. Clinical pastoral training, units on the aging within pertinent courses already in the curriculum, and other educational experiences can be incorporated into the professional preparation of the clergy (Moberg, 1970). Continuing education programs similarly can help to improve the quality of pastoral ministries of those who are already clergymen.

The Role of Gerontology in Adult Education*

David A. Peterson

Just as there can be religion without churches and politics without legislative buildings, there can be education without schools or colleges. Indeed, many elderly persons spend a great deal of time reading books, browsing in public libraries, and attending lectures and other educational presentations. Nevertheless, our educational institutions, ranging from public schools through universities, have a great deal to offer the elderly, at the same time that the elderly have a great deal to offer the students and faculty of these institutions.

Adult education can occur in many forms and in many places. The obvious one is at the school itself, in the evening when the full-time students

*Edited from "The Role of Gerontology in Adult Education," by D. A. Peterson. In S. M. Grabowski and W. D. Mason (Eds.), *Learning for Aging.* Copyright 1974 by the Adult Education Association/U.S.A., 810 Eighteenth Street, Washington, D.C. 20006. Reprinted by permission.

are not around. But older people frequently will not go out in the evenings, partly through fear of crime, partly through having transportation difficulties (public transportation is inadequate and some elderly have visual problems with night driving). Also, a local college or university campus is usually seen as "unknown turf" to older residents of the community, and they may prefer to have programs in areas in the community which they know well.

As a result, some colleges have established outreach programs, holding courses in retirement communities, local churches, wherever appropriate space is available. Then, as the participants become more familiar with the procedures and feel more a part of the school, they are encouraged to come to the campus to take additional courses.

Similarly, some older persons fear that they will be embarrassed by "these bright young kids" if they attend regular college courses, but this fear usually disappears after they have taken a course or two designed particularly for them. They realize that they still have the capacity to learn and to enjoy their learning. And the mystique associated with college students tends to disappear when you have taken a few college courses yourself.

Educational programs do not need to be restricted to traditional approaches. The well-known SAGE program, developed in Berkeley, is a good example of applying highly sophisticated and innovative personal growth instruction to the needs of older persons. The SAGE program consists of a combination of relaxation and sensory awareness procedures, including biofeedback, yoga, meditation, breathing exercises, massage, and similar processes (Elwell, 1976). Similar programs are evolving throughout the United States and Canada.

Heightened sensitivity and concern for older people has led to recognition of their educational needs. Educators and gerontologists are now beginning to focus on these needs and to develop educational programs which will provide the skills, knowledge and experience to assist older people in meeting these needs.

This developing interest and concern has led to a new role for adult education—a role which has been almost totally disregarded in the past and even now is receiving only minimal attention. This role is to provide education for the later years of life, those years when new problems combine with old to form an altered life situation, and where increased leisure time provides for growth opportunities of uncommon means.

EDUCATIONAL BACKGROUND OF OLDER PEOPLE

Older persons in this country face numerous problems. Health, income, housing, transportation, role loss, isolation, loss of friends, and impending death are some of those placing new demands on aging individuals. At the same time, many have needs to express their creative abilities, to continue to grow, to explore new areas of knowledge and geography.

The ability to cope with these problems and to continue their intellectual growth is partially a function of the previous educational experience of older people. In general, the greater the individual's age, the less formal education he has had. The median number of years of school completed by persons over 65 in 1972 was 9.1 years. This means that nearly half of today's older population has had no high school education whatsoever. Table 1 shows the number of years of school completed by persons at various ages.

At least half the persons in the older population must be viewed as undereducated, and nearly 3 million are categorized as functionally illiterate. It is important to note, however, that the limited exposure to education is primarily restricted to persons over age 55, and especially prevalent in those over 65. Each of the groups between 25 and 55 has an average of slightly over twelve years of schooling. Put another way, the average person under 55 has completed high school, and age is not significantly related to the amount of schooling. The group of persons between ages of 55 and 64 is the transition group, showing an increase in schooling over the older group, but less formal education than the younger group.

Another way of showing the significance of the change taking place is to review educational levels in the past. Table 2 shows that persons over the age of 65 in 1940, 1950, 1960, and 1972 have had approximately the same number of years of formal education—slightly more than eight years. The only exception is women 65–74 in 1972 who have nine and one-half years of education.

Up to this time, the young old and the old old have been generally equal educationally. There has been little difference between the oldest and the youngest of those over age 65. However, this is about to change. Persons age 55 to 64 in 1972 have a significantly higher education level than do those already retired, and the 45 to 54 age group have education approximately equal to each of the younger groups.

Table 1. Years of School Completed, March 1972*

| | *Years of School Completed (% distribution)* | | | | | | | |
| | *Elementary School* | | | *High School* | | *College* | | *Median* |
Age	*Less than 5 Years*	*5–7 yrs*	*8 yrs*	*1–3 yrs*	*4 yrs*	*1–3 yrs*	*4 or More*	*School Years Completed*
25–29 years	0.8	2.7	3.1	13.6	43.8	17.1	19.0	12.7
30–34 years	1.4	3.4	4.7	16.7	43.9	13.6	16.5	12.5
35–44 years	2.5	5.4	6.9	18.5	41.5	11.5	14.7	12.4
45–54 years	3.4	7.3	10.8	18.6	38.6	10.6	10.7	12.3
55–64 years	5.6	11.6	17.3	18.9	29.3	8.5	8.8	11.3
65–74 years	9.9	16.0	23.6	15.3	20.1	7.2	7.8	9.1
75 years and over	16.0	18.3	27.1	11.8	15.2	6.1	5.6	8.6

*U.S. Bureau of the Census, "Educational Attainment: March 1972." *Current Population Reports,* 1972.

Table 2. Median School Years Completed by Age and Sex for the United States, 1940, 1950, 1960, 1972*

	Age					
	25–34	35–44	45–54	55–64	65–74	75 and Over
Males						
1972	12.7	12.5	12.3	11.1	8.9	8.4
1960	12.2	12.0	9.9	8.6	8.2	8.0
1950	11.8	10.0	8.7	8.4	8.1	8.8
1940	9.7	8.7	8.4	8.2	8.1	7.8
Females						
1972	12.6	12.4	12.3	11.5	9.5	8.7
1960	12.2	12.1	10.6	8.8	8.5	8.3
1950	12.1	10.6	8.9	8.5	8.3	8.2
1940	10.3	8.8	8.5	8.4	8.2	8.1

*U.S. Bureau of the Census, *Eighteenth Census, 1960; Seventeenth Census, 1950;* and *Sixteenth Census, 1940;* and *Current Population Reports,* 1972.

The quality of the education received by older persons must also be considered. With teachers who were ill-trained, materials which were scarce if available at all, a curriculum which deviated little from the three R's, and a class atmosphere which typically stressed discipline above learning, it is probably not accurate to equate a year of schooling in the early 1900's with a year today.

Thus, persons over age 65 are less well prepared by formal education to meet the challenges that face them than are those at any younger age. Although they have doubtless profited from their years of experience, they may well have neglected the development of those skills which are increasingly needed to adjust to the constant change which impinges upon all of us.

Since education may provide a person with the skills which help him understand the world in which he lives and equips him to make better decisions regarding the options that are open to him, older people may be expected to be less successful in adapting to changes around them than are younger persons.

OLDER PERSONS' EDUCATIONAL NEEDS

One of the needs of older people is that of education to overcome these deficiencies. This education should provide the basic learning skills that are needed as well as specific information and experiences which will help meet the new challenges of old age.

Education for older people must also begin to be preventive rather than totally ameliorative. As persons with increased education reach the retirement years, they may face fewer of the crises with which current retirees have been plagued. They will have different needs and education can begin to play different roles in assisting them.

There are several categories of educational need. These have been conceptualized in a variety of ways by different writers, but one of the most useable sets of designations is provided by McClusky (1971), who identifies four educational need categories—coping needs, expressive needs, contributive needs, and influence needs. Each of these is described in terms of its programmatic implications and relevance to the older group.

Coping needs refer to that group of requirements which must be met in order to continue adequate social adjustment, psychological health, and physical well-being. McClusky includes such programming as adult basic education; health education; and training for economic improvement, legal arrangements, housing choices, family adjustments, and successful use of leisure time.

The second category, expressive needs, refers to those areas where individuals engage in activity for its own sake, activity which has intrinsic meaning and pleasure. This educational activity may include physical education, liberal education, or hobby and personal interest areas.

Contributive needs are those which encourage older persons to repay society in some way for its past generosity. Many older people feel that they need to serve in some way, to help others less fortunate than themselves, to repay a past debt. This need can be translated into educational programming through in-service, leadership, and community awareness education.

The fourth area of need is referred to as influence need. This identifies the desire of older people to be able to affect the direction and quality of their lives. Educationally this has been approached through civic and political organization and the accompanying education for leadership, community action, and problem solving.

Awareness of the usefulness of these several kinds of education for older people is not currently widespread. In fact, it is often overlooked as a resource which could be of significant service to older people. When education is mentioned, it is typically accorded low priority, both by adult educators and by older people themselves (Peterson, 1971). This has led to low participation rates by older people in educational activities and limited interest in this type of programming by adult educators.

It is well documented that age is inversely related to participation in continuing education (Johnstone & Rivera, 1965). That is, the older the person, the less likely he is to be engaged in any organized adult education program. A 1969 study by the Bureau of the Census (USDHEW, 1971) showed that 11.0 percent of the total eligible population over 17 years of age participated in adult education. Eligible population was defined as those who were not full-time students. However, participation was not evenly spread over the total age range. As age rose the percent of adult education participation declined (Table 3).

Of an eligible 18.6 million people over 65 in 1969, only 263,600 or 1.6 percent actually participated in adult education activities of any kind. No reason for this decline is provided in the study, but it was shown that the

Table 3. Participants in Adult Education as a Percentage of the Total Population by Age—United States, May 1969*

Age	Population in Each Age Group	% Who Participated in Adult Education
17–24	24,800,000	18.0
25–34	23,600,000	18.2
35–44	22,700,000	13.5
45–54	22,700,000	9.4
55–64	17,900,000	4.5
65 and over	18,600,000	1.6

*U.S. Department of Health, Education and Welfare. National Center for Educational Statistics. *Participation in Adult Education,* 1969; Initial Report.

decline is approximately parallel for men and women, as well as for whites, blacks, and other racial groups.

A NEW ROLE FOR ADULT EDUCATION

Adult education is a diverse and comprehensive field. It includes a wide variety of educational methods, clientele, and content which are not easily integrated into a single statement covering the enterprise. The goals of adult education also include a wide variety of programs and philosophy. A. A. Liveright (1968) has attempted to derive the goals of the field by inductively surveying programming in the field. He concluded that there are four major goals: "occupational, vocational and/or professional competence; personal and family living competence; social and civic responsibility; and self-fulfillment" (p. 4).

These goals include virtually all of what we know as adult education. The problem, however, is not in the breadth of the definition, but in its implementation. It is clear that in some areas, the implementation is not complete and some segments of the population are perhaps inadvertently excluded from participation in adult education activities. As indicated earlier, the lack of participation by older persons in adult education activities may be the result of lack of interest, lack of motivation, costs, or a generally negative attitude toward their capabilities.

The reasons may be multiple, but the result is singular. Participation in activities defined as basically educational is almost totally disregarded by the older population. Their needs for adjustment and growth are evident, but education is not utilized to meet these needs.

Gerontology's Role in Adult Education

In order to respond to the challenge of the various educational needs of older adults, it will be necessary for the field of adult education to adjust in at least five ways. These include expansion of programming, adjusted emphasis in the psychological base, alternative financing mechanisms, expanded recruitment, and a changed philosophical stance.

Programming. The first major adjustment that will need to be made is in the area of programming. Older persons have tended to avoid the type of programming typically provided by adult education agencies. Although adult courses are generally open to older people, senior citizens do not participate. They typically find the courses designed for younger people, competition greater than they desire, and fees beyond their means. Adult education agencies have failed to develop programs specifically for older people. Consequently participation rates are extremely low.

In order to change this situation, adult educators will need to revise their view of older people as potential clientele and begin to program for their needs and interests. McClusky's four categories of need may be advantageously used to determine which types of educational experiences should be provided. The category of coping needs is an appropriate one to give priority. Londoner, who uses the term instrumental education to refer to this type of programming, points out that the needs of older people can best be approached by education which provides the skills and information needed to help solve problems (Londoner, 1971).

Heimstra has built on this theoretical position by surveying the expressed educational interests of older people and has found that instrumental education if presented in convenient locations is much desired by older people (Heimstra, 1972). Our own work at the University of Nebraska at Omaha in offering a three-day education festival for older people with nearly 70 one-hour courses supports this position. Older persons responded very well to instrumental types of education, in fact they were likely to choose it over other types which were offered.

Courses which fall into McClusky's second category—expressive needs of older people—are also highly appropriate. These would include many offerings in the liberal education area as well as arts and crafts, current affairs, and such special interest areas as genealogy. These are the courses that older people are likely to take in the general adult education program, but have been shown to be of special interest when they are offered primarily for older people.

Expressive activities offer the greatest potential for growth and continued social engagement of older persons, since they allow individuals to renew or continue their contact with the world of learning. Too often this area of educational growth is discontinued in earlier years. A concerted effort needs to be made to re-engage these people in educational activities which will allow them to examine and explore areas of knowledge which have held the attention of mankind for hundreds of years—philosophy, literature, history, politics.

Courses which would prepare persons for the contributive role are also needed. The retirement of the breadwinner, loss of children, and decline in income frequently make older people feel less sure of their value and place in society. Educational offerings which can provide insight into their role in the community, emphasize their skills, and develop new competencies which can be provided to community groups would allow the senior citizen to find a role which has meaning to both him and the community.

Finally, the influence need has been evidenced by an increasing number of older people turning to political activity as the means to improve their position in this country. Too often, this activity is less than optimally effective because of the limited experience and skills which older people have developed. Instruction and assistance by adult education agencies is needed and appropriate to assist the formation of older people's groups and to facilitate the expression of their desires to elected officials who can provide services or stimulate programs that will be of direct benefit to them. Little of this type of leadership training has been undertaken to date, but the need and desire for it will hopefully lead to expansion in the future.

In programming, then, there is a definite need for education experiences which are prepared and directed exclusively toward older people. Some adult educators and some older people will object to this type of age-segregated programming, but the alternative of including meaningful numbers of older people in courses designed primarily for the general public has been an unqualified failure. An alternate approach is needed, and the experience of a number of public schools, colleges, and informal organizations has shown that age-segregated programming can prove very successful.

Psychological base. The second adjustment that must be met by adult educators is in the psychological bases on which programming is built. Current training of adult educators in the psychology of adult learning tends to overlook or underemphasize the learning ability that people retain into their 60's and 70's. Just as college courses in human development tend to terminate before dealing with adulthood, so courses in adult psychology tend to conclude before confronting old age. This instructional inadequacy has been a factor in limiting the insight of adult program planners.

Too many persons continue to believe that psychological development ends in young adulthood, that persons past their "prime" are not able to change their behavior or to learn new material. This is clearly not the case. Society, however, generally accepts the stereotype that increased age correlates positively with increased rigidity, inflexibility, and mental decline. There are older people who are rigid; but there are many others who have kept their flexibility and can benefit from learning experiences.

The concept of the teachable moment is especially appropriate in this context. Since education per se is not a high priority item for older people, we must look to the developmental stages that are being experienced and identify the adjustments that are forced upon them. These adjustments will identify areas where certain types of new skills and information will be desired. This will be the time when the educational experience will be most likely to succeed.

A second psychological area which should be emphasized is that of the group process involved in the instruction. Hixson (1969) emphasizes the need for a non-threatening educational setting. It is necessary, however, to go even beyond this level of psychological safety and consciously attempt to build a supportive instructional environment, one which conveys in concrete terms that the individual is foremost and content secondary. When this type of setting is achieved, the involvement of older persons may be expected to be at its peak.

This supportive setting appears to be most likely to develop when the clientele of the educational experience are segregated by age. Even though age-integrated instruction has much to recommend it, in general it is viewed as more threatening, more competitive, and less supportive by older persons. Consequently, at least some understanding of the value of age-segregated programming is needed by adult educators.

Expansion of the adult educator's view of the psychology of older learners should also include the physical conditions under which older people learn best. Lighting, size of print, loudness of speakers, audio interference, the type of furniture, and the approach of the instructor are all variables which will need to be carefully considered in programming for older persons.

Alternative financing. Financial support for most adult and continuing education programming comes from client fees. Although the administrative overhead may be borne by the sponsoring institution, operational costs typically must be covered by course income.

This financial arrangement is very difficult to implement in programming for older people who often are unwilling or unable to pay ten to twenty-five dollars or more for a course or workshop. Because the median family income of the older group is so low, purchase of non-essential products and services is generally avoided; education is too often viewed as non-essential. Consequently, educational programming simply does not enroll many older people because of the costs involved. Regular fee schedules limit attendance to a minority of more well-to-do older people.

An alternative approach to funding programs for older people will be required if the majority of the older population is to participate. This will need to be, at the least, a combination of fees and other sources of funds. Federal dollars present one alternative, but at the present time these are generally very limited.

Perhaps, the continually expanding discussions on the necessity for life-long learning may hasten the implementation of some type of voucher or educational credit system whereby adults are provided the equivalent of cash to buy the education they desire from any available agency. Tax credits, tax reductions or released time from work are other possibilities which governmental units may promote in the not too distant future.

Other alternatives include the use of private funds. Groups such as the American Association of Retired Persons—National Retired Teachers Association have developed programs in many parts of the country and appear willing to work cooperatively with public and private agencies in developing education and especially preretirement education for older persons. Local communities may also be developing a willingness to invest some monies in this kind of program. In addition, colleges, especially community colleges, appear more willing to provide some funds also.

Another source of potentially extensive funding is from business and industry. Retraining and job upgrading programs have long been a part of industry's activities and more recently, preretirement education has gained increased support. Some companies offer their own classes or counseling while others contract with local educational agencies. The future, however, may hold greatly increased participation with business and industry supporting preretiree and retiree clubs, programs, and hobbies.

Whatever the source, some financial assistance is needed. This is not to suggest that most older people will not be willing and able to pay a small fee for an educational experience. They will be and often desire to pay something, but the fee must usually be minimal—under five dollars if the average older person is to take part. If this adjustment in funding can be made, a significant obstacle to programming for older people will have been overcome.

Expanded recruiting. The older population, like other low-participant groups, will need a great deal of encouragement to enter the adult education area. It will require more recruiting on the part of the adult educator, more outreach, and a developed system of personal contact with groups of older persons.

It will probably never be sufficient to announce educational offerings for older people in the local newspaper and expect an extensive response. Too many older people do not act on information presented in such a manner. It will be necessary to meet with groups of older people, to involve them in planning the experiences, to develop a group of voluntary recruiters, and to utilize the existing communication networks in the aging community if the information is to really reach the right people.

These communication networks vary markedly from one community to the next, but often include a number of senior citizen centers which operate one or more days per week; clubs which meet in churches or homes; agencies such as Family Services, Red Cross, Visiting Nurse Association; institutions like nursing homes, hospitals, and homes for the aging; and governmental organizations like Departments of Housing, Health, Mental Health, Social Services, Social Security, Education, and Human Resources. Contacts with these groups lead to increased awareness of activities and needs of the aged and mechanisms for coordination.

The problem of recruiting older people is no more difficult than it has been in recruiting other groups which have traditionally been non-participants—the undereducated, minorities, etc. Additional time and energy are required; adjustments in program locations, fees, and hours are necessary; but if the additional effort is expended, the rewards in terms of community relationships, individual good will, public relations, and repeat business will be well worth the effort.

Philosophical stance. The final adjustment which adult educators will need to make is in the philosophical stance of the agency and the adult educator. The needed change is in the perception of the agency staff. They must begin to view people in later maturity as having the ability to grow and develop, as being appropriate to include in adult education activities, as being desired clientele. Then, adult educators must begin to program in accordance with this perception.

In the final analysis, the greatest educational barrier that older people must overcome lies in the stereotypes, folk-wisdom, and ignorance that label senior citizens as unworthy clients for the field of adult education. Until this prejudicial attitude is revised, it will be unlikely that real change in the participation rates of older people will occur.

If adult educators wait for older people to demand educational services, they may be slow in coming. On the other hand, if adult educators will take the lead as societal change agents, the milieu is now ready, and rapid development of education for this neglected segment of society can be rapidly implemented.

CONCLUSION

The role of gerontology in adult education is to bring to light a neglected clientele group which should be served, to point out the need for expanding educational understanding of the abilities of older people, to identify the financial and recruiting realities in implementing such programming, and to identify the need for an adjustment in the attitudes of the adult education programmers which will allow all of this to occur.

Gerontology is pointing to the potential of education to meet numerous growth and maintenance needs of the older population. Education for older people has been sorely neglected in the past. It must not be so in the future.

The Role of Television*

Richard H. Davis

It was not many years ago when Bill Cosby began to play a sustaining role in the television show, I Spy. Today we are so likely to accept the idea that Blacks perform leading roles in television and movies that we have trouble recalling how recently Cosby established that first. Although old people have not historically fared as poorly as Blacks in the entertainment media, they almost never play leading roles. One delightful show some years ago, starring two older women as accidental but competent detectives, lasted only through the summer.

Who will be the Bill Cosby of the elderly? Do you feel that this has already been taken care of with "The Waltons" or "Sanford and Son" or another show?

Before moving on to the discussion, it seems appropriate to mention that television, of course, is not the only example of the media in which older people can play some part. There is radio, the record industry, newspapers, and magazines as well. But for the moment, the emphasis is on television. And, as I write this, there are plans being implemented to change the status of the elderly person as the forgotten member of the small-screen industry.

The communications media most easily available for mass dissemination of information are print and broadcast facilities. Surveys too numerous to list have indicated that the use of print media for information service by those of little education, the culturally disadvantaged, and the elderly is significantly less than use by other segments of the population. Loss of visual acuity as well as possible financial limitations may explain why the elderly are included with these other disadvantaged in this statement.

The Roper National Surveys have asked for an indication of the primary source of news "about what is going on in the world" (Roper, 1971). The print media are much less utilized by the general population than broadcast media. Television consistently ranks as a first choice with the majority of the respondents who represent a cross-national, age-diversified sample. In two other surveys of both a well-educated old sample in Long Beach and an urban Los Angeles older population with fewer educational advantages, television also ranked as first information source (Davis, 1971; 1972). The percentage of elderly choosing television as first source was significantly greater than for the general population. A comparison of the ranking of news sources as indicated by the 1968 Roper Sample, the 1969

*Reprinted by permission from November/December 1973 issue of *Perspective on Aging*, published by The National Council on the Aging, Inc.

Long Beach sample, and the 1971 Urban Los Angeles Sample appears in Table 1.

Table 1. Preferred News Sources

	Roper National Sample—1968		Long Beach Elderly Sample—1969		Los Angeles Urban Elderly Sample—1971	
	No.	*%*	*No.*	*%*	*No.*	*%*
Television	59	40.7	89	56.2	145	55.8
Newspapers	49	33.8	42	26.2	38	14.6
Radio	25	17.3	14	8.5	76	29.2
Magazines	7	4.8	12	7.5	1	0.4
People	5	3.4	1	0.6	0	0.0
	145	100.0	158	100.0	260	100.0

Not only is television the most frequently chosen source for news, additional research indicates that as one ages, the choice of program type is more likely to be information programs than entertainment programs. Schramm (1969, pp. 352–375) reported that 48% of programs viewed by those age 65 and over were information programs as compared to 20% of programs viewed by those under age 25. Davis (1976) surveyed 215 persons age 65 and over and found that the entire sample population viewed news and public affairs consistently. Using a Nielsen audience measurement technique, this sample was found to view news programs in greater number than did younger age groups (c.f. Nielsen, 1973). Table 2 compares the Davis response with Nielsen responses for the same broadcast day and time. (Nielsen data do not tabulate age groups above age 64). The survey indicated further that older people viewed local news programming in still greater numbers than network national news.

Upon contemplating the problems of communicating both with and about older persons, one must turn to the preferred media, broadcasting, to assess their potential.

Table 2. Viewing of Network News by Three Age Groups. (Figures show percent of the designated audience with sets turned on who are viewing either NBC or CBS, 7:00 p.m. network news on Wednesdays, 1973.)

	Nielsen Sample		Davis Sample
Sex	*Age 25–49*	*Age 49–64*	*Age 65–95 (mean = 76)*
Male	37.2%	38.7%	52.4%
Female	31.5%	40.0%	56.4%

BROADCASTING AND THE OLDER AUDIENCE

What are the apparent positive aspects of broadcast communication? Radio and television are communication channels especially suited to their audiences because of what Otto Kleppner (1966) calls "a sense of participation, personal access and reality which approximate face-to-face contact." In addition to this, the two media reach virtually the entire population, including groups such as the very old, the very young, and the less well-educated, all of whom, by virtue of their status do not have easy access to the print media.

Radio

Table 1 shows television as the preferred broadcast medium and it outranks radio by a large percent. Radio, it might seem, is the medium of the young, music-oriented generation and the commuter who finds it companionable through his long stints on the freeways. This is not to imply that radio is less effective in influencing audience behavior. Far from it; under certain conditions, it is a more powerful agent than television. Primarily, the employment of listener imagination and subsequent subjective involvement is more likely to happen through radio communication. But when the communicator wishes to imprint a visual identification in the recipient's consciousness, obviously television will be superior.

Television

Existing studies in the specific area of the older population as a broadcast audience are few, but they do offer some generalizations regarding the older television audience.

1. The older population is a dependable, constant, often house-bound and captive audience.
2. It has a high status of availability.
3. The audience has been called "embracers" because of a demonstrated tendency to accept without question, and with gratitude, whatever programming is available to them.
4. It is the basis of shared experience, a valuable common denominator with the rest of society.
5. The television is a companion; the performer or personality is a nonjudgmental friend.
6. Finally, and perhaps most significant, the television provides for the older audience the single and strongest, the most preferred source of news and information.

Television communication, if it is to be regarded in any sense as a service, must be regarded as such only in a special sense. It is a public service designed to serve a large and undifferentiated society. The offerings are non-fragmented. Nevertheless, because of the diversity of broadcast outlets in many areas, the population served does benefit from freedom of choice.

Although a public service mandated by the Federal Government to operate in "the public interest, convenience, and necessity," broadcasting is a service controlled by profit making organizational structures. Within these structures the decision makers must choose carefully how they utilize air time to satisfy the public service qualification and still make money. Although older people find certain benefits in television viewing, the system does not define them as a primary target. They are seldom intended recipients of specific communications. In the broadcast world target audiences are thought of in gross market terms: children (4-12), teenagers (13-19), young adults (20-30), mature consumers (31-55). Any audience beyond age 55 is not of particular interest to the broadcast business.

THE VALUES OF TELEVISION

Television viewing serves varying functions with varying audiences. There is some commonality, to be sure, in the value placed on this activity by all viewers regardless of age, income, education or other variables. However, the relative weight of these values varies greatly according to viewer demographics. For example, education is a primary determiner of certain viewing behaviors as it is a determiner of other social behaviors. For older viewers it should be recognized that a dependency factor exists for them that is extremely important as an underlying determinant of viewing behavior. Older viewers are often characterized by a captive status (Steiner, 1963; Berelson & Steiner, 1964; Meyersohn, 1961). The world has shrunk for many older people and their choices of activity may become more and more limited. But television ownership is now universal and the decision-making processes regarding which channel to tune in are simple.

Involvement

What are the values and benefits that may be said to accrue to the older viewer? The first is obvious; the older viewer relies on television to remain involved and to continue to be a part of the mainstream of life (Glick and Levy, 1962). The elderly viewer's dependency on television for news reflects the dependency of the general population. Media surveys have indicated again and again that most people in our society rely first of all on television, secondly on radio, and thirdly on newspapers for information about world events. This is especially true of the older viewer and is quite understandable. Reading the newspaper is often a more difficult task for the elderly than viewing and listening to televised news. The older viewer finds that the action seen in television news keeps him involved. It is the connecting link with the affairs of society, and it means that, by sharing common knowledge, the older viewer is still a member of the club.

Companionship

The older viewer finds television a beneficial source of companionship (Meyersohn, 1961; Glick & Levy, 1962). When friends depart and there are fewer people with whom one can relate, substitutions must be found. Those people whose images appear regularly on the television screen are readily available substitutions. (Of course, this value, like all listed here, applies also to the general population. One of the premises in writing programs is to create characters who, by the force of their personality, will attract regular viewers. A program's success is often determined solely by the personality of the major character, or the host person in the case of talk and game shows.) Older viewers may be using the real and fictitious characters in a series, a variety show, or a newscast to relate to as they would to visiting families and people had they such real people available. It should be noted too that by and large one has the choice of many accepting, nonjudgmental, safe personalities to relate to on the television screen.

Demarcation of Time

Television acts as a way to mark off time (Meyersohn, 1961). Because of the programming schedule of television there is an available logical time demarcation. We live our lives marking off time into certain significant spaces. We get up and go to work at a certain time. We stop for lunch. We stop work and go home at five o'clock. These are time demarcations that have significance for us during a large part of our lives. The older person who has moved out of the labor force does not have the same kinds of ways to mark off time so a day becomes comparatively unstructured. However, if one is going to watch a program daily at 2:30 p.m., then the time 2:30 has special significance. The day can be marked off as to the events that happen before 2:30, and those events that happen after three o'clock. This has special significance for many older people because they can look forward to something happening at a certain time. Many people have a need for scheduling time so that they may feel that their life has a strong dimension of structure.

Time Structure

The fourth value of television viewing for older people is that it fills time (Christensen & McWilliams, 1967). Not only does it mark off time in significant segments, but it simply fills time. For many older people this enormous amount of uncommitted time is difficult to fill.

Television is an easy way to fill time. In this sense, television has been said to have a narcotizing effect. The dependent viewer may become "hooked." It seems, however, that for the older audience the time-filling value is "a doing something" as opposed to "a doing nothing."

Existing Broadcasting
Services to the Elderly

Because it has been determined that, comparatively speaking, the older audience is not economically advantaged, it is not wooed by broadcast interests. What programming is targeted to the older audience is apt to be sporadic, lacking in focus and dropped into any public service time slot. Under such conditions, its impact is apt to be less than strong. Nevertheless, changing population patterns, an increasing social awareness on the part of the industry, and developing technologies in communications are factors that should and will influence new philosophies regarding the elderly as an audience that should be attended to by communicators in broadcasting.

CONCLUSION

There are questions to be raised about the older person's dependency on television as indicated by the importance the older viewers place on the values listed above. What are the opportunities for older people to see on television other people like themselves dealing with problems which are like the problems they deal with? How can positive role models be incorporated into current television programming?

When the rapid technological changes in television broadcasting are contemplated it is possible to predict greater and more diverse information dissemination activity through this channel of communication. The older viewer will eventually have the opportunity to derive more easily the specific kinds of information necessary to improve the quality of life. Cable television and closed circuit television will provide programming for special audiences that differs from current programming for mass audiences. The values for the older audience may remain the same, but this "captive" older audience may recognize an even greater therapeutic value from viewing as television broadcasting changes to reflect the changing times.

Chapter 8

Using Physical Space:
Housing and Transportation

A man's home—and a woman's as well—is his castle—or hers. But for older men and women, housing can become a very large problem. Many older people live in houses that were purchased when their children were at home, so often they have more space than they need. At the same time, rising property taxes and home-maintenance costs require that they spend an increasing amount of their income to keep the residence going.

For many people, the decision is simple and obvious: They move to smaller, less expensive and less physically demanding quarters. For others, this is not the answer. Either financial circumstances make it impossible to obtain appropriate living arrangements, or their attachment to their *castle* is so great that leaving would cause too much of an emotional wrench.

Young people who are still transient in their living and working arrangements may not be sensitive to the importance of attachment to things. We all understand attachment to people, or to ideals, or to organizations, but there is something about attachment to things that may seem unduly materialistic. Yet the sense of loss some people feel when they move down the street, or to another neighborhood, or to another community is often acute. Older people (and of course many nonelderly) resist such change with an intensity that may seem extreme in light of the apparent value of what they must surrender. But more than the purely physical attributes they lose, people most miss the familiarity of the old place. The familiar is predictable and comfortable. It is often easier to deal with change when we can return to a place where we feel at home. We know where things are; we know the neighbors and the neighborhood; we are secure and in control. Of course, as neighbors and neighborhoods change, people lose that sense of the familiar and may feel that it is time to leave. So, while one segment of the elderly population seeks to maintain familiar attachments, another segment is willing and ready to relocate, particularly if the new setting provides them with more of what they need and want in terms of cost, neighborhood, convenience, comfort, and also access to getting where they want to go when they want to go there.

The title of this chapter is Using Physical Space. Housing forms only one part of the physical environment. We not only function within a given space, but we also need to move through space. The pleasure provided by a home can only be understood in terms of the location of that house, the neighborhood, the community, and (immensely important) the available transportation. For an older person who no longer drives, a beautiful home in a lovely neighborhood may become a prison if the nearest public transportation is two miles away. Your mother, who never learned to drive, loved living on the farm until your father died, and suddenly the beloved home is twice-lonely: no husband and no access to friends. The story is familiar, and you undoubtedly know similar stories yourself.

The Housing Patterns of Older People*

James E. Montgomery

Where do older people live? Why? What are their alternatives? For those who have the financial resources and who are in good health, the possibilities are virtually limitless; for those on limited incomes or who have physical problems, the alternatives are few. But this, of course, is true for any age group. What makes the elderly unique is that their income often is diminishing and there is little hope of any significant increase. But also, the elderly generally are limited by physical weaknesses, poor health, and risk of poor health.

The immediate environment looms large in the lives of most older Americans. Hansen (1971) has estimated that persons over 65 spend 80 to 90 percent of their lives in the domestic (home) environment. Of all people, only small children, the chronically ill, and those institutionalized are so house and neighborhood bound. Others have indicated that the life space of the elderly tends to diminish with age (Birren, 1969; Clark, 1968). Eventually older persons cease to journey to and from work and to range by car over the United States. As energy and health decline and financial resources shrink, countless numbers of older Americans limit the physical space they occupy to the neighborhood grocery store, nearby church, and to their dwelling. Indeed, for the enfeebled and the ill, life space is reduced to a house or an apartment, to a room and ultimately to a bed within four restricting walls.

Therefore, the quality of the housing environment becomes increasingly significant in the lives of many aged families and individuals. And the quality of this limited world largely determines the extent to which they will retain their independence; the amount of privacy, auditory and visual, they will experience; how often they will visit with friends; their sense of place; and their ability to exercise a measure of control over the immediate environment. Housing often is a major variable, physically, socially and psychologically, in the lives of older persons.

Since around 1950 a new vocabulary has come into usage to designate types of housing available to the aged population—condominiums, town houses, cooperatives, "prefabs," public housing, mobile homes, retirement

*Edited from "The Housing Patterns of Older Families," by J. E. Montgomery, *The Family Coordinator,* 1972, *21*, 37–46. Copyright 1972 by the National Council on Family Relations. Reprinted by permission.

communities, congregate homes, nursing homes, intermediate care facilities, and geriatric hospitals. Undoubtedly a reason for this emerging pluralistic approach to housing is a growing recognition that on many counts those "65 and over" constitute a wide variety of personalities, life styles, and needs. This "group," representing an age span of more than 35 years, differs in sex, education, health, marital status, income, race, life style, geographic location, aspirations, and "behavioral maps" (Kent, 1971; Montgomery, 1965).

The purposes of this section are to provide an overview of income and housing of older persons, to identify housing needs, and to examine housing alternatives.

Low fixed incomes (not fixed against the erosion of the dollar) mean that many of the aged simply cannot afford even to buy modestly priced homes or to rent modestly priced apartments. Mobile homes are virtually the only form of new housing within the economic reach of many older persons. Other alternatives are to continue to live in but neglect the maintenance of their homes, to rent rundown quarters, or to live in dwellings subsidized in one way or another by the federal government. Older Americans value decent housing as evidenced by the fact that they spend a larger percentage of their income for shelter than does any other age group (Ellis, 1964).

The dwelling units occupied by the aged are frequently old, in a state of disrepair, and lacking in one or more plumbing and heating amenities. Usually older persons do not live under crowded conditions. In fact, in many instances, they are "over-housed" in terms of the numbers of rooms and square footage. In 1970, 69.5 percent of the aged owned their dwellings compared with 64.0 percent for all household heads.

Today there is an over representation of the proportion of older families who live in central city and rural areas and an under representation of those living in the suburbs. Birren (1970) has observed that millions of aged persons have been unable to escape substandard housing and limited services commonly found in central city by following younger, more affluent families to the suburbs. Meanwhile, Clark (1971) has noted that geriatric ghettos as well as ethnic ghettos are increasingly developing in the central areas of many urban communities.

In rural areas many older families also live under highly adverse conditions despite the fact that in recent years the spotlight of concern has become increasingly focused upon urban problems. In Appalachia, in much of the rural South, on Indian reservations, and among Mexican Americans are large numbers of aged persons whose life space is almost completely devoid of decent housing and community support services—health, recreation, transportation, and other necessities (Hansen, 1970).

For a variety of reasons, older persons do not change their place of residence as frequently as do younger individuals and families. For the period 1955–1960 only four percent of older persons moved to another state contrasted with nine percent of the total population (Lenzer, 1965). Many older persons have a bias against changing their place of residence despite undesirable housing conditions and isolation on the one hand and better housing and a greater opportunity for social amenities on the other (Robbins, 1971).

Montgomery (1965), in a study of older persons who lived in a small community in central Pennsylvania, found that the respondents had not recently moved and did not wish to move. Sixty-eight percent of those interviewed were born in or near the community and 81 percent had lived in their present dwellings for ten or more years. Seventy-eight percent of the 512 older persons stated that they liked their neighborhood very well; 76 percent liked their houses very well.

A recent survey (Institute for Interdisciplinary Studies, 1971) of 3053 older persons revealed that 82.6 percent of the national sample were happy with their neighborhood.

In the absence of facts one can do little more than speculate as to why older families, no longer tied to a place of employment, are so relatively immobile. One can hypothesize that anchoring variables include limited incomes, declining health, a strong sense of place, and an unwillingness to face adjustment problems occasioned by moving.

Housing Needs

Traditionally Americans, including researchers, architects, planners, housing officials, and consumers, have viewed housing in a restricted sense—as a dwelling unit, house, or apartment. At the same time those who produce shelter usually regard housing more as a tool or commodity than as a small private world in which intimate and day-to-day familial interaction and activities take place. But more recently social and psychological dimensions are being ascribed to housing; increasingly it is being considered a part of each family's life space—physical, social, and psychological. But, as Birren (1969) has said, it is easier to focus upon housing than upon a larger aspect of the environment of which housing is merely a part.

Robbins (1971) also recognized the larger scope of housing when he observed that the problem is to provide housing consistent with a variety of life styles rather than merely to produce a large number of dwelling units. Variety in housing implies that older families no less so than younger families should be allowed to exercise as much freedom of choice as possible.

If housing is to be a viable support system for a wide variety of life styles and conditions, it is mandatory that it be planned, designed, built, and operated in a manner that will maximize older people's chances to realize certain basic needs. Here some of these fundamental needs highly relevant to housing will be identified and briefly discussed.

Independence. Almost without exception older couples and individuals wish to live independently as long as possible. This implies types of housing and social services which will enable them to be masters of their own households, to care for themselves, to be free to entertain friends, to go and come as they please, and to perform roles to which they have grown accustomed.

Safety and comfort. As older persons are highly vulnerable to falls and other accidents (Lawton, 1965), their dwellings should be so planned, constructed, and equipped as to minimize injury. The aged are less tolerant of extreme temperatures than younger persons. Therefore, heating, cooling, and ventilation take on added significance. Inasmuch as visual and auditory reception declines with age, special attention should be given to lighting and noise control.

Wholesome self concept. A basic characteristic of human beings is a need to think well of themselves. Recently several writers have stated that the housing environment is closely linked to the way persons feel about themselves (Carp, 1966; Montgomery, 1970). In American society it is commonplace to judge people by their income, occupation, and material possessions. Older persons judge themselves and are judged by others in terms of their dwellings and their neighborhoods. Perhaps the desire to think well of themselves explains in part why older families spend a relatively large proportion of their income for housing and why they so often attempt to remain in larger dwellings.

A sense of place. Fromm (1963) has written that people have a basic need to feel that they belong to their environment. Regardless of where older persons live, they seem to have a fundamental need to identify with a place—a dwelling, a neighborhood, a village, a city, or a landscape. Fried (1963), following his study of older persons who were forced to move from familiar surroundings in West End Boston, concluded that human functioning requires a sense of spatial identity.

Relatedness. People, regardless of age, have a need to relate to and interact with other human beings. The extent to which older spouses interact with one another, with their children, with their grandchildren, and with friends is affected by the design, size, and location of their dwellings. In commenting on the behavior of older residents of Victoria Plaza, a public housing facility in San Antonio, Texas, Carp (1966) stated that older residents of the enriched environment seemed to respond to their housing by reengaging in social life.

Environmental mastery. Individuals have a need to exercise some measure of mastery over their environment. This may include gardening, decorating, and furnishing the dwelling unit, displaying accessories, or otherwise making changes within the dwellings. Obviously, for many aged families and individuals the house is the major part of the environment over which they can exercise a modicum of control. Dumont (1968) has stated that failure to manage or control some aspect of the environment can lead to serious frustration.

Psychological stimulation. Increasingly there is a beginning understanding that the individual has a need for psychological stimulation, for a variety of stimuli. As Dumont (1968) has observed, sensory deprivation can lead to psychosis. As the older person's life space is reduced, as a result of declining health, the loss of significant others, and limited income, his major source of daily stimulation is derived from his housing environment. But often his immediate world becomes drab at the very time his sensory intake mechanisms decline.

Privacy. Human beings daily need to engage and then disengage socially. And following retirement of the husbands, older couples have a pressing need to be apart no less so than to be together. This involves auditory as well as visual stimulus breakers. In a real sense, houses are indispensible regulators of human association and withdrawal. Doors, windows, walls, closets, and the like do much more than enclose space and conceal: they also serve the crucially important function of privacy.

Housing Alternatives

Each community, in cooperation with governments, should strive to provide a variety of housing options for older persons. Nevertheless, at least half of all the aged have no real freedom of housing choice. Options that might be, but usually are not, available to older persons, include: continuing to live in one's present dwelling in comfort and dignity, moving into congregate housing, nursing homes, or extended care facilities.

Remaining in one's own home. It is an American ideal that older persons should continue to live in their familiar environments for as long as possible. Many aged do cling to the familiar beyond the point in time when reason might dictate a change, and moving may be a major life disruption, socially and psychologically. The limitations of economic resources often militate against repairing and improving dwellings and against moving to more suitable environments. Generally, programs and services which enable older people to remain in their present dwellings would be a wise course to follow for most, but by no means all, aged persons. To make every effort to enable an impoverished and enfeebled widow to continue to live in her run-down house or apartment is questionable. At the same time, older persons who are in good health, have financial resources, and who are accustomed to living in a larger dwelling may be better off remaining than moving.

Age-mixing or age-segregation. An issue that cross-cuts a large variety of housing is whether there should be age-mixing or age-segregation. Rosow (1967) examined the influence of varying proportions of aged persons on patterns of friendship. His subjects included 1,200 older persons in Cleveland. He regarded apartment buildings which contained from one to fifteen percent of older persons as normative, 33 to 49 percent as concentrated and 50 percent or more as dense. Rosow found that friendship patterns varied in direct proportion to the number of the aged peers living nearby. Age-homogeneity yielded the larger number of friendships.

To date the most thorough and methodologically rigorous study made of the change of behavior of older persons as a result of moving into a public housing complex exclusively occupied by the aged is Carp's (1966) investigation of life in Victoria Plaza, San Antonio, Texas. In 1960, Carp made a baseline study of 352 aged persons who had applied for admission to the facility which had eight stories of apartments and a senior center on the ground floor. From twelve to fifteen months after the structure was occupied, she studied 204 applicants who had moved into Victoria Plaza and 148 applicants who remained in their substandard dwellings in San Antonio. In her effort to assess the impact of an enriched environment on the feelings and activities of the aged, she collected data on a variety of dimensions, including activities, friendship patterns, health, personal adjustment to problems, attitudes toward life in the new setting, changes in life style, self-concept, and morale. Her data indicated decisively that by and large the enriched and age-segregated environment had produced many positive effects in the lives of older residents. In broad outline, Carp found that the enriched, age-segregated environment of Victoria Plaza promoted social involvement and enhanced morale and the self image.

Recently Sussman and Steinberg (1970) examined the experiences of older persons who were living in public housing projects in New York City. Their account of the experiences of older persons was quite different from Carp's (1966). They have reported that many changes, usually of an adverse nature, characterized older residents of age-segregated public housing. In structures occupied almost exclusively by the aged, they observed that the aged developed their own culture. When persons from different walks of life were concentrated under one roof, former life styles tended to disintegrate. The familiar—old neighbors, shops, landscape, and patterns of interaction—was swept aside when the aged moved into the public housing units. Self-images appeared to metamorphose from those of an adult to that of a senior citizen. Sussman and Steinberg also stated that medical problems reached great proportions and that, in reality, the housing environment became old age homes in which life trickled at a low ebb.

Sussman and Steinberg did not describe the structures in which they made their observations, how the tenants were selected, nor indicate how long they had lived in their present apartments. Therefore, one can only speculate why their conclusions differ so greatly from those of Carp. One suspects that the facilities were older and less well designed than was Victoria Plaza. Too, it may well be that the New York City residents were much older than Carp's respondents.

Messer (1967) has examined the level of interaction and morale of 88 older persons who lived in public housing projects occupied exclusively by the aged and of 155 aged persons who lived in age-heterogeneous public housing projects. He found that the level of interaction and morale were significantly higher among those who lived in age-homogeneous environments than among those who lived in age-heterogeneous settings. From his findings, he concluded that not only were interaction opportunities greater for those living in age-segregated environments but also that a normative system developed which seemed to facilitate adjustment to old age.

This review of recent literature on the question of age-mixing versus age-segregation has dealt almost exclusively with older persons who lived in public housing. Age-segregation of older persons appears to run counter to a major American ideal. Nevertheless, research to date seems to tip the scale in favor of age-concentration in that age-homogeneous environments appear to increase the number of friends and the extent of social interaction, to increase morale, and to contribute to a normative system in which the aged are spared competition and possibly conflict with the life styles of younger persons. It must be noted, however, that at present relatively little is known about how age-mixing or age-concentration affects middle-and-upper-income groups, and the younger aged. Therefore, at present the question remains unsettled. To the extent that the aged are culturally impelled to form a sub-culture, age-segregation on balance may be highly functional. At the same time, to the extent that negative attitudes toward old age are attenuated, thereby enabling older Americans to be partners to other age groups, age-segregation may become dysfunctional. Finally, economic factors appear to exert more pressure toward age-segregation than do stated policies. Specifically, migration of younger persons from rural areas and from central cities, low-incomes of the aged and a limited desire to move all are creating age-concentrations of older Americans.

Retirement communities. Since the 1950s there has been a rapid increase in the number of communities planned and built for the aged, and the controversy as to whether the aged should be segregated from or mixed with other age groups and whether such new environments are suitable for the aged has continued. In the late 1960s, Bultena and Wood (1969) made a study of 521 retired men of whom 322 lived in four planned, age-segregated communities in Arizona. The educational and pre-retirement occupational status of residents in each group was higher than for the national aged population. Residents of the four retirement communities held a number of advantages over those living in age-integrated (regular) communities.

The study revealed that morale, as determined by Neugarten's Life Satisfaction Scores, was significantly higher for men living in retirement communities than for those who lived in regular communities. Residents in neither community appear to have encountered any difficulty in establishing and maintaining friendship ties. Nevertheless, a smaller proportion of residents in retirement communities than of those in age-heterogeneous communities experienced a decline of close friends and expressed dissatisfaction with their new setting. Bultena and Wood (1969) concluded that planned retirement communities not only had provided many opportunities for social activities but also support for those who had a commitment to a retirement life style of leisure-orientation. The authors recognized the fact that persons choosing to live in retirement communities were more likely to desire social and recreational activities than were those choosing age-mixed communities.

Today most older persons do not wish to live in retirement communities, many cannot afford to do so, and the health of many will not permit it. But the leisure-oriented who possess the health, the money, and the desire seem to find these communities highly satisfactory. One may confidently expect the number of retirement communities to increase as the financial resources and education and health status of the aged increase.

Congregate homes. Historically, the destitute older person often was sent to the poorhouse. But gradually, in the last 50 years or so, there has emerged a number of congregate care facilities that focus upon older persons who are not able to continue in their private homes but who do not need to live in a skilled nursing home. Congregate homes vary greatly in size and in the nature of services provided. At one extreme are smaller facilities with individual and shared rooms for the residents with a central dining room and with minimal health services. At the other extreme are larger institutions, which provide apartments equipped for independent living, individual rooms, a nursing and hospital unit, dining facilities, and an array of social, counseling, and therapeutic services.

In recent years congregate housing has begun to provide an environment in which husband-wife relationships are fostered and one in which health, social, and psychological needs are considered. Better planned and operated homes for the aged provide facilities for husbands and wives, single rooms, infirmaries, and an array of social services. Too, they are being located in a manner that will enable the residents to have access to such community facilities as churches, shops, and recreational establishments. In former days, of course, old folks homes, the forerunner of today's congregate housing, were often located in areas characterized by a high degree of isolation from the mainstream of life and, meanwhile, provided few health and social services (Zelditch & Bram, 1965; Weiss, 1969).

Increasingly the public is becoming aware of the potential of congregate housing for many persons who need some daily assistance in order to prolong independence. (See Chapter 9 for a comprehensive discussion of nursing homes.)

Conclusion

In conclusion, perhaps this examination of housing and life space needs, and housing alternatives of the older family and individuals will alert the reader to some of the conditions and problems encountered by the elderly. Today, large numbers of the aged live under conditions of expedience which all too often ignore needs and in settings in which they are regarded more as old products to be processed than as human beings to be accorded dignity. Tomorrow perhaps each of the types of housing on the continuum noted in this paper will become truly enriched environments.

Current programs of action on behalf of older Americans, while making a positive impact, hardly begin to meet the pressing environmental needs of countless older persons. The closing of the gap between biological and behavioral potentials will require a number of steps—finance, technology, services, education, and a change of attitudes toward and by the elderly. In the long run, however, even more imperative is a commitment to basic research designed to reveal which older persons respond to what kinds of environments. Unless the horizon of knowledge is extended, the nation shall continue to steer a course by myths while plying the waters of the River of Meander.

*Planning Physical Space**

M. Powell Lawton
Thomas O. Byerts

This section picks up where the last one left off. It includes discussion of several considerations that emerge in planning for housing the elderly, including group housing and mobile-home living. It also touches on matters of policy for the elderly, and policy, together with planning, is the keystone of any program for social improvement. Therefore, much of the effort of gerontologists and of other advocates of older people is to influence planning and policy in directions that they believe will improve the world of the elderly— the world in which we all live.

FACILITIES AND RESOURCES

Perhaps the most important physical resource for the elderly is the *existing housing stock*. Most national effort, however, has been devoted to the building of new planned group housing, to the neglect of the 70 percent of elderly who are homeowners, the great majority of whom (70 to 90 percent, by various estimates) wish to remain where they are. Some problems that make it difficult for old people to use their owned homes more effectively have been:

—Lack of information about loan and grant availability.
—Lack of assistance (through outreach, or ombudsman) in fording the governmental bureaucracy.
—Lack of *immediate* access to funds and manpower for small or emergency home repairs.
—Lack of total dollars for grants, rather than loans.
—Lack of assistance in getting the person who needs more space in touch with the elderly head of household who has too much space.

*Edited from *Community Planning for the Elderly,* by M. P. Lawton and T. O. Byerts, with F. Carp, S. Howell, R. Steiner, M. Wylie, and E. Kahana. Gerontological Society. Washington, D.C.: U.S. Government Printing Office. (Copies available through National Technical Information Service, U.S. Department of Commerce, Springfield, Va. 22151, # PB 232-000/AS.)

—In urban centers, the psychological discouragement in seeing one's
neighborhood deteriorate and crime increase.
—Cash outlays required to pay property taxes and basic utility costs.

New and creative measures are clearly required to preserve the older
housing and by so doing, give the independence of self-determination to the
many who do not wish planned housing.

The local planner might well explore the possibilities of organizing
home repair services with some control over fair charges, possibly utilizing
semi-retired workmen with the required skills. He might also use his influence to persuade nonprofit housing groups to think of rehabilitating scattered older housing sites, rather than focusing only on the production of new
group housing.

Other varieties of housing have their uses, particularly in the light of
rapid changes in population, in housing styles, and in housing preferences.

Mobile Home Parks

Mobile home parks seem to be a fact of life today, and the planner
would do well to determine whether case-finding and supportive services
would be available to elderly residents of a proposed park. The impression
seems to be, however, that elderly residents of such communities are self-
selected in terms of general competence. Barrier-free layout of the space
between trailers and pathways to important common facilities should,
under most conditions, be easy to attain, and not particularly costly, though
barrier-free access to the mobile unit itself would be difficult. A major planning question is that of the age mix desirable in a park. It is known that
very few people 80 and over live in trailer parks and that many are forced to
relocate when their health declines. There has not been a satisfactory empirical evaluation of the trailer park in terms of the quality of life it supports
for the elderly person. Substantial questions remain regarding the effect of
such problems as the lack of construction standards, uniform safety codes, or
the lack of a clearly specified service role of the management. Anecdotal
evidence points to the age-segregated, carefully planned, relatively high-
cost trailer park in a mild climate being an entirely acceptable living environment for the healthy older person. However, a close inquiry into
management practices, access to services, and impact on the surrounding
community has yet to be made.

Boarding Houses

Boarding houses and communal living arrangements have grown up
spontaneously, especially in marginal areas of inner cities. Again, informal
observation suggests that they serve a real need. Lifelong isolates and psychologically maladjusted people do grow old, and such people seem to constitute some of the clientele of the boarding houses. Thus, despite their nega-

tive social image and frowns of civic boosters, they constitute a positive resource that must be protected.

Housing for the elderly takes many forms, some of which involve the use of structures originally built for other purposes. The major primary question that must be asked, "Is it really suitable for the elderly?" There is a strong tendency to view the housing needs of the elderly in terms of anything being preferable to the rock-bottom level at which many older people are presently living. The low social valuation of the elderly is prominent in this thinking: "They should be grateful for improvement, even if those structures have been rejected by everyone else." The choice of slum clearance sites or sites never utilized because of their poor location for new senior housing projects is one frequent example of this thinking. Major examples of the use of older structures for this purpose are the conversion of old hotels and a flurry of interest in trying to use now-vacant college dormitories as residences for the elderly. Neither is intrinsically a bad idea. Any such instance must be carefully evaluated, however, in terms of the site selection criteria described below, and in terms of the internal structure modifications and the service packages proposed by the developer or sponsor. *No such conversion should be countenanced without the assurance of a committed sponsor who has the capacity to take responsibility for the quality of life of the tenants as well as their shelter.* It is possible for low-cost conversions to be made that are both commercially viable and at least moderately enriching to the tenants, though for the future it seems increasingly clear that some subsidy with public funds will be necessary to prevent the choice of impossible sites for this purpose. Hotels frequently have no kitchens, thus limiting them to *congregate* use. To deprive fully independent older people of the possibility of continuing their lifelong instrumental tasks of cooking and housekeeping, and their accustomed privacy, by housing them in this style is unacceptable today. Location of older people on a college campus certainly has much to recommend it, but interaction between the elderly and the college community will not take place without a strong assist from the college administration. The locational requirements for students will often be totally unsuited for the elderly in regard to public transportation, neighborhood shopping, and even physical security. No information is yet available on the economics of such conversions, or of the market appeal of these arrangements.

Another type of conversion that may be proposed is to use state mental hospital buildings for older people. Such buildings are likely to be uniformly undesirable as living environments, though some hospitals have building ground that might be suitable for new construction.

A great variety of *new purpose-built group housing* exists that is familiar to all planners:

—The high-rise apartment dwelling, usually in urban centers, variously
   financed under the HUD programs, or under privately financed nonprofit and limited-profit sponsorship.
—Low-rise structures as above.

—The "retirement village," financed under some of the above arrangements, but frequently built outside urban centers as relatively self-sufficient communities offering many facilities and services, including health care on the site. Costs are usually high.

—"Congregate housing," under a provision of the 1970 housing act that authorized use of federal funds for personal care facilities such as common dining rooms, central kitchens, and limited out-patient medical facilities within a housing structure.

With the exception of some poorly planned high-cost economic failures and some poorly sited social failures, these age-segregated housing facilities have been successful from most points of view.

Major issues for the planner include the size of the project, the relationship of community services to the housing (and the changes to be anticipated over a period of years), population mix, as well as topics not discussed here: need for the housing, locational decisions, zoning and community support, and consumer involvement in planning.

Size

Definitive answers are not yet available on the consequences of size. Some research is beginning to suggest that there are some distinct advantages to small size (up to 100 units) in terms of smallness being associated with greater social activity, higher tenant morale, and less separation from the community. This tendency seems to be in direct opposition to economic considerations, which favor larger projects. Sponsors consider 100 units a minimum size to justify a full-time manager; many smaller successful public housing projects exist where one manager handles several projects. Housing sites that attempt to provide on-site meals in a common dining room may have to be even larger to be able to make this service financially viable. Research suggests that large sizes (200 to 300 or more units) risk having more tenants disappear into anonymity. It seems clear that the planner should attempt to adjust size downward to the fewest financially viable number of units, but this number will be larger as the service package grows.

Services and Housing

Services such as on-site medical care and common dining rooms are relatively expensive, as are social programs that go beyond the one-afternoon-a-week Golden Age Club. Few low- and moderate-cost housing environments are able to afford these without a subsidy, whether by direct contribution by the sponsor or through local agencies. On-site meals, in particular, are available primarily because they are made mandatory or because local subsidy makes the service financially possible. It is economically desirable to broaden the consumer base for on-site services by including older people in the surrounding community as potential users. This practice, if successful, has the even greater advantage of providing inter-mingling between community residents and housing residents. Thus, in the future, one can expect financial incentives to be made available for agencies and housing willing to make the effort to center community services in housing projects for the elderly. An essential element of such services would be their two-way character: community residents coming to the housing for services and the same or different services traveling to the homes of the less mobile people in the neighborhood.

Medical care is a somewhat different proposition. Economic factors, state licensing regulations, and the aversion of some tenants to the sight of relatively sick people in housing have caused most housing to avoid imbed-ding any medical care into the service package. Research shows, however, that tenant need is very strong for a doctor's office on the site, with regular hours by physician and nurse. Housing combined with a physically sepa-rate, longterm care facility has been successful in other situations, though infrequently for moderate cost.

There is relatively little experience thus far with congregate housing that has no kitchen facilities in individual apartment units. This concept appears to be a satisfactory alternative for people coming from nursing home situations.

Changes to Be Expected over Time

No matter how independent the original tenants of housing are, they will grow older and presumably less competent. Replacements for original tenants may or may not match the originals in health. Thus, there is bound to be some decline in the average competence of the tenants over time, which must be accounted for in planning. Common space for eventual use as dining, recreational and medical clinic space should be included in every plan; expansion space on the site would serve similarly. In general, proxim-ity to a longterm care institution and administrative ease of access to the institution provide a sense of security for the housing tenant, even though he may not wish to acknowledge it.

However, there is not yet enough experience with the aging of a hous-ing project and its tenants to know just what kinds of physical and pro-grammatic adjustments may have to be made to make such environments more functional for use by less competent people.

It is the easiest thing in the world to say that effort should be made to locate new housing in proximity to stores, a bank, or churches. It is much more difficult to preserve these resources in neighborhoods where old people are clustered, but whose socio-economic vigor is gone. It is also much more difficult to "treat" a community where resources were always sparse or distant, but whose population only recently grew old. In fact, the best the planning process can do with these two more difficult situations is to think in terms of adequate transportation of people to resources, or vice-versa, which is discussed in the following section.

CIRCULATION ROUTES

Research has indicated that, like other age groups, the aged perceive driving their own cars as the most satisfactory means of transportation. However, for both economic and biological reasons they are far less likely to own or drive their own cars. Therefore, walking and public transportation are the most frequent forms of transportation for the elderly.

Walking

While walking is frequently done for pleasure, it can be a burden when done by necessity under less than optimal conditions. Some criteria for pedestrian design and housing location should be:

—Existence of paved sidewalks leading to the several critical neighborhood facilities, e.g., grocery store, drug store, bank, and public transportation.
—Designated pedestrian crosswalks at street intersections.
—Traffic light timing somewhat slower than average, especially at complex or wide intersections.
—Community-supplied benches placed in safe locations adjacent to sidewalks, preferably with a view of high-activity areas.

Relatively independent older people report the length of an average daily walk to be about 15 to 20 minutes. Around two-thirds of them experience no difficulty in walking one-half mile (or 8 blocks). Thus, facilities located within 6 blocks will be accessible to the great majority of older people, though carrying heavy bundles or making the walk in bad weather will cause problems.

The concept of "ideal distance to facilities" has been attractive to planners, probably because a research project done some years ago by the planner Paul Noll resulted in a neat table that has been frequently reproduced. He asked public housing managers to estimate ideal distances from housing site to various facilities (listed in descending order of importance):

Grocery store	1 block
Bus stop	adjacent to site
House of worship	one-half mile
Drug store	1 block
Clinic or hospital	1 mile
Bank	one-quarter mile
Social center	on site
Library	one-half mile

It is important to understand that these are managers', rather than elderly tenants', estimates. Our information from tenants would indicate a much greater importance being attached to proximity to medical care of some kind, and to some safe check-cashing facility.

The topography of these main access routes is a more critical factor to older adults than to others. Some standards specify no more than a 5% grade in access to a housing site, while others stretch it as far as 10%. The extent of grade in housing access of circulation route will act as a filter. The 10% grade would be no great problem to the most competent, but there will be a percentage of people of marginal competence whose mobility will be reduced by any incremental departure from level.

A more important barrier to circulation is the fear of crime, which has become a major preoccupation of urban residents, regardless of their age. Much older public housing suffers from its location in out-of-the-way parcels of land that have no built-in surveillance along the deserted streets between the project and the nearest business artery. For new construction, such sites should be rejected out of hand. Large-scale planning can, of course, transform an entire pedestrian route so that safe passage is enhanced.

Parks are especially important resources for older people, though they may act either negatively or positively on the person's mobility. Small city plazas located in areas of high activity can be especially favorable aspects of the urban environment. Such locations will be certain to attract less desirable marginal people as well as older people, but the gain is worth the price if:

—enough pedestrian traffic occurs to provide natural monitoring of behavior
—a minimum level of police surveillance occurs
—benches are placed orienting the sitter to views of high density of human behavior
—other benches are placed so as to give choice of sun or shade, low-behavior density orientation, and right-angles (social) orientation vs. parallel or isolated (non-social) orientation
—the location is within easy walk of some basic shopping facilities
—a safe toilet is nearby

Larger parks are notorious for crime risk, and are far less utilized by the elderly. However, park edges facing busy streets (or occasionally an inner park center located near amusements, museums, or refreshment stands) may, at least during daylight hours, be as actively used as the city plaza. The essential element here is also enough surveillance, natural or official, combined with landscape design that provides tree shade without the dangerous cover of shrubs, winding wooded paths, walls, or unfrequented buildings. Such a park edge near concentrations of the elderly can be greatly enhanced in value to the aged if regularly patrolled and if some small recreational facilities are provided, such as chess and card tables and recreational equipment.

It is very difficult to do anything about a park edge in terms of its psychological effect on night pedestrian travel. If this is a necessary route to public transportation or night-time recreation, the elderly will remain shut in, unless alternative counteractive measures are taken, such as escort service, continuous police visibility, or organized group walks.

Public Transportation

Public transportation planning for the elderly has received considerable attention recently. More than 100 localities are reported to have instituted reduced-fare travel arrangements for the elderly, usually limited to non-rush-hour times. Those plans are typically subsidized by public funds. Sometimes the reimbursement is close to the actual amount of total fare reductions. It seems far more reasonable however, to calculate the required subsidy on the basis of estimated lost income, or even appeal to the empty-seats-give-no-extra-cost argument to justify a token subsidy in the name of public service. One carefully conducted study of New York City bus lines estimated the immediate increase in ridership following the institution of a reduced-fare plan as 27%.

Alternative transit arrangements for the elderly include:

—Special bus routes or extension of existing routes to include a high density elderly area (such as a new clustered project) or a resource utilized frequently by such a group, such as a hospital.
—Extra or tailor-made routes geared to critical times of day, such as the change-of-shift time at an institution that is otherwise isolated.
—Nonprofit-agency subsidized special routes similar to the above.
—Door-to-door pickups, either on regular routes, or by special order.

All such specially designed means are relatively expensive. The door-to-door pickup, for instance, has been estimated to require a minimum of 30 minutes per person (round trip), where assistance must be given in mounting and dismounting and in negotiating the route between the dwelling unit and the vehicle.

The Mobility of Retired People*

Frances M. Carp

This chapter began with a discussion of housing, moved on to a section on planning that included both housing and transportation, and now offers a description of the kinds of transportation older people use. Unlike most of the selections in this book, the present material is taken from one research project, conducted in San Antonio, Texas. You must, of course, keep in mind that the specific results would differ in other cities. But in writing about the mobility of 709 elderly San Antonio residents, author Carp outlines the transportation requirements of older people. You might wish to investigate how the use of transportation by older people in your community would compare with this Texas city.

GROWING OLD IN THE CITY

As population increases and technology advances, more people live in urban areas. As cities grow, transportation problems increase for most persons within them (Mumford, 1970), and especially for the elderly. The mobility of older persons is greatly affected by the increasing complexity of transportation systems, especially as they involve speed. Age-related physiological, psychological, and social changes interact with transportation changes and disproportionately increase the hazards and discomforts of getting from one place to another. There are many reasons for the accentuated impact of modern transportation systems on the aged. Some of them involve the automatism of habits practiced over a lifetime, sensory-perceptual-motor changes occurring with age, and the societal "devaluation" of the aged.

The Tyranny of Habit

Over a lifetime, a person builds up a repertory of cognitive maps and motor skills which enable him to navigate his world and go where he wants to go; however, as transportation systems change—and as he must change from one mode of transportation to another or from one set of destinations to another—his deeply ingrained learnings become inappropriate. They may interfere with, rather than facilitate, the new skills which must be acquired if he is to be mobile. Relearning usually is more difficult than learning. A particular hazard is the "spontaneous recovery" of behavior patterns which have been "unlearned." Old habits reappear at inappropriate times—as, for

*Edited from "The Mobility of Retired People," by F. M. Carp. In E. J. Cantilli and J. L. Shmelzer (Eds.), *The Mobility of Retired People*. Washington, D.C.: U.S. Government Printing Office, 1970.

example, when an older person responds to the green traffic light straight ahead, rather than to the new arrow low on the left, and makes a left turn into oncoming traffic (Lawton, 1967).

Sensory-Motor Changes

Because of changes in sensory and motor capabilities, the elderly person is likely to be at some disadvantage both in learning new transportation skills and in simply continuing to perform old ones. Generally, as people age, sensory acuity diminishes, strength and agility decline, and responses slow (Birren, 1964). Perceptual-motor changes decrease the ability for a correct response to complex stimuli. This decrement is emphasized in any situation in which there is pressure for speed. Body balance becomes less secure, both when walking and when standing in place, and there is an increasing tendency to lose equilibrium and to fall. The consequent loss of confidence may accentuate inadequacy of mobility behavior and reduce willingness to embark on trips.

Complexity and Speed of Transportation

Changes in transportation systems interact with aging processes to augment older people's difficulties in going places. Laboratory studies have demonstrated that perceptual-motor task complexity and the pressure for speed penalize the older person. As traffic patterns and signals become more complex and as traffic speed increases, vehicular and pedestrian activities become increasingly more hazardous to older people and deterrent to their mobility. Older people become less able and willing to leave their homes or immediate vicinity.

Income

The transportation problems of many older people are magnified by low income. Older persons are likely to be poor. Almost universally, even for those in comfortable financial circumstances, there is a sharp reduction in income at the time of retirement. Transportation options are few for those with little money, and they are at least narrowed for those who have less money than they have been accustomed to.

Availability of Transportation Facilities

Bracey points out that: "In America, the ability 'to go places' depends so very much on the ability to drive an automobile without which you can be literally marooned in your own house" (Bracey, 1966, p. 185). The retired person may not be able to afford a car. He may be unable to renew his driver's license. Even if he has both automobile and license, the perceptual-motor demands of superhighways may deter him from many activities theoretically available to him, because he does not trust himself in freeway traffic. His children may fear for his safety or consider him a menace on the road and therefore persuade him not to drive, even though he can meet the requirements for a license.

Public transportation facilities and pedestrian accommodations are of particular importance to older persons because of the limitations on their use of automobiles. In New Orleans, Bracey found "46% of all . . . pensioner households with no car in the garage" (Bracey, 1966, p. 186). Among applicants for public housing for the aged in San Antonio, individuals whose incomes were similar to those of most persons receiving Social Security benefits, only one in five had an automobile (Carp, 1966). Brotman (1969) has reported that while 84% of U.S. households headed by younger persons own automobiles, only 56% of the households headed by older persons owned at least one automobile.

Household car-ownership may overestimate the extent to which automobiles meet the needs of older people. As Brotman points out: "Older households tended to own older automobiles" (Brotman, 1969, p. 6). In addition, it is not clear that an older member of a household has unlimited access to a car owned by a younger, working member of that household. Even when an automobile is freely available, other factors may set limits on the times or places to which the older person may drive. Difficulties with vision, particularly at night, may limit older persons to day-time trips. New expressways and rerouting of traffic on familiar streets may inhibit even daylight driving.

Consequently, if they are to be met at all, transportation needs must increasingly be served by public transportation systems and by walking. Ironically, however, some of the same factors that reduce driving ability—decreases in strength, agility and endurance, loss of visual and auditory acuity, perceptual-motor decrements, etc.—also reduce capability for getting about by means of public transportation systems or on foot. An older person may find it difficult to cope with the physical demands or the confusion and rush of the subway or bus, and of pedestrian traffic. As a result, he may be increasingly confined to his home. On his first visit to the United States in 1959, Bracey commented on "how few old people we saw about the streets" (Bracey, 1966, p. 185).

When transportation problems arise, individuals in most segments of the population have the support of some institution such as the place of employment or the school. These institutions not only provide information and assistance to persons with respect to transportation, they also influence transportation systems. Often, roads are built and repaired, and buses routed to meet the needs of business and industry and of educational institutions. Retired persons, on the other hand, do not usually have institutional assistance with their transportation needs and problems, and seldom are transportation systems influenced by their viewpoints.

The Role of Transportation

Transportation is the mediator between the person and much of his environment. It determines whether the community is a useless facade or a dynamic social system. Housing, medical, financial, and recreational services for older people are useful only to the extent that transportation is workable—for the people who need and want the services. Informal social contacts with family members and friends are possible only if access to these other persons is available.

Lack of appropriate transportation constricts the life-space of any person, limits his capacity for self-maintenance, restricts his activities and his contacts with other people, and may contribute to his disengagement or alienation from society, and his experience of anomie. Adequate transportation is not only humane to the older person, it is of economic value to society in that it supports the individual's capacity for independent living and thus assists in postponing or obviating institutional care. Many older people identify transportation as their most serious problem (Carp, 1966).

Either innovations or modifications of existing types of transportation must be based on information about where people need and want to go, and about the characteristics of transportation which make it easy or difficult to get there. Transportation must be viewed in light of age-related physiological changes and in view of the preferences of older persons and the purposes for which they use and would like to have transportation. To be truly useful, transportation must not only be properly engineered, but must also provide access to the places people want to go and in ways they find convenient and comfortable. In the final analysis, older persons themselves can assist in defining the transportation problems, needs, and preferences of the elderly, of those whose lives are no longer structured by work.

THE STUDY OF TRANSPORTATION NEEDS, HABITS, AND PREFERENCES OF OLDER PEOPLE

The study discussed here represents a direct approach to understanding the mobility and transportation habits, needs, problems, and preferences of older people. One goal is to describe the transportation habits of retired people in specific terms—where they go, for what reasons, how often, and by what means. Another goal is to ascertain their transportation needs, problems, and preferences. How well do present arrangements satisfy their needs? To what extent is present transportation inadequate or inappropriate, and in what ways? Where do retired people want to go and cannot because of transportation? For each mode of transportation, what are the advantages and problems?

To be useful, this description of transportation habits, needs, problems, and preferences must be categorized according to location within the urban complex and for important population subgroups. Mobility behaviors and transportation facilities are not the same for persons in the inner city as for those in the suburbs. A concentration of same-age people in the immediate vicinity or residence in a minority-group neighborhood may affect transportation needs and facilities (Stringfellow, 1966). Mobility and transportation may be different for men and women, and for retired people of different ages or conditions of health.

This section presents an overview of mobility and transportation behaviors and attitudes of a city-wide sample of retired people. It is a description of how the "average" retired person gets about outside his home, and how he feels about his mobility and transportation, or lack thereof. The report is limited to findings from the first phase of the study, which was conducted in San Antonio, Texas, 1968–1969.

Data were collected from a sample of 709 persons, approximately 1.3% of the city's retired population. Three ethnic groups were represented: Afro-American (17%), Anglo-American (57%), and Mexican-American (26%). All were self-identified as retired people or as wives of retired men. The mean age was 67.5; 82% were 65 or over. The group was comprised of 283 men and 426 women. The median yearly income was close to the national median for persons 65 and over. During working years, most of the men and/or the women's husbands had held jobs in the middle levels (McGuire, 1949).

MOBILITY BEHAVIORS AND ATTITUDES

Where did these retired people go? How often? How did they get there? How well did the transportation facilities available to them meet their needs? What did they say they would do more often if transportation were not a problem?

Visiting Friends

The most frequent trips were made to visit friends: over 10% of the retired people said they habitually paid one or more visits to friends daily, and over one-third said they visited friends at least once a week. An even larger number, however, "never" went to see friends, and only half visited a friend more often than "several times a year" (see Table 1). An automobile was the most common means of transportation for going to visit friends. Half of those who made such visits drove themselves or were passengers in a car (see Table 2). Most of the remainder walked.

Most of those who visited friends seemed fairly well satisfied with their transportation for these trips. About one visitor in ten, however, was highly critical of it. One in four said he would make more visits to friends if he had better transportation. Reasons given for not going to see friends varied. The friends were too far away, or funds were insufficient, or no automobile was available and the bus did not go there, or the trip was too complicated or tiring, or it was impossible because of some physical handicap. Any of these may be a rationalization for having no friends. All may express a need to disengage from other people (Cumming & Henry, 1961). On the other hand, each may result from lack of *suitable* transportation. Most people who "never" went to see friends thought they would do so if they had transportation which was convenient and which they could afford.

Visiting Children

Trips to see children were not quite as frequent as those to friends. This is not to say that the old people saw their friends more often. Probably, adult children go to see their parents more frequently than vice versa. Nevertheless, it is interesting that only about five percent of these retired people said they usually paid visits to their children on a daily basis, and only a quarter of them said they usually visited children at least once a week.

The number of respondents who "never" paid visits to children was slightly larger than that which "never" visited friends. Being childless was the only explanation for "never" seeing children. Though a small number of the old people had children whom they had not seen for many years, they did not use the term "never," as they might in the case of friends seen so infrequently.

Generally, parents were favorable in evaluating their transportation for visits to children. About 15% said they were not satisfied with their means of transportation for these visits, but twice that number said they would go to see their children more often if they had a way to get there. Generally, the transportation—usually by car—was very satisfactory, but parents would like it to be offered more frequently.

Visits to Other Members of the Family

Less than five percent of the retired people paid a daily visit to some relative other than a child, and only about one person in five visited such a relative at least once a week. Nearly half "never" made such visits, usually because they had no relatives who lived nearby. Driving and being driven in a car by someone else were tied as the most common forms of transportation to visit these kin, and automobiles provided well over half the transportation. The majority of those who made family visits said that they were well satisfied with the transportation, but a quarter said they would go more often if they had better transportation. Most who "never" saw kinfolk would like to, but could not manage the necessary long trips.

Doctor

The typical frequency for going to see the doctor was several times a year but less than once a month. Generally, people who went to the doctor were driven or drove themselves in private automobiles. About one person in five went by bus, and nearly as many walked. A small number took a taxi.

Church

Over half of the group attended church at least once a month. Weekly attendance at church was the most common pattern, though nearly as common as the weekly attenders were those who had not been inside a church

Table 1. Percent of Older People Visiting Indicated Destinations, by Frequency of Trips*

				Frequency					
Destination	Daily	2–3 per week	Weekly	2–3 per month	1 per month	Several per year	Once a year	Every 2–3 years	Less often; never
Friends	12	11	12	8	8	8	2	<1	40
Children	6	7	12	5	6	9	7	2	45
Other kin	4	5	10	6	8	10	8	3	46
Doctor	0	1	4	8	15	34	20	6	13
Church	2	7	39	6	4	5	2	1	33
Grocery	5	28	36	8	5	<1	0	0	18
Other stores	1	3	11	10	20	26	6	<1	23
Meetings	<1	3	4	6	12	2	<1	<1	71
Entertainment	0	1	2	2	5	8	2	0	79
Senior center	<1	2	2	1	1	2	0	0	91
Library	1	2	2	2	2	2	1	0	87
Sports	0	1	2	0	1	5	1	1	89
Travel	0	0	0	1	4	20	25	11	39

*Sample of 709 retired older people, San Antonio, Texas, 1968–1969.

for more than three years. Automobiles provided transportation for the majority of church-goers: over a quarter drove themselves and one-third were passengers in cars.

Grocery Shopping

The most typical pattern of grocery shopping was once a week, though nearly as many people went more frequently, a few of them every day. Nearly one fifth said they "never" went grocery shopping. Usually, a relative or friend did the shopping. Almost without exception, these non-shoppers said they would prefer to go out and buy their own food, but could not manage the trip carrying their purchases. Cars provided transportation for most grocery shopping trips. Nearly a third of the shoppers drove themselves, and an equal number were driven in automobiles. A similar number usually walked to the grocery store. The bus and taxi were seldom used for this purpose, the bus because of the inconvenience, and the taxi because of the cost.

Again, little dissatisfaction with transportation was expressed by those able to go out to shop: one shopper in five expressed serious dissatisfaction. Twenty percent said they would shop more often if better transportation were available—and an equal number would go less often if they had a way to transport more groceries at one time. Two out of every five shoppers thought they would change their food shopping habits if their transportation were better.

Other Shopping

Several times a year, but less frequently than once a month, was the most typical pattern of shopping for items other than food. Nearly a quarter of the group "never" did much shopping, but 15% went at least once a week. Most shoppers (53%) drove themselves or were driven in a car by someone else. Nearly a quarter walked, and a similar number took the bus.

Unfortunately, "window-shopping" was not systematically investigated. Mention of "just going downtown" was frequent and suggested the importance of this type of outing. It seems that even people who cannot afford to make purchases enjoy going downtown.

Table 2. Percent of Older People Visiting Indicated Destinations, by Mode of Transportation*

| | *Transportation* | | | | | |
| | *Automobile* | | | | | |
Destination	*Driver*	*Passenger*	*Bus*	*Walk*	*Taxi*	*Train and Plane*
Friends	29	21	8	42	—	<1
Children	24	45	8	16	—	7
Other kin	30	31	15	16	<1	7
Doctor	28	32	20	16	4	—
Church	26	32	7	34	<1	—
Grocery	31	31	4	31	3	—
Other stores	29	24	23	23	—	—
Meetings	32	34	6	25	2	—
Entertainment	26	32	10	31	<1	—
Senior center	16	38	<1	45	—	—
Library	19	6	6	67	1	—
Sports	37	36	16	8	1	1
Travel	22	32	22	—	—	23

*Based on sample of 709 retired older people, San Antonio, Texas, 1968–1969. N varies with destination.

Senior Centers

Few (9%) of the respondents ever went to a senior center, and some of them went rather infrequently. Walking was the most common mode of transportation, and most of the rest of the people were driven by someone else in a private automobile.

The low rate of attendance at senior centers has been a cause of concern to gerontologists. The results of the present study suggest that low utilization may be largely due to the inability of older people to get to centers. The large majority (86%) of these respondents who used senior centers said they would go more often if they had transportation, and as large a proportion of those who did not go to senior centers thought they would go if they had a way to get there.

Travel

Half of the people interviewed usually took a trip at least once a year, though about 40% "never" traveled. Cars provided transportation for slightly over half the travelers. A quarter went by bus, and the remainder by plane and train. The most typical trip was about half a day each way. Half of those who traveled said they would take more frequent trips if they had transportation, and practically all of the non-travelers said they would like to take trips if they had a way to take them.

Duration of Trips

One of the striking findings of this study is the brevity of the trips taken by older people. By far the majority of local trips took less than half an hour each way, and most took less than 15 minutes.

An important question remains: To what extent is this home-boundness a normal consequence of the aging process, and how much of it is due to environmental constraints? To what extent is the low rate of mobility personally frustrating and socially impoverishing, and to what extent is it welcome to the individual because of a need to disengage? Further, and of prime importance for transportation planning: To what extent *could* changes in transportation facilities affect this behavior and, if mobility can be increased, *should* it be? Would greater mobility on the part of retired people be individually and socially desirable?

OLDER PEOPLE'S USE OF VARIOUS MEANS OF TRANSPORTATION

Before considering these questions it seems useful to review the information about the San Antonio retired people in terms of their use of various modes of transportation. Table 2 presents data on the modes used by the individuals traveling to different types of destinations. In order to obtain a realistic view of transportation facilities in relation to the mobility of retired people generally, it is necessary to view utilization of transportation modes also in terms of the entire sample.

Automobile

Hopefully, the previous discussion has made it clear that the automobile provided more transportation than any other mode, and that car owners had relatively few transportation problems. It is important to repeat, however, that among this group, access to automobiles was limited. Only one-third of the respondents were drivers, and less than half the drivers felt free to drive "anywhere." The majority of drivers recognized or set some limitation on their driving. A significant proportion either had been issued licenses for daytime driving only or had decided that they should no longer drive because of poor night vision. Even in daylight, many would not drive on expressways, or downtown, or in new parts of town. Some drove only within their immediate neighborhoods. Two-thirds of the respondents "never" drove, and less than 15% were freely able to meet their needs to go places by driving automobiles.

Most people who had cars were well satisfied with their present ability to get about, but they expressed strong negative feelings in anticipating being unable to drive. The most common reason for this apprehension was that they did not see how they could get to the places they needed to go. The second most often named reason for negative feeling was loss of independence.

For the nondriver, going by car as a passenger was the most common means of transportation to every destination which was discussed. Indeed, when all respondents are considered, drivers and nondrivers together, riding as a passenger in a private automobile was second in incidence only to driving oneself. Approximately one-third of the trips these respondents made were in private automobiles as passengers. Nearly everyone (88%) was given a ride, at least upon occasion. The outstanding problem in regard to being a passenger in an automobile was the lack of opportunity to be so more often. Most nondrivers, and many drivers, said they needed and wanted more such rides. In addition to infrequency of opportunity, there were the problems of dependency and of obligations which could not be repaid, and the inconvenience of tailoring times and destinations to fit the plans of the driver.

The results of the present study indicate that some drivers cannot come and go freely by car to do what they want during their years of retirement, and that rides with others are not sufficient. For the large majority of people beyond the work years, automobile transportation is not available to meet the need to go places. This situation has serious implications in a society so highly dependent upon this form of transportation.

Bus

San Antonio's major public transportation mode is a bus system. Over 40% of the present sample "never" took a bus and only one person in five usually went somewhere on a bus as often as once a week. Obviously, for the majority of the group who never rode one, the bus was irrelevant to transportation needs.

Walking

Nearly half the respondents used walking as a means of transportation several times each week, and one person in five went somewhere on foot "every day." On the other hand, nearly as many habitually walked to some destination less often than once a month, and some who considered themselves walkers had not done so for several years. Approximately a quarter of the group usually walked to fetch their food, and the same number went on foot to visit friends.

EXPRESSED AND LATENT TRANSPORTATION NEEDS

Generally, the data of this study indicate that retired people go out infrequently, that they make little use of community resources except for basic maintenance (medical and food), and that they are minimally mobile in regard to informal social contacts. Private automobiles provided most of the transportation for these respondents, but only about a third of the people could drive "everywhere." The public transit system had many disadvantages and was "never" used by nearly half the group. Most respondents used their feet to get places, but many destinations were too far for walking.

How satisfactory is this situation? Would retired people go about more if transportation were less of a problem? Would provision of suitable transportation facilities improve the quality of life in retirement?

In assessing transportation to the various places they went, usually 10% to 20% of the travelers expressed serious dissatisfaction (see Table 3). Typically, however, twice that number or more said they would go to that place more often if transportation were not such a problem. This difference does not reflect a simple response tendency to unthinkingly say yes to a question posed in a particular way. Differences between satisfaction with transportation facilities and estimate of changed rate of going vary from destination to destination (see Table 3). For example, less than a third of those who rate their transportation to the physician "very poor" feel that better transportation would increase their contact with the doctor.

The estimate of change in rate of going is probably a more valid score than the rating of transportation for the simple reason that much of the difficulty with transportation was the *amount* available. For example, being driven by a friend may be an excellent means of transportation to the stadium, but the invitation may be extended only once a year which is disappointingly seldom. Generally, the majority of people who did not go to a place indicated that they would or might go if transportation were available. If the anticipations of non-goers are added to those of goers, the majority of people thought they would be more mobile if suitable transportation facilities were available.

Statements of "would do" under projected conditions are not necessarily predictive of behavior should those conditions come to pass. Furthermore, it may be argued that old people really want to be left alone and that it is wrong to force mobility upon them. Such arguments are seductive because they would excuse society from improving transportation facilities for old people and alleviate guilt which the immobility of oldsters may arouse in younger people; however, there is considerable question as to whether these arguments are appropriate.

Table 3. Percent of Older People Visiting Indicated Destinations by Their Evaluation of Their Transportation*

| | Evaluation of Transportation | |
Destination	Dissatisfied	Would Go More if Better
Friends	11	25
Children	14	30
Other kin	15	25
Doctor	20	6
Church	13	21
Grocery	20	20†
Other stores	15	15
Meetings	9	25
Entertainment	10	37
Senior center	9	86
Library	11	45
Sports	11	68
Travel	21	50

*Based on sample of 709 retired older people, San Antonio, Texas, 1968–1969.
†An additional 20% would go less often.
N varies with destination.

It is distinctly possible that older people have a fairly accurate idea of what they are likely to do, given certain circumstances. Certainly, verbal statements are not the same as mobility behavior. But logic does suggest that deviance may be in *either* direction and psychology suggests that verbal expression may overestimate satisfaction with the status quo. When people know that they are trapped in a situation, they may have an ego-defensive need to put the best possible face upon it. This tendency is so common that it has been named the "sweet-lemon" rationalization.

In regard to their mobility, old people know that they are not going to become more agile or gain in physical endurance, and that their incomes are unlikely to keep up with inflation. They have little reason to expect that transportation facilities will become better suited to their needs. Indeed, recent trends suggest that the opposite is more likely to be true. Then the low rate of direct expression of dissatisfaction with transportation may be a defensive distortion; the projection of behavior "if suitable transportation were available" may be more nearly accurate; and both may underestimate the "latent need" to get about in their communities. When circumstances are strongly inhibiting and unchangeable, the only adaptive response possible may be the "sweet lemon" rationalization and a limitation on "felt needs." In order to endure and maintain self-respect, the individual may allow himself to express and be aware of little beyond subsistence demands.

Life Space and the Urban Elderly*

Marjorie H. Cantor

More older people live in New York City than in any other city in the United States or Canada. How well do they live there? We hear so much about how isolated, frightened, and abandoned the urban elderly are that this selection might be somewhat surprising.

Today's large American cities originated as trading settlements along the nation's major natural and artificial transportation routes. The Industrial Revolution added manufacturing to the cities' economic functions and led to the emergence of a mobile industrial working class detached from the land and living in smaller family units. Eventually, service industries joined manufacturing as a major economic focus of urban centers.

In general, the early city residents rarely lived much beyond their productive years and so were not faced with the problem of being a nonworker in an urban environment. Increased longevity coupled with economic pressures to introduce younger more productive workers resulted in a growing group of retired elderly urbanites no longer directly involved in the economics of the city. Initially, the needs of this group were the responsibility of the family or private charity but, increasingly, the government has become a partner with the family in providing for the economic and social supports of the elderly urban population.

The question then arises: Is the city a viable place for those no longer actively involved in the labor force to live out their years? Or do the very qualities which make the city such a successful economic hub and convenient service center mitigate against a decent life for those lacking the physical, social, and financial resources of youth?

THE ELDERLY IN THE INNER CITY

This section is based on some selected findings of a comprehensive cross-cultural survey of the elderly living in the inner or central city of New York (Cantor, 1975). For purposes of the study, the inner city was defined as New York's 26 poorest neighborhoods, and the study's probability sample of 1552 respondents is representative of the more than 400,000 noninstitutionalized elderly 60 years of age and over who live in these areas. Inner City elderly comprise approximately 35% of all older New Yorkers.

*Edited from "Life Space and the Urban Elderly," by M. H. Cantor, *The Gerontologist*, 1975, *15*, 23–27. Reprinted by permission of the Gerontological Society.

The study sample is clearly not a homogeneous, middle-class, white population. Rather it is a low-income urban elderly sample encompassing three distinct ethnic groups. Although New York's neighborhoods are increasingly nonwhite, at the present time, among both young and old alike, whites still predominate. Thus, 49% of the respondents are white, 37% black, and 13% Spanish-speaking, principally of Puerto Rican origin.

FINDINGS

The question of the viability of New York as a place of residence for older people can be approached from many vantage points. This paper will confine itself to three aspects which are among the most crucial: the life space of the Inner City elderly; the extent to which they possess a functioning social support system; and their perception of city life—its strengths and weaknesses.

Life Space and the Use of Time

The elderly of the Inner City are long-term residents. Virtually all have lived in the neighborhoods at least 10 years or more and over half have 20 or more years of neighborhood residency. As they cease to work, grow older, frailer, and as incomes become more limited, they are increasingly neighborhood-based and often neighborhood-bound.

First, what is a neighborhood in the eyes of older people? By analyzing the services respondents considered in and outside the neighborhood in terms of the distance from the homes, it became clear that for New York's Inner City elderly a neighborhood is consistently defined as having a maximum radius of ten city blocks.

Next, what services are provided in the neighborhoods and for which must the elderly leave the area? As expected, the most frequently used service by the largest group of respondents is shopping for food (87% visited the grocery store). Virtually everyone walks to the grocery several times a week; almost one-quarter food-shop daily. Food stores are only one to three blocks from their homes.

Almost 80% of the respondents patronize a drug store and make at least two or three visits per month for drugs. Again, drug stores are in the neighborhood, usually within one to three blocks of the home. Churches and synagogues are also to be found in the neighborhoods—71% of the sample attend a religious institution, usually weekly. Three-fourths of the churchgoers attend neighborhood institutions four to six blocks from their home. Banks and clothing stores are used by half of the sample. Banking is mainly a neighborhood-based activity with banks also within a four to six block radius of home.

Clothing shopping on the other hand, at least among black and white elderly, mainly occurs outside the neighborhood. Only the Spanish report using local stores. Shopping for clothing occurs far less frequently, usually only a few times a year, and is an occasion for going downtown to a major shopping center, usually by bus or sometimes by subway.

As persons grow older the need for medical services increases sharply and there is considerably less discretion in either the frequency or timing of such visits (Cantor & Mayer, 1972; Shanas, 1961). Given the high rate of utilization of health services by the elderly, it is not surprising that 86% of the sample report going to a doctor or clinic. Although medical services are not used as frequently as other types of facilities—generally only once per month or less—it is the one critical service for which half of the elderly leave their neighborhoods. Distances travelled for medical services are often considerable. Most respondents use public transportation to reach their doctors. Somewhat more of the Black respondents than either white or Spanish go to doctors outside the neighborhood.

Far smaller proportions of the sample report participation in recreational or employment activities (from 15% to 35% depending upon type of activity). Parks are usually in the neighborhood but other recreational facilities and employment involve leaving the area.

Niebanck and Pope (1965), in setting forth criteria for the selection of a housing site for the elderly, generalize that facilities used regularly or those which are critical when needed are most essential to have in close proximity. They further rank facilities in order of need as stores, bus stops, health, and religious facilities.

Using these criteria, it can be seen that the Inner City neighborhoods of New York provide within easy proximity most of the essential services needed by the elderly, with glaring exceptions of medical care. For elderly not physically able to use public transportation or even for many who can use it only with difficulty, getting to medical services can mean a considerable hardship. It is highly unlikely, given the economics of medical care and shortage of personnel, that doctors can always be provided within the immediate neighborhood. What is suggested, however, is the need for an alternative means of medical transportation for older and handicapped people, even in high density areas like New York City with extensive public transportation systems.

Social Support System

The data presented thus far suggest that the city, even in its more deteriorated residential areas, is capable of meeting most of the day-to-day physical needs of the nonhomebound elderly. But does city life provide equally well for important social needs for interaction and personal support in time of stress? Perhaps the very ability of the city to provide goods and services mitigates against social interaction and instead enhances isolation and alienation, particularly in the case of the more neighborhood-bound very old and very young.

In urban industrial society, the support system of the elderly increasingly involves an amalgam of services provided by the family and significant others, and services offered by large scale organizations, be they governmental or voluntary. As kinship structure evolves from the extended family to the modified extended family the importance of the familial versus societal role shifts. Thus, today it is government which provides the floor of basic services for older people in such crucial areas as income maintenance, health, and transportation. But the family and significant others still retain considerable importance, particularly in meeting the more idiosyncratic human needs of the individual. Three levels of the personal support system were examined in the study: children, close friends or intimates, and neighbors.

Children

Contrary to myths that circulate widely about today's parent-child relationships, two out of three Inner City elderly have at least one living child and they have not been abandoned by their children. Familial bonds are strong and there is evidence of mutual affection and assistance between the generations.

In view of the frequently described flight of children to suburbia, it is significant to note that 28% of all children are within walking distance, while 26% live elsewhere in the five boroughs of New York. Only 13% reside in the suburbs, and 32% are beyond the metropolitan area. According to the respondents, they see half of their children at least once a week and two-thirds at least monthly.

Contact between parents and children is not limited to mere visiting or "checking up," valuable as this type of support may be psychologically. In attitudinal questions the respondents expressed strong feelings about the appropriateness of assistance within the kinship structures and the desirability of mutual interdependency between parents and children. The behavior of the generations appears consonant with these attitudes.

Assistance between Generations

Over three-fourths of the elderly report helping children in some manner, while the level of involvement of children with parents is even higher—87%.

Gift-giving ranks first as the most important form of child-parent assistance just as it does in the flow of support from parents to children. Approximately 80% of the elderly of all three ethnic groups receive gifts from children (78% black elderly, 84% white and Spanish).

At least two-thirds of the parents received help from their children in the case of illness, and again the proportions of respondents receiving crisis intervention is virtually identical among the three ethnic subgroups.

Whereas parents are not apt to help children in the running of their homes, about two-thirds of Inner City elderly receive substantial assistance from their children in the chores of daily living. Half of the respondents report children shop for them. Spanish and black children tend slightly more often to shop for parents (58%), but even among whites, 42% have children who help with the shopping. Approximately 40% of all respondents have children who fix things in the house and almost one-third have children who drive them to the store or doctor.

The amount of help parents receive from children is positively related to the age of the respondents and the paucity of income, suggesting that as older people in the Inner City become more vulnerable, their children respond with more of the needed assistance.

Intimates and Neighbors

To turn now to the secondary levels of a social support system, friends and neighbors, as noted, the majority of Inner City respondents have one or more children as a foundation for a support system. But one-third of the elderly have no living children and, even among those with children, 19% do not have a child within the metropolitan area. For such older people, close friends and neighbors could, if they exist, substitute as primary social supports.

But even if older people are fortunate enough to have a weekly or even biweekly visit from a child, such visits do not replace their need for intimacy and interaction on a day-to-day basis. Blau (1973) argues that people who have friends have less to fear from significant role losses since they can continue to feel needed and influence others, and other studies indicate that morale in old age may be even more highly related to association with friends than association with children (Rose, 1965; Shanas et al., 1968; Townsend, 1957).

Our data support the importance of friends and neighbors in the life of urban elderly. They further suggest that city living, with its high density and accessible transportation, is encouraging to extensive interaction between the elderly and those living around them.

Slightly over half of the respondents reported having at least one "intimate." Most often persons designated as intimates are not related to the respondents. Slightly over one-half of the intimates (56%) are younger than the respondents and 60% live in the immediate neighborhood. With so many intimates living in the neighborhood, contacts between respondents and their intimates are frequent—68% of the close friends are seen at least weekly, while 39% are seen daily.

In addition to the persons designated as intimates, the respondents receive considerable support and interact extensively with neighbors living in the same or nearby buildings. Most of the sample live in mixed-age housing. Thus for three-quarters of the respondents, neighbors are generally younger than themselves.

But the fact that neighbors are usually younger did not prevent over 60% of the respondents from knowing at least one neighbor well and the mean number of neighbors known well is 2.5. Interestingly enough the "live alones" are significantly more likely to report knowing at least one neighbor well.

It would appear that the younger age of neighbors is no barrier to close supportive relationships arising between the elderly and those around them. Respondents were asked what neighbors do for them, what they do for neighbors and what types of activities they shared together.

Interaction with Neighbors

The most important category of neighboring activities is that of emergency assistance or crisis intervention. Two-thirds of those who know neighbors well state that neighbors help them when they are ill and that they help neighbors in turn. In addition, about 22% of the neighbors accompany respondents to the doctor or clinic, while almost one-fifth of the elderly escort neighbors to medical services.

With respect to assistance in chores of daily living, the flow of assistance also tends to be mutual. Neighbors shop for older people in 45% of the cases, while 42% of the respondents shop or watch children for neighbors.

The importance of the neighborhood as a socialization center for older people is seen by the fact that Inner City elderly's relationships to neighbors are by no means limited to mutual helping activities. There is a strong friendship cast to many of the activities. Over 80% "sit and talk" together with neighbors either in front of the building or in parks or open spaces. Almost two-thirds have a visiting relationship with neighbors. For a smaller, but significant group, relationships with neighbors become even more close, 28% eat together, 25% shop together, and 18% go to church together.

Although the study data do not address the question of age preference with respect to friends or neighbors, they strongly support the notion that close intergenerational relationships are possible and in fact do take place in urban society. Thus the absence of a majority of peer-age residents in the building or area does not appear to interfere with the development of meaningful supportive sharing relationships. Rather, the high population density in urban areas offers a large reservoir of persons living within the immediate vicinity from whom to draw on as intimates and friends. And the elderly in the Inner City appear to be friendly with and receive support from many of those around them, regardless of whether such persons are younger or their own age.

Persons without a Viable Social System

There was, however, a small but significant group of elderly—8% of the sample—who appeared to have no personal support system of any kind and were entirely "on their own." Some of these persons may be in touch with community organizations or religious institutions, but the absence of any "close other" suggests that they are likely to be true isolates.

As a matter of fact, the proportion of "live alones" among the study sample (39%) is significantly greater than is true for the city as a whole, or for the elderly in the low income areas of Philadelphia (Kent, 1971, 1972) and Los Angeles (Gelwicks, Feldman, & Newcomer, 1971).

The City: A Viable Place in Which to Live?

The discussion so far has stressed the neighborhood as a provider of services, as the locale for a viable personal support system, and as an arena for socialization. But there is yet another facet of the city beyond the urban village and that is the broad cosmopolitan nature and vitality of city life. What does city life mean to the elderly?

Like most New Yorkers, the majority of older people reported many things they liked about the city and some which worry and upset them. However, on balance, although living in the most deteriorated, changing neighborhoods of the city, respondents expressed more optimism than pessimism about city life (61% feel the city is a good or fairly good place of residence for older people; 39% said it is not too good or not good at all).

What specifically, do older people react to about New York City? First of all, they in no way gloss over the problems of the city. Most often cited is crime and the general lack of personal safety; followed by comments on deteriorating conditions of the neighborhoods, dirt and noise, and the high cost of living. In addition, the elderly are also often fearful of persons different from themselves—be they of different ethnic background or life styles.

Their negative feelings, particularly fears about personal safety, are deeply rooted in reality. Over 40% of the sample report being victims of personal crime at some time in the past ranging from purse-snatching to forcible entry into their homes. And New York City is certainly one of the most difficult places in the country in which to survive on a limited income.

But offsetting these negative aspects of city life were the positives we tend to overlook. First, and foremost, is the fact that most people (especially the old) are more favorably inclined to the place they presently live in—to what is familiar and known; what they can navigate and encompass. But in addition to their sense of rootedness, older people verbalize specific reasons why they rate the urban environment so highly. They talk about the ease and availability of desired facilities and services, the opportunities for work and a sense of privacy in a big city. City life means having at one's fingertips most of the services needed and wanted, including both the necessities of life and the special cultural and recreational facilities found in a large cosmopolitan city. Thus, the density of people and spread of activities appears to be of great benefit to people as they retire and age.

When one looks at responses of older people to the question of the viability of the city as a place of residence, we find they mirror the values attributed by urban planners to cities over the years. Among older people the services and amenities become more important than opportunities for economic advancement. But the vitality of city life surging around them and its potential for satisfying personal tastes are as important to the old as to the young. New York City is apparently considered a viable place to live in by a majority of the respondents despite its recognized problems because it offers an environment rich in choices and capable of satisfying needs.

Chapter 9

Social and Health Services

It takes more than medicine and physicians to provide health-care services in our complex society; it takes more than social workers and psychologists to provide social and psychological care. It requires physical structures and complex networks of social interaction—integrated transportation services, extensive record-keeping systems, government and private agencies, immense piles of regulations, financing plans, and insurance companies. Services must be provided in the home, in the hospital, in the social agency, in the office of the psychologist, on the way from home to hospital or on the way home from the hospital (which may occur in stages involving nursing homes, board-and-care facilities, welfare agencies, and other facilities).

Some major policy issues must be resolved in the provision of health and social services. First, we wish to put as much money into direct services and as little into administrative overhead as possible; yet, if we ignore effective administration, the service program may collapse or become undependable. Second, we wish to avoid politics as much as possible; yet the major sources of funding often are government agencies (for example, state public health, county welfare), and appointments to decision-making positions in such agencies often are made by political figures, not infrequently with political motives. Third, we are more concerned with the needs of the elderly for whom services are developed, than with the people who run those programs; yet if we ignore the needs of the staff or of others in the community, we can run into trouble.

A particularly difficult issue is establishing to what extent we will utilize *outreach* programs to get to people who do not actively seek available services. Obviously it is important to reach those people who do not have access to information sources that the rest of us tend to use. Elderly people may be isolated from newspapers, from informed peers, and from social agencies and health facilities. At the same time, we should take care not to manipulate the elderly into accepting services that we (you and I, as workers in the field) believe they need but that they don't particularly want. It is all too easy for a well-meaning service-provider to get older people to become so dependent that they lose their autonomy. Further, Margaret Blenkner, a social worker herself, has shown that those elderly who receive extensive social and other services are more likely to end up in institutions, and even to die slightly sooner, than those who remain in the community and on their own (Blenkner, Bloom, & Nielsen, 1971).

Blenkner's research is, as you can imagine, highly controversial. Do we really "kill elderly people with our kindness?" We know there is a danger in destroying the autonomy of the elderly through too many services, but we also know of the danger in destroying their autonomy by not providing enough support. The task of knowing when "not enough" becomes "enough" and of stopping before it becomes "too much" is extremely difficult, and the decision must be made for each individual and each service. Also, over the years many well-intentioned people have opposed any sort of meaningful help for the elderly on the basis that "They don't need it; it will only lead to early dependency." Still others oppose support programs saying, "They don't deserve it; they should have worked harder when they were young."

We talk a great deal about a continuum of services, so that each elderly person can obtain what he needs: On the one hand, no person would be kept from services that are important to him or her; on the other hand, no one has to accept more than is necessary. Perhaps this requires some additional explanation. Assume that you can set up only one kind of mental health facility for the elderly. Perhaps you decide on a crisis-intervention walk-in center where older people can come to discuss emotional problems requiring immediate and short-term care. One morning, Mrs. Samuelson comes in wanting to talk about her feelings of loneliness since the recent death of her husband, and you feel very good that the center is there to meet her need. But later, Mr. Pickett walks in with some questions about filling out his Medicaid form. You don't know anything about Medicaid forms, but you realize that that is his immediate and pressing problem. So, you call a doctor you know, but he is in the emergency room. You call another physician, and he refers you to Mr. Pickett's personal doctor—the one who asked the man to complete the form in the first place. Now where should you call? You have spent an hour trying to help this man, and two other clients are waiting to see you. Your center just isn't set up to deal with this kind of problem. You are frustrated and angry, and Mr. Pickett is still confused.

Worse still, after a few minutes of discussion with a new client, Mrs. Vance, you realize that she will require extensive psychotherapy, probably lasting several months, and your center is not equipped for long-term care.

So, to meet the continuum of mental health needs of the elderly, ranging from the very demanding to the undemanding, you must learn what other facilities are available in the community. If certain services are lacking, you may wish to join other workers to try to develop them.

The sections that follow will discuss health, social, and psychological services for the elderly.

Health-Care Services*

Anthony Lenzer

Old people, as author Lenzer points out, are not as unhealthy as we often assume, but there is no doubt that poor health is of immense concern to the elderly, as well as to those who provide services and those who help pay for those services (which, in final analysis, means almost everyone).

The nature of health-care services, the distribution of these services (that is, the extent to which they receive the facilities, personnel, equipment, and funding they need), and the delivery of health-care services are all part of the same package. Most people who work with the elderly know that in most instances this package is not adequate, but there is a great gap between having such knowledge and knowing what to do about it.

How well are old people, and how likely are they to maintain health throughout old age? While not as healthy as the young, most are, for all practical purposes, quite healthy and are likely to maintain this state of health until very near the end. Many members of the helping professions find this statement difficult to accept.

Some reject the claim because they themselves are illness-oriented. They define health as the absence of clinical pathology. Seen this way, old people are indeed sick, and the older they get, the sicker they become. Eighty-six percent of persons over 65 have at least 1 chronic condition. When one adds acute illness and accidental injuries, practically every old person has something wrong with him.

Other professional workers reject the statement because it contradicts their own experience. Most of the aged persons whom they are trying to help are ill, frail, disabled or dependent. They assume their clients are typical of old people, but in reality they are atypical. The old do not usually turn to community agencies for help until they, their families, and friends can no longer cope with a problem. By that time the problem is serious and complicated.

HEALTH STATUS OF OLD PEOPLE

In these terms, old people seem to be pretty healthy after all. The National Center for Health Statistics indicates that only 5 percent of persons over 65 are so ill or function so poorly that they must live in nursing homes, homes for the aged, mental hospitals or other institutions. Even at

*Edited from "Health Care Services," by A. Lenzer. In *Working With Older People: A Guide to Practice. Vol. III: The Aging Person: Needs and Services.* United States Department of Health, Education, and Welfare. Washington, D.C.: U.S. Government Printing Office, 1970.

age 85, 8 of 10 persons are still living in their own or relatives' homes and *not* in institutions. But how well do the noninstitutionalized aged function? Chronic or long-term conditions are the major source of disability for old persons, and 85 percent report at least 1 chronic condition. Yet only 14 percent of the noninstitutionalized aged report that they are totally unable to work or keep house due to a chronic condition. An additional 25 percent can work but are somewhat limited in the amount or kind of work or house work they can undertake. Even at age 75, only 24 percent are totally limited and 30 percent partially limited in work capacity because of chronic illness.

One additional measure of health is the number of days per week in which the person has restricted activity or is confined to bed. This measure of "disability days" counts *all* such days, whether due to chronic illness, acute illness or accidents. National Center for Health Statistics data indicate that old people have more disability days than young or middle-aged people. But even the old are, on the average, restricted in activity only 35 days per year and are confined to bed on only 12 of these days.

Despite this encouraging view of the health of the aged, there are aging process realities to be considered.

TYPES OF HEALTH SERVICES

In general, health services for old people should be comprehensive, coordinated, and continuous.

Comprehensive Health Services

Comprehensiveness means that a total range of services is available and accessible to meet all known needs of the old person and his family. These include: (a) health promotion; (b) prevention and detection of illness; (c) ambulatory care; (d) hospital and other institutional care; and (e) home care. They also include: (f) evaluation of the patient's status and needs; (g) counseling and referral to sources of help; and (h) continuing surveillance so that care plans change as needs change. In addition, they should include: (i) help in restructuring family, job and avocational plans; and (j) emotional support over the months or years that illness or disability persist.

Coordinated Health Services

Coordination means that services are assembled into an appropriate package for each individual. When several agencies are involved, it is sometimes difficult to reach full agreement on what the package should contain. Other problems arise when the practitioner understands some patient and family needs but ignores others. Planners of care create additional problems by trying to fit the needs of the patient to the resources they are familiar with instead of finding resources to fit needs.

Continuous Health Services

Continuity means that services are provided without interruption. Continuity should be assured whether patients are brought to services or vice versa; whether one receives all services from a single agency or a number of agencies; and whether care is financed through one or several sources.

PREVENTION OF ILLNESS AND DISABILITY

Preventive services should aim for the maintenance or development of healthful living habits, elimination of sources of illness or injury, and protection against their hazards.

Healthful Habits

The following habits are important to health maintenance in old age: eating in such a way as to meet all nutritional requirements while avoiding overweight; exercising regularly to maintain full functioning capacity; getting enough rest to wake refreshed and function well throughout the day; correcting minor defects which could reduce ability to walk, talk, eat, see or hear; avoiding or eliminating cigarette smoking.

Eliminating Hazards

Environment includes the immediate environment of the home as well as the larger social environment. Many home accidents could be prevented by changes in the structure or arrangements of the home. Home safety inspections by firemen, building officials or neighborhood aides might help sensitize old people to home hazards. Groups or classes on home safety might also be helpful.

Within the home, increasing illumination levels, using large readable labels on containers of hazardous products, and keeping electrical and gas equipment in good repair all serve to protect the old against hazards. Installation of air conditioning can also be beneficial. Recent studies of heat waves show the aged to be the major victims.

Air pollution and unsafe crossing zones on busy streets are two types of social hazards to be removed so as to benefit old people. Heavily polluted air has been shown to cause excessive illness and death among the old; poorly regulated traffic strikes down the old as well as young.

Detection of Illness

Health workers believe that early detection followed by correct diagnosis and prompt treatment reduces the likelihood that a disease will lead to disability or death. This requires that the condition be discovered prior to the time when the average person becomes sufficiently alarmed by symptoms to go to a doctor.

Three principal methods of early detection are periodic health exams, screening and sensitizing people to symptoms.

Periodic health exams. Health exams include a health history, "physical," and whatever laboratory work the physician feels is indicated. The physician gives the physical, interprets findings and gives instructions as necessary.

Periodic exams have their greatest value when they are comprehensive and are done by the same physician throughout the person's lifetime. Under these circumstances, the physician has a baseline (information on what the old person was like as a young and middle-aged adult) and an accumulation of data on which to base judgments. However, relatively few adults have regular exams, and they are rarely of the type suggested.

Screening. Screening is the use of simple tests and procedures for rapidly discovering signs of illness in large populations. Theoretically, at least, screenees should be unaware of the presence of illness and should believe that they are in good health. Screening can be aimed at uncovering one condition or several possible conditions in "multiple" or "multiphasic" screening.

While screening has the virtues of being fast, inexpensive and applicable on a mass basis, it also poses difficulties. For example, a number of the serious chronic conditions cannot be detected by known screening tests. Neither has it been scientifically established that most existing screening programs lead to significantly reduced disability or death rates. Apparently it is of *proven* value for only a limited number of conditions such as anemia, cataracts, otitis, rheumatoid arthritis, hernia, TB, overweight and cancer of the uterus, bladder, skin, and mouth.

Sensitizing people to symptoms. Another approach is to familiarize people to symptoms which may indicate the presence of certain diseases. The most extensive and oldest symptoms campaign centered around cancer's "Seven Danger Signals."

The basic shortcomings of the "danger signals" approach are the confusion likely to ensue if the public is expected to remember symptoms of even half a dozen serious diseases and the fact that by the time symptoms are apparent to the person, a disease may already be beyond the early stage. Then too, knowledge of symptoms per se is insufficient to motivate people to action.

AMBULATORY CARE

Even if prevention and detection systems were excellent, illness would still occur and old people would need diagnosis and treatment. Ambulatory care is primarily diagnosis and treatment which is given in doctors' offices, clinics or group health settings. Aside from medical care provided in hospitals or other institutions, about two-thirds of all physician contacts with old people are at the doctor's office. Approximately 9 percent of such contacts occur in hospital clinics and 8 percent are by phone. Seventeen percent represent visits by doctors to the old person's home. Old people have approximately the same pattern of contact with physicians as the total population, with one important exception: physicians visit old people at home three times as often as any other age group, according to 1963–64 data. To obtain care, the individual must be able to get to where it is given. At least on the surface, most old people manage to do so on their own or with the help of relatives, friends, or taxi drivers.

HOSPITAL CARE

The general hospital is usually seen as provider of maternity care and inpatient care for persons with serious, acute conditions. Yet, the aged make heavy use of hospitals—they are hospitalized more often and stay longer than any other age group.

Hospitals today are concerned with the entire spectrum of illness, from its earliest to its last stages. Stimulated in part by Medicare, hospitals are increasingly establishing screening and diagnostic services and rehabilitation departments.

Some leaders in the hospital profession believe that these changes are just the beginning of the transformation of the acute hospital into a community health center in which public and private health activities, acute, chronic and psychiatric care would be available on a single health campus. Whether this becomes the new pattern or not, the aged are likely to be among the chief beneficiaries of experimental approaches to the integration of health services.

OTHER INSTITUTIONS SERVING THE AGED

Mental hospital admission rates increase with age, as do mental illness rates. Yet the evidence suggests that most old people are mentally competent and they do not become irresponsible or befuddled in their last years.

Institutionalization for the Mentally Ill Aged

Where are the mentally ill aged? Recent national studies indicate that there are almost as many people with "mental disorders" in nursing and personal care homes as there are in mental hospitals. In 1968, there were approximately 120,000 people over age 65 in state and county mental hospitals, plus thousands more in Veterans Administration and other facilities. In 1967, nursing homes contained an estimated minimum of 186,000 mentally ill aged (Kramer, Taube, & Redick, 1973).

Does institutionalization mean the end of the road for the aged? Not necessarily. A Public Health Service report on *Mental Disorders of the Aging* indicates that response to treatment by patients 65 and over is virtually the same as for other age groups: a third recover or nearly recover; a third improve considerably; and a third remain the same or grow worse. The trick is to get *treatment* for the old, rather than custodial care.

Old people should not be placed in mental hospitals or other long-term institutions until they have been given a thorough evaluation at an appropriate center. Evaluation provides the opportunity to ask: Why does the old person behave as he does? Can anything be done to correct this condition? Does he really need to go to the State mental hospital, nursing home or whatever other institution we had in mind for him? What alternatives might better meet his needs and those of his family?

Psychiatric units in general hospitals are often more appropriate places for treatment of the mentally ill aged than are long-term care institutions and should be used whenever possible. As of mid-1967, there were over 700 psychiatric units in general hospitals, and almost all of these were certified to provide services under Medicare. In fact, Medicare regulations encourage the use of such units in preference to custodial mental hospitals. General hospitals are more likely to have the specialized medical resources which older people need and are usually more accessible to friends and relatives. There is also less stigma and a greater sense of hopefulness associated with care in these institutions.

Nursing Home Type Facilities

Extended care nursing homes and homes for aged offer care and protection from the stresses of independent living when the aged become too ill, frail or dependent to manage on their own and when family members cannot or will not assume such responsibilities. These facilities vary enormously in their objectives, their names, ownership and administration, bed capacity, staffing, services, quality and cost of care. For an up-to-date analysis of facilities of this type, the reader is advised to contact the National Center for Health Statistics of the U.S. Public Health Service since there are rapid changes currently taking place nationally.

The *extended care* facility is a newer type of facility created by Medicare legislation. Its purpose is to provide short-term, skilled nursing and active, rehabilitation-oriented care for old people, following discharge from the hospital. The basic orientation of the ECF is quite unlike that of the traditional nursing home, which still has a custodial flavor and a passive approach to care. While the ECF emphasizes rehabilitation, the term has a somewhat different meaning than when applied to young people. For young people, rehabilitation usually means a return to the community, to school or to the job. For old people, it often means, essentially, prevention of further disability. The criterion for success is not return to "productivity," but the ability to care for one's own needs while making fewer demands on social resources.

It is hard to consider nursing homes and homes for the aged as two separate types of facilities, since many homes offer a mixture of skilled nursing and room, board and assistance in activities of daily living. Also, State licensing laws often fail to adequately distinguish between facilities on the basis of the services which they offer.

Nursing homes have, in general, improved greatly in recent years due to increased professionalism, licensing, accrediting and certification. Licensing laws have begun to include standards for nursing and other care and require certain minimum qualifications for personnel. By 1972, the States were required to establish minimum standards of training and experience for persons wishing to enter nursing home administration.

Accreditation is a further method for raising standards. Accreditation, unlike licensing, involves voluntary compliance with a set of standards which an industry or occupation sets for itself or which is set by an impartial accrediting body. In January 1966, the Joint Commission on Accreditation of Hospitals agreed to serve as the accrediting body for nursing homes. Certification as an ECF under Medicare imposes still more quality standards on the institution.

Another approach is to devise more sophisticated systems for classifying old-age institutions. Such systems should take into account intensity and amount of service and the quality of care provided.

Traditional homes for the aged are nonprofit institutions sponsored by churches or fraternal organizations. They have served as homes for old people who, though physically well, were socially dependent and unable to maintain themselves.

Although the traditional type still exists, most homes have either become: (a) medical facilities for the physically or mentally ill; or (b) parts of larger institutional complexes which are designed to meet a wide range of needs. Such institutions frequently are affiliated with universities or medical centers and foster research and training in addition to serving the aged.

Adult foster homes serve people who, because of physical, mental or emotional problems, are unable to live independently, but who need and desire the security of family living. The foster family is expected to provide a family-like role.

Boarding homes for the aged are similar to foster homes except that they are larger, serve more people, and have less of the intimate family atmosphere. They are often used for former mental hospital patients and others who are not self-sufficient but cannot tolerate the intimacy of family living.

HOME CARE

Home care has numerous forms. It varies from programs offering a single service such as nursing care of the sick at home, homemaker-home health aide, or meals on wheels to multi-service patterns, the most sophisticated of which are coordinated home care programs.

Prior to the advent of Medicare, the most widespread program of home care was nursing care of the sick at home, whether provided by a voluntary nursing agency, an official health department or other source. With the passage of Medicare and its "Conditions of Participation of Home Health Agencies," emphasis is on providing services in addition to nursing, and today the multi-service home health agency predominates.

In June 1971, there were 2,256 home health agencies certified for participation in the Medicare program. Of this number, 3 out of 5 were in official health departments, 1 in 4 in visiting nurse associations, and about 1 in 13 was administered by a hospital. The range of services offered by these agencies varied. Of the total, 73 percent provide physical therapy; 48 percent, home health aid services; 20 percent, medical social services; 22 percent, speech therapy; and 16 percent, occupational therapy.

Although the intent of the law is for the attainment of comprehensive services in the home health agencies, Social Security data show that in January 1969, half of the certified agencies were at minimum certification level, and that 43 percent of these agencies had staffs of only one or two nurses. Thus while some progress has been made in expansion of home health programs, much remains to be accomplished with regard to a sharp increase in the number of agencies and diversification of services offered.

BARRIERS TO ADEQUATE HEALTH CARE

"Potential" barriers become "real" to the extent that the old lack the skills or energy needed to overcome them and communities fail to provide necessary help. Barriers within old people, health practitioners, the health care system and society may keep the aged from obtaining health services.

Some aged people believe that symptoms of illness are normal and inevitable results of aging and therefore do not seek help. Others are aware of their need for help but lack the knowledge or energy required to reach available services. The poor and poorly educated lack skills needed to manipulate the system to their advantage.

Health professionals in general are oriented toward acute illness or the acute phase of chronic disease and have limited experience in management of long-term conditions. Some feel that they have little to learn from an old patient and that they cannot do much about his problems. Increasing demands for health care result in more pressure upon practitioners, who in turn give low priority to the needs of the aged.

The term "health care system" implies an unreality, namely, that most communities have an integrated network of health services and facilities and someone doing planning to meet health needs of the population. Most communities contain many services and facilities which offer potential aid to the aged person. Yet few have any mechanisms for assessing patient or family needs, determining how and where such needs can best be met, and helping people obtain the appropriate services. Some practitioners are willing and able to perform these time-consuming "medical management" functions, but many are not.

The autonomy of providers of care is another barrier. Most agencies are independently administered, and the linkages between them are fragile or nonexistent. Because old people need a variety of services, they must knock on many doors to obtain help. Many health agencies define their mission in a rigid, narrow fashion and vigorously defend their territory against real or imagined encroachment by others. Fragmentation of information about the patient often occurs when he receives service from different agencies. Finally, the system creates particular hardship for old people in small towns, rural areas and the inner core of large cities. These are precisely the areas with the greatest shortages of health resources.

The major social factor affecting access to health services is the generally low social valuation of the aged compared with other age groups. When resources are scarce relative to demand, aged persons and other low-priority groups will be the last to receive them. Negative social valuation is reinforced by the fact that many old people are not only old but are also poor and ill educated and thereby possess low social status.

A Brief Look at Medicare*

The United States is one of the few so-called "developed" nations that does not have government-subsidized health care for all its people. Medicare (and the related Medicaid programs) provides health care for the elderly and for many other persons. The next section offers a brief overview of the services provided by Medicare.

WHAT IS MEDICARE AND
WHO ARE ITS PROVIDERS?

Medicare is a health insurance program for people 65 and older and some people under 65 who are disabled. It is a Federal Government program run by the Social Security Administration. Medicare has two parts. One part is called hospital insurance. The other part is called medical insurance.

Medicare's hospital insurance (sometimes called Part A) can help pay for medically necessary inpatient hospital care, and, after a hospital stay, for inpatient care in a skilled nursing facility and for care in your home by a home health agency.

Medicare's medical insurance (sometimes called Part B) can help pay for medically necessary doctors' services, outpatient hospital services, outpatient physical therapy and speech pathology services, and a number of

*Edited from *Your Medicare Handbook*. U.S. Department of Health, Education, and Welfare. Washington, D.C.: U.S. Government Printing Office, 1975.

other medical services and supplies that are not covered by the hospital insurance part of Medicare. Medical insurance also can help pay for necessary home health services when hospital insurance cannot pay for them.

You are responsible for part of the cost of some services covered under Medicare. As general health care costs rise, these amounts may increase. If you cannot pay these amounts or for other health care expenses, you may be able to get help from the Medicaid program in your State.

Medicare payments are handled by private insurance organizations under contract with the Government. Organizations handling claims from hospitals, skilled nursing facilities, and home health agencies are called *intermediaries.* Organizations handling claims from doctors and other suppliers of services covered under the medical insurance part of Medicare are called *carriers.*

To help make sure that health care furnished to Medicare beneficiaries is of acceptable quality, persons or organizations providing services must meet all licensing requirements of State or local health authorities. Persons and organizations shown below also must meet additional Medicare requirements before payments can be made for their services:

—Hospitals
—Skilled nursing facilities
—Home health agencies
—Independent diagnostic laboratories and organizations providing X-ray services
—Ambulance firms
—Chiropractors
—Independent physical therapists (those who furnish services in your home or in their offices)
—Facilities providing kidney dialysis or transplant services

All hospitals, skilled nursing facilities, and home health agencies participating in the Medicare program also must comply with title VI of the Civil Rights Act, which prohibits discrimination because of race, color, or national origin.

Except for certain situations, Medicare cannot pay for care you get from a non-participating hospital, skilled nursing facility, or home health agency.

You should always make sure that the persons or organizations providing services are approved for Medicare payments. If you are not sure, ask them.

Two Important Rules

Under the law, Medicare does not cover care that is not "reasonable and necessary" for the treatment of an illness or injury. Medicare also does not cover care that is "custodial."

If a doctor places you in a hospital or skilled nursing facility when the kind of care you need could be provided elsewhere, your stay would not be considered reasonable and necessary. So Medicare could not cover your stay. If you stay in a hospital or skilled nursing facility longer than you need to be there, Medicare payments would end at the time further inpatient care is no longer reasonable and necessary.

To help Medicare decide whether inpatient care is reasonable and necessary, each hospital and skilled nursing facility has a Utilization Review Committee, which is made up of at least two doctors. And in some parts of the country there are Professional Standards Review Organizations, which are made up of local doctors who review the care prescribed by their fellow doctors.

If a doctor (or other practitioner) comes to treat you or you visit him for treatment more often than is the usual medical practice in your area, Medicare would not cover the "extra" visits unless there are medical complications. Medicare cannot cover more services than are reasonable and necessary for your treatment. Any decision of this kind is always based on professional medical advice.

Some health care services and supplies are not generally accepted by the health community as being reasonable or necessary for diagnosis and treatment. This includes acupuncture, histamine therapy, and various kinds of medical equipment, for example. Medicare cannot cover services and supplies unless they are generally recognized as safe and effective by the health community.

Care is considered custodial when it is primarily for the purpose of meeting personal needs and could be provided by persons without professional skills or training; for example, help in walking, getting in and out of bed, bathing, dressing, eating, and taking medicine. Even if you are in a participating hospital or skilled nursing facility or you are receiving care from a participating home health agency, Medicare does not cover your care if it is mainly custodial.

YOUR MEDICARE HOSPITAL INSURANCE

Medicare's hospital insurance helps pay for three kinds of care. The three kinds of care are (1) inpatient hospital care; and, when medically necessary after a hospital stay; (2) inpatient care in a skilled nursing facility; and (3) home health care.

There is a limit on how many days of hospital or skilled nursing facility care and how many home health visits Medicare can help pay for in each benefit period. However, your hospital insurance protection is renewed every time you start a new benefit period.

Medicare hospital insurance will pay for most but not all of the services you receive in a hospital or skilled nursing facility or from a home health agency. There are covered services and non-covered services under each kind of care. Covered services are services and supplies that hospital insurance can pay for.

When You Are a Hospital Inpatient

Medicare's hospital insurance can help pay for inpatient hospital care if *all* of the following four conditions are met: (1) a doctor prescribes inpatient hospital care for treatment of an illness or injury, (2) you require the kind of care that can only be provided in a hospital, (3) the hospital is participating in Medicare, and (4) the Utilization Review Committee of the hospital does not disapprove your stay.

Major inpatient services covered. Medicare hospital insurance can pay for these items:

1. A semiprivate room (2 to 4 beds in a room)
2. All your meals, including special diets
3. Regular nursing services
4. Intensive care unit costs
5. Drugs furnished by the hospital during your stay
6. Lab tests included in your hospital bill
7. X-rays and other radiology services, including radiation therapy, billed by the hospital
8. Medical supplies such as casts, surgical dressings, and splints
9. Use of appliances such as a wheelchair
10. Operating and recovery room costs
11. Rehabilitation services, such as physical therapy, occupational therapy, and speech pathology services

Some inpatient services not covered. Medicare's hospital insurance *cannot* pay for these items:

1. Personal convenience items that you request such as a television, radio, or telephone in your room
2. Private duty nurses
3. Any extra charges for a private room, unless you need it for medical reasons
4. The first 3 pints of blood you receive in a benefit period

Inpatient Care
in a Skilled Nursing Facility

Medicare's hospital insurance can help pay for inpatient care in a participating skilled nursing facility after you have been in a hospital. Hospital insurance can cover this care if you no longer need all the services that only a hospital can provide, but your condition still requires daily skilled nursing or rehabilitation services which, as a practical matter, can only be provided in a skilled nursing facility.

Hospital insurance can help pay for care in a skilled nursing facility if *all* of the following five conditions are met: (1) you have been in a hospital at least 3 days in a row before your transfer to the skilled nursing facility, (2) you are transferred to the skilled nursing facility because you require care for a condition which was treated in the hospital, (3) you are admitted to the facility within a short time (generally within 14 days) after you leave the hospital, (4) a doctor certifies that you need, and you actually receive, skilled nursing or skilled rehabilitation services on a daily basis, and (5) the facility's Utilization Review Committee does not disapprove your stay.

As we said, *all* five conditions must be met. But it's especially important to remember the requirement that you must need skilled nursing care or skilled rehabilitation services on a daily basis.

By skilled nursing care, we mean care that can only be performed by, or under the supervision of, licensed nursing personnel. Skilled rehabilitation services may include such services as physical therapy performed by, or under the supervision of, a professional therapist. The skilled nursing care and skilled rehabilitation services you receive must be under the general direction of a doctor.

Major services covered in a skilled nursing facility. Medicare's hospital insurance can pay for these items:

1. A semiprivate room (2 to 4 beds in a room)
2. All your meals, including special diets
3. Regular nursing services
4. Rehabilitation services, such as physical, occupational, and speech therapy
5. Drugs furnished by the facility during your stay
6. Medical supplies such as splints and casts
7. Use of appliances such as a wheelchair

Some services not covered in a skilled nursing facility. Medicare's hospital insurance *cannot* pay for these items:

1. Personal convenience items you request such as a television, radio, or telephone in your room
2. Private duty nurses
3. Any extra charges for a private room, unless you need it for medical reasons
4. The first 3 pints of blood you receive in a benefit period

YOUR MEDICARE MEDICAL INSURANCE

Medicare's medical insurance can help pay for (1) doctors' services, (2) outpatient hospital care, (3) outpatient physical therapy and speech pathology services, (4) home health care, and (5) many other health services and supplies which are not covered by Medicare's hospital insurance.

When a Doctor Treats You

Medical insurance can help pay for covered services you receive from your doctor in his office, in a hospital, in a skilled nursing facility, in your home, or any other location in the U.S.

Radiology and pathology services by doctors. While you are an inpatient in a hospital, medical insurance pays 100 percent of the reasonable charges for services by doctors in the fields of radiology and pathology.

Outpatient treatment of mental illness. Doctors' services you receive for outpatient treatment of a mental illness are covered, but medical insurance can pay *no more than* $250 in any one year for these services.

Podiatrists' services. Medical insurance can help pay for any covered services of a licensed podiatrist, except for routine foot care.

Dental care. Medicaid insurance can help pay for dental care *only* if it involves surgery of the jaw or related structures or setting fractures of the jaw or facial bones.

Major doctors' services covered. Medicare's medical insurance can help pay for:

1. Medical and surgical services
2. Diagnostic tests and procedures that are part of your treatment
3. Other services which are ordinarily furnished in the doctor's office and included in his bill, such as:
   —X-rays you receive as part of your treatment
   —Services of your doctor's office nurse
   —Drugs and biologicals that cannot be self-administered
   —Medical supplies
   —Physical therapy and speech pathology services

Some doctors' services not covered. Medicare's medical insurance *cannot* pay for these services:

1. Routine physical examinations
2. Routine foot care
3. Eye or hearing examinations for prescribing or fitting eyeglasses or hearing aids
4. Immunizations (unless required because of an injury or immediate risk of infection)
5. Cosmetic surgery unless it is needed because of accidental injury or to improve the functioning of a malformed part of the body

Outpatient Hospital Services

Medicare's medical insurance helps pay for covered services you receive as an outpatient from a participating hospital for diagnosis or treatment of an illness or injury.

Major outpatient hospital services covered. Medicare's medical insurance helps pay for these items:

1. Services in an emergency room or outpatient clinic
2. Laboratory tests billed by the hospital

3. X-rays and other radiology services billed by the hospital
4. Medical supplies such as splints and casts
5. Drugs and biologicals which cannot be self-administered
6. Physical therapy
7. Speech pathology
8. Independent laboratory services
9. Ambulance transportation
10. Prosthetic devices
11. Durable medical equipment such as oxygen equipment and wheel-chairs
12. Portable diagnostic x-ray services
13. Medical supplies

Some outpatient hospital services not covered. Medicare's medical insurance *cannot* pay for these items:

1. Routine physical examinations and tests directly related to such examinations
2. Eye or ear examinations to prescribe or fit eyeglasses or hearing aids
3. Immunizations (unless required because of an injury or immediate risk of infection)
4. Routine foot care

HOME HEALTH CARE UNDER MEDICARE

Sometimes people are confined to their homes because of an illness or injury and need skilled health services only on a part-time basis. These services may be medically necessary, for example, after treatment in a hospital or skilled nursing facility. Or, part-time skilled care provided at home could help avoid an inpatient stay.

If you need part-time skilled health care in your home for the treatment of an illness or injury, either hospital insurance or medical insurance can help pay for covered health care services furnished by home health agencies[1] participating in Medicare.

Medicare does not cover home care services furnished primarily to assist people in meeting personal, family, and domestic needs. These services include general household services, preparing meals, shopping, or assisting in bathing, dressing, or other personal needs.

When care in your home is covered by Medicare, the services you receive are counted in visits. For example, if you receive one home health service twice in the same day, or two different home health services in the same day, two visits would be counted.

Home health services covered by Medicare. Medicare can pay for:

---

[1]A home health agency is a public or private agency that specializes in giving skilled nursing services and other therapeutic services, such as physical therapy, in your home.

1. Part-time skilled nursing care
2. Physical therapy
3. Speech therapy

If you need part-time skilled nursing care, physical therapy, or speech therapy, Medicare can also pay for:

—Occupational therapy
—Part-time services of home health aides
—Medical social services
—Medical supplies and equipment provided by the agency

Home health services not covered by Medicare. Medicare *cannot* pay for:

1. Full-time nursing care at home
2. Drugs and biologicals
3. Meals delivered to your home
4. Homemaker services

The Effects of a Decade of Medicare Benefits*

Philip Meyer

The first section of this chapter outlined the scope of health services and some of the institutions that provide these services. How to pay for them is very much related, and yet it is a very different issue. Do we deny necessary health care to people who cannot pay for it? What is necessary? Who decides? When Medicare legislation was passed, now more than a decade ago, many people thought that the financial aspects of health care for the elderly had been taken care of. Not so.

The health-care system must be financed, and the costs are immense, with disproportionate costs falling on the elderly. The money to pay for health services comes from taxes (distributed through Social Security/Medicare and welfare), from individual private insurance with commercial carriers, and from personal savings. In a much more personal context, a long illness can wipe out a lifetime of accumulated savings along with available funds of family members, even with Medicare and Medicaid.

Medical costs have been skyrocketing, partly because of increased services, partly because of general inflation, partly because of rising insurance

*From "The Effects of a Decade of Medicare Benefits," by P. Meyer. San Francisco *Sunday Examiner & Chronicle,* April 4, 1974. Reprinted by permission of Knight News Wire.

*rates for physicians and hospitals, partly because of a variety of other reasons.
And since the health needs of the elderly are the greatest, the health costs are
also the greatest.*

The benefits of Medicare, won by older citizens in 1967 after years of
political struggle, are slowly but surely being taken away from them. One
tragic result is a gathering political struggle of young against old as Congress tries to hammer out a new national health insurance plan for
everyone.

Inflation and direct cutbacks in the Medicare program have depleted
the benefits to older persons so that they are now only slightly better off
than they were when Medicare was established to help them cope with
medical bills that eat away at fixed incomes. The best years for that program were 1968 and 1969. The average out-of-pocket medical costs for persons 65 and over took a sharp drop at a time when most other living costs
were rising. In the last year before Medicare, direct medical costs (those paid
by the patient) were 10.3 percent of income for persons 65 and over. As the
program gained momentum, the share of older persons' income that was
paid out for direct medical costs shrank to 6.3 percent within the next three
years. Then inflation and stricter bookkeeping by the administration turned
everything around. In 1971, for the first time, the average senior citizen's
health costs were higher than they had been before Medicare. Incomes were
higher by then, so Medicare users were still paying a smaller proportion of
their total income for medical expenses than in the old days. But even that
advantage now is fading. Direct medical costs take an ever higher proportion of elderly income and were approximately 8 percent in 1973—compared
to 6.3 percent at the low point and 10.3 percent before Medicare.

Lobbyists for older Americans are worried that proposed new health
insurance plans will accelerate this trend by gearing all insurance to the
needs of younger persons or families. The basic difference is one of
philosophy about which medical dollars should be covered by insurance: the
first or last. Both the Nixon Administration plan and the Democratic coun-
terproposal emphasize the last dollars, those spent on catastrophic illnesses.
Older people, whose incomes are smaller, are more concerned with front-end
medical costs, those that steadily and regularly nibble away at their income
and savings to pay for the predictable illnesses of the elderly.

Insurance, says Nelson H. Cruikshank, president of the National
Council of Senior Citizens, "should be designed to protect the great majority
of the covered population against the most common risk, rather than just
the exceptional cases." Younger people are more likely to be able to pay the
common, everyday expenses, and they need insurance against the rarer but
more devastating risks, such as kidney failure, paralysis, or cancer, which
require lengthy and expensive care. Spokesmen for the older people say they
want that protection too, but restoring the original basic goals of Medicare
should take first priority.

The main barrier against that goal is the spiraling cost of health care.
Government outlays per elderly person have more than doubled since Medicare's first year. And yet, Medicare's proportionate share has been dropping:

from 46 percent of the total health bill for old people in 1969 to only 40 percent in 1973. Changes in the rules for extended care facilities accounted for most of the drop. These facilities were originally intended as a cost-cutting device, places for long-term patients to recover when they did not need full hospital services. But the demand for this nursing home-type care was much higher than Medicare's designers had anticipated, and in fiscal 1970, the Nixon Administration changed the rules to reduce the kind of extended care that Medicare would pay for.

Another cost-cutting ploy was to slow down the revisions in Medicare's official list of "reasonable charges" which it pays physicians. If a doctor wants to collect more than the official "reasonable charges," he has to get it from the patient. And more doctors are doing just that. In 1969, doctors in three cases out of five accepted direct payment from Medicare on a "reasonable charge" basis. Now only about half do.

The government now faces the prospect of medical costs going up even faster than in the past if price controls are lifted. Boosts in hospital charges of 16 to 17 percent a year have been predicted. Nursing home charges would go up 14 percent a year. Even if price controls are continued for health services, there will continue to be some increases as the doctors and hospitals pass their inflation costs through. With controls, government economists estimate, hospital charges might still go up 10 to 11 percent a year while nursing home charges increase 6.5 percent.

Some government analysts think that older people are getting better care for the extra money they are having to spend. But they have no data to prove it. Average hospital stays by older people have decreased slightly in the past few years, and that might be because patients are getting well faster. But it might also mean that people who can't pay are being shoved out faster.

Increase Since 1966

Here's how average incomes and direct medical payments of persons over 65 have increased since 1966—the last year before Medicare. The numbers are derived from sources in the Social Security Administration and the Bureau of the Census.

Year	Medical Payments	Income	Medical Payments as Percent of Income
1966	$236.72	$2304*	10.3
1967	196.14	2421	8.1
1968	166.92	2639	6.3
1969	181.16	2854	6.3
1970	228.67	2991	7.6
1971	251.81	3289	7.7
1972	288.59	3590	8.0
1973	311.40	3841*	8.1

*Projections: government figures not available.

Social Services in the Community*

Dorothy K. Heyman
Grace H. Polansky

In the last decade, there has been a significant increase in community services for the elderly. Such services have undoubtedly permitted large numbers of old persons to remain out of institutions, but—more important, I feel—these services have enriched the lives of many older persons. In the selection that follows, the authors discuss the role of social work and social services in enabling the elderly to lead more satisfying lives in their own communities. Because of the overlap with other segments of this book, discussions of legal services, senior centers, adult education, and extended-care facilities have been omitted.

In many communities there is a growing awareness of the needs of the elderly and a new willingness to take responsibility for more adequate services to these citizens. Welfare agencies provide basic financial assistance to those in need in all areas of the country. In addition, other social services in local communities as well as on state and national levels are expanding.

While the medical needs of the elderly have been properly emphasized, it must also be made clear that their needs are far more extensive than for medical assistance alone. The bedridden are only a small fraction of the total older population, and most older people continue to live active and independent lives. They continue to function in their accustomed ways until a crisis or change occurs profound enough to challenge their equilibrium. The crises of old age may take various forms, and they are usually multiple in nature. At such times of distress, older persons are turning increasingly to social workers for help.

SOCIAL CASEWORK WITH OLDER PERSONS

The basic problems of the aged are in the areas of emotional and physical health, retirement and finances, physical living arrangements, marital and family relationships, relationships between generations, and problems connected with the use of leisure time—all of which relate to a sense of worth and belonging. Many older persons struggling with these problems, singly or in combination, can use social casework help. Interest-

*Edited from "Social Casework and Community Services for the Aged," by D. K. Heyman and G. H. Polansky. In E. W. Busse and E. Pfeiffer (Eds.), *Behavior and Adaptation in Late Life.* Copyright 1977 by Little, Brown and Company. Reprinted by permission.

ingly, some of these problems do not require intensive intervention but respond to assistance of a superficial nature. Unfortunately, the aged are often unaware of the resources available to them. For this reason it is extremely important that information about such resources be widely disseminated to the aged themselves and to those in contact with them. Applications for help may be received by agencies from older persons themselves, from immediate family or other relatives, or from friends and neighbors. Referrals are frequently made by physicians, clergymen, nurses, and other professional persons. Usually only a simple telephone call is needed to initiate the process of obtaining assistance for a troubled elderly person.

Although it is obvious that social workers in public and private agencies must be familiar with community resources, it is equally important that the full range of community supportive social, home, health, and financial assistance be known to the social worker based in an institution. These resources can make a critical difference in the quality of the client's adjustment to an institution or in his transition back to the community (Brody et al., 1975).

Goals

Social casework has as its goals helping the older person in his adaptation, in his social functioning, and in maintaining or reestablishing psychic equilibrium. Old age is a time when crises involving losses and changes coincide with diminishing strength and energy. The impact of multiple losses may result in a depletion of personal resources, and a supportive relationship and other restitutive measures may be needed. Casework tries to aid the person in adapting his environment to his diminishing functional abilities, or in lessening external stress. If these adjustments are not possible or sufficient, he is then assisted in moving to a new setting in which physical, emotional, and social needs can be met more adequately (Wasser, 1966). At all points the older person is helped to maintain or regain his self-image, to maintain a sense of mastery and control over his environment, and to be relieved of immobilizing fears and anxieties.

Casework frequently involves not only the older person but also the spouse, adult children, grandchildren, and other relatives, as well as interested friends. Professionals such as the physician, nurse, attorney, clergyman, banker, and other social workers may participate in planning and treatment. Landlords, neighbors, staffs of institutions and home care facilities, paramedical personnel, and others are additional resources. The person may need the help of an increasing variety of people. At the same time the emotional involvements of some of these people, particularly of family and friends, need to be taken into account.

Settings

The setting for social casework may be in a counseling service for older persons, a sectarian or nonsectarian family agency, a public welfare department, an institution for the aged, or a general, geriatric, or psychiatric hospital. Other settings are senior centers, community centers, and housing projects or other locations easily accessible to older persons. Agencies such as public welfare departments that perform many supportive functions also use casework concepts and techniques. Here, at the frequently painful point of applying for help, dignity and sense of self-worth can be maintained or increased while a determination is made as to what services are needed. Continued individualized interest in the person and the experience of a positive relationship can be as helpful as the concrete financial or other assistance provided.

Problems

The specific focus of counseling and the specific services to be provided are generally determined by multiple, interrelated needs. For example, personal adjustment to actual and threatened changes and losses, as well as marital and extended-family relationships, are areas in which help is frequently requested. These problems are often accompanied by inadequate income and by the necessity to change physical living arrangements. At other times, physical and mental disability or retirement, with its possible loss of social and economic roles, may necessitate treatment intervention by a caseworker. A brief case history may serve to illustrate the problem:

> Mr. B., age 82, and his wife, who was six years younger, each were experiencing difficulties because of Mr. B.'s progressive brain disease. He was showing memory loss, increasing suspiciousness, disorientation, and lack of judgment. His increasing dependence on Mrs. B. was becoming intolerable to her, especially as it represented a reversal of their previous roles. She herself was feeling vigorous and full of plans and activities but was prevented from carrying them out because of Mr. B.'s unwillingness or inability to participate. Although depressed with her "babysitting" role, Mrs. B. felt guilty about her thoughts of placing her husband in a home for the aged. Friends, too, reinforced her guilt by hinting that he would die sooner if placed in an institution. Her husband clearly opposed any discussion of such placement, and their son obviously was uneasy with the idea of having his father in a home for the aged. Mrs. B. was clearly conflicted in her feelings about the problem. She and her husband had gotten along well during 53 years of marriage. She was afraid she would miss him greatly if he were to leave. In fact, she hardly knew whether the present situation was not better than the guilt she might feel if she placed him in an institution.
>
> A caseworker met with Mrs. B. and her son over a period. On one occasion the psychiatrist who had evaluated Mr. B. joined them. In these sessions Mrs. B. and her son were given emotional support and guided toward realistic planning. The caseworker suggested the possibility of hiring an attendant who could relieve Mrs. B. from time to time, thus freeing her for her own activities and interests and for an occasional vacation. This plan was more acceptable than the institutional solution, and the caseworker told them of the resources for such help.
>
> For his part, Mr. B. was experiencing fears of abandonment, which he expressed through concerns that his wife might die before he did. He said that he regretted being such a "burden" to her. His past occupational

success and his previous sexual prowess became important elements in his conversation. At one point he made a sudden attempt to have sexual relations with his wife, after 15 years of inactivity. This proved upsetting to Mrs. B., and she retaliated at first with threats of proceeding to institutionalize him. In casework, Mrs. B. was helped to see the meaning of these developments and to be more understanding. She was also helped to anticipate her own emotional reactions to having someone else caring for her husband for periods of time, and she also grew somewhat more comfortable with the idea of temporary or permanent placement of her husband if the present plan did not work out. She was able to make good use of professional support. The son, too, became freer to look at the needs of each parent without overidentifying with his father's wishes.

Clients

A study of the whole person, with concern for his individual physical, emotional, and social needs, is the basis for treatment. The older person may be identified as the primary client, or he may be seen as part of a family unit that can then be considered "the client," with the needs of each family member taken into account. Thus, treatment can be either client-centered or family-centered.

Casework Treatment

Identification of the problem is followed by treatment planning. The goals of treatment may be limited to helping the person deal with the immediately stressful situation. On the other hand, increased self-awareness and self-understanding, with consequent behavior modification, may be sought (Wasser, 1966). Treatment is basically ego-supportive, with the caseworker sustaining and developing the healthy personality aspects and useful defenses of the client. The essential ingredient is the relationship between caseworker and client. Past achievements and present strengths are given recognition. Physical and emotional supports within the family and the community are utilized to promote self-mobilization and independence. Depending on the ego strength of the client, confrontation, clarification, and interpretation may also be used on a selective basis. Sometimes role shifts occur in old age that require the establishment of new or changed relationships and a redefinition of social identity.

Casework continues as long as it is needed. It may be resumed at any time when a new crisis arises. For the elderly, need, rather than motivation for behavioral change, is the primary indication for intervention. A prompt response to requests for service is essential for the older person whose self-esteem may be depleted. Caseworkers cannot expect to see all their elderly clients in the customary office settings; many will have to be visited in their own homes or in hospitals and nursing homes. Interviews cannot be hurried, and repeated contacts may be needed to accomplish what might be accomplished in a single sitting with a young person. Personal warmth and positive affect are essential (Wasser, 1966).

Among specific problems often referred for treatment are marital problems. Possible causes for disruption in the marriage are many; for instance, retirement and new uses of leisure, or changing financial and health situations. Primary family roles often shift from a focus on child care to mutual nurturance between the two marriage partners. If the marriage has been essentially sound, it can become even more satisfying in old age. If there have been deficiencies in closeness, perhaps camouflaged by the presence of children in the household, these tend to increase when children move out and family roles change. Casework assistance may then be needed to reestablish a satisfying balance (Wasser, 1966).

A second area for casework help is the relationship between the aged parent and his adult child. Old problems between parents and children may be reactivated as help from adult children is needed. Because disabilities in old age often progress at an uneven pace, the adult children may themselves become confused and require help in modifying their own roles and changing relationships to their parents. Alternating feelings of dependency and hostility are not uncommon responses on the part of the older person.

A poignant and possibly traumatic situation requiring casework intervention occurs when a decision must be made about a change in living arrangements or placement of an older person in a rest home, nursing home, or other institution. Careful evaluation is made of the desirability and necessity of placement, along with its meaning to the older person and those close to him. Caseworkers must be aware of all the alternative placement possibilities in a given community for the best matching of the specific services required by the aged person to the services available in specific institutions. Sometimes a seemingly intolerable home situation can be ameliorated and the aged person maintained in his own home, with the provision of added supports, such as skilled home nursing care.

The most common reason for relocating an older person is the development of mental deterioration in the absence of adequate supervision in his own home. Organic brain changes may result in severe memory loss and disorientation; the older person may wander away from home, or forget to turn off the stove, thereby creating a fire hazard; or he may become offensive in his personal hygiene. Dramatic personality changes may take place, with loss of inhibitions, irritability, or paranoid ideation. A rest home may provide adequate care in some instances; in others, admission to a psychiatric hospital may be required.

A second common reason for considering placement is the presence of a physical disability requiring extensive care. The individual who has suffered a stroke or is for some other reason bedridden, who may require special medication or is in need of physical assistance that cannot be provided at home, may need to be admitted to a nursing home or extended care facility. There are some elderly who are not significantly deteriorated either mentally or physically but who are socially isolated and require an environment in which social interaction is again possible. A day care center or a rest home may provide enough satisfaction to prevent or reverse emotional problems. As of this writing, not all of the types of facilities mentioned are available in all communities. But it is hoped that eventually each community will be able to provide a full range of coordinated alternatives to serve the elderly.

Older persons often find the change to completely new settings very disturbing. The older person, as well as members of his family, may experience feelings of ambivalence, anger, rejection, depression, and guilt. A caseworker can often be of help with these feelings, not only in the planning of the move but also after the aged person has moved to a new setting.

Thus casework helps the older person and his family to handle as comfortably and effectively as possible changes resulting from those internal aging processes that affect each one at different rates and in different areas of functioning. For those elderly persons who are not in need of the kinds of services that have been described, there exist many valuable supportive structures in the community that may be used as tools to bolster the drive to remain independent and to maintain a continuing role in society.

COMMUNITY SERVICES FOR THE AGED

As Shanas et al. have pointed out, it is often assumed that the community, through the provision of social services and voluntary organizations, has supplanted the family and its functions, providing the elderly with a "kind of comfortable seclusion." However, these investigators go on to state that the evidence suggests "that the social services tend to complement rather than replace informal community and family associations and that they tend to reach those in genuine need" (Shanas et al., 1968).

Comprehensive Services by a Single Agency

Probably the most important element in a community program for older persons is to have available resources that enable older people to remain independent with a maximum degree of self-determination. A central referral service, with caseworkers able to work with the older person on his own terms, going into the home if necessary, is of great importance.

Nutrition Programs for the Elderly

In 1972, federal funds were authorized for the establishment and operation of nutrition projects that would provide low-cost, nutritionally sound meals in congregate settings to persons over 60 years of age and their spouses, regardless of age. Several goals are thus achieved simultaneously: provision of nutritious meals to elderly persons who are malnourished as a result of poverty or physical or mental incapacity; social interaction and the breaking of barriers for the lonely and isolated older person; and facilitation of the delivery of supportive services.

Federal funds are provided to local programs through designated state agencies, and specific regulations are defined in the federal guidelines. In addition to providing at least one hot meal per day that meets the nutritional criteria established by the Food and Nutrition Board of the National Academy of Sciences–National Research Council, the grantee agency must provide the following supportive services: transportation, information and referral, health and welfare counseling services, nutrition education, shopping assistance, and recreational activities.

Another aspect of providing proper nutrition is the training of personnel who understand the biological nutritional requirements of the elderly, the importance of ethnic and cultural food patterns, and the socioeconomic constraints facing this population.

Protective Services

Older persons without close and interested relatives or friends are often in need of protective services, since they are not capable, physically or mentally, of either planning or caring for themselves or of protecting whatever resources they may have. Serious legal and financial problems may be involved and require the services of experts (Hall & Mathiesen, 1973).

The nature of protective services for the elderly is not generally understood, and responsibility for protecting those in need of such services has not as yet been clearly allocated. To date, it is generally considered that the elderly person who needs protective services from some agency is one who is so mentally ill that he cannot make rational decisions; who is scarcely able, or unable, to care for himself physically and financially; who may harm himself or others; or who manifests seriously disturbed behavior (Wasser, 1966).

In many states the department of public welfare assumes legal responsibilities. Professional persons working with older people recognize the deficiencies in this field (Wasser, 1971). There is also a need to establish protective devices for the elderly person who may not be irrational or totally incompetent but is nevertheless helpless in the face of complex problems (Hemmy & Farrar, 1961).

A study of a group of cases of persons requiring protective services revealed that: (1) old persons in need of such services often do not or cannot seek the help of an agency; (2) service must continue for a long time, possibly the balance of the client's lifetime; and (3) the client's helplessness, demands, and needs may require that the caseworker assume a preponderant amount of responsibility. It was concluded from the study that to meet the needs of these elderly, resources of many kinds must be readily available, to be dispensed as needed: medical and psychiatric care, legal services, nursing care, hospital and nursing home care, family home care, housekeeper and homemaker services, drugs, ambulance service, and money for rent, clothing, food and the like (Hemmy & Farrar, 1961).

Retirement Planning

Services for the aging are concerned in a major way with the problems of retirees, i.e., those facing a readjustment that "involves filling the gap in social relations, the day-to-day or hour-by-hour contact with other persons which was provided by the work situation" (Friedman & Havighurst, 1954). In recognition of the fact that retirement can be problematical, widespread efforts are being made by industry, labor, and communities to prepare the preretiree to accept and enjoy the years after 65. Classes are held, sometimes years before a man is scheduled to retire, to help him face the implications of retirement with its possible financial, social, personal, and family problems. Typical preretirement courses may include management of financial resources, budgeting, and health information, along with adult education classes, hobby shops, and a variety of other subjects.

The role of the wife of a retiree is often overlooked. Although retirement is a different experience for the wife than for the husband, and although she may feel herself less deeply involved (Kerckhoff, 1966b), her attitudes undoubtedly will affect the satisfactions both derive from the retirement years (Heyman & Jeffers, 1968). Thus wives must be included in planning for retirement.

Volunteer Services

A central volunteer bureau staffed by older persons is needed in many communities. Elderly persons who are in good health should be encouraged to serve as volunteers: as visitors to other elderly people at home or in institutions; as Girl Scout or Boy Scout leaders or assistant leaders; or as hospital auxiliary or ward aides, helping to write letters and passing out books.

Programs designed specifically to encourage intergenerational contacts have been established. Children's wards in hospitals or custodial institutions have volunteer programs in which elderly people regularly visit the wards to read to and play with the children, thus providing love and individual attention.

Young people on some college campuses have established programs in which visits are made to homes for the aged or to elderly persons in their own homes at regular intervals. Often a grandparent is "adopted." Birthday parties are held, entertainment provided, and trips outside the home arranged. Both these programs appear to provide mutually shared satisfactions.

The Friendly Visitor is another volunteer program open to persons of all ages; this activity offers opportunities for healthy older persons to be of service. It can provide much satisfaction to both the visitor and to the persons visited. A friendly visit with a contemporary may be especially enjoyable. Activities should be mutually satisfying and may include table games, gardening, sewing, knitting, reading, crafts, going for rides, shopping, movies, lectures, or any interests that appeal to both.

Friendly Visitors, either to institutions or to people in their own homes, should operate under the supervision of a social agency for the protection of both the person visited and the Friendly Visitor. Although the volunteer is anxious to be helpful, this quality is not necessarily innate, and the volunteer should be carefully selected, trained, and supervised. Perhaps the most satisfying results are obtained when there is not too great a difference between the volunteer and the person visited in educational or intellectual level, socioeconomic status, and interests.

Friendly Visitors assume certain minimum responsibilities. They obligate themselves to serve clients' needs rather than their own, to be dependable in making regular visits, to be good listeners and interested in the client as a person, to refrain from comments that may be upsetting or depressing, and in general to be welcomed with pleasure in another's home. The goal is a very worthwhile one, and together with social workers and other professionals, such volunteers can help to bring satisfaction and meaning to an isolated or unhappy older person.

Telephone reassurance programs are widespread. Volunteers check on regular "clients" to be sure they are managing as usual. Arrangements are generally made before hand to alert someone to assist should there be no satisfactory response to the phone call.

Following the recommendations of the 1971 White House Conference on Aging, a program was organized under the Administration on Aging to provide opportunities specifically for older persons to volunteer their services in community projects. ACTION, the sponsoring agency, has developed a variety of programs jointly supported by federal and local funds. Older persons are presently involved in the Retired Senior Volunteer Program (RSVP), which serves many community needs; in Foster Grandparents, who give "tender loving care" to children in institutional settings; and in Senior Companions, who "sit" with the ill or disabled. Senior Corps of Retired Executives (SCORE) and Active Corps of Executives (ACE) offer the services of volunteers to businessmen for advice and Vista Volunteers join a variety of programs, usually educational in nature.

Employment Opportunities

Although many older people retire from work with a sense of relief, others in good health would, if given the choice, enjoy continuing to work, for many reasons: financial needs, a continued sense of usefulness, and participation in the mainstream of life. Older people cannot easily find jobs in the open market, but employment opportunities can be located or even created by a skilled employment counselor matching the job opportunity to a selected individual.

Employers often have openings that do not appeal to younger people and yet are suited to the capacities or interests of the older man or woman. Jobs offering only part-time or seasonal work or unusual hours may be more appealing or more acceptable to an older person than to a younger one, particularly because of the Social Security limitations on yearly earnings. Employers must often be convinced of the value of hiring older persons in appropriate positions, and the importance of experience, stability, and reliability must be emphasized to them. Vocational guidance is a helpful adjunct to job placement, even with older persons.

Vocational Rehabilitation

The Vocational Rehabilitation Agency, while geared primarily to the needs of the handicapped "of working age," may be of assistance in rehabilitating older persons. Disabled housewives have been accepted for help and assisted in learning better ways of managing a household (U.S. Department of Health, Education and Welfare, 1967). Older persons who cannot be retrained for employment in the open market may find employment in the sheltered workshops utilized by this agency.

Homemaker Services

Although most older people continue to live in environments that allow them to be independent, some of the aged, particularly the widowed, single, and divorced, live in isolated and lonely circumstances. Provision of specialized services to these elderly, as well as to elderly couples, may enable them to live independently in the community. To keep the elderly functioning in their own homes, homemaker services are available in some communities, supported by public welfare or private social agencies.

The trained homemaker assigned by the caseworker as the need arises is usually responsible for the general housework, shopping, and cooking. She also gives some personal care, such as helping with bathing, shampoos, and dressing. This is an expensive service and is therefore generally used only on a part-time basis. When necessary, this service may be supplemented by visits by a public health nurse.

Meals-on-Wheels

Many of the elderly living and eating alone lack motivation for proper meal planning and preparation. They soon deteriorate in energy and in interest, and continued poor nutrition often leads to illness. Some communities have therefore established programs in which appetizing and balanced meals are delivered to the homes of elderly persons at modest cost. The program must be subsidized, even though much of the food preparation and delivery is done by volunteers. Arrangements are sometimes made to have meals prepared in the kitchen of an institution, such as an old-age home or a church, with delivery before noon. Two meals are provided, one of which is to be eaten hot and one cold.

Home Nursing Care

County health departments in many areas maintain a staff of registered nurses to make home visits and evaluations, to perform nursing duties, and to educate the patient and family in nursing care procedures. There are also private organizations, religious and secular, which provide visiting nurse services at modest fees, including The Visiting Nurse Association of America, the nursing services of Metropolitan Life and other insurance companies, and Catholic nursing orders. In some large cities, all of these organizations provide nursing services.

Physical Therapy

Many hospitals now have physical therapy departments with extensive exercise and retraining programs, but these services are not often available to the homebound elderly. However, county health departments often have graduate physical therapists on their staffs who will make regular visits for evaluation and treatment. There are also a number of therapists in private practice who accept patients on referral by a physician.

The physical therapist, after an evaluation of the facilities of the home, devises an individualized program to help the handicapped person adapt to his setting and to maintain or regain maximal functioning. Often, equipment is improvised with whatever resources the home setting provides. All the prescribed exercises and planned activities are oriented toward achieving physical independence. The physical therapy program that is designed to prevent chronic invalidism may begin with simple instructions on transferring from bed to chair, the use of a walker or techniques for self-care.

The aged confined to the home can be helped to move out into the community by learning simple methods of managing steps and curbs and entering a taxi or a bus. Progress in self-help, even when measured by small achievements, leads to a sense of independence and is valuable in combating depression and self-devaluation.

Occupational Therapy

Although there are not enough trained occupational therapists to maintain a home visiting program, the skills of this discipline are appropriate to services in the home. Self-maintenance can be taught to the partially disabled, so that they can prepare meals and carry out other chores satisfactorily. The goals are not to teach arts and crafts per se, or to provide entertainment, although these are often pleasurable by-products. Through individually designed occupational therapy programs, the aged may be assisted in regaining physical and emotional strength while learning to adjust to their limitations and disabilities.

CONCLUSION

Although the services that have been described are many and varied, few communities now provide all of them to their elderly populations. Funding new programs and accommodating the demand are always difficult. Accessibility to the facilities is also a problem in that some of the elderly dislike traveling to various centers or offices or are not physically able to do so. As have a few other states, Pennsylvania has established a rural transportation system. However, such programs are scarce in some locations, perhaps because of community inertia or lack of awareness—not, it is hoped, because of lack of interest. When communities are small or unable to provide sufficient financial support, strong volunteer efforts are needed; or else the resources of several communities should be combined into regional programs.

Future planning for the needs of older persons should envision the extension of comprehensive and coordinated services to ever-increasing numbers. It is important to help not only those whose needs are critical but also those in somewhat less difficult financial circumstances. For them, the availability of these programs would serve to enhance the quality of life and help to reintegrate them into the larger society, thus avoiding a painful sense of marginality.

The Senior Center, Individuals, and the Community*

Joyce Leanse

The senior center is most often thought of as a place where the elderly go to play cards and gossip, the geriatric version of the high school hangout. Undoubtedly, cards and gossip are important factors in its appeal, but they are only a small part of what a center can provide. And the philosophy of the senior center movement is turning centers into more dynamic organizations providing more comprehensive programs.

The Multipurpose Senior Center concept was developed in 1942, initially to address the needs of older persons in New York City who sought a place to come together with their peers. The first center was organized under the sponsorship of the Welfare Department to serve low-income persons, but the concept of providing a place for older persons of every income level, where services and activities are geared to their needs and interests, took hold. Soon San Francisco, Philadelphia, and the suburban community of Menlo Park, California, developed senior centers with support from the private sector. Today, nearly 5,000 such operations function in communities throughout the United States. These centers operate under the sponsorship of public and/or private community agencies, generally with funding from government and voluntary dollars and sometimes even with corporation dollars.

The Multipurpose Senior Center has come to be recognized as a major component in the network of community resources. As such, the facility in which it is housed and the extent of the budget allocated for its work are measures of the depth and sincerity of the community's concern for people. The image of the senior center projects the community's value of people as people, without considering their productive potential.

THE CONCEPT OF THE MULTIPURPOSE SENIOR CENTER

Over the years senior centers have developed and adapted according to the needs and resources of individual communities, their size, and the availability of transportation. More recently, such centers have adapted in response to a changing concept of service delivery that emphasizes not merely making services available, but also having services that are accessible and acceptable to the people for whom they are intended. The first senior centers tended to be organized, as all service agencies were in the 1940's and 1950's, as places downtown where people could come for services, for activities, and for social interaction with their peers. In the 1960's, however, many communities came to recognize that services are needed by people who are unable to get to a downtown facility, and by those who are too inexperienced or too frightened to seek out public supports for personal needs. So service networks for older persons began to be developed, usually with one centrally located or downtown facility serving as the organizational center, with satellite facilities located in neighborhoods. Often the satellite centers operated from such existing facilities as churches, schools, and community space in housing projects. In a national study of senior centers, we found that 52 percent of the reporting centers were in multisite networks, and the average number of sites was nine. Senior center networks sometimes cover an entire county or several counties or portions thereof. Jurisdictional arrangements vary according to assessments of regional need.

Obviously, the development of neighborhood sites has enhanced accessibility, but an equally important use factor is acceptability of senior center programs. Community centers must be responsive to people's values and expectations, which are greatly influenced by their socioeconomic and racial or ethnic backgrounds. Since housing patterns often conform to these characteristics, programs in neighborhood centers can be focused on the special needs and interests of persons in a given neighborhood.

The advantages of a central unit to which neighborhood programs can relate cannot be overemphasized. The primary center serves as a focal location for community services provided by senior center staff members as well as by personnel from other agencies that maintain a desk or an office at the center full- or part-time. Such arrangements make services more accessible for older persons, and also serve an integrating function. With centralization of community agencies, citizens are better served as agencies take a coordinated, comprehensive approach within a central facility. The use of such a center also creates a climate of acceptance, so more older people will be encouraged to seek and to accept the services they see provided to others. The central location also provides a base from which a concerted attempt can be made to reach out and help isolated and friendless older individuals like the "loners" who live in downtown hotel rooms.

Another major purpose of the senior center is its function as a bridge within the community. Some people suggest that senior centers can isolate older people from the community; what is nearer to the truth is that the community has isolated older people from it. A senior center is needed to bridge the chasm which the community has permitted to develop. The purpose of the senior center is to tap the resources of the elderly by creating opportunities for them to find new roles and to develop latent or new skills. By providing an environment in which older people feel safe to test new ideas and behavior, a community center or a neighborhood satellite can facilitate development of an important new source of trained capacity and leadership for the community. It also serves as a bridge linking the loose-knit senior community to the community-at-large and at the same time permitting older people to create a special community of their own without isolating them from the larger community. The senior center thus becomes a bridge over which people and ideas, services and resources pass freely, back and forth, to the benefit of the entire community.

WHY SENIOR CENTERS—AND FOR WHOM?

Among the concerns which accompany retirement is the problem of unobligated time. What to do today? While one worked on a job or was a homemaker with a family, one's day was structured by one's responsibilities. Not only the direct tasks of the job, but the myriad related obligations would keep one wistfully dreaming of long hours with nothing to do. But, when that day finally arrives, the luxury of no routine too soon becomes a burden for many people. They seem to need structure for their day and seek activities to fill the hours. If they are to maintain self-respect and to continue feeling worthwhile, people must be involved in activities that are more than just *busy work*. They need to be productive in some way—either for themselves or for the benefit of others. Furthermore, activities in retirement should provide opportunities that aren't readily available to people outside the work force.

Work not only provides income and a place to go each day, but also a means for recognition and for maintaining self-esteem, colleagues with common interests, and the feeling of being part of a group working toward shared objectives. All of these are important to one's sense of well-being, and at retirement, individuals usually need to find new ways to bring these elements to their daily lives.

Senior centers are intended to meet these needs by providing a place where older people can come together and have available opportunities for meaningful activities. As a focal point in the community for activities relating to the older individual, the senior center can become a substitute work site, a place where he or she can come for structure and for meaning.

Too often, the senior center is viewed merely as a place where older people come to spend some time and wile away the hours. In some places, unfortunately, this image is the actuality. But, the potential is there, and the greatest strength of the senior center is its malleability. Since it was developed to meet the needs of retired persons, its programs, structure, and focus can change as those needs change and as participants help to bring about change.

Today, the senior center is more than just a place for recreational and leisure-time activities. It is also the place where educational programs are offered, social services are provided, employment opportunities are made available, social and political action groups are coordinated and from which community services can be organized to serve all age groups. Though the senior center is a community facility to be used by older people, its function is not to isolate the elderly from the community, but, rather, to involve them in the community by dealing with its concerns and enhancing its services, by reacting to its youth, as well as to its old age.

Whether we are ready to accept it or not, one of the issues that faces people in their retirement years is how to grow old. Does one stagnate or continue to develop, does one despair or integrate his capacities with his goals? Senior center programs can assist older people in their adaptation to retirement and in their continuation of their personal growth and development.

The center provides the opportunity to meet with people at a similar stage in life with similar concerns. The awareness that comes from such interaction that one is not unique or peculiar can be among the most beneficial of the experiences offered. A new group identity can begin and, perhaps, a new individual one as well.

A retired doctor, businessman, or carpenter can continue using his specific skills through the senior center or he can become an artist, a chef or a surrogate grandfather. A housewife, retired teacher, or social worker will find that the need for her talents is endless at the center. But she, too, has the opportunity to learn new roles and try out new skills. She can become involved with other members in social action to get reduced bus fares in the community, she can follow legislation at the state and national level or she can learn carpentry skills.

One of the traits which often needs reinforcing at this stage of life is self assertiveness. At one senior center, a class was organized to help people learn or relearn this attribute. They practiced such things as saying no to adult children who wished to make them into full-time babysitters. What the class didn't offer and which may have been equally necessary was practice in learning to say no to some of the programs offered. Of course, participants have a responsibility to say more than no, they need to involve themselves in the planning process and to assert their preferences. The give-and-take between staff of a center and the people it serves can lead to creative programs that encourage opportunities for continued involvement and development for all concerned.

Perhaps unique to the senior center is the opportunity it provides for older persons to learn to be gracefully dependent. In the group setting with their peers, retired persons can learn that it's not a disgrace to be dependent. Everyone is to some degree. As people age, their dependencies become more overt. Older people—like all of us—must learn to be able to ask for help and to accept it without bitterness.

Through personal counseling or in group discussion or problem-solving sessions at the senior center, older persons can learn how to adjust their life-styles to reduced income, to determine if their housing arrangements are realistically related to their current use, and to understand when symptoms related to personal health require attention and are not to be glossed over because one is, after all, aging.

Practical classes in cooking for two or one, learning to mend or caring for an elderly relative are available at senior centers. Similarly, there are opportunities to expand one's creative abilities, to explore current literature, or to delve into the unlimited opportunities for learning.

Senior centers offer an opportunity for the action-minded to organize around issues and to provide a community base for social or political action. Current-events classes, discussions on issues in aging, and legislative study groups all contribute to the increased awareness of the membership and, in turn, of the larger community. The energies of interested persons can be directed toward local, state, or national issues. Change has occurred within many communities and at the higher levels of government because of the persistent action of senior center participants around the country.

Ways to supplement income are sometimes sought by retired persons who find their Social Security or pension benefits too meager to supply even the basic necessities, not to mention the extras they could wish to enjoy. Some centers have established employment-referral services or job banks that link potential retirees with temporary, part-time, or even full-time job opportunities. Other centers provide job opportunities through the center itself by offering catering services, geriatric aides, home-maintenance services, the sale of handcrafted items, and other income-generating activities.

Besides creating opportunities to earn additional income, senior centers also help to stretch dollars. Trips are very popular at centers, and travel is always less expensive in a group than individually; it is also usually more fun. For older individuals who are alone, the center's trips can be particularly meaningful, providing opportunities to see new places and meet new people. Senior centers also assist participants by informing them of benefits to which they may be entitled, such as reduced taxes or food stamps. For those older people who have no grandchildren of their own or who are separated from them by great distances, senior center programs provide endless opportunities for the fun and satisfaction of relating to young people. Even when one's grandchildren are close by, the availability of a new audience for old stories can be very appealing.

Some people ask if a senior center is a priority need of the elderly in the community. I think that's an inappropriate question. A senior center is not a need of the elderly; it is a vehicle for meeting their needs—like a hospital or drug store—it is developed to provide a certain range of services to a particular portion of the population. Our study suggests that programs serving the elderly which are part of multigenerational facilities do not meet the needs of older persons as comprehensively as separate senior centers do. There is no substitute for an identifiable facility and a staff that focuses its total concern on improving the quality of life for older persons. If that is your goal, there is no better way.

Psychotherapy with the Aging*

Muriel Oberleder

It's amazing how many things that we know can't possibly work with the elderly do work when we try them out. In Berkeley, California, a program for older persons has been developed that focuses on body awareness and deep relaxation and includes biofeedback, massage, yoga, Tai Ch'i, and meditation; with a very small paid staff and many volunteers, both young and old, this program has been successful with both healthy and alert older persons and those in nursing homes.

Individual psychotherapy with the elderly is also assumed to be impossible or irrelevant. It often is, not because of the age of the client but because the therapist is unable to be flexible enough to adapt traditional approaches to the needs of the elderly. Dr. Oberleder's article was written over a decade ago, but it describes the present situation quite accurately.

There is no logical basis for the therapeutic discrimination against the older patient; it is a prejudice. The emotional disorders of aging are neither intractable, nor untreatable, and in fact are not even peculiar to old age. The syndrome of "old age," namely fear, frustration, anger and depression, may manifest itself at any life stress period, whether it be college graduation, one's 30th, 40th or 50th birthday, retirement or menopause. Conversely, all

*Edited from "Psychotherapy with the Aging: An Art of the Possible?" by M. Oberleder, *Psychotherapy: Theory, Research, and Practice*, 1966, *3*, 139–142. Reprinted by permission.

the various neuroses and psychoses appear in the later years. Paraphrasing a medical aphorism, "There are no emotional problems peculiar to old age, and none from which it is free." The work of Goldfarb (1955), Wolff (1962), Wolk (1965) and many others shows that aged patients are capable of change, redirection and rehabilitation through psychotherapy. The therapist who is trained to work with adults has had his basic training for work with the aging.

Why then does an illness-oriented approach with institutionalization as the goal still prevail in the treatment of the mental and emotional problems of the aging? And why does a "hands off" policy still prevail among psychotherapists of all persuasions?

"SENILITY" SCARES THE PSYCHOTHERAPIST AWAY

Many erroneous and stereotyped attitudes toward aging persons are held by therapists. The aging are viewed as uncooperative, rigid and with inevitable mental deterioration. These subtle attitudes are so often unconscious that when the patient of 60 or even 50 complains of inability to concentrate, forgetfulness or feelings of persecution, the therapist (who may be 60, or perhaps 70 himself) immediately begins to entertain possibilities of cerebral arteriosclerosis. If the patient is 70 or 80, the diagnosis may be changed to "chronic brain syndrome." And when brain damage is ruled out by physical examination, there is always the gnawing doubt that a "small stroke" has occurred leaving no trace except in the aforementioned symptoms.

Usually, treatment for older patients is not considered until an emergency state of mental and personality breakdown has developed. While symptoms of depression, sleeplessness, irritability and anxiety may justify psychotherapy for the younger patient, they are considered "par for the course" in old age, and are not likely to attract attention. The older person must qualify on the basis of loss of memory, disorientation, or incontinence before he is considered for the same treatment, at which time, paradoxically, its feasibility may indeed be questioned (Butler, 1963).

The psychotherapeutic point of view has not yet been appreciably influenced by the findings of studies which suggest that full mental ability may be retained in old age, and that many of the "senile" symptoms are remediable, and represent the panic and regression of the defenseless ego rather than an irreversible organic state (Oberleder, 1964).

The criterion sample of the older population perceived as representing the whole still remains the 2 to 3% of the aging who are in institutions, or the 20 to 30% of the elderly psychiatric population who evince signs of organic brain damage. Small wonder the therapist (regardless of orientation) is quick to think of hospitalization when confronted with the elderly patient. Even more unfortunately, individuals of ages 60 and 90 are usually regarded as equally poor therapeutic risks for the same reasons.

Frequently underlying the reluctance to take an older patient into therapy is the feeling that his life is almost over, and professional efforts might be "wasted." Aside from the philosophical considerations implicit in this point of view, one can say that such "waste" is intrinsic to any type of effort with the older patient. Psychotherapy may, in fact, be less wasteful than other approaches to aging because of its broadly beneficial effects on health, functioning and general well being, as well as the emotional and economic relief for family, friends and community.

Obviously, if disturbed behavior is reactive to a specific, identifiable external stress, an economic or situational approach may be more feasible. Moreover, psychotherapy with the aging should never be undertaken without consideration of health status. The relationship between physical disease and mental disease in the aging is so profound that one cannot be sure which is cause and which is effect. Restoration of health status has had corresponding effects on psychological status and the reverse is also true (Dovenmuehle, 1965).

In general, however, behavioral and emotional problems of the elderly are within the province of psychotherapy, and promising results have been obtained in group and individual therapy (usually in institutional settings) utilizing directive, supportive and activity-oriented approaches (Oberleder, 1964). Even deep analytic therapy and complete personality reconstruction are possible with the elderly although such an intense therapeutic relationship may be ill-advised because of the patient's sense of personal loss when therapy ends (Da Silva, 1965).

In any case, total personality reconstruction of the older patient is rarely necessary or even called for. In most instances therapy with the aging has two main goals, the alleviation of anxiety and the maintenance (or restoration) of adequate psychological functioning.

ANXIETY—THE AFFLICTION OF AGING

If there is a mental "state" peculiar to aging, it may well be anxiety. While it may be true that the disturbances which occur in old age (and middle age) are quite characteristically profound, possibly because there is an attrition of coping resources, or possibly because of the accrual of stresses with the years, the confounding effects of anxiety are almost incalculable. Because of the anxieties attendant upon the inevitable physical, emotional, and socio-economic losses of old age, as well as the anxieties in anticipation of these losses, the aging person is always in a precarious position. In our society, at least, it seems there can be no aging without anxiety.

The older person's psychological vulnerability is analogous to his physiological vulnerability. "The fewer cells possessed by the aging must work longer and under more compulsion. Not as many can be spared or rested compared with youth when there are fewer organ handicaps" (Freeman, 1965b).

Although generally speaking most older people are capable of maintaining function without decrement in the absence of extra stress, all are in danger of breakdown in the presence of such stress. Anxiety is the extra stress of aging. Successful aging may depend upon the successful management of anxiety (Kuhlen, 1959).

Even the signs of aging are identical to the signs of anxiety: tremor, fatigue, clumsiness, unsteadiness, facial tics, quavering voice, palpitating heart, to list a few. Fear of death is the fear of the anxious and the aged alike (Roche Labs, 1963).

LOSS OF SELF-CONTROL . . . THE SPECTRE OF OLD AGE

"Regression in defense of the ego" is a privilege we do not extend to older people. We have no faith in their recovery powers and neither do they. Consequently older people are ruled by the fear of loss of impulse control. In their panic they may actually retreat to states of confusion and incontinence just as they do to other less serious stereotyped behavior when they are threatened.

Kahn, who has described dramatic recovery in advanced cases of vegetative deterioration in old people, suggests that the disoriented old person is really "unoriented," the helpless, terror-ridden victim of an accretion of psychological insults (Kahn, 1965).

Many other studies confirm that mental breakdown in the elderly is usually associated with such "panic periods" as retirement, widowhood and relocation (Dovenmuehle, 1965). Conflicts which are readily identifiable in younger people become distorted and unrecognizable in the older patient because of the spiralling effects of "senility" which in itself may be in large part a panic reaction.

In treatment, the alleviation of anxiety involves ventilation of feelings of anger, fear, isolation and rejection. The older patient, just like his younger counterpart, is restored by the knowledge that he is not alone in his symptoms, that he is not evil, that he is sane. Insight formation, at least during the therapeutic hour, is not as necessary. Sometimes it is therapeutic simply to siphon off immobilizing tensions by allowing expression of petty complaints (Rustin and Wolk, 1963).

In therapy older people should be helped to come to grips with the realities of diminishing physical capacities, personal loss, role changes and death itself. A tolerance for loss must be developed because loss *is* the reality of old age. Only in this way can the rational replace the irrational in aging.

ACTIVITY IS THERAPY WITH THE AGING

One of the therapist's primary responsibilities is to prevent the deterioration which results from withdrawal and disuse. The need for continuing human contacts, social participation and meaningful work in order to maintain function cannot be minimized. The symptoms of the isolated older person are often indistinguishable from those elicited experimentally in studies of sensory deprivation, and may be reflected in loss of mental function, personality disintegration and psychotic symptoms.

Therapy often must be reinforced with a concrete activity program, and the therapist must be prepared to assume the role of social planner, family consultant, recreational or vocational adviser, or just plain good friend (Zinberg, 1964).

When deteriorated mental processes need bolstering, a program of perceptual and conceptual retraining adapted from methods used successfully with brain-damaged children should be considered (Levi, 1965). The sense of mastery and renewed self-esteem accomplished in such "perceptual therapy" make it an appropriate and effective adjunct to more orthodox treatments.

THERAPIST, CURE THYSELF

Rarely is the older patient as resistant to dealing with the emotional problems of old age as is the therapist. The personal feelings of the therapist about old age and old people are usually greater obstacles to the successful course of therapy than the feelings of the patient.

The therapist must overcome his hesitation about discussing sex with the older patient. The old person's fear and shame in respect to sex frequently underlie his symptoms. Somatic ills and bodily preoccupations may be related to sexual needs. The relationship with the therapist may have frankly sexual components. Touching the older patient is urged. A handshake, a friendly arm about the shoulders, an understanding pat, not only encourage discussion about human contact needs, but also clear the air, as it were, of the cloud of guilt and shame which burdens the old person.

No less burdensome are the blocked-off aggressive needs of the older person which become turned against the self in depression, unaccountable hatreds and ego-alien behavior. The therapist may be viewed as a parental figure, as a spouse or other close relative, or as a symbol of authority or of rejection by society. Regardless of the role attributed to the therapist, even sheer ventilation of pent-up anger and resentment can release the patient's resources for constructive adjustments. When there is reduction of guilt and anxiety, the older patient is surprisingly alert to the displacements of these repressed feelings.

Motivating the older patient may be another major challenge for the therapist. Like the adolescent, the old person's difficulties often stem largely from frustrations of basic drives due to restrictions outside himself. His deep-seated and justifiable conviction of his own normality makes him resent his position all the more, and this is hardly conducive to rapport. He tests out the therapist in many ways—and does so constantly. Worst of all, because he has a legitimate "out" in senility, his use of senile symptomatology may eventually convince both therapist and patient that all efforts are futile.

In the end, it is the therapist's uncritical acceptance, his uncontaminated view of the patient which can lead to the self-interest necessary to make motivation possible in the elderly.

The real enemy is the feeling of futility with which we tend to regard psychotherapy with the older patient.

Psychological Barriers to Getting Well*

Don R. Lipsitt

We spend most of our time wondering how to get health-care services to the elderly at a cost they can afford. A handful, however, turn the tables on us. They continue to show up for services they don't really seem to need. Why do they do this? If they don't need health care, what do they need?

Aging is welcomed by some people as an opportunity to indulge in postponed as well as new pleasures. Others, who have had lives of hardship and disappointment, see it as a time of even greater deprivation, isolation, and misery. They experience a sense of increased helplessness and depreciation, become more dependent on others for the provision of their needs and wants. The anguish arising from emotional starvation is profound and lingering, and it ultimately leads to despair, preoccupation with bodily functions, reliance upon others, physical and mental deterioration, hospitalization, and even death.

Before giving up, geriatric individuals often turn pleadingly to their physician for the alleviation of their misery and pain. But when the physician does not acknowledge that treatment of helplessness, dependency, and depression is part of his professional task, he unwittingly may drive these patients into deeper despair. They may feel that while they can afford a physician's services, they really cannot afford (psychologically) to be well, to "lose" their symptoms, lest in the bargain they forfeit the relationship that sustains them.

In the usual model of medical practice, the physician confronted with a complaining patient initiates a series of fairly routine steps including

*Edited from "A Medical-Psychological Approach to Dependency in the Aged," by D. R. Lipsitt. In R. A. Kalish (Ed.), *The Dependencies of Old People* (Occasional Papers in Gerontology, #6, 17–25). Copyright 1969 by the Institute of Gerontology, University of Michigan— Wayne State University. Reprinted by permission.

history-taking, physical examination, and selected laboratory studies. In this way he tries to establish the clear-cut presence or absence of known diseases. When a thorough work-up fails to disclose an etiologic explanation (usually organic) for the complaint, the doctor may reassure the complainant (and perhaps himself) that "there is nothing physically wrong" and therefore "no need to worry." Or he may minimize and dismiss the complaint with the benign explanation that "there's a lot of it around," or "maybe you strained a muscle," etc. On rarer occasions he will indicate the lack of positive findings, offer symptomatic remedies and hope that "this will take care of your problem." Satisfying himself that organic disease is ruled out, he may be reluctant to offer a return appointment.

Seldom does he acknowledge the aging person's increasing sense of helplessness, need for dependent relationships, and bid for attention as the generating force behind the physical complaint and request for a doctor's appointment. If and when these factors *are* recognized, there may be even more reluctance to treat the patient because the physician does not regard helplessness, dependency, and depression as "illness."

When a doctor considers treatment of physical ailments his sole function, patients are in danger of being deprived of the support, interest, and understanding that could help alleviate depression, fulfill their dependent needs, and restore their sense of worth, autonomy, and hopefulness.

Some patients find this approach satisfactory, with its emphasis on the ruling out of physical illness and provision of routine reassurance. But many of them, particularly among the aged, are decidedly not relieved of their anxieties, not rid of their symptoms, not reassured by such measures. Discharged because no demonstrable organic disease has been found to explain or justify their complaints, they continue to complain and seek relief for their ill-defined distress, sometimes wandering from physician to physician or hospital to hospital in search of assistance. Neither the patient nor the doctor apparently realizes that the key to effective treatment lies not only in ruling out organic illness, but also in the medical practitioner's ability to tolerate the increased dependency of the "ailing" aged individual.

Burdened by the realities of time and the pressures of an overloaded medical practice, physicians tend to be puzzled if not annoyed by the persistence of complaints in persons who manifest no organic disease. It is not only a sense of frustration at having failed to explain or cure their problems that prompts the physician to reject them, but also his personal definition of what he feels constitutes real illness.

Unable to turn to usual sources of support, understanding, and comfort, the elderly individual has fewer opportunities to realign the disrupted dependence-independence balance. Preoccupied with concern about a body which is failing him, he often turns to his physician. The latter is in a particularly strategic position to help the patient reassess himself, reclaim his strengths, and reassert his capacity for self direction—in short, to reaffirm the self-sufficiency that keeps his self-esteem from sagging, keeps him from becoming depressed. When the doctor accepts the hurting individual and provides interest, help, and reassurance, he simultaneously meets the patient's need for a dependent relationship that allows him to make use of his own resources to solve his problems.

The task of assessing how much help is needed is a difficult one. It requires a careful inventory of the patient's capacity for self-direction, prior achievements, and expectations for the future. Without such assessment, physicians are prone to judge their patients to be capable of more or of less than they actually can achieve. The pitfalls in treatment, then, are those of over-control or under-concern.

It is the dilemma of having to make such difficult judgments that may precipitate abrupt or inappropriate responses by the physician. He may resent being asked for more than he feels he can provide. He may regard dependency as "bad," or feel that if he gives in he will never rid himself of the clinging patient. Or he may feel that getting involved in the patient's emotional life would open a Pandora's box. He may be angry that the patient does not seem willing to accept help in the form the doctor deems best.

All outpatient departments and practicing physicians know patients whose symptoms defy treatment, who visit clinics more often than appears justified by objective findings, and who simply will not get well. The well-meaning and competent physician who enthusiastically starts treating them may be the same one who, months or years later, finds himself referring to them as "crocks," chronic complainers, management problems, or hypochondriacs. He may be unable to refrain from writing in their record such notes as "essentially positive review of systems," or "patient is a triple A-1 crock," or "patient comes here to waste my good time." The discouragement, frustration and anger evident in such entries appear in more disguised forms in requests for further studies, referrals, or discharge from the clinic. In many cases, it appears, he would almost prefer to believe that they enjoy being sick rather than acknowledge their need to be dependent upon someone.

It is difficult to believe that anyone truly seeks suffering as a goal in itself, puzzling that one would persist in utilizing facilities that do not provide symptomatic relief. Perhaps patients are satisfied with visits that their doctors call useless. Perhaps they come not to waste the physician's time, but in the hope that repeated contacts will reveal to them and to him an explanation and remedy for what really ails them.

To explore some of these issues, an experimental outpatient facility was inaugurated at the Beth Israel Hospital in Boston. It previously had been found that patients referred to Psychiatric Service from outpatient clinics usually were older women who experienced their distress more in physical than emotional terms. They had long histories of vague somatic complaints resistant to usual medical treatment, and they were reluctant or unable to use "talking treatment" when it was offered. Because of their anti-psychiatry bias, these patients could be studied and treated only in ways that they viewed as acceptable and useful. Therefore, the new clinic brought psychosocial evaluation and treatment to these patients in a medical setting that was familiar and preferred by them. Physicians in other clinics were asked to refer their problem patients, management problems, chronic complainers, or others considered to need psychological assessment, to the new facility. The designation "Integration Clinic" distinguished it from psychiatry, and suggested that efforts would be made to integrate or correlate prior attempts at treatment.

Emphasis was on physical history rather than psychological autobiography. The treatment objective was maximum psychosocial adjustment within the limits of each patient's healthy assets and pathological findings. Techniques and services included supportive measures, personal and environmental manipulation, advice-giving when appropriate, laboratory studies, referral to selected clinics, clarification, and adjunctive psychopharmacology. Appointments were scheduled according to the patient's need and tolerance, not at arbitrary intervals; they varied from fortnightly to monthly.

Special attention was focused on the relevance of dependency to the development of problem patients and styles of seeking and obtaining treatment. It clearly was of greatest importance to assess not only the need for a dependency-supporting relationship but also the capacities and strengths of the individual for relatively independent functioning currently and in the past.

Of 800 referrals in four years, about 50 percent were over 50 years of age and 25 percent were over 65. While the mean age of all patients was 45, those who qualified as "thick chart" or problem patients usually were over age 60; they used more clinics and made more visits than did younger patients. These patients tended to establish close, clinging relationships with doctors, similar to that established with a spouse; at the same time, they seemed to promote the failure of these relationships by maladaptive, alienating behavior. Psychiatrically, they were described as long-suffering, self-sacrificing, masochistic, dependent persons.

The usual reason given for referring patients to the Integration Clinic was somatic complaints without organic basis. The psychiatrist's most frequent diagnosis, however, was depression. This suggests basic discrepancy in the way the two physicians assessed the same patient.

Since patients with significant masochistic, dependent, and depressive features are the most difficult for the general physician to tolerate and manage, these became the major therapeutic responsibility of the Integration Clinic. Great expenditure of time, effort, and resources in outpatient departments create the clinical impression that problem patients exist in great abundance, yet only 8–10 percent of all referrals to the Clinic would be called hard-core problem patients. The distorted clinical impression probably is a result of the average doctor's low tolerance for the demanding, dependent patient.

While treatment approach to these patients acknowledged their need to talk about somatic concerns, it was not the physician's expressed goal to alter these concerns. The patient was assured of a continuing (but not continuous) relationship regardless of symptom fluctuation. In patients who develop intensely dependent relationships, all responsibility usually is relinquished to the physician. To forestall this with problem patients, their participation and autonomy was supported and encouraged by allowing them some latitude in regulating the frequency of appointments as they felt the need. Their unfamiliarity with this approach to medical management resulted in some preliminary testing, ultimately followed by security and comfort in the knowledge that appointments could be made upon request without risk of reprimand or discharge from the clinic.

It would appear that when these patients recognize that acceptance by the physician is not regulated according to complaint or symptom intensity, complaining diminishes and other topics are discussed (even by opponents to "talking treatment"), over-all adaptation improves, masochistic traits are channeled into more productive areas, and utilization of services drops because the flow of dependency satisfactions is not shut off. A continuing flexible relationship with the Integration Clinic is accepted because it never threatens patients with discharge for being either cured or untreatable. It allows gratification of dependency needs in a way that does not divest the patient of his autonomy, self-control, and therefore self-esteem.

I would now like to return to the point made earlier that these patients, before their Integration Clinic experience, "could not afford" to get well. In conventional medical practice, patients learn that it is their symptoms that entitle them to medical attention. In a sense, this is the price they pay to be dependent upon the use of hospital facilities when no organic disease is found. Eligibility for medical care, therefore, requires that patients retain their symptoms.

Yet the most frequent visitor to ambulatory units and practicing physicians is the patient with no significant physical disease. People with discomforts of all sorts seek solace from the physician because he represents a powerful, knowing person who can help them overcome their miseries, whatever the source. They expect him to help. Such expectations may be unrealistic, but they do not know it; and berating them for it only sends them scurrying elsewhere—to another hospital, another clinic, another doctor, even a quack.

When the physician believes that patients expect or demand from him something that he does not define as medical care, he feels misused, offended, or duped. He may not regard talking or listening as authentic tools of the medical profession; he may define the doctor's job in purely biomedical terms. "No organic disease" to the physician often means "no treatment" for the patient. Without the admission ticket of symptoms, he is not allowed to depend upon the physician.

In treating the elderly, it must be recognized that many of the discomforts of old age come not only from physical illness, but also from changes in adaptation and self-regard, and from feelings of helplessness and dependency engendered by the experience of loss and decline. The physician who requires his patients to show demonstrable physical disease may deprive them of a sense of worth, autonomy, and productivity, unwittingly commit them to a course of unremitting somatic complaints.

When the doctor's job includes the assessment and treatment of psychological as well as organic illness, a powerful force can be exerted to relieve depression and restore a sense of pride and value in the elderly. Patients *can* afford to be well, if thereby they do not forfeit their doctor's interest and concern and their own freedom to be appropriately dependent.

Chapter 10

Institutional Living

Although institutions for the elderly house only 5% or so of those over 65 at any one time, a much larger proportion of people will enter such a facility at one time or another during their lives. Because of the large numbers of persons affected and because of the immense amount of money required, institutions for the elderly have received (and certainly have deserved) a great deal of attention.

Institutions fall into three categories of ownership or control, and decisions as to where an older person might be referred may be influenced by who operates the facility. One type is public facilities and institutions. These are both owned and operated by some governmental agency, such as the county, the city, the Veteran's Administration, or the state. Often the services of the institution are not limited to, or even primarily for, the elderly. State mental hospitals and Veteran's Administration domiciles are not geriatric institutions, but a high proportion of their services are provided to the elderly.

Another type of ownership is by voluntary organization, including social or fraternal organizations (Masonic order, Moose lodge), religious groups (all major denominations run institutions for the elderly), and unions and professional groups (facilities for retired teachers, actors, union members).

A third type is under private ownership, and such facilities are often referred to as proprietary because they are run for a profit and are increasingly under corporate, rather than individual, ownership. Privately owned institutions serve the greatest number of older persons, some through arrangements with local social welfare agencies providing payment through tax dollars and some through individual arrangements with payments coming from a combination of Medicare and personal payment.

Proprietary homes, which receive neither tax advantages as nonprofit organizations nor financial support through contributions or government backing, often have difficulty in providing their residents equivalent services for equivalent money. At the same time, as private businesses, they have greater freedom from regulations and therefore more flexibility than nonprofit institutions.

In the materials that follow, there are both attacks against and defenses of institutional care, particularly with regard to proprietary homes. All the authors, however, would probably agree that institutional care must be improved and can be improved, both within the existing institutions and by providing more options—Goldfarb (1969) uses the term *equivalents*—to institutional care.

The issue is not whether institutions are needed, because they are. Rather, the issue is that they be used to care only for those who need such care. It is ironic that an elderly woman, prevented from cooking by arthritis and afraid to leave her apartment because of a high crime rate, must be institutionalized at great financial cost to the community and personal cost to her, when a combination of homemaker service, escort service, and bus service would permit her to remain in her home. Development of such options, however, is more expensive and more complex than it may appear to be. More to the point, taxpayers and government officials are more willing to provide money for institutional care than they are for home care or community facilities.

There are styles in social programs, just as there are styles in music or clothing, and one of the contemporary styles is to get people out of large institutions and back into their home communities. Essentially this is a good idea, assuming that whatever condition got them into the institution in the first place will receive equivalent or better attention in their home communities. And, as you may well imagine, that assumption often proves false. Unfortunately, the motivation for getting people out of institutions is all too often to reduce financial costs or to shift the financial burden from one level of government to another, while the welfare of the individual is secondary.

For the most part, gerontologists are eager to see the elderly living as close to their friends as possible, preferably in the home environment they themselves choose. This does not mean that a somewhat confused, poverty-stricken old man or woman is left to his or her own resources. Yet, many elderly people who apparently could not possibly make it on their own, do somehow survive. They may not eat the best diet; they may get cheated and ripped off; they may live in a style that would make their friends of twenty years ago cringe. But somehow they make it.

The Institutionalized Elderly:
A New Challenge*

Leonard E. Gottesman

Who should be in what, if any, type of institution for the elderly, under what circumstances, paid for by whom, for how long, with what kinds of treatment? This is one of the most important issues facing not only those concerned with aging, but the entire health-care system.

Moving people who don't need to live in an institution into the community requires more than giving them a few lessons on the local transportation system and a housing allowance. This is especially true for those elderly who have spent many years in a mental hospital; they are so accustomed to being cared for that independent living may be extremely difficult. With careful planning and effective support systems, however, even these individuals can become autonomous again.

A great deal has been said and written about the upsets caused by moving elderly institutionalized people from one setting to another. In some instances this appears to lead to a more rapid decline and even death, whether or not the new accommodations are physically better than the previous ones. Research results are not clear, however. Those who suffer seem to be those who are the most ill and most confused. Losing familiar surroundings distresses some people greatly, even though those surroundings may be viewed by others as substandard. And this returns us to the issue, discussed in the previous chapter, regarding the extent to which attitudes and feelings and self-esteem may affect an elderly person's physical health.

Treatment is an attempt to change a person's feelings or behavior by altering his capacities, his expectations, the expectations of significant people around him, or the expectations or opportunities in his world. Of all types of treatment, the most desirable is self treatment—sometimes called adaptation or adjustment. In self treatment the person changes his own behavior to meet the realistic demands of life. This is the usual way people behave. For example, we know that many people stop driving at night as a direct reaction to natural changes of vision with age. The least desirable and most extreme form of treatment is institutionalization, because it removes the person into an encapsulated portion of the world, and in doing so it generally removes almost all autonomy.

*Edited from "The Institutionalized Elderly: A New Challenge," by L. E. Gottesman. This section originally appeared in George L. Maddox (Ed.), *The Future of Aging and the Aged*, a book in the Southern Newspaper Publishers Association Foundation Seminar Series published in 1971 and distributed by The Duke University Center for the Study of Aging and Human Development. Reprinted by permission of the SNPA Foundation and The Duke University Center for the Study of Aging and Human Development.

Today institutions offer almost the only formal type of treatment available to older people. Despite all the furor about community mental health centers, only 2 percent of mental health center clients are over 65 (Kramer, 1970). In a recent study, only 3 percent of the clients of 30 east coast psychoanalysts were over 50 years old (Weintraub and Aranson, 1968). Community centers which care for the physically disabled aged are almost non-existent.

One advantage postulated for institutional treatment is that because of its radical nature—cut off from the world—it can efficiently replicate under controlled conditions many of the therapeutic techniques available in the outside world. A major question is whether any program which aims at enhancing independence can be carried out in a setting which requires giving up freedom as a ticket of admission. Most evidence suggests that people enter institutions as a place to live when they lack the support necessary to stay in the community. There is little evidence that institutions cure.

I

Only 5 percent of all old people are residents of long-term institutions (Riley et al., 1968). We must be careful not to assume that they are representative of older people in general. We must discover what institutionalized old people are really like, and whether there are people like them living outside. The answer to how the community group "makes it" may solve the riddle of care for the disabled aged.

Society cannot ignore the institutionalized old person. To begin with, he (or more likely she) is in every sense as worthy as any other person. In aggregate (Kramer, 1968), the institutionalized aged are over 610,000 persons. One-hundred eight thousand of them are in mental hospitals and nearly three times that many are in nursing homes and homes for the aged. We must bear in mind that few of us could afford a long institutional stay for ourselves or our parents. Almost all institutional residents are paid for by public monies. The recent Medicare and Medicaid laws, in fact, have even moved most residents of church-operated homes for the aged onto the public rolls (Goldfarb, 1969).

Though only a small part of the aged are institutionalized, institutionalized persons are disproportionately old. Eighty-eight percent of nursing home patients and almost all residents of homes for the aged are over 65. One-third of mental hospital admissions and a quarter of residents are old. To the professional who works in an institutional setting, the aged seem to be a very sick lot. Not only are their numbers troublesome, but also their lack of community ties.

Most people who enter institutions at any age are marginal people. This is no less true among the old. In one mental hospital, for example, the long-stay elderly patients were more poorly educated, more often single, more likely to have been marginally employed, and many long-term geriatric patients had been admitted to a mental hospital directly from their parents' homes decades earlier without ever having really gone out into the world (Gottesman, Donahue, Coons, & Ciarlo, 1969).

This same marginality is also true of people who are first admitted to institutions in their old age. A large-scale study in San Francisco (Simon, Lowenthal, & Epstein, 1970) found that elderly first admissions mental patients were poorer, more alone, and had not worked for many more years than the typical older person. In addition, they were physically sick. Four out of five new admissions were found to need supervision for physical ailments and 53 percent to be suffering from acute brain syndrome. Most of these patients were elderly people who had become unable to manage for themselves.

There is a pecking order among institutions. Homes for the aged receive richer, younger residents who are less physically and mentally disordered. Mental hospitals get old people who are more disturbed mentally, physically, and socially. Nursing home patients today are the most ill physically, mentally, and socially—the most cast out of all. Lest we miss the main point, however, let me reiterate that there is considerable overlap among settings and their residents (Goldfarb, 1969). The major differences are between inside and out.

II

Today we are all interested in alternatives to institutions. In our research at Michigan (Gottesman et al., 1971), we have tried a variety of placements for elderly ex-mental patients who averaged 19 years of hospitalization. On the basis of two years of study, we can characterize their assets and deficits. Some ex-patients went to large rooming houses, some to independent apartments. Large rooming houses, often viewed as skid row by professionals, came off quite well. They offered considerable freedom and encouraged residents to handle their own clothes, money, and living quarters. Their residents behaved in normally responsible ways. Small-room-and-board living was intimate, but quite demanding. Especially where families ate together with the ex-patient, they were often very intolerant of deviant behavior. Our return rate was low overall, but highest in these settings.

Not surprising, in view of their histories, few patients were able to return to their own families. But when they did (and our sample is quite small) families were generally at least moderately tolerant of deviance and encouraged lots of normal behavior. The returning grandma was sometimes able to take on important family-helper responsibilities. One old woman went home to take care of her disabled adult son.

Private apartment living was possible for a few old ex-patients. In them, the ex-patient (either alone or with a roommate) was forced to handle all aspects of life. The few patients who tried this always seemed precarious, but all but one in twelve made it through two years, and several were so independent that they refused to let our follow-up interviewers in.

Nursing homes restricted their patients most and permitted little normal behavior within them or with the outside world. Sometimes ex-patients were placed in nursing homes instead of a more normal setting because funds were available only for nursing home care. In some instances, patients who had been very active in the hospital were prevented from doing things they had been capable of just a few days previously. A patient who had been working and earning money when she left was found staring into space at the nursing home. She complained that her money had been taken (it was, and put away for safe-keeping). A few days later she returned to the mental hospital by Greyhound bus, saying she preferred her old home to being "in the community."

III

Naturally different kinds of patients went to each type of setting, and some had a better chance of getting out than others. Schizophrenic patients admitted in their 30s often grow old in the hospital, because there is nowhere else to go. In our experience, and in that of others, release has far less to do with treatment than with social characteristics of the patient and with opportunities for placement. Our patients were mostly long-term schizophrenics. In 18 months we released 41 percent of the patients. Only four percent died. Women were more likely to get out than men. Those 65–69 had a better chance of getting out than either older or younger patients. The older ones were too physically ill. Patients under 65 had no one to pay the tab, since they were not covered by Medicare or Medicaid.

A patient's social participation influenced whether he was kept in or released from the hospital. Active younger patients who stayed in the hospital were often kept on the experimental ward to await placement. The older, less active, patient was likely to be returned to a regular hospital ward.

Drs. Bourestom and Bok (Bok, 1971) have shown that more active patients of all ages have a higher likelihood of getting released. But even active patients were not likely to be released if they worked off their ward and out of sight. Patients were more likely to be released if they had been in the hospital a shorter time. If they had even mild interest shown in them by a family and even if they did not return to their families, they were also more likely to be released. It should be clear that few of these factors which influence release could have resulted from treatment.

Blenkner (1968) has written that "the flow of care of the aged follows the public dollar," and even in 1964 it was clear that changes in federal regulations would move the elderly mentally ill from mental hospitals into nursing homes (Gottesman, 1964). This has happened. From 1950 to 1960 residents of nursing homes increased 31.5 percent while those over 65 in state hospitals declined 12 percent, and first admissions also went down. There has not been a marked increase in deaths nor in success of therapeutic programs. These shifts have been administrative transfers. A different decision could move the old back to the mental hospital, to the poor house, or to the community.

When institutionalized old people are sick and socially marginal, to expect their return to normal life as you and I know it may be unrealistic. The institutional resident seems not to have been very social before coming in. Generally, entering is viewed by all as a final step down brought on by the failure of a tenuous support system. Nearly always, the move is thought of as a permanent one (Glaser & Strauss, 1968).

Many people blame institutions for damaging people, but it is possible that the deficits which we see in institutional residents were there when they were admitted. After an exhaustive review of over 30 years of research, Lieberman concluded that there is no evidence that institutionalization has either harmed or helped the aged (Lieberman, Green, & Lieberman, 1968). Institutions are primarily a place to live for people who have nowhere else to go.

Since 1953, when Maxwell Jones founded a therapeutic community for veterans returning from World War II, many programs for the young and old have been tried in mental hospitals. Their results are also relevant to other institutional settings. These programs fall into three general classes: those which try to individualize patient care; those which try to overcome the isolation of institutions and tie them into the outside world; and those which try to cure the deficits which are so very obvious in institutional residents. The results of these programs have been quite consistent, and I shall cite only three examples.

George Fairweather (1964) divided a group of hospitalized patients who averaged 37 years of age into small groups, each of which performed tasks together. When released from the hospital, patients who had been members of such groups were socially active and adjusted better than did other released patients who had not had the group experience. But, the former group members often became upset after a short time out of the hospital without continuing social support. Fairweather then showed in a new study that similar patients could do well in a group outside the hospital, when such support was available (Fairweather, Sanders, Kressler, & Maynard, 1969).

Saunders, Smith, and Weinman (1967) worked with a wide-range of patients who had been hospitalized an average of nine years. They compared three programs which differed in the amounts of structured activity they offered. In this study, patients from the three treatment groups were more social, had higher release rates and did better in the community than a control group. But the ones who did best were the older, chronically ill patients. These patients, the investigators concluded, were the ones who were the easiest to involve either because they had few interfering drives or because they had learned to allow themselves to be shaped by their environment (Appleby, 1969).

Group therapies, behavior therapies, psychotherapy and drugs have all been used effectively in institutions and in non-institutional settings. Re-motivation and occupational therapies are often used to create in the institutional setting aspects of society which the institution itself took away initially.

In our own program in Michigan we offered 240 patients a sheltered workshop and other planned activities in and out of the hospital (Gottesman et al., 1969). Both with pay and without, in both highly staffed and normally staffed wards, between 87 and 94 percent of patients were involved in productive activities five to ten hours per day (Gottesman, Bourestom, & Flug, 1971). A regular hospital ward of 80 patients similar to ours was used to compare our results. It, too, involved 78 percent of its patients in some activities, but only a few star patients did most things, while the others sat or slept during most of the day.

Patient performance on the special wards was unrelated to their sex, age, marital status, living arrangements prior to hospitalization, education, or job history. In other words, our programs were beneficial in spite of the deficits which symbolize marginality and bring chronic patients into the hospital. Patients did do better if they already had work experience in the hospital. They were less active if they were severely disoriented, but even patients with organic disturbance were usually active when opportunities were available.

Increased activity was not the only benefit of our program. The most active patients were more popular with their fellow patients. They saw their wards as more complex, orderly, and less distorted with personal meanings (Guttman, Gottesman, & Tessler, 1968). These mental patients were able to see their problems as psychic and interpersonal and expected to deal actively with them. In a milieu which more closely approximated normal life, since it had work and pay for work, as well as time for inactivity, patients were happier than on a traditional ward.

We found that when no programed activities were available, patient activities stopped. Like most people outside of hospitals, patients did not make their own opportunities. They required social supports to behave more normally.

We were disappointed that release from the hospital appeared to be independent of treatment. Our data also showed that neither psychotic symptoms nor confusion were markedly ameliorated by treatment. What we did was provide a humane environment which increased opportunities to use skills which patients had before they entered the research wards. . . .

V

Today many elderly patients who might benefit from home care are being treated in nursing homes. With the availability of federal money to pay for institutional care, nursing homes are attracting some older people who might otherwise be cared for at home. Even some homes for the aged are revising their programs to become eligible for the public dollar.

We have recently undertaken a project (Gottesman, 1970) which we hope will help nursing homes to avoid some of the mistakes mental hospitals have just begun to overcome. Our staff spends an entire week in each of a group of 50 nursing homes representing all sizes, types of ownership and proportions of public-pay patients. We are satisfied that we are beginning to understand nursing home care. As expected, every home is on its best behavior when company is there, but we are around from 6:30 in the morning to 7:30 at night. We observe and record the total patient experience; we interview owners, administrators, directors of nursing, aides and patients. We do not come expecting to find the worst, and our staff is trained to understand old people and their needs. Our impression is that many nursing homes are doing a really outstanding job. But there are problems which severely impede them in doing what they want to do. I would like to summarize some of the impediments we have discovered in our study so far.

While mental hospitals are reorganizing into smaller units, nursing homes are becoming larger. In Michigan, between 1950–54 only 20 percent of new licensed homes had over 100 beds; in 1965–69, 46 percent were this large. While the mental hospitals were decreasing centralized control, nursing homes have been moving toward increased control by a few corporations. In the Detroit area, six corporations control 18 percent of 168 homes and 30 percent of the beds. While mental hospitals have been encouraging more contact with the non-institutional community, nursing homes are becoming more isolated. Current legislation forces nursing homes to create distinctly separated parts with narrowly defined patient populations and rigid staffing patterns. Homes must be either skilled, intermediate or basic-care specialists or they cannot qualify for the federal funds which support 87 percent of nursing-home care. For example, a nursing home could not be paid if it shared the care of a patient with a family in a program which exchanged the patient between the home and the nursing home every three weeks or so. Yet, such a program is being highly successful in England.

Some mental hospitals provide milieux which increase a resident's opportunity for independence. On the other hand, nursing homes are paid more if their patient is sick. If a patient were to make her own bed, the home would either have to send her away (recall that nursing-home patients generally are there partly because they have no home) or lose payment for her.

Residents of nursing homes have medical, nursing and personal care needs. Goals are set and fees ostensibly paid for curative, restorative and maintenance services related to these needs. But nursing-home patients have only three conditions with substantially greater frequency than non-institutionalized persons with physical handicaps. According to a national survey of nursing-home residents, these three are: mental conditions (43.9 percent vs. 14.0 percent), vascular conditions affecting the central nervous system (36.0 percent vs. 7.0 percent) and paralysis due to stroke (15.7 percent vs. 5.2 percent). For all other diseases, the rate for non-institutionalized old people either equals or exceeds the institutionalized. Except for these three conditions, the main differences between people in nursing homes and those outside with similar conditions is that the former have no families to care for them.

Table 1 summarizes data from the National Health Survey (U.S. Department of Health, Education, and Welfare, 1967) which show the percentage of nursing-home patients who have each major condition mentioned

Table 1.

	Condition % With	Receive Intensive Care	Nursing Other	Personal	Neither
Mental condition	43.9	31.3	23.3	18.8	2.7
Vascular lesion	36.0	51.5	27.0	23.5	7.5
Paralysis	15.7	22.9	10.1	6.1	2.6
All conditions	100.0	31.0	28.7	26.9	13.5

above and the nursing care these patients receive. For all conditions only one-third of nursing home patients get intensive care, one-quarter other nursing care and one-quarter less intense personal care. Fourteen percent require none of these forms of care.

Sixty-five percent of patients in nursing homes stay in them over one year; 17 percent stay five years or more. They are not there to obtain acute intensive care. If one estimates even grossly, all of the services that any patient receives require only a very small part of a day to give. Yet, almost no nursing-home patients make their own beds, cook, wash, iron, clean, shop, go for walks or engage in any other significant activity of life. Most sit from arising to bedtime, with only meals and medication to punctuate their day.

There is no doubt that nursing homes are replaying the tragedy which mental hospitals have been trying to overcome—the tragedy of people with years filled with nothing to do. Nursing homes, like mental hospitals, have no cures to give and nursing care fills only small parts of each day. Nursing homes must be recompensed for bringing life back to their residents. Dull as it seems, life for most of us is cleaning, cooking, dressing, working, socializing, and helping others. Of these activities, many are within the capability of many nursing-home patients. There is no reason to suppose a priori that the nursing care needed could not be so distributed in the day as to leave room for other activities. The goal is not cure but a meaningful life. Projects which were successful in mental hospitals should be tried in nursing homes. These programs could provide opportunities for patients to take part in individual and group activities. They could also tie the nursing home more closely into the larger community.

VI

Despite sincere governmental attempts to encourage private institutions to offer adequate programs and despite the real needs of their highly specialized populations, many programs for the disabled elderly have faltered through severe lack of funds and through misunderstanding of the impossibility of their appointed tasks.

One cannot create a normal environment when the essential element of normality—freedom—is removed. Yet, if freedom is not removed, if residents are not described as sick and in need of constant supervision and surveillance, then funds for their care are denied by the families or by government agencies which pay the bill.

Our interpretation of the data summarized here suggests that treatment efforts should be directed toward keeping people at home if possible. When home care is impossible, then an institution, by whatever name it is called, should be allowed and encouraged to permit as much freedom as possible to those it serves. Often this can be accomplished by programs like those discussed. Let me give a final example.

A three-year program in England explored ways to share the care of 73 elderly patients between their families or community services and psychogeriatric wards of a mental hospital. This sharing was found to have advantages for the patient, the family and the institution (Lear et al., 1969).

The patient spent approximately a month at the hospital and a month at home. The treatment team consisted of both hospital and community personnel, with the social worker providing the vital link between home and hospital. All team members were involved to some extent on a continuing basis with the patient, and the family had opportunities to have discussions with the ward staff. Where needed, the hospital provided help at home, such as laundry service for incontinent patients and home-helps.

Though the idea of sharing was sometimes resisted by families, and more often by general medical practitioners, it was advantageous to all parties. With a greater emphasis placed on personal needs than on symptoms, the patients were seen more as persons and less as cases. Even on the hospital wards the atmosphere of depression and stagnation was reduced. In addition, the patients were able to retain their places in the family and community. Families, knowing that they could count on help and periodic relief from the very real burdens imposed by the care of a helpless old person, were better able to mobilize their resources and were freed from the guilt that usually accompanies the permanent institutionalization of an aged parent. Professional staff members were provided a valuable learning experience in their contact with families and insights into family relationships. Finally, the plan has clear economic advantages, for each hospital bed can be used by two families instead of one.

Referral: Hospice*

Sylvia Lack

In the final analysis, it seems impossible that institutions for the elderly will disappear. There are health-related and care tasks that cannot be appropriately performed in people's homes and need not be performed in the very expensive acute-care hospitals. The issue becomes not that of eliminating institutions but of finding less expensive and more personally satisfying options when it is possible and utilizing institutions most effectively when options are impossible.

In recent years, people have gone to hospitals when they became acutely and, eventually, terminally ill, but there is good evidence that the majority of people, in contemplating their own death, would rather die at home than anywhere else (Kalish & Reynolds, 1976). Unfortunately, for a variety of reasons ranging from lack of support persons who can stay home to the necessity of constant medical supervision, dying at home is often not a possibility. Another option has recently been developed, the hospice. The hospice is not a "place to die," it is a support system for the terminally ill and their families.

Hospices can be established as parts of hospitals or other facilities or as independent entities. The initial hospice just outside of London is not affiliated with any specific hospital, and the building that houses it is also apart from any other medical facility. So far, no hospice in the United States or Canada has its own building, although a hospital in Montreal has turned one ward into a hospice and a program in New Haven, Connecticut, has begun an out-patient program and is rapidly progressing toward getting the funds for its own building.

Hospice is a health care program designed to meet the special needs of terminally ill patients and their families. This program offers the kind of care that will enable them to live out their lives as fully and comfortably as possible. The Hospice program, based on sophisticated medical and nursing care, employs new pharmaceutical and other treatment methods to control pain, nausea, loss of appetite—conditions that deprive patients of strength, will, and sometimes even their human dignity.

Hospice considers the basic unit of care to be the patient and family and offers its services to both. Hospice ministers to their medical, emotional, social and spiritual needs. Teams of professionals and volunteers help them to mobilize their own resources to cope with their difficulties. Most importantly, the team—qualified not only by their knowledge and skill, but also by their humanity and dedication—listens to the patient/family and offers constructive help with their problems.

*Edited from *Referral: Hospice,* by S. Lack. Reprinted by permission of Hospice, Inc., New Haven, Connecticut.

HEALTH CARE GAP

Hospitals are, practically and philosophically, oriented to the cure of disease. This immediate urgency guides the hospital's efforts. The staff and most of the other resources are devoted to helping the patient recover from disease. When disease cannot be cured, the hospital has few resources to help the patient live as fully and completely as possible; nor can it give the patient's family the skilled care and support they need to understand and cope with the effects of this continuing illness.

Most nursing and convalescent homes are not equipped to give additional priority attention to the physical and emotional needs of the terminally ill, much less to their families. These institutions are designed primarily to provide long term care for the elderly and to conclude a recuperative period or rehabilitative program for patients. For patients recovering from an illness or accident, rehabilitative services are necessary to prepare for re-entering the community. For the terminally ill, cure is an unrealistic goal, and many rehabilitation programs refuse admission to those with a short prognosis.

At the same time, other health care professionals are dedicated to the treatment of disease and to the life extending philosophy promoted in our society. Hospitals and other facilities reflect this philosophy. When professionals come face-to-face with the reality of a dying patient, his needs, life style, and specific requests, they must often struggle with the biases of past training, the orientation of health care agencies, and their concern for the patient and for the family. Health care professionals, like many people, have difficulty coming to terms with the inevitability of dying. Yet, this must be done in order to think and act in a way that helps and comforts a patient in the midst of this struggle.

The care of the terminally ill is incomplete without counseling—both to the patient and the family. Often the focus has been only on the patient. But the acceptance of death can be more difficult for the patient's family than it is for the patient himself. Help must be available for both. Counseling—financial, practical, emotional—is often unavailable, especially on an ongoing basis. Death involves more than prayers and tears—it is a web of insurance policies, bills, attorneys, physicians, guilt, loss of income and funeral preparations. To help the patient/family cope with the reality of impending death, supportive relationships during the illness are necessary. To ease the pain of separation and grief and to assist in creating a new life for the family, this care must continue during their time of bereavement. These are services that can appropriately be provided through a hospice.

HOSPICE IN NEW HAVEN

St. Christopher's Hospice, a 54-bed facility in London, England, and St. Luke's Hospice, a 25-bed facility in Sheffield, England, are the prototypes for the Hospice currently being planned for construction in Branford, Connecticut, a suburban New Haven community. Though modified to reflect our particular culture and ethic, America's first Hospice will incorporate many of the principles of care already demonstrated as viable by the English models. These principles include a comprehensive, coordinated program of home care and in-patient care. Particular medical expertise in pain control, the management of nausea and other symptoms, maintenance of alertness and mood will be stressed. Pharmacological consultation and research will be important. Expert nursing care will be given, but in addition, nurses will be specifically trained, and given the time, to attend to the needs of the patient and family. Social work, psychiatric consultation, clergy services, and volunteer activities will be offered to support patients and families and to include them in an ongoing living process designed to maximize their valuable contribution and participation.

These concepts have application in general health care, but nowhere are they more important than in terminal care. In the process of dying and bereavement, it is vital that relationships are lived out and concluded as productively as possible. Families will be included as important members of the Hospice team, whether the patient is at home or in the in-patient facility.

This emphasis means that the patient/family is involved in teaching the staff about their needs, and in the decision-making regarding their treatment. Hospice will assist the patient and family to maintain their own lifestyle and a sense of their own responsibility while receiving supportive services.

One of the supportive services now in operation is the Hospice volunteer program. Volunteers, well-oriented to the Hospice program, are an integral part of the care-giving service, fulfilling a wide variety of needed tasks, including patient care, family support and assistance to the staff in planning and community education.

For the past several years, numerous groups have asked Hospice to provide programs of general information about its work, and to participate in specialized workshops and seminars. We will continue to develop these and other educational aspects of our program for health care professionals, religious groups, students, and the general public. We know that all persons will not be served by Hospice, but what we learn will be shared.

Another shared aspect of our program is in the field of research and program evaluation. Although some research has focused on the terminally ill, this population has never been observed in a comparative controlled environment such as Hospice will provide. Present research has documented the physical and psychological trauma experienced by the dying and given valuable insights into their special needs. Since Hospice will offer a situation where these needs are known and generally met, research can concentrate on comparative modes of care.

Any new part of a health care system does not effectively work in isolation. If it is to be most useful to the person in need, it must be integrated into the total fabric of the health care system of the community. Hospice includes approximately 250 people—health professionals from all disciplines and lay people from the community—on the task forces carrying out its planning and development. Many of these individuals have important primary responsibilities in the acute general hospital, the university teaching hospital, the Veteran's Administration Hospital, the Visiting Nurse Association, community medicine, nursing homes, or community agencies in Greater New Haven.

The care that patients will receive in Hospice, although highly personal and specialized, will cost appreciably less than services in an acute care hospital. Care in Hospice is expected to cost approximately 40% less per day than general hospitals in Connecticut. In addition, the Home Care Program enables the patient to remain home for an extended period, shortening the patient's stay in the facility, and further reducing the cost of care.

HOME CARE PROGRAM

The home is the natural place to die. Here a patient is surrounded by loved ones and cherished possessions. The dying can gain much by being cared for in this familiar environment. They are better able to maintain their individuality and dignity, and avoid the anonymity that is devastating to the dying hospital patient. By remaining at home, patients need not doubt that they are still part of their family. They can participate, even in a limited way, in home life. Many patients long to go home—and many families long to have them there.

In the home, lack of communication and support can be distressing to the family. A sense of abandonment is often felt, not only by patients, but also by their families. Doctors rarely make house calls, yet many patients are too sick to endure office visits. Too often, a patient, suffering from pain and weakness, must struggle to go to a hospital miles away from home. Once there, the patient may be required to wait three or four hours only to see an unknown resident physician for a few brief minutes.

It is the troubled and crisis-prone nights which make home care by relatives impossible. Professional health care is not readily available at these times when it is needed most. Without this necessary support, families feel helpless and overburdened, and sadly realize that the only alternative is to admit the patient to the hospital.

Since March 1974, Hospice has provided a coordinated Home Care service to patients and their families who are facing such problems. This program, the working application of Hospice's philosophy, is administered by the full-time Hospice physician. The team includes medical, nursing, social, volunteer (professionals and lay), physical therapy, and pastoral care workers, as well as other professionals as needed. This multidisciplinary program of specialized attention insures against fragmented and incomplete care for the terminally ill.

The team is available for regular daytime visits to patients in their homes, and is on-call for emergencies at night and on weekends. This round-the-clock, on-call availability of the Home Care team has proven invaluable in combating nighttime anxiety and in dealing with medical problems that would ordinarily result in a 2 A.M. dash to the emergency room.

Patients and families have the comforting assurance that the team can be called upon—at any time—for help. The goal of the program is to extend the periods of time in which patients can be safely, comfortably and inexpensively cared for in their own homes.

Patients are referred to Hospice Home Care by physicians, nurses, social workers, families, hospitals, and health agencies, as well as by patients themselves. When a new patient is admitted to the Home Care Program, the team, with the attending physician, evaluates the needs of the patient and family. Applying the resources of the team, and in collaboration with the local agencies, a schedule of care is programmed to meet the patient's needs.

Subsequently, the entire team is kept up-to-date on the patient's condition in daily and weekly review sessions. Visits are scheduled from one a week to as many as three a day. The patient's physical condition is not the only criterion for determining the number of visits—the family situation is always taken into account: loneliness and anxiety are as serious as the disease. The team monitors the patient's condition, checks to see if the medication is properly and regularly administered, and, most importantly, evaluates the response to the treatment.

For the patient, the home visit is more than a routine check-up—it is time spent with a person who sees him as an individual. For the team members, the home visit is more than an exercise in specialized medicine—it is an opportunity to help a fellow human being at the end of life. The visit may provide supportive counseling—emotional, psychological, physical—for both the patient and the family. It may give guidance and instruction in self-help to enable their active participation in the plan of care. It may offer volunteer services to free more time for the family to draw closer to the patient and to themselves.

After the patient's death, the Home Care team continues to care for the family in an effort to reduce the vulnerability to mental and physical illness associated with bereavement. When the team is satisfied that the family is successfully coping with bereavement, and adequately supported from other sources, the family is discharged from the program.

Case Study

Mrs. Angela Campobello* was 57 years old when she was referred to the Hospice program in January. Four years earlier she had had a radical mastectomy of her left breast because of infiltrating ductal cell carcinoma, which, since that time, has been asymptomatic. Her progress had been followed in the breast clinic of the hospital. The clinic's attending physician had requested Hospice services because, like the patient,

*Names have been changed to preserve anonymity.

he realized that her physical and mental condition had deteriorated, and that she, as well as her family and friends, needed help to face the months ahead.

Severe pain had begun the previous Christmas Eve during a family party. That night, she awoke with a severe pain in her neck. During the week, she tried everything—heat pad, drugstore remedies, even a vibrator. Nothing helped.

We first saw her as she walked down the clinic hall with a heavy, slow step. When she turned around, her eyes were brimming with tears. She began by telling what a bad mood she was in, "Boy, as we drove in this morning, I said, 'The doctors are going to put me in the looney bin, if I jabber the way I did this morning.' I'm so upset." Her daughter, Mrs. Arntella, looked up quickly. The air was heavy with the tension between them.

After the examination, medication was prescribed for the immediate relief of pain. The physician cautioned that if this medicine did not help to ease the pain within a week, she was to let him know and x-ray treatments would be started. Her eyes filled with tears, "I know what that means."

But by the time the prescriptions were filled, mother and daughter had begun to relax. Before leaving, both were laughing at how terribly upset Mrs. Campobello had been and how she had threatened to "let the daughter have it." They expressed relief that the Home Care staff would soon visit.

The next month was difficult. Mrs. Campobello's anxiety mounted, and her breathing, already impaired by the metastases to her lung, became labored.

During the first home visit, the nurse found Mrs. Campobello sitting immobilized in a darkened room. Pain and fear had interrupted her sleep and kept her housebound. Although she sat with the telephone directly in front of her, she was reluctant to call her family because they became so frightened by her symptoms and felt helpless in responding to her complaints.

In the next six weeks, the home visits of the Hospice nurse, psychiatric consultation, collaboration with the Hospice pharmacists, and palliative x-ray treatments resulted in improvement in her condition. Mrs. Campobello was able to enjoy a good night's rest, her breathing eased, the pain was reduced. She now turned to the Hospice team for help for her family.

She was the center of a large Italian family of four children, twelve grandchildren, several sisters, numerous in-laws, cousins and a beloved aunt and uncle. She also had a wide circle of friends anxious to help. A priest joined the Hospice team of physician, nurse, and pharmacist, to provide services and support for her, for her husband, and for her children.

She wanted to talk about her illness but her family found this very difficult. Her worry about what would happen to her family was compounded by her estrangement from her husband two years earlier. She was also concerned that, alone, she would not have the physical strength to suffer the discomforts that surely would come. "What will it feel like?" "Will I be alone?" "What will happen next?" These were questions that the Hospice team discussed with her.

The time from our first encounter to the last was long—eight months. During the first few months, holidays and family celebrations were overlooked; the family was afraid to plan for fear that they would be disappointed. Soon they relaxed and began to enjoy birthdays, anniversaries and family get-togethers. As her fears diminished, her feeling of well-being increased, her zest for life and courage returned, and her sense of humor blossomed.

Easter was an important turning point. After long and thoughtful consideration, Mr. and Mrs. Campobello decided to reunite. In preparation for his return, the house was spruced up. For the first time in months, the duster came off the sewing machine, and Mrs. Campobello made new curtains for the front room. She splurged on a new dress for the 50th wedding anniversary party for her aunt and uncle. That celebration, Mother's Day, and the Fourth of July were great days.

In between there were times when pain, breathlessness, weakness and depression rose to the surface, and treatments were changed to meet these problems. The more Mrs. Campobello became at ease in talking about life coming to a close, the more the children and grandchildren needed Hospice's help for comfort and reassurance.

Her last night was the kind of Saturday evening she always loved: dinner with the whole family, poker until midnight, then a good night's sleep. The next day, her daughter hesitated to wake her at 9 A.M.—her breathing was so easy, her sleep so peaceful. At 10:30 A.M., her daughter called the Home Care Office. Mrs. Arntella found her mother had stopped breathing just a few moments before.

Mrs. Campobello once described what she felt: "I've had a hard life. But it has been a good one. During this illness, I've found so many new and wonderful friends. And my family is all together. They'll manage."

THE FACILITY

In order to provide specialized care and support for those patients who cannot be cared for at a home, a Hospice facility has been designed. The social, psychological and physiological aspects of patient care have been carefully considered.

Good transportation facilities, by private and public systems, were a paramount consideration. The Hospice has been centered in a fifteen-mile radius of the community it will serve with easy access to the supporting general hospitals and home care services.

The reception room will give the sense that this is a pleasant place to be. A feeling of quiet activity will be conveyed by color, furnishings, and decorations. Every room, every corridor, every space is designed with the patients' and families' care and comfort as the first priority.

The design permits mobility whether a patient is confined to a bed or a wheel chair. The entire patient area is on a single level, with sliding glass doors to outdoor courtyards. An oversized corridor between the courtyard and the patient rooms allows even the individual whose mobility is severely limited to "leave" his room. The corridors are lined by deep window boxes containing plants and flowers, and enclosed by large windows, suggestive of a greenhouse. The use of free-standing walls between the rooms permits the patients to be aware of the staff's presence, and, likewise, permits the staff to be aware of all the patients from any part of the patient wing. Families can visit with patients in the rooms, in the courtyards or in a comfortable living room in each of the two patient wings. These living rooms, each with a fireplace, also double as dining areas where patients and families share meals together.

The majority of patient rooms will have four beds to foster communication between patients and families. The peer support offered by patient to patient and by family to family is fostered by the special design of the rooms. It is comforting to a patient to learn, by the example of the high quality care received by those near him, that his needs will be met whenever he also experiences difficulties. Adequate space around the bed is also important so that several members of a family can be with the patient at the same time as the staff.

The feeling of home—not just any home, but the particular home from which the patient comes—must be conveyed. Belongings—a picture, an art object, something from home—can be brought with the patient.

When weather permits, patients can enjoy the outdoors. The large terraces are at grade level to enable staff to move patients in their own beds if necessary. This architectural feature solves many of the problems of managing patients who are not easily moved in wheelchairs. The gardens will contain flowers, fruits and vegetables to be cultivated by staff, volunteers and patients when they can. There will also be walks, retreat spots and bird watching areas.

A space frequently absent in health care facilities is an area where the workers can retreat to replenish themselves for continual effectiveness. Spaces where a nurse may be alone or with others on the team, where a family can retreat or meet with nurse or doctor, are necessary parts of the total system of care for Hospice patients.

An integral part of the Hospice family concept is inclusion of children as visitors and as part of the community. A day care nursery will permit mothers of small children to work at Hospice and offer the children the opportunity to join them at mealtimes.

While the need for technical support facilities will be limited, certain services are essential: a pharmacy with a full-time pharmacist; diagnostic radiology, oxygen and suction systems at every bed; and a small laboratory for frequently administered tests. Other services which are needed only occasionally, palliative x-ray, for example, will also be provided. Arrangements with other hospitals and institutions to provide back-up services are being completed.

Swope Ridge Nursing Home: Prevention and Rehabilitation*

Hospice is not directed particularly at the elderly, although this new form of institution will undoubtedly influence the lives of many older persons. It is nursing homes to which most disabled old people go, and it is the nursing home that has come under a great deal of attack from both professionals in aging and from politicians. The image of "the nursing home" is certainly unfavorable; they are accused of being dirty, depressing, uncaring, impersonal, money-oriented, the "end of the line." Yet few if any of the complainers expend time and effort to make changes; even more significant, few would themselves administer or work in a nursing home. As one administrator commented, "Society considers these deteriorated old people as their garbage, and we are the garbage-collectors." The work has very low status; pay, except for top administrators and professionals, is low; few people enjoy visiting the homes.

Now read about Swope Ridge Nursing Home in Missouri. Read it not only to see the kinds of things that can be done in a nursing home, but for the tone of the article. Note also the integration between the physical structure and the social program, as well as between the activities inside the home and what is going on in the world outside.

The prevailing public image of the nursing home is that of a place where old people wait for death. Families rush through dutiful Sunday visits, eager to be away from the depressing atmosphere, and older residents too often appear to wait out their days in almost apologetic hopelessness.

Though nursing homes have traditionally cared for the chronically ill, the disabled and the mentally impaired elderly, even the best of these facilities have provided little in the way of therapeutic social activities, arguing that since their patients are among the oldest and most impaired of the elderly population, the best one can offer them is nursing care, some medical attention, cleanliness, comfort, food and kindness—until they die.

Swope Ridge, a non-profit nursing home in Kansas City, Missouri, has been challenging this concept of custodial care since it opened its doors in 1957. At Swope Ridge, the mood and purpose are far different from the great majority of nursing homes across the country. That purpose is reflected in the words of the Executive Director of the Home. "No resident of Swope Ridge is admitted with the idea that he is a 'terminal patient.' The emphasis is on rehabilitation—not vegetation. Residents come to this home to live, not to die."

*Edited from "Swope Ridge Nursing Home: A Case History." Congressional Record. Washington, D.C.: U.S. Government Printing Office, 1971.

Swope Ridge offers each resident a range of physical and psychological therapeutic programs designed to foster mental and physical health. Here residents are encouraged to satisfy their needs for work, recreation, education, religious expression, social and personal relationships, as independently as they might in the outside community.

Meaningful social activity is basic to the mental health of the elderly, as with any age group. When such activities are linked with physical and psychological therapy programs, administered by a staff trained to understand and treat special problems, even the oldest, sickest and most disabled elderly patients can hope for improvement.

A PHYSICAL ENVIRONMENT DESIGNED TO PROMOTE SOCIAL ACTIVITY

The focal point of this 50,000 square foot building is the activity area. All of the living areas, residential wings and lounges (living rooms) surround a sheltered patio, which opens into a "social center." The social center includes the central dining room, two lounges, and a large, multi-purpose room which serves as an auditorium, chapel, social hall, hobby shop and recreation room. A recent annex is equipped with its own lounges and patios, to enable the most severely mentally and physically impaired patients (who are housed here) to participate in recreational and social activities. The physical therapy department (recently expanded), beauty and barber shops, are on the lower (or basement) level.

A building such as this, designed for social and therapeutic activity, is the first step in alleviating the patient's feeling of isolation and fear. The activity areas are but a few steps from each resident's room. It is difficult to avoid social interaction in such a setting.

PRIMARY PHASE—PHYSICAL REHABILITATION

Nothing is so discouraging to a person (of any age) as physical disability. To the older person who was once an active, vigorous human being, the loss of previously held skills can be devastating.

Even the smallest gains can have a positive effect on the emotional outlook of older patients. Therefore, physical therapy is considered the primary phase of the rehabilitation program at Swope Ridge. Today, 80% participate and physical therapy is provided five days a week.

A calisthenics program is provided to all patients, no matter what their level of disability. The exercises are geared to individual needs, and they range from very mild for the most severely impaired, to quite strenuous for those who can (and wish to) participate. Dance classes are provided as part of the calisthenics program—even for those who manipulate wheelchairs for Folk dancing.

Speech therapy is available at the Home (supervised by qualified professionals). Speech therapy takes place every day and has proved especially helpful to victims of stroke (who are frequently mentally impaired). A number of patients, who were never expected to speak again, have shown remarkable recovery of speech through this continuous treatment program.

Inhalation therapy is yet another innovative aspect of the physical therapy program at Swope Ridge, and provides an opportunity for physical rehabilitation to tuberculosis patients and persons suffering from emphysema.

AN OPPORTUNITY TO LEARN NEW SKILLS AND RE-LEARN OLD ONES

Occupational therapy is an integral part of the Home's activity program. The two occupational therapists direct sheltered workshop activities and other such programs. This treatment serves a definite psychological purpose. For example, the woman who once was a skilled seamstress but can no longer use her hands, or the man who was once a skilled laborer but can no longer attempt such strenuous activity, have been deprived of skills which gave them a feeling of worth, of usefulness. The re-learning of such skills, or the training for new ones, can do much to rebuild their damaged feelings and can also prevent depression and dependence.

RECREATIONAL ACTIVITIES THAT PROVIDE A REASON FOR LIVING

Many nursing homes are medically rehabilitative and a number have introduced physical therapy programs, but few supplement these services with meaningful psycho-social activities. It is this type of supplemental activity that can provide the older patient with a psychological reason for living and improving.

At Swope Ridge, the term "diversional activities" describes a wide variety of psycho-social programs. At breakfast each day in the central dining room, the Director of the Home broadcasts the "News of the Day" over the loudspeaker, reading from the daily newspaper. This creates breakfast table conversation among the patients and staff, and helps bring the outside world into the nursing home. The broadcast also reaches those patients who cannot take their meals in the dining room. Nurses and nurses' aides have been encouraged to discuss the news with these patients, as they are helping them with their morning meal, so that they, too, may begin their day with friendly and meaningful conversation.

A listing of the activities offered during one month (each month a new Calendar of Events is posted on the bulletin board outside the Social Center, and sent to families of patients) from the Calendar of Events, will best illustrate the range of services available at Swope Ridge:

Highlights of the Month, April, 1969

(All activities at 7:00 P.M. unless notified otherwise)

1   What's Cookin'—session in Hobby House
2   Spring Fashion Show (2:30 P.M.)
2   "Artist with a Camera," Slides by Bob Cunningham, professional photographer
3   (PASSOVER) Movie Nite: "He is Risen"; "On This Mountain" (King Solomon)
4   (GOOD FRIDAY) Easter Egg Dye in Hobby House—daytime (No evening program)
6   (EASTER)
7   Come Play Guggenheim (quiz nite)
8   Lecture—Rae Ann Nixon, Costume Curator, K.C. Museum—slides and display of Victorian costumes
9   Program in Terrace Annex
10 Movie Nite: "Dynamic Maturity"; "The Name of the Game is Fun!"
11 Joan Lang Dance Studio
13 "An Evening with Kay Dennis" (7:00 P.M.)
14 Birthday Party honoring Harriet Tompkins, Betty LaBar, Mary Fryer, Blanche Sartaine, Marion Imbs, Myrtle Pederseon, Marion Drought, Georgene Kynette, Eleanor Kennaley, Nathan Fischer, Pauline Banta, Vita Saladino and Katharine Ridgway. Musical entertainment by Edna Lashbrooke.
15 "The Good Old Days"—L.W. Henderson, Downtowners Toastmaster Club
17 Feature Film: "The Gunfighter" (6:30 P.M.)
18 Sports/games—bowling and others
21 Spring Arts Festival begins—Southeast High Drama Presentation
22 Accordian Ensemble, drum, guitar—Pauline Wright Music Studio, students 8–13 years
23 Loretto High Glee Club—60 girls
24 Movie Nite: "Sunkist in Motion"; "Building the Golden Gate Bridge"
25 Residents' Sing-a-Long/Talent Show
28 Surprise program
29 Book Review—Margaret Hart, Head Librarian, Southeast Library
30 Out-trip: Drive thru Swope and Loose Parks

Regular Activities

Question of the Week
News of the Day: 8:15 A.M. to 8:45 A.M.—Every Morning
Hobby House: 9:00 A.M. to 4:30 P.M.—Mon. thru Sat.
Physical Therapy: 9:00 A.M. to 4:00 P.M.—Mon. thru Fri.
Current Events Class: 10:30 A.M. to 11:30 A.M.—Tues.
Book Reading: 2:30 P.M. to 3:15 P.M.—Mon. thru Fri.
Music Appreciation in Terrace Annex: 2:30 P.M. to 3:30 P.M.—Friday
Room Visits/Craft Cart: Afternoons—Mon. thru Fri.
Terrace Annex Fellowship: 3:15 P.M. to 4:00 P.M.—Mon. thru Fri.

Group Exercises: 3:30 P.M. to 4:00 P.M.—Mon.-Wed.-Fri.
Chinese Culture Class: 4:00 P.M. to 5:00 P.M.—Friday
Bingo: 2:30 P.M. to 4:00 P.M.—Every Saturday
Use the Library: Every Day

Some other unusual programs include:

—Audio Visual: Slides, showing scrapbooks and albums representing a patient's lifetime hobby, such as stamp collecting or photography, may provide an evening's entertainment.
—Ballroom dances for all residents who wish to attend—even those who are wheelchair-bound.
—Discussion groups: Once a month, the Home invites local "celebrities" (civic leaders, television personalities) to come and lead the discussion.
—Dramatics: Residents put on playlets, poetry readings.
—Gardening: During warm weather, members of the resident Garden Club work in the patios, planting flowers and bushes. The plants are brought indoors during winter months so that gardening may continue throughout the year.
—Sports events: Wheelchair races, and ballgames.
—Outings: Occasional night club trips are offered to those who are able to drink (physician's recommendation).[1]

The purpose behind all activities is to motivate the residents to an active participation in the affairs of the world—both inside and outside the home. As the activities list indicates, several events occur simultaneously. This is planned so residents may have a choice and vary their routine occasionally, just as they would if they lived in the outside community. Every effort is made to encourage freedom and to avoid regimentation.

A ROLE IN THE DECISION-MAKING PROCESS

When an elderly individual enters a nursing home, his feelings of status and self-worth are usually at low ebb. He most likely has no say in the decision to place him in the Home. In order for these feelings to be strengthened, it is important that the patient have a voice in the management of his new "home."

The Residents' Council at Swope Ridge gives each resident a role in the decision-making process through committee participation, and encourages them to perform voluntarily, some function that is useful to others. The Council consists of a chairman, a secretary, and the heads of seven committees, who meet with the Executive Director of the Home to point out needs and suggest improvements.

---

[1]All activities require a physician's recommendation. The Home informed the Committee that physicians have been quite enthusiastic about allowing their patients to participate.

The Recreation Committee meets with the Recreation Director to help organize and plan social events, such as entertainment, birthday parties, theater parties outside the Home, sing-a-longs, picnics and other outings.

The Hobby and Crafts Committee is made up of individuals who have (or have had) special skills in this area. They are actively involved in the planning of the program, and also encourage other residents to participate.

A Hospitality Committee escorts visitors on tours of the Home, and staffs the information desk and gift nook (where residents' handiwork is sold).

The Food Committee meets with the Dietitian to help plan menus for the week, informing her of special or favorite dishes other residents may have suggested.

Religious Committee members remind residents of the various religious services available and also help the most severely impaired residents attend. Clergymen from Protestant, Catholic and Jewish faiths conduct services on a voluntary basis.

A Welcoming Committee calls on new residents to acquaint them with Swope Ridge, helping make them feel "at home" soon after admission.

The "Guys and Dolls" Committee gathers news and helps write the bi-monthly newspaper.

The Council and Committee members are not selected by the staff because they are the "healthiest" residents. They are elected by all residents in the Home, and many are wheelchair-bound.

A VOLUNTEER PROGRAM THAT BRINGS THE COMMUNITY INTO THE NURSING HOME

Perhaps the greatest barrier to the mental health of an institutionalized patient (and nursing homes are also institutions) is isolation. He often feels "put away," and abandoned by family and friends. This feeling of isolation can lead to depression, dependence, confusion and finally, complete withdrawal from the world around him. Sunday visits from the family are not enough to prevent deterioration.

Swope Ridge has long made a practice of opening its doors to family and friends any time they wish to visit, and patients are frequently taken out into the community on field trips.

But the administrators of the Home recognized that even this was not enough. What was needed was constant participation in the home's activities by community residents of all ages.

Therefore, in 1964 a Volunteer Program was developed with community organizations, such as girl scouts, boy scouts, teenage service groups, and church organizations. The home has more than 250 volunteers under the supervision of a paid Director of Volunteers. The volunteer training program has been accepted by the Red Cross. Outside community organizations are also brought into the program through the use of the Swope Ridge Volunteer Community Advisory Board.

COMMITMENT TO LEARNING—A WELL-TRAINED STAFF

The achievements which can be gained from providing comprehensive, life-giving care to nursing home residents can be great, but such care cannot be achieved without the services of a well-trained professional staff and an effective in-service training program for all levels of staff. The success of any therapeutic program depends to a great extent on those who administer the therapy and care for the patients.

At Swope Ridge, the entire staff is exposed to a continuous in-service education program. The Director of Physical Therapy conducts weekly training sessions to keep the nursing staff abreast of new techniques so that they may offer physically therapeutic services to the patients continuously. For example, the nurse or nurses' aide may help the resident exercise upon waking in the morning, to loosen up brittle joints and sore muscles, help patients move properly while escorting them to meals or activities, remind patients suffering from emphysema or tuberculosis to breathe correctly, or work on a patient's speech defects while engaged in idle conversation.

A nursing instructor from the University of Missouri conducts training classes for nurses' aides (approximately 60 hours a month). The classes instruct not only in the administration of drugs and treatments, but are designed to orient the staff to the unique physical and mental problems of the elderly residents.

The professional personnel at Swope Ridge conduct classes during employees' off-duty hours, enabling those who are high-school drop-outs to earn the equivalent of a high school diploma.

Scholarship aid is arranged for employees while on leave to attend one of the local schools of health-field professions. The Home pays tuition and stipends so aides can participate in nurses training.

Human Relations Seminars are presented at Swope Ridge by the University of Missouri, to help improve working relationships among employees.

The entire staff meets periodically with psychologists from the University of Missouri, to discuss ways of dealing with the mentally impaired residents and methods of preventing decline.

A NEW DIMENSION—OUTPATIENT SERVICES

Large numbers of elderly persons residing in the community are in need of services—psychiatric, medical and social—but for a variety of reasons are not receiving them. The administrators of Swope Ridge have opened the doors of the nursing home to elderly individuals in the community who may be in need of help and care, but who are still able to function independently. Since January, 1970, Swope Ridge has provided the following outpatient services to the community: physical therapy, including speech and inhalation therapy, occupational therapy, and diversional activities.

Outpatient services are available every day of the week and to all income levels. Referrals are solicited from private physicians, general hospitals, state mental hospitals, Department of Public Welfare, religious organizations, private social agencies, and neighbors, relatives and friends of the potential patients.

The difference between this and other outpatient clinics is that the outpatients (community residents) and in-patients (nursing home residents) will receive treatment at the same time, in the same place. In other words, the services are integrated with those provided to residents of the Home.

The purpose of this plan is two-fold: (1) to provide outpatient community services in a non-regimented manner; and (2) to provide residents with further personal contact with the outside community.

FUTURE THRUSTS—
A HEALTH COMPLEX FOR THE ELDERLY

Swope Ridge is planning the development of a Health Care Complex which will provide several levels of comprehensive care to the elderly, including: a facility to house the "well" aged, who need a semi-protective living arrangement; a building for the mentally-impaired elderly, which will offer specialized care and treatment; another facility for the chronically ill, long-term patients; and finally, Home Care for those individuals who wish (and are still able) to remain in their own homes, but who need some help and care.

References

Advisory Council on Social Security. Report of the Quadrennial Advisory Council on Social Security, Committee on Ways and Means, U.S. House of Representatives (94th Congress, 1st Session). Washington, D.C.: U.S. Government Printing Office, 1975.

Appleby, L. (Review of *Chronic psychoses and recovery* by R. Sanders, R.S. Smith, & B.S. Weinman). *Contemporary Psychology,* 1969, *14,* 188–189.

Ash, P. Pre-retirement counselling. *The Gerontologist,* 1966, *6,* 97–99.

Atchley, R.C. Retired women: A study of self and role. (Unpublished doctoral dissertation, The American University, Washington, D.C., 1967.)

Atchley, R.C. Recreation and leisure. In R.C. Atchley (Ed.), *Understanding American society: An institutional approach.* Belmont, Calif.: Wadsworth, 1970.

Back, K., 1965. *Cited,* in R. Kastenbaum. Meaning of time in later life. *Journal of Genetic Psychology,* 1966, *109,* 9–25.

Back, K., & Guptill, C.S. Retirement and self-ratings. In I.H. Simpson, K.W. Back, & J.C. McKinney (Eds.), *Social aspects of aging.* Durham, N.C.: Duke University Press, 1966.

Barfield, R., & Morgan, J. *Early retirement: The decision and the experience.* Ann Arbor: Institute for Social Research, University of Michigan, 1969.

Barron, M. *The aging Americans.* New York: Thomas Y. Crowell, 1961.

Becker, E. *The denial of death.* New York: The Free Press, 1973.

Berardo, F.M. Survivorship and social isolation: The case of the aged widower. *The Family Coordinator,* 1970, *19,* 11–25.

Berelson, B., & Steiner, G. Chapter 13. In B. Berelson (Ed.), *Human behavior.* New York: Harcourt, 1964.

Binstock, R.H. Interest-group liberalism and the politics of aging. *The Gerontologist,* 1972, *12,* 265–280.

Birren, J.E. *The psychology of aging.* Englewood Cliffs, N.J.: Prentice-Hall, 1964.

Birren, J.E. The aged in cities. *The Gerontologist,* 1969, *9,* 163–169.

Birren, J.E. The abuse of the urban aged. *Psychology Today,* 1970, *3,* 37–38; 76–77.

Blau, Z.S. *Old age in a changing society: New viewpoints.* New York: Franklin Watts, 1973.

Blenkner, M. The place of the nursing home among community resources. *Journal of Geriatric Psychiatry,* 1968, *1,* 135–150.

Bok, M. Some problems of milieu treatment of the chronic older mental patient. *The Gerontologist,* 1971, *11,* 141–147.

Bracey, H.E. *In retirement: Pensioners in Great Britain and the United States.* Baton Rouge: Louisiana State University Press, 1966.

Brody, E.M., et. al. *A social work guide for long-term care facilities.* National Institute of Mental Health. Washington, D.C.: U.S. Government Printing Office, 1975.

Bromley, D.B. *The psychology of human ageing.* Baltimore: Penguin Books, 1966.

Brotman, H.B. A fact sheet on home ownership aspects of the economics of aging (July). Washington, D.C.: Administration on Aging, U.S. Department of Health, Education, and Welfare, 1969.

Bultena, G.L., & Wood, V. The American retirement community: Bane or blessing? *Journal of Gerontology,* 1969, *24,* 209–217.

Busse, E.W. Changes in thinking and behavior in the elderly: An interdisciplinary study. Paper presented at the meeting of the American Psychiatric Association, Detroit, May, 1967.

Butler, R.N. Psychiatric evaluation of the aged. *Geriatrics,* 1963, *18,* 220–232.

Cain, L.E., Jr. Life course and social structure. In R.E.L. Faris (Ed.), *Handbook of Modern Sociology.* Chicago: Rand McNally, 1964.

Cameron, P., Stewart, L., & Biber, H. Consciousness of death across the life-span. *Journal of Gerontology,* 1973, *28,* 92–95.

Campbell, A. Politics through the life cycle. *The Gerontologist,* 1971, *11,* 112–117.

Cantor, M.H. *The elderly in the inner city.* New York: New York City Office for the Aging, 1975.

Cantor, M. H., & Mayer, M. *Health crisis of older New Yorkers.* New York: New York City Office for the Aging, 1972.

Carp, F.M. *Factors in utilization of services by Mexican-American elderly.* Palo Alto, Calif.: American Institute for Research, 1968.

Carp, F.M. *A future for the aged: Residents of Victoria Plaza.* Austin: The University of Texas Press, 1966.

Cartwright, A., Hockey, L., & Anderson, J.L. *Life before death.* London: Routledge & Kegan Paul, 1973.

Chen, Y.P. Economic poverty: The special case of the aged. *The Gerontologist,* 1966, *6,* 39–45.

Chen, Y.P. Making a theory work: The case of homeownership by the aged. *Aging and Human Development,* 1970, *1,* 9–19.

Christensen, R.M., & McWilliams, R.D. *Voice of the people.* New York: McGraw-Hill, 1967.

Christenson, C.V., & Gagnon, J.H. Sexual behavior in a group of older women. *Journal of Gerontology,* 1965, *20,* 351–357.

Clark, M. Is dependency in old age culture bound? Paper presented at the Annual Meeting of the Gerontological Society, St. Petersburg, Fla., November, 1967.

Clark, M. The anthropology of aging: A new area for studies of culture and personality. In B.L. Neugarten (Ed.), *Middle age and aging.* Chicago: University of Chicago Press, 1968, 433–443.

Clark, M. Patterns of aging among the elderly poor of the inner city. *The Gerontologist,* 1971, *11,* 58–66.

Clark, M., & Mendelson, M. Mexican-American aged in San Francisco: A case description. *The Gerontologist,* 1969, *9,* 90–95.

Clark, R.N. Age structure changes and intergenerational transfers of income. Durham, N.C.: Duke University Press, 1975.

Clemente, F., & Kleiman, M.B. Fear of crime among the aged. *The Gerontologist,* 1976, *16,* 207–210.

Cottrell, W.F. *Technological change and labor in the railroad industry.* Lexington, Mass.: D.C. Heath, 1970.

Cottrell, W.F., & Atchley, R.C. *Women in retirement: A preliminary report.* Oxford, Ohio: Scripps Foundation, 1969.

Cowgill, D. Trends in the ecology of the aged in American cities, 1940–1950. *Journal of Gerontology,* 1957, *12,* 25–80.

Cowgill, D. The demography of aging. In A. Hoffman (Ed.), *The daily needs and interests of older people.* Springfield, Ill.: Charles C Thomas, 1970, 27–70.

Cumming, E., & Henry, W.E. *Growing old: The process of disengagement.* New York: Basic Books, 1961.

Damianopoulos, E. A formal statement of disengagement theory. In *Growing old: The process of disengagement,* by E. Cumming & W.E. Henry. New York: Basic Books, 1961.

Da Silva, G. Loneliness and death of an 81-year-old man. *Geriatric Focus,* 1965, *4,* 7.

Davidson, J.D. Religious involvement and middle age. *Sociological Symposium,* 1969, *3,* 31–45.

Davis, R.H. Television and the older adult. *Journal of Broadcasting,* 1971, *14,* 153–159.

Davis, R.H. A descriptive study of television in the lives of an elderly population. Unpublished doctoral dissertation. University of Southern California, 1972.

Davis, R.H., Edwards, A.E., et al. Assessing television viewing behavior of older adults. *Journal of Broadcasting,* 1976, *20,* 69–76.

Deutscher, I. The quality of postparental life: Definitions of the situation. *Journal of Marriage and the Family,* 1964, *26,* 52–59.

Diggory, J.C., & Rothman, D.Z. Values destroyed by death. *Journal of Abnormal Psychology,* 1961, *30,* 11–17.

Donahue, W. Psychological changes with advancing age. In *Planning welfare services for older people.* Papers presented at the Training Institute for Public Welfare Specialists in Aging, Cleveland, June 13–24, 1965. Washington, D.C.: U.S. Government Printing Office, 1965.

Donald, M.N., & Havighurst, R.J. The meanings of leisure. *Social Forces,* 1959, *37,* 355–360.

Dovenmuehle, R.H. Psychiatry: Implementation. In J.T. Freeman (Ed.), *Clinical features of the older patient.* Springfield, Ill.: Charles C Thomas, 1965, 266–272.

Dublin, L.L. *Factbook on man.* New York: Macmillan, 1965.

Dumont, M. *The Absurd Healer.* New York: Science House, 1968.

Duncan, L. Ecology and aging. *The Gerontologist,* 1968, *8,* 80–83.

Eisdorfer, C. Discussion. In F.M. Carp (Ed.), *The Retirement Process.* Washington, D.C.: U.S. Government Printing Office, 1968, 97–104.

Ellis, M.J. Spending patterns over the life cycle. Paper presented at the 42nd Annual Agricultural Outlook Conference, Washington, D.C., November, 1964.

Ellison, D.L. Work, retirement, and the sick role. *The Gerontologist,* 1968, *8,* 189–192.

Elwell, C.C. The SAGE spirit. *Human Behavior,* (March) 1976, *5,* 40–43.

Erskine, H.G. The polls. *Public Opinion Quarterly,* 1963, *27,* 133–141.

FHA report, quoted in *U.S. News & World Report,* August 10, 1969, 76.

Fairweather, G.W. *Social psychology in treating mental illness: An experimental approach.* New York: Wiley, 1964.

Fairweather, G.W., Sanders, D., Kressler, D., & Maynard, H. *Community life for the mentally ill.* Chicago: Aldine, 1969.

Feaver, J.C., & Boyd, D.R. Attitudes of the elderly toward religion and death. In *Working with older people* (Vol. III). Washington, D.C.: U.S. Government Printing Office, 1970, 81–85.

Feifel, H. Older persons look at death. *Geriatrics,* 1956, *11,* 127–130.

Feifel, H., & Branscomb, A.B. Who's afraid of death? *Journal of Abnormal Psychology,* 1973, *81,* 282–288.

Freeman, J.T. Body composition in aging. In J.T. Freeman (Ed.), *Clinical features of the older patient.* Springfield, Ill.: Charles C Thomas, 1965, 3–43.

Fried, M. Grieving for a lost home. In L.J. Duhl (Ed.), *The urban condition.* New York: Basic Books, 1963, 151–171.

Friedmann, E.A., & Havighurst, R.J. (Eds.). *The Meaning of Work and Retirement.* Chicago: University of Chicago Press, 1954.

Fromm, E. *The Art of Loving.* New York: Bantam Books, 1963.

Fukuyama, Y. The major dimensions of church membership. *Review of Religious Research,* 1961, *2,* 154–161.

Fulton, R.L. Comments, symposium on attitudes toward death in older persons. *Journal of Gerontology,* 1961, *16,* 63–65.

Gallup, G.H., Jr., & Davies, J.O., III. *Gallup opinion index: Special report on religion.* Princeton, N.J.: American Institute of Public Opinion, 1969.

Geer, J.H. The development of a scale to measure fear. *Behavior Research and Therapy,* 1965, *3,* 45–53.

Gelwicks, L., Feldman, A., & Newcomer, R.J. *Report on older population: Needs, resources, services.* Los Angeles: Gerontology Center, University of Southern California, 1971.

Gilbert, G.M. Stereotype persistence and change among college students. *Journal of Abnormal and Social Psychology,* 1951, *46,* 245–254.

Glaser, B.G. The social loss of aged dying patients. *The Gerontologist,* 1966, *6,* 77–80.

Glaser, B.G. & Strauss, A.N. *Awareness of dying.* Chicago: Aldine, 1965.

Glaser, B.G., & Strauss, A.N. *Time for dying.* Chicago: Aldine, 1968.

Glenn, N.D. Aging, disengagement, and opinionation. *Public Opinion Quarterly,* 1969, *23,* 17–33.

Glick, I.O., & Levy, S.J. *Living with television.* Chicago: Aldine, 1962.

Glock, C.Y., Ringer, B.B., & Babbie, E.R. *To comfort and to challenge.* Berkeley: University of California Press, 1967.

Glock, C.Y., & Stark, R. *Religion and Society in Tension.* Chicago: Rand McNally, 1965.

Goldfarb, A.I. Psychotherapy of aged persons. *Psychoanalytic Review,* 1955, *42,* 180–187.

Goldfarb, A.I. Institutional care of the aged. In E.W. Busse & E. Pfeiffer (Eds.), *Behavioral adaptation in later life.* Boston: Little, Brown, 1969.

Goldscheider, C. Differential residential mobility of the older population. *Journal of Gerontology,* 1966, *21,* 103–108.

Goldsmith, J. Community crime prevention and the elderly: A segmental approach. *Crime Prevention Review,* 1975, *2,* 18–19.

Gottesman, L.E. Needed research on the mental health of the aged. In *A report of the Governor's Task Force on Aging.* Lansing: Michigan Commission on Aging, 1964, 15–20.

Gottesman, L.E. Organizing rehabilitation services for the elderly. *The Gerontologist,* 1970, *10,* 287–293.

Gottesman, L.E. Milieu treatment of the aged. *The Gerontologist,* 1973, *13,* 23–27.

Gottesman, L., Donahue, W., Coons, D., & Ciarlo, J. Extended care of the aged. *Journal of Geriatric Psychiatry,* 1969, *2,* 220–249.

Gottesman, L., Quarterman, C., & Cohn, G. Psycho-social treatment of the aged. In C. Eisdorfer & M.P. Lawton (Eds.), *Psychology of adult development and aging.* Washington, D.C.: American Psychological Association, 1973, 378–427.

Grannis, G. Demographic perturbations secondary to cigarette smoking. *Journal of Gerontology,* 1970, *25,* 55–63.

Gray, R.M., & Moberg, D.O. *The church and the older person.* Grand Rapids, Mich.: Eerdmans, 1962.

Gutherie, H.W. Intergenerational transfers of wealth and the theory of saving. *Journal of Business of the University of Chicago*, 1963, *36*, 97–108.

Guttman, D., Gottesman, L.E., & Tessler, S. A comparative study of ego functioning in geriatric patients. Paper presented at the Annual Meeting of the Gerontological Society, Denver, Colorado, November, 1968.

Hall, G., & Mathiesen, G. *Guide to development of protective services for older people*. Springfield, Ill.: Charles C Thomas, 1973.

Hammond, P.E. Aging and the ministry. In M.W. Riley, J.W. Riley, Jr., & M.E. Johnson (Eds.), *Aging and society, Volume II: Aging and the Professions*. New York: Russell Sage Foundation, 1969, 293–323.

Hansen, G.D. Meeting housing challenges: Involvement—the Elderly. In *Housing issues. Proceedings of the Fifth Annual Meeting, American Association of Housing Educators*. Lincoln: University of Nebraska Press, 1971.

Hansen, N.M. *Rural poverty and the urban crisis: A strategy for regional development*. Bloomington: Indiana University Press, 1970.

Harris, I. (Ed.) *Final report: Homemaker—public health nurse demonstration project serving incapacitated adults*. San Diego: Homemaker Service of San Diego, Inc., 1968.

Havighurst, R.J. The social competence of middle-aged people. *Genetic Psychology Monographs*, 1957, *56*, 297–375.

Havighurst, R.J. The nature and values of meaningful free-time activity. In R.W. Kleemeier (Ed.), *Aging and leisure*. New York: Oxford University Press, 1961, 309–344.

Havighurst, R.J. Successful aging. In R.H. Williams, C. Tibbitts, & W. Donahue (Eds.), *Processes of Aging* (Vol. I). New York: Atherton, 1963.

Havighurst, R.J. Research and development goals in social gerontology: Part II. *The Gerontologist*, 1969, *9*, (4, Part II).

Havighurst, R.J., & De Vries, A. Life styles and freetime activities of retired men. *Human Development*, 1969, *12*, 34–54.

Havighurst, R.J., Munnichs, J.M.A., Neugarten, B.L., & Thomae, H. *Adjustment to retirement: A cross-national study*. New York: Humanities Press; Assen, Netherlands: Van Gorcum, 1969.

Havighurst, R.J., Neugarten, B.L., & Tobin, S.S. Disengagement and patterns of aging. In B. Neugarten (Ed.), *Middle age and aging*. Chicago: University of Chicago Press, 1968.

Heimstra, R.P. Continuing education for the aged: A survey of needs and interests of older people. *Adult Education*, 1972, *22*, 100–109.

Hemmy, M., & Farrar, M. Protective services for older people. *Social Casework*, 1961, *42*, 16–20.

Heyman, D.K., & Jeffers, F.C. Wives and retirement: A pilot study. *Journal of Gerontology*, 1968, *22*, 488–496.

Hinton, J. *Dying*. Baltimore: Penguin Books, 1967.

Hixson, L.E. Non-threatening education for older adults. *Adult Leadership*, 1969, *18*, 84–85.

Howard, W. Population change in SMSA's and central cities, 1960–1970. Unpublished paper, Duke University Center for Demographic Studies, 1971.

Hsu, F.L.K. *The challenge of the American dream: The Chinese in the United States*. Belmont, Calif.: Wadsworth, 1971.

Institute for Interdisciplinary Studies. *Tabulations of community forum questionnaires for 1971 White House Conference on Aging*. Minneapolis: American Rehabilitation Foundation, 1971.

Jaffe, A.J. Has the retreat from the labor force halted? A note on the retirement of men, 1930-1970. *Industrial Gerontology,* 1971, *9,* 1-12.

Jaffe, A.J. Pension systems—How much myth? How much reality? Paper presented at the 10th International Congress of Gerontology, Jerusalem, June, 1975.

Jeffers, F.C., Nichols, C.R., & Eisdorfer, C. Attitudes of older persons toward death: A preliminary study. *Journal of Gerontology,* 1961, *16,* 53-56.

Johnstone, J.W.C., & Rivera, R.J. *Volunteers for learning: A study of the educational pursuits of American adults.* Chicago: Aldine, 1965.

Jones, M. *The therapeutic community.* New York: Basic Books, 1953.

Kahn, R.L. Emotional needs of older people. Paper read at American Psychological Association, Chicago, September, 1965.

Kalish, R.A. Sex and marital role differences in anticipation of age-produced dependency. *Journal of Genetic Psychology,* 1971, *119,* 53-62.

Kalish, R.A. Of social values and the dying: A defense of disengagement. *Family Coordinator,* 1972, *21,* 81-94.

Kalish, R.A., & Johnson, A.I. Value similarities and differences in three generations of women. *Journal of Marriage and the Family,* 1972, *34,* 49-54.

Kalish, R.A., & Reynolds, D.K. *Death and ethnicity: A psychocultural study.* Los Angeles: University of Southern California Press, 1976.

Kastenbaum, R. As the clock runs out. *Mental Hygiene,* 1966a, *50,* 332-336.

Kastenbaum, R. On the meaning of time in later life. *Journal of Genetic Psychology,* 1966b, *109,* 9-25.

Kastenbaum, R. Death and bereavement in later life. In A.H. Kutscher (Ed.), *Death and bereavement.* Springfield, Ill.: Charles C Thomas, 1969, 28-54.

Katz, D., & Braly, K.W. Racial stereotypes of 100 college students. *Journal of Social and Abnormal Psychology,* 1933, *28,* 280-290.

Kent, D.P. Aging: Fact and fancy. *The Gerontologist,* 1965, *5,* 51-56.

Kent, D.P., & Hirsch, C. *Needs and use of services among Negro and white aged, Vols. I & II.* University Park: Pennsylvania State University, 1971 & 1972.

Kerckhoff, A.C. Family patterns and morale in retirement. In I.H. Simpson & J.C. McKinney (Eds.), *Social aspects of aging.* Durham, N.C.: Duke University Press, 1966a, 173-192.

Kerckhoff, A.C. Husband-wife expectations and reactions to retirement. In I.H. Simpson & J.C. McKinney (Eds.), *Social aspects of aging.* Durham, N.C.: Duke University Press, 1966b, 160-172.

Kimsey, L.R., Roberts, J.L., & Logan, O.L. Death, dying, and denial in the aged. *American Journal of Psychiatry,* 1972, *129,* 161-166.

Kimura, Y. War brides in Hawaii and their in-laws. *American Journal of Sociology,* 1957, *63,* 70-76.

Kinsey, A.C., Pomeroy, W.B., & Martin, C.E. *Sexual behavior in the human male.* Philadelphia: Saunders, 1948.

Kinsey, A.C., Pomeroy, W.B., Martin, C.E., & Gebhard, P.H. *Sexual behavior in the human female.* Philadelphia: Saunders, 1953.

Kitano, H.H.L. *Japanese Americans: The evolution of a subculture.* Englewood Cliffs, N.J.: Prentice-Hall, 1969.

Kleppner, O. *Advertising procedure.* Englewood Cliffs, N.J.: Prentice-Hall, 1966.

Kogan, N., & Wallach, M. Age changes in values and attitudes. *Journal of Gerontology,* 1961, *16,* 272-280.

Kramer, M., Taube, C.A., & Redick, R.W. Patterns of use of psychiatric facilities by the aged: Past, present, and future. In C. Eisdorfer & M.P. Lawton (Eds.), *The psychology of adult development and aging.* Washington, D.C.: American Psychological Association, 1973, 428-528.

Kramer, M. Mental health of the aged. *Psychiatric Research Reports,* 1968, *23.*

Kramer, M. Problems in psychiatric epidemiology. *Proceedings of the Royal Society of Medicine,* 1970, *63,* 553–562.

Kreps, J.M. (Ed.) *The employment, income, and retirement problems of the aged.* Durham, N.C.: Duke University Press, 1963.

Kreps, J.M. The economics of intergenerational relationships. In E. Shanas & G. Streib (Eds.), *Social structure and the family: Generational relations.* Englewood Cliffs, N.J.: Prentice-Hall, 1965.

Kubler-Ross, E. *On death and dying.* New York: Macmillan, 1969.

Kuhlen, R.G. Aging and life-adjustment. In J.E. Birren (Ed.), *Handbook of aging and the individual.* Chicago: University of Chicago Press, 1959.

Lawton, A.H. Accidental injuries to the aged. *The Gerontologist,* 1965, *5,* 96–100.

Lawton, A.H. Accidental injuries to the aged and their psychological impact. *Mayo Clinic Proceedings,* 1967, *47,* 685–697.

Lear, T.E. Sharing the care of the elderly between community and hospital. *Lancet,* 1969, *2,* 1349–1353.

Lenzer, A. Mobility patterns among the aged, 1955–1960. *The Gerontologist,* 1965, *5,* 12–15.

Levi, A. Treatment of disorder of perception and concept formation in a case of school failure. *Journal of Consulting Psychology,* 1965, *29,* 289–295.

Lieberman, P., Green, R., & Lieberman, V. Outpatient group therapy with geriatric patients. *Geriatrics,* 1968, *22,* 148–153.

Linton, R. A neglected aspect of social organization. *American Journal of Sociology,* 1940, *45,* 870–886.

Liveright, A.A. *Study of adult education in the United States.* Boston: Center for the Study of Liberal Education for Adults, 1968.

Londoner, C.A. Survival needs of the aged: Implications for program planning. *Aging and Human Development,* 1971, *2,* 113–117.

Lowi, T.J. *The end of liberalism.* New York: Norton, 1969.

Maddox, G.L. Persistence of life style among the elderly. In B.L. Neugarten (Ed.), *Middle age and aging.* Chicago: University of Chicago Press, 1968.

Madsen, W. *The Mexican-Americans of South Texas.* New York: Holt, Rinehart & Winston, 1964.

Man and his years. An Account of the First National Conference on Aging, sponsored by the Federal Security Agency, 1951.

Martin, D., & Wrightsman, L. The relationship between religious behavior and concern about death. *Journal of Social Psychology,* 1965, *65,* 317–323.

Martin, J., & Doran, A. Perception of retirement: Time and season. University of Liverpool, 1966. Unpublished paper.

Mathiesen, G. Current status of services to the aging. In J.L. Gorn (Ed.), *Social work education for better services to the aging. Proceedings of seminar on the aging,* Aspen, Colo., 1958. New York: Council on Social Work Education, 1959.

Maves, P.B. Aging, religion, and the church. In C. Tibbitts (Ed.), *Handbook of social gerontology.* Chicago: University of Chicago Press, 1960.

McClusky, H.Y. *Education: background and issues.* White House Conference on Aging. Washington, D.C.: U.S. Government Printing Office, 1971.

McGuire, C. Index of status characteristics. In C. McGuire, *Social status, peer status, and social mobility.* Chicago: University of Chicago Press, 1949.

McKain, W.C. *Retirement marriage.* Storrs, Conn.: Agricultural Experiment Station, The University of Connecticut, 1969.

McNevin, T.E., & Rosencranz, H.A. Racial differences in life satisfaction and adjustment between welfare and non-welfare, non-institutionalized, aged males. In *Long-range program and research needs in aging and related fields.* Hearings before the Special Committees on Aging, December 5-6. Washington, D.C.: U.S. Government Printing Office, 1967.

Merriam, I.C. Implications of technological change for income. In J.M. Kreps (Ed.), *Technology, manpower, & retirement policy*. Cleveland: World Publishing, 1966.

Messer, M. The possibility of an age-concentrated environment becoming a normative system. *The Gerontologist*, 1967, *7*, 247–251.

Meyersohn, R. An examination of commercial entertainment. In R.W. Kleemeier (Ed.), *Aging and leisure*. New York: Oxford University Press, 1961.

Midwest Research Institute. *Interim report—crimes against aging Americans—the Kansas City Study*. 1975.

Miller, R. Social Security: The cruelest tax. *Harper's Magazine*, 1974, *248*, 22–27.

Miller, S.J. The social dilemma of the aging leisure participant. In A.M. Rose & W.A. Peterson (Eds.), *Older people and their social world*. Philadelphia: F.A. Davis, 1965.

Moberg, D.O. Church membership and personal adjustment in old age. *Journal of Gerontology*, 1953, *8*, 207–211.

Moberg, D.O. Religiosity in old age. *The Gerontologist*, 1965, *5*, 78–87; 111–112.

Moberg, D.O. Aging and its implications for theological education. *Journal of Pastoral Care*, 1970, *24*, 127–134.

Moberg, D.O. *Spiritual well-being*. White House Conference on Aging Background and Issues. Washington, D.C.: U.S. Government Printing Office, 1971.

Montgomery, J.E. *Social characteristics of the aged in a small Pennsylvania community*. State College, Pa.: College of Home Economics Research Publication 233, The Pennsylvania State University, 1965.

Montgomery, J.E. Living arrangements and housing of the rural aged in a central Pennsylvania community. In F.M. Carp (Ed.), *Patterns of living and housing of middle-aged and older people*. Washington, D.C.: U.S. Government Printing Office, 1966, 83–96.

Montgomery, J.E. Housing imperatives. In *Proceedings of a Conference on Housing Today and Tomorrow*. University of Maryland, 1970, 1–10.

Morgan, J. Economic problems of the aging and their policy implications. Paper presented for a conference on Public Policy Assessment of the Conditions and Status of the Elderly, February, 1975.

Morris, R. Principles and processes of community planning, coordination, and development. In *Planning welfare services for older people*. Papers presented at the Training Institute for Public Welfare Specialists in Aging, Cleveland, June 13–24, 1965. Washington, D.C.: U.S. Government Printing Office, 1965.

Mumford, L. The highway and the city. In G. DeBell (Ed.), *The environmental handbook*. New York: Ballantine Books, 1970.

Myers, G.C. Changing mortality patterns and sex imbalance among the aged. Paper presented at the 10th International Congress of Gerontology, Jerusalem, June 22–27, 1975.

The nation and its older people. Appendix A in *Report of the White House Conference on Aging*, Washington, D.C.: U.S. Government Printing Office, 1961.

National Center for Health Statistics. *Final Mortality Statistics, 1974*. Vol. 24, February 3, 1976.

National Council on the Aging. *The myth and reality of aging in America*. Washington, D.C.: Author, 1975.

Neugarten, B.L. Age groups in American society and the rise of the young-old. *Annals of the American Academy of Political and Social Science*, 1974, *415*, 187–198.

Neugarten, B.L. (Ed.) *Personality in middle and later life*. New York: Atherton, 1964.

Neugarten, B.L., Moore, J.W., & Lowe, J.C. Age norms, age constraints, and adult socialization. *American Journal of Sociology,* 1965, *70,* 710–717.

Niebanck, P.L., & Pope, J.B. *The elderly in older urban areas.* Philadelphia: Institute for Environmental Studies, University of Pennsylvania, 1965.

Nielsen, A.C. NSI Los Angeles instantaneous audimeter: Television audience estimates. Chicago: Media Research Division, A.C. Nielsen Co., 1973.

Oakes, C.G. Conclusion: Aging in perspective. In R.R. Boyd & C.G. Oakes (Eds.), *Foundations of practical gerontology.* Columbia, S.C.: University of South Carolina Press, 1969, 217–235.

Oberleder, M. Aging: Its importance for clinical psychology. In L.E. Abt & B.F. Riess (Eds.), *Progress in clinical psychology.* New York: Grune & Stratton, 1964, 158–171.

O'Reilly, C.T. Religious practice and personal adjustment of older people. *Sociology and Social Research,* 1957, 42, 119–121.

Ostfeld, A. Frequency and nature of health problems of retired persons. In F.M. Carp (Ed.), *The retirement process.* Washington, D.C.: U.S. Government Printing Office, 1968.

Pattison, E.M. Help in the dying process. *Voices: The Art and Science of Psychotherapy,* 1969, *5,* 6–14.

Peterson, D.A. Education and the older American. *Adult Leadership,* 1971, *19,* 263.

Pihlblad, C.T., & Rosencranz, H.A. *Social Adjustment of Older People in the Small Town, 4,* No. 1. Columbia: University of Missouri Press, 1969.

Pressey, S.L., & Pressey, A. Two insiders searching for best life in old age. *The Gerontologist,* 1966, *6,* 14–16.

Reichard, S., Livson, F., & Petersen, P.G. *Aging and personality.* New York: John Wiley, 1962.

Riley, J.W., Jr. What people think about death. In O.G. Brim, Jr., H.E. Freeman, S. Levine, & N.A. Scotch (Eds.), *The dying patient.* New York: Russell Sage Foundation, 1970.

Riley, M.W., Foner, A., et al. *Aging and society.* New York: Russell Sage Foundation, 1968.

Robb, T.B. *The bonus years: Foundation for ministry with older persons.* Valley Forge, Pa.: Judson Press, 1968.

Robbins, I.S. *Housing the elderly. Background and issues.* White House Conference on Aging, Washington, D.C.: U.S. Government Printing Office, 1971.

Roche Laboratories. Aspects of anxiety #1: "Flight or fight": the nature and meaning of anxiety. New Jersey: Roche Laboratories, 1963.

Roper, B.W. *An extended view of public attitudes toward television and other mass media, 1959–1971.* New York: The Roper Organization, 1971.

Rose, A., & Peterson, W.A. (Eds.) *Older people and their social world.* Philadelphia: F.A. Davis, 1965.

Rosow, I. Old age: One moral dilemma of an affluent society. *The Gerontologist,* 1962, *2,* 182–191.

Rosow, I. *Social integration of the aged.* New York: The Free Press, 1967.

Rossi, P. *Why families move.* Glencoe, Ill.: The Free Press, 1955.

Rubel, A.J. *Across the tracks—Mexican-Americans in a Texas city.* Austin: The University of Texas Press, 1966.

Rubin, I. *Sexual life after sixty.* New York: Basic Books, 1965.

Rustin, S.L., & Wolk, R.L. The use of specialized group psychotherapy techniques in a home for the aged. In J.L. Moreno (Ed.), *Group psychotherapy, Vol. XVI.* Beacon, N.Y.: Beacon House, 1963.

Ryser, C., & Sheldon, A. Retirement and health. *Journal of the American Geriatrics Society,* 1969, *17,* 180–190.

Sauer, H., & Donnell, H. Age and geographic differences in death rates. *Journal of Gerontology*, 1970, *25*, 83–86.

Saunders, R., Smith, R.S., & Weinman, B. *Chronic psychoses and recovery.* San Francisco: Jossey Bass, 1967.

Schramm, W. Aging and mass communication. In M.W. Riley, *Aging and society, Vol. II: Aging and the professions.* New York: Russell Sage Foundation, 1969.

Schulz, J.H. Some economics of aged home ownership. *The Gerontologist*, 1967, *7*, 73–74; 80.

Schulz, J.H. *The economics of aging.* Belmont, Calif.: Wadsworth, 1976.

SERVE's success invites imitation. *Aging*, 1968, *170*, 7–10.

SERVE's volunteers help the mentally ill. *SERVE Newsletter*, 1970, *14*, 1; 6–7.

Shanas, E. *Family relationships of older people.* Health Information Foundation Research Series, No. 20. New York: Health Information Foundation, 1961.

Shanas, E., Townsend, P., Wedderburn, D., Henning, F., Milhoj, P., & Stehouwer, J. *Old people in three industrial societies.* New York: Atherton, 1968.

Shapiro, H.D. *The New York Times Book Review*, Nov. 15, 1975, 8.

Sharma, K.L., & Jain, U.C. Religiosity and fear of death in young and retired persons. *Indian Journal of Gerontology*, 1969, *1*, 110–114.

Simmons, L. *The role of the aged in primitive society.* New Haven: Yale University Press, 1945.

Simon, A., Lowenthal, M.F., & Epstein, L. *Crisis and intervention.* San Francisco: Jossey Bass, 1970.

Simpson, I.H., Back, K.W., & McKinney, J.C. Continuity of work and retirement activities. In I.H. Simpson & J.C. McKinney (Eds.), *Social aspects of aging.* Durham, N.C.: Duke University Press, 1966a, 106–119.

Simpson, I.H., Back, K.W., & McKinney, J.C. Work and retirement. In I.H. Simpson & J.C. McKinney (Eds.), *Social aspects of aging.* Durham, N.C.: Duke University Press, 1966b, 45–54.

Sotomayor, M. Mexican-American interaction with social systems. *Social Casework*, 1971, *5*, 321.

Spengler, J.J. *Stationary population and changes in age structure: Implications for the economic security of the aged.* Durham, N.C.: Duke University Press, 1975.

Stark, R. Age and faith: A changing outlook or an old process? *Sociological Analysis*, 1968, *29*, 1–10.

Statistical Bulletin. *Diverse longevity trends for older men and women.* New York: Metropolitan Life Insurance Company, (Oct.) 1964, *45*, 3–6.

Steglich, W.C., et. al. *Survey of needs and resources among aged Mexican-Americans.* Lubbock: Texas Technical College, 1968.

Stehouwer, J. The household and family relation of old people. In E. Shanas et al., *Old people in three industrial societies.* New York: Atherton, 1968.

Steiner, G.A. *The people look at television.* New York: Knopf, 1963.

Streib, G.F. Family patterns in retirement. *Journal of Social Issues*, 1958, *14*(2), 46–60.

Streib, G.F., & Schneider, C.J. *Retirement in American society.* Ithaca, N.Y.: Cornell University Press, 1971.

Stringfellow, W. The representation of the poor in American society. *Law and Contemporary Problems*, 1966, *31*, 142–151.

Suchman, E., Streib, G.F., & Phillips, B. An analysis of the validity of health questionnaires. *Social Forces*, 1958, *36*, 223–232.

Sussman, M.B. Relationships of adult children with their parents in the United States. In E. Shanas & G.F. Streib (Eds.), *Social structure and the family.* Englewood Cliffs, N.J.: Prentice-Hall, 1965, 62–92.

Sussman, R.B., & Steinberg, F. The aged in public housing. Unpublished paper.

Swenson, W.M. Approaches to the study of religion and aging. In *Religion and aging.* Los Angeles: Andrus Gerontology Center, University of Southern California, 1967, 59–84.

Templer, D.I., Ruff, C., & Frank, C. Death and anxiety: Age, sex, and parental resemblance in diverse populations. *Developmental Psychology, 1971, 4,* 108.

Thompson, W.E., & Streib, G.F. Situational determinants: Health and economic deprivation in retirement. *Journal of Social Issues,* 1958, *14*(2), 18–34.

Thompson, W.E., Streib, G.F., & Kosa, J. The effect of retirement on personal adjustment: A panel analysis. *Journal of Gerontology,* 1960, *14,* 165–169.

Thornton, R., & Nam, C. The lower mortality rates of nonwhites at the older ages: An enigma in demographic analysis. *Research Reprints in the Social Sciences,* 1968, *11,* 1–8.

Townsend, P. *The family life of old people.* London: Routledge & Kegan Paul, 1957.

Townsend, P. Welfare services and the family. In E. Shanas, et al. (Eds.), *Old people in three industrial societies.* New York: Atherton, 1968.

Treanton, J.R. Comments, Symposium on Attitudes Toward Death in Older Persons. *Journal of Gerontology,* 1961, *16,* 63.

Tunstall, J. *Old and alone: A sociological study of old people.* London: Routledge & Kegan Paul, 1966.

U.S. Bureau of the Census. *Current population reports,* Series P-20, No. 243. Educational attainment: March, 1972. Washington, D.C.: U.S. Government Printing Office, 1972.

U.S. Bureau of the Census. *Current population reports,* Series P-23, No. 43, Some demographic aspects of aging in the United States. (By Jacob Siegel). Washington, D.C.: U.S. Government Printing Office, February, 1973.

U.S. Bureau of the Census. *Current population reports,* Series P-23, No. 59, Demographic aspects of aging and the older population in the United States. (By Jacob Siegel). Washington, D.C.: U.S. Government Printing Office, May, 1976.

U.S. Census of Housing. Homeowner properties. *Residential finance,* 1960, *5,* 1.

U.S. Department of Health, Education, & Welfare, National Center for Health Statistics. *National health survey.* Washington, D.C.: U.S. Government Printing Office, 1967.

U.S. Department of Health, Education, & Welfare, Vocational Rehabilitation Department. *For the disabled: Help through vocational rehabilitation.* Washington, D.C.: U.S. Government Printing Office, 1967.

U.S. Department of Health, Education, & Welfare, National Center for Education Statistics. *Participation in adult education: Initial report, 1969.* (By Imogene E. Okes), Washington, D.C.: U.S. Government Printing Office, 1971.

U.S. Senate, Committee on Labor and Public Welfare, Subcommittee on Aging, and the Special Committee on Aging, *White House Conference on Aging Reports, 1973.* Washington, D.C.: U.S. Government Printing Office, 1973.

Vital and Health Statistics, National Health Survey. Prevalence of chronic conditions and impairments among residents of nursing and personal care homes. National Center for Health Statistics, Series 12, No. 8, 1967.

Wasser, E. *Creative approaches in casework with the aging.* New York: Family Service Association of America, 1966.

Wasser, E. Protective practice in serving the mentally impaired aging. *Social Casework,* 1971, *52,* 510–522.

Weintraub, W., & Aranson, H. A survey of patients in classical psychoanalysis: Some vital statistics. *Journal of Nervous and Mental Disease,* 1968, *146,* 98–102.

Weiss, J.D. *Better buildings for the aged.* New York: Hopkinson and Blake, 1969.

Wenger, D.L., & Fletcher, C.R. The effect of legal counsel on admissions to the state mental hospital: A confrontation of professions. *Journal of Health and Social Behavior*, 1969, *10*, 66–69.

Wickenden, E. *The needs of older people*. Chicago: American Public Welfare Association, 1953.

Williams, R.H., & Wirths, C.G. *Lives through the years*. New York: Atherton, 1965.

Wolff, K. Group psychotherapy with geriatric patients in a state hospital setting: Results of a three year study. *Group Psychotherapy*, 1959, *12*, 218–222.

Wolff, K. Group psychotherapy. *Journal of the American Geriatric Society*, 1962, *10*, 1077–1080.

Wolk, R.L., Reder, E.L., Seiden, R.B., & Solomon, V. 5-year psychiatric assessment of the patients in an out-patient geriatric guidance clinic. *Journal of the American Geriatric Society*, 1965, *13*, 222–229.

Wood, V. Age-appropriate behavior for older people. *The Gerontologist*, 1971, *11*, 74–78.

Zinberg, N.E. Geriatric psychiatry: Need and problems. *The Gerontologist*, 1964, *4*, 130–135.

Zelditch, M., Jr. Role differentiation in the nuclear family: A comparative study. In N.W. Bell & E.F. Vogel (Eds.), *A modern introduction to the family*. New York: The Free Press, 1968.

Zelditch, M., & Bram, H.B. The modern home for the aged. *The Gerontologist*, 1965, *5*(2), 67–73.

Appendix A

The Contributors

Robert C. Atchley is Professor of Sociology, Miami University, Oxford, Ohio, and Director of the Scripps Foundation Gerontology Center. Author of a well-known text on aging, Dr. Atchley uses his time writing, doing research on aging and migration, and teaching gerontology.

Vern Bengtson received his Ph.D. from the University of Chicago, then migrated West to the University of Southern California where he is now Associate Professor of Sociology and Laboratory Chief in the Andrus Gerontology Center.

Allen Bernard was a journalist who became interested in aging many years ago and developed a bi-monthly publication, *Geriatric Focus,* under the sponsorship of Knoll Pharmaceutical Company. For many years, until shortly before his death, he was a well-known figure at any meeting that concerned the field of aging, and his work gained the respect of both professional gerontologists and the health community for which he wrote.

Robert H. Binstock earned a doctorate in political science from Harvard University. He is presently Louis Stulberg Professor of Law and Politics at Brandeis University, Waltham, Mass., and is associated with both the Department of Politics and the Graduate School of Social Welfare. He served as President of the Gerontological Society in 1975–1976, and as Director of the White House Task Force on Older Americans under President Lyndon B. Johnson in 1967–1968.

When *Margaret Blenkner* died in 1973, she left a large gap in the field of social gerontology. Her writing and her research in social work and aging earned her a national reputation, based in part on her leadership at the Benjamin Rose Clinic in Cleveland, Ohio.

The only architect represented in this volume, *Thomas O. Byerts* is Director, Architecture and Environment, for the Gerontological Society in Washington, D. C. He received a Master of Architecture degree from the University of Southern California in 1970. Mr. Byerts has recently co-edited *Community Planning for an Aging Society* with Drs. Powell Lawton and Robert Newcomer. He also serves as chairman of the U.S. Editorial Board of the *Journal of Architectural Research.*

Marjorie H. Cantor is presently Director of Research, Planning, and Evaluation in the New York City Department for the Aging, with which she has been affiliated since 1968. Prior to that, she was on the faculty of the Fordham University School of Social Work. Ms. Cantor has been an active advocate for the inner city elderly, having succeeded in obtaining several substantial grants from the federal government to support and study such projects as an alternative transportation system for the elderly and the handicapped and a program for the mentally frail elderly.

Frances M. Carp received her doctorate in clinical psychology from Stanford University in 1950 and subsequently served for 12 years as professor and chairman of the Department of Psychology at Trinity University in San Antonio, Texas. She later was affiliated with the National Institute of Child Health and Human Development in Washington, D.C., the University of California, San Francisco Medical Center, and the University of California, Berkeley. Writer and editor of four books and over 100 professional articles and book reviews, she is now at the Wright Institute in Berkeley.

One of the few economists who has had a long-standing interest in aging, Dr. *Y. P. Chen* held a Brookings Research Professorship and was subsequently on the faculty at the University of Wisconsin and the University of Washington. He is presently Associate Professor of Economics at UCLA.

Richard H. Davis is Director of Publications and Media Projects for the Andrus Gerontology Center at the University of Southern California. He has developed courses in media and aging at this university, where he also received his Ph.D., and where he has conducted a series of research projects with older viewers. His community activities include consultation on major television specials about aging for all networks.

Carl Eisdorfer received the doctorate in psychology from New York University in 1959 and a medical degree from Duke University in 1964. After 16 years on the faculty at Duke University, where he was also Director of the Center for Studies of Aging and Human Development, he was appointed Chairman of the Department of Psychiatry and Behavioral Sciences, University of Washington. A past president of the Gerontological Society, Dr. Eisdorfer is also chairman of the Advisory Committee for *Over Easy,* the educational television program directed at an audience of persons in their later years.

Elliott Feigenbaum is a psychiatrist in private practice in San Francisco, where he also serves on the City's Commission on Aging. Before entering practice on a fulltime basis, Dr. Feigenbaum was on the faculty of the Department of Psychiatry, University of California, San Francisco Medical Center.

A University of Chicago Ph.D., *Leonard E. Gottesman* was associated with the Institute of Gerontology, University of Michigan, for several years. He is now Senior Research Psychologist at the Philadelphia Geriatric Center where he directs several research and community-service projects.

Well-known in the field of childhood education, *Robert J. Havighurst* has also had a lengthy involvement in gerontology. His extensive writings, research activities, and community involvements have spanned a 40-year period, and today, at an age when most people are retired, he continues to be active and to serve as Professor of Education and Human Development at the Graduate School of Education, University of Chicago.

Dorothy K. Heyman, M.S.W., is a Research Social Worker in the Geriatrics Research Project at the Duke University Medical Center. Since 1971 she has also been Assistant Professor of Psychiatric Social Work and Executive Secretary of the Center for the Study of Aging and Human Development at the same institution.

Mark H. Ingraham is Dean Emeritus of the College of Arts and Sciences, University of Wisconsin. Dr. Ingraham is a former trustee of the Teachers University of Wisconsin. A mathematician by training, Dr. Ingraham has published extensively and has also served in advisory capacities for numerous public organizations.

Presently Associate Professor of Medical Sociology, Department of Psychiatry, Duke University School of Medicine, Dr. *Jacquelyne J. Jackson* earned the doctorate in sociology from the Ohio State University in 1960. Her recent work has been particularly concerned with aging among Black Americans, and she has been active in research, writing, and advocacy.

After receiving a doctorate in social psychology at Case-Western Reserve University, *Richard A. Kalish* joined the faculty at the University of Hawaii and later taught at California State University, Los Angeles, and at UCLA. He is now associated with the Graduate Theological Union in Berkeley, where he spent three years as a National Institutes of Health Research Fellow.

Prior to her appointment by President Carter as Secretary of Commerce, *Juanita Kreps* was James B. Duke Professor of Economics and Vice-President of Duke University. Among her numerous writings are books on work and income and on the impact of women in the labor force.

A British physician, *Sylvia A. Lack* worked with St. Christopher's Hospice in London prior to becoming Medical Director of Hospice, Inc., the first United States venture with hospice.

A clinical psychologist with a doctorate from Columbia University, *M. Powell Lawton* has been Director of Behavioral Research at the Philadelphia Geriatric Center since 1963. Dr. Lawton has written and edited several books and innumerable articles, most recently focusing his attention on environmental psychology and aging, with particular emphasis on housing the elderly. He has served as Secretary of the Gerontological Society and as President of the Division of Adult Development and Aging, American Psychological Association.

After receiving her M.A. in Public Health at UCLA, *Joyce Leanse* moved to Washington, D.C., where she is now with the National Council on the Aging as Director of their National Institute of Senior Centers. Ms. Leanse co-authored a national study on senior centers and is currently directing a project to develop standards for senior centers.

Anthony Lenzer earned a doctorate in sociology from the University of Michigan where he taught at the School of Public Health for several years before he became Professor of Public Health and Human Development at the University of Hawaii. There he also serves as Director of the Gerontology Training Program, a joint project of the Schools of Public Health and Social Work. Dr. Lenzer is particularly interested in health services and health institutions as they involve the elderly.

Don R. Lipsitt is Chief of Psychiatry, Mount Auburn Hospital, Cambridge, Massachusetts, and also serves as Associate Professor, Harvard Medical School. He is also Psychoanalyst, Boston Psychoanalytic Society and Institute, and Editor of the *International Journal of Psychiatry in Medicine,* which he founded in 1970.

David Maldonado, Jr., is Assistant Professor, Graduate School of Social Work, University of Texas, Arlington. His doctorate in social welfare was recently granted by the University of California, Berkeley, where he began his present involvement with the extended family and the impact of ethnicity on social services.

Philip Meyer is a journalist whose writing covers a variety of topics and is frequently carried in syndicated articles through the Knight News Wire Service.

David O. Moberg joined the faculty of Marquette University in 1968 as Professor of Sociology and Chairman of the Department of Sociology and Anthropology. After he received a Ph.D. from the University of Minnesota, Dr. Moberg taught at Bethel College in St. Paul, at the University of Washington, and as Fulbright lecturer in both the Netherlands and West Germany. He has authored or co-authored four books, one of which, *The Church and the Older Person,* was published in revised form in 1977.

At the time he wrote this article, *James E. Montgomery* was Professor and Head of the Department of Management, Housing, and Family Development, Virginia Polytechnic Institute and State University. In 1976, he moved to Athens, Georgia, where he became Chairman of the Gerontology Faculty, University of Georgia.

After completing her doctorate in sociology at the University of Southern California, *Sharon Moriwaki* taught at USC and conducted research on suicide prevention with the Veteran's Administration. She recently accepted the position of Director of Training for the California Department of Aging.

James M. Mulanaphy is a Research Specialist with the Teachers Insurance and Annuity Association and its companion organization, College Retirement Equities Fund.

Demographer *George C. Myers* is at Duke University, where he is Director of the Center for Demographic Studies, a Professor of Sociology and a Senior Fellow of the Center for the Study of Aging and Human Development. He also serves as a member of the Aging Review Committee of the National Institute on Aging.

Paul S. Nathanson, an attorney, is Executive Director of the National Senior Citizens Law Center in Los Angeles.

Muriel F. Oberleder is a long-time New Yorker. She received her doctorate in clinical psychology from Columbia University in 1957 and has been in private practice since that time. She also holds a clinical appointment at the Albert Einstein College of Medicine at Columbia University.

David A. Peterson received the Ph.D. in Adult Education from the University of Michigan where he later served as chairman of the Department of Educational Gerontology. He is now Director of the Gerontology Program at the University of Nebraska at Omaha.

At the time her contribution was written, *Grace H. Polansky,* M.S.S.A., was Associate in Psychiatric Social Work, Department of Psychiatry, Duke University School of Medicine. Ms. Polansky died in 1975.

Physician *Manuel Rodstein* is the Chief of Medical Services and Director of Cardiology, The Jewish Home and Hospital for the Aged, New York City. He is also affiliated with the Albert Einstein College of Medicine as Associate Clinical Professor, and is Director of the Zeman Center for Instruction in the Care of the Aged.

Sylvia Sherwood, Ph.D., is Director of Social Gerontological Research at the Hebrew Rehabilitation Center for Aged, Boston. A sociologist by training, she is particularly interested in action research as a laboratory for testing theories of behavior. Her on-going interest in nutrition for the elderly is one of several active concerns she maintains in gerontology.

Herbert Shore came to Golden Acres, the Dallas Home for the Jewish Aged, in 1953 as its first director. Now, nearly a quarter of a century later, he and Golden Acres have both become nationally recognized as leaders in the field. Dr. Shore has been President of the National Association of Jewish Homes for the Aged, President of the Texas Gerontological Society, and President of the American Association of Homes for the Aged.

Beth J. Soldo is the Assistant Director of the Center for Demographic Studies, Duke University, where she received a Ph.D. in Demography. Dr. Soldo has a primary interest in developing a demographic perspective on gerontological research problems.

Recently appointed Graduate Research Professor at the University of Florida, *Gordon F. Streib* was on the faculty of the Department of Sociology at Cornell University for many years. He has written and edited several books and innumerable articles, primarily on topics related to aging.

C.J. Tupper is Professor of Internal Medicine and Dean of the School of Medicine at the University of California, Davis. He was formerly at the University of Michigan where he was active in the gerontological research program and the Faculty Periodic Health Appraisal Program.

One of the very few authors in this volume who is neither a gerontologist nor affiliated with a university or research institute, *Evelle Younger* is Attorney General for the State of California, an office to which he was elected in 1970 and re-elected in 1974. Prior to that, Mr. Younger was district attorney for the County of Los Angeles.

Appendix B

Some Organizations Serving the Elderly in the United States

The *Administration on Aging* is part of the United States Department of Health, Education, and Welfare. It provides funds to carefully selected programs dedicated to improving the physical and personal conditions of the elderly. Among its recent concerns are improved nutrition, alternatives to institutionalization, and better housing and transportation. Although the AOA headquarters are in Washington, D.C., there are regional offices in major cities throughout the country. In addition, each state has a department on aging, funded partly through the AOA and usually located in the state capital.

The *American Association of Homes for the Aging* represents nonprofit homes for the aging, including those that are under the auspices of churches, communities, one or another branch of government, or fraternal orders such as the Elks and Masons. The profit-making version of the AAHA is the *American Nursing Home Association,* whose member facilities are owned by individuals or corporations.

The *American Association of Retired Persons,* in conjunction with the *National Retired Teachers Association,* is a private, nonprofit organization operated for the benefit of its membership, almost all of whom are elderly. It distributes a highly readable publication, offers health and automobile insurance, has its own travel agency, supplies low-cost pharmaceuticals by mail, and does some lobbying on behalf of the elderly. Dues are very low, and its membership numbers in the millions.

The *American Geriatrics Society* restricts its membership to physicians with an interest in practice, administration, or research with the elderly.

The *Gerontological Society* has a membership consisting primarily of academics and other professionals concerned with the elderly and with the aging process. Most members participate in one of its four sections: Biological Sciences, Clinical Medicine, Behavioral and Social Sciences, and Social Research, Planning, and Practice. Some are members-at-large without sectional affiliation. Its headquarters are in Washington, D.C., but its annual meetings have been held in such cities as Miami, San Juan, Toronto, and Portland, Oregon.

The *Gray Panthers* are a political pressure group with a membership consisting largely but not exclusively of older persons. As their name suggests, they are often militant in their demands, which include improved economic conditions and better health care.

The *National Caucus on the Black Aging* was initiated a few years ago in response to the feelings of many people that the Black elderly could best be represented by other Blacks. Its leadership consists of Blacks, and its efforts are directed toward the problems of the Black aging, but it simultaneously serves as advocate for elderly people in general, and it has many non-Black members. Its headquarters are in Washington, D.C.

The *National Council on the Aging,* a volunteer agency headquartered in Washington, D.C., is a membership organization of professionals in the field of aging. Both individual and organizational memberships are available. The NCOA attempts to improve the condition and the image of all elderly people through providing information, holding national and regional meetings, planning and conducting educational and training programs, undertaking research, and publishing relevant materials. It is also involved in formulating public policy and in providing technical assistance to private and public agencies.

The *National Council of Senior Citizens* is primarily a membership organization of groups of retired people who are involved in advocating help for the elderly. They have a low-cost travel program, a low-cost drug-buying club, and low-cost insurance.

The *National Interfaith Coalition on Aging* attempts to disseminate information on aging and the elderly to church groups. The organization is very recently formed and has recently conducted a major national study of resources, both present and potential, that exist for the elderly within various church denominations.

Senior Advocates has been recently instituted as a membership organization whose goals are to provide services for the elderly and to serve as their advocate in increasing available resources through both public and private sectors.

Other organizations include the Division of Adult Development and Aging, American Psychological Association; the Western Gerontological Society; the International Congress of Gerontology; the United States Senate Committee on Aging; and the National Institute of Aging, part of the National Institutes of Health.

Author Index

387

Subject Index